A LIFE AT LAW

Isie Maisels

A LIFE AT LAW

Foreword by Sydney Kentridge

Edited by
Keith Maisels and Benjamin Trisk

JONATHAN BALL PUBLISHERS · JOHANNESBURG

ISBN 1 86842 065 5

Front cover photography by courtesy of the Maisels family
Design by Michael Barnett, Johannesburg
Typesetting and reproduction of text by Book Productions, Pretoria
Typesetting and reproduction of cover and picture section by Ince (Pty) Ltd, Johannesburg
Printed and bound by National Book Printers, Drukkery Street, Goodwood, Western Cape

CONTENTS

Foreword *vii*

Preface *ix*

Acknowledgements *xi*

CHAPTER 1 Early Days in Johannesburg *1*

CHAPTER 2 Daisy de Melker *10*

CHAPTER 3 A Busy Junior Practice *26*

CHAPTER 4 Marriage, War and 'White Mischief' *36*

CHAPTER 5 Courts Martial, the Middle East and Taking Silk *47*

CHAPTER 6 Fighting Verwoerd and Farm Labour *67*

CHAPTER 7 Municipal Vices and the Tobacco Case *77*

CHAPTER 8 Burnt Stamps and a Rusted Bolt *83*

CHAPTER 9 Murder and Madness *93*

CHAPTER 10 The South West Africa Diamond Case *108*

CHAPTER 11 Race and Rape *125*

CHAPTER 12 The Treason Trial 1956–1961 *129*

CHAPTER 13 Two Civil Trials with Unusual Features *217*

CHAPTER 14 Rhodesia *223*

CHAPTER 15 After Rhodesia *237*

CHAPTER 16 Return to the Bar *246*

CHAPTER 17 On the Bench in Neighbouring States *257*

CHAPTER 18 Rhodesia Revisited *270*

CHAPTER 19 Jewish Affairs *280*

CHAPTER 20 Recollections *307*

Notes *325*

Index *331*

FOREWORD

Reminiscences of advocates are sometimes no more than a dry account of long forgotten (and often justly forgotten) court cases. These memoirs of Isie Maisels are something completely different. First, many of Isie's cases, especially during the long years of apartheid, were not merely cases between two litigants. They were cases about the sort of country we were then living in. The notorious Bethal farm labour cases of the 1950s and the great treason trial which ran from 1956 to 1961 are only two examples. Secondly, Isie seemed to attract to his practice cases which, even without any political dimension, were of extraordinary interest, such as the De Melker case or the Bubbles Schroeder murder case. What is more, the stories of these cases are told in Isie's individual voice. He was a great raconteur, and this talent is vividly present on the printed page.

This is not a book simply for lawyers. No reader, I think, can fail to find it fascinating and, indeed, compulsively readable. For a lawyer it is enthralling. Over the years South Africa has known great advocates, whose names survive in legal legend – Beauclerk Upington and Graeme Duncan of Cape Town, Graham Mackeurtan of Natal and Harry Morris of Johannesburg. Isie Maisels is among these greats and, I suspect, as an all-round advocate the greatest of them all. I say 'all-round' because Isie was known to the public during his years of practice at the Bar primarily as a formidable cross-examiner. That he was, but he was much more. His forensic skills were based on sound knowledge of the law. If I have a favourite case in this book it is Rex *v* Manasawitz, which Isie describes in Chapter 3. I shall not give away the story, which Isie tells so well. The reader will find that it illustrates perfectly the combination of legal acumen and sheer forensic panache which made Isie the advocate he was. And he was not yet 30 years old when he argued that case.

Isie's power as a cross-examiner does, however, deserve more than passing mention. It is not easy to describe, let alone analyse. In some uncanny way Isie would from the outset achieve domination over the unfortunate witness, which usually enabled him to extract exactly the answers he wanted. A prime example of this was his cross-examination of Professor Andrew Murray, the prosecution's expert on Communism in the treason trial. In that instance he used a weapon of cross-examination which young advocates are not advised to imitate but which could be deadly in Isie's hands – good natured humour at the expense of the discomfited witness. All in all I have never seen Isie's equal as a cross-examiner in any jurisdiction in which I have practised.

Isie sat as a judge for a time on the High Court of Southern Rhodesia and for many years he held part-time appointments on the Appeal Courts of Botswana, Swaziland and Lesotho. He was never appointed to the Bench in South Africa. This was undoubtedly a loss to the South African judiciary but it was a considerable gain to the Bar. While Isie was a good and conscientious judge he was so extraordinary an advocate as to be an inspiration for his profession.

Isie was a lawyer, not a politician, but his fierce detestation of apartheid was unconcealed. Time and again he appeared in the courts to vindicate the rights of the individual against the oppression of the apartheid state. The reader may learn from Isie's life in the law what it is that goes to make a truly great advocate – legal learning, eloquence combined with lucidity, wise judgment – but above all, courage. We are fortunate to have had him amongst us.

SYDNEY KENTRIDGE, QC
London

PREFACE

It is in some ways surprising to me that this book was written at all, because my father was strenuously opposed to writing it. However, he was persuaded to do so by me, and in particular by my brother-in-law, Benjamin Trisk, whose contribution to the book in terms of his experience in publishing and editing – and, indeed, in terms of the enormous amount of work he put into editing the chapter on the treason trial – has been considerable. After Benjamin introduced Isie to Jonathan Ball, author and publisher had a number of discussions over a glass or two, which both found enjoyable – and so the book was born. In July 1994, when the book was complete, but for two chapters that Isie wished to write about attorneys he had known and colleagues at the Bar, he was seriously injured in a car accident. This prevented him from resuming work on the manuscript until October that year, when, whilst actually at work on it, he suffered a stroke, became completely incapacitated, and died a couple of months later, in December. The stroke rendered him incapable of speech or writing, which for him of all people must have been terrible.

No doubt the two outstanding chapters would have been as zestful and interesting as the rest of the book, and would have completed the picture he painted of his world – but they are lost to us. Nevertheless, this circumstance gave us, his editors, an opportunity to add some valuable touches to the portrait that emerges of the man himself. I wrote therefore to a number of his colleagues and associates, who gladly furnished us with the anecdotes and recollections that form the final chapter. Having been in the position of briefing him myself from time to time, I am also privileged to have been able to contribute some anecdotes to this 'endpiece', a tribute to a remarkable personality of our times.

In reading his memoirs, it must be remembered that Isie was putting them down at a time of rapid changes and adjustments in the fabric of South African society, politics, and government. The reader will notice certain instances where mention is made of institutions with which we lived for so long – the 'homelands', for instance – that now no longer exist; and in other instances, mention is made of circumstances that have changed in the few years since Isie's death. Although the editors have adjusted the details where appropriate, a certain authenticity – a flavour of the period – is retained by leaving as they were aspects of his usage or details of circumstances as they were at the time.

Because he was essentially a Victorian in manner and approach – somewhat formal, even austere – the many forms of deep kindness and generosity of sentiment, experienced not only by his family, but by many outside it, are hardly reflected in the text. Indeed, my late mother, having read some of the manuscript, wondered whether readers would realise that my father actually had a family life in addition to his practice at the Bar. But she really knew, and we know, better. His generosity extended to giving free advice to and acting *pro amico* for people in need, or whom he perceived as having a special claim on his time and skills. Some of these instances I, taking the liberty of an editor, have had the satisfaction of incorporating into the text where appropriate.

KEITH MAISELS

ACKNOWLEDGEMENTS

Our thanks go to a number of people, without whose input and contributions it would not have been possible to produce this book. It has involved contributions of various kinds from a number of people in the legal world. Special mention must be made of Lourens Ackermann, who, under Isie's guidance, made a major contribution in research of all types for the book, and of Mr Justice Edwin Cameron, who also contributed to the research. We thank also those who contributed the anecdotes and reminiscences that make up the final chapter, most of whose names are recorded there.

In terms of the famous treason trial, an immense amount of information had to be considered, and an invaluable contribution to the details of the text came from Isie's esteemed colleague, Mr Justice Chris Plewman, now a member of the Appellate Division, whose informed view of the case derives from his maintaining, as a very able junior, a watching brief over the case while the more senior members of the defence team busied themselves with the ongoing business of their practices. His ability to recall the most minute detail and the sublety of crucial exchanges in court, as well his record of the sequence and strategy of the planning of the trial, were invaluable to Isie. We mention with appreciation Michelè Pickover, Curator of Manuscripts in the Library, University of the Witwatersrand, who on many occasions made available some of the numerous volumes of the treason trial proceedings – assisting the research with a gracious willingness to interrupt her other responsibilities. Isie also expressed his indebtedness in terms of this chapter to Professor Thomas Karis, for use of the material recorded in *A Guide to the Microfilm Record of the Treason Trial* (Johannesburg, Contra, 1998), and in Thomas Karis & Gwendolen

M Carter (eds), *From Protest to Challenge* (Stanford, Hoover Inst Press, 5 vols, 1972-1997). Isie wrote: 'The complete record of the trial, from the arraignment of the accused in August 1959 to the conclusion of evidence in October 1960, amounted to over 18 000 pages. This does not include the argument addressed by the Crown and the defence after evidence had concluded. As I was obviously not able to read the full record, I was fortunate to be granted the kind permission of Professor Thomas Karis to utilise the *Guide*, as well as of *From Protest to Challenge*, vol 3, to which I have made many references during the course of the chapter. Indeed without his permission I would not have been able to write certain parts of my account of the treason trial.'

Notably, we record our indebtedness to the publisher, Jonathan Ball, who in the end takes credit for persuading Isie to commit himself to paper, and to his production and design team, who have contributed their time and skills to producing a handsome volume worthy of its subject. Our thanks also to Lindsey Morton, the copy-editor, who efficiently refined the enormous amount of information with which she was presented. A difficulty to be overcome in the process of recording Isie's memoirs was his intractability in refusing to use a dictaphone. (His son Jeffrey had years before bought him one so that he could reminisce for the family on tape – but to no avail. In conversation with Keith – then 59 – he dismissed such equipment as 'one of these machines you young fellows use'.) So Jonathan Ball provided a 'shorthand writer', as Isie termed her, in the form of Mrs F Gamsu, who conscientiously took down his dictation.

Of course, these acknowledgements would be incomplete without paying tribute to the quiet supportive influence in the background of Muriel, Isie's devoted wife, who regrettably did not survive to see the book in print, having passed away on 8 June 1997.

Chapter One

EARLY DAYS IN JOHANNESBURG

My father, Henry, came with his parents, two sisters and the youngest brother of the family to the Transvaal in the last decade of the last century. A younger brother of my father (who had come to South Africa during the previous year) had found the land good, and as a result, the remaining members of the family came to South Africa and settled in Johannesburg.

They had lived in Pokroy, a small village in Lithuania, and they emigrated to escape from the oppression and anti-semitism of Tsarist rule. Thousands of Jews left Russia around this time, the majority of them going to the United States and Canada and a comparative minority coming to South Africa. They came with no knowledge of English or Afrikaans, their home language being Yiddish. They had no secular education – it was not available to them as Jews – but they had a Hebrew education and they remained loyal to their Judaism.

My mother, Andzia, emigrated with her family, the Sieradzkis, from Lodz in Poland, also in the latter part of the century. Anti-semitism was, of course, always endemic in Poland and her family no doubt had the same reasons for emigrating that motivated Jews leaving Tsarist Russia.

My parents were married in January 1905, and on 19 November of that year I was born in Johannesburg, in a house at the corner of Smit and Loveday Streets, in the suburb of Wanderers' View (now part of Braamfontein). My brother and sister, twins, were born on 6 October 1908, but they pre-deceased me. Our family lived in the same house for many years until we moved further north to 136 Loveday Street.

The doctor attending at my birth was a Dr Abelheim, of whom my mother, as I recall it, was terrified. A very able physician with a practice in Johannesburg, he in later years lectured at Wits Medical School. The story is told of him that he lectured students on medical ethics and cautioned them as to the necessity of being polite to patients whether rich or poor; pointing out, so it is said, that the poor may one day be rich.

The first school that I attended, Spes Bona, was a government preparatory school. There I spent a year doing my first and second grades. When I was seven, my father took me to the Marist Brothers' School, which was situated at the corner of Koch and Claim Streets, just north of the railway line. I well remember his taking me there early one morning and introducing me to the headmaster (whose name I cannot recall) and then leaving me to fend for myself. I remained at that school until I matriculated in 1922.

The great Harry Morris, KC, recounts in his memoirs, *The First Forty Years,* that he too went to this school. He refers to certain of the brothers by name, one of whom – Brother Dominic – was at the school when I was there, many years after Harry Morris had left it. He also refers to Brother Valerian, who had died by the time I came to the school; but there was a book prize called the Valerian Prize, awarded in the Junior Matriculation class. I was the fortunate recipient of that prize in 1921. Morris wrote: 'The Brothers seemed to take a personal interest in every individual scholar'.[1] I can fully endorse this remark, as the following instances will demonstrate.

Shortly after the Second World War I took a tram to Yeoville. When I got off the tram, I saw a Marist brother – whom I recognised as Brother Vital – trying to catch the tram as it went off, but failing to do so. I went up to him and said, 'Brother, I don't suppose you remember me?' He looked at me for a moment, then said: 'Yes, I remember you. I remember when you got the Valerian Prize and I wrote down your name as Isaac instead of Israel and I had to correct it.' He asked me to come and see him at the school, which had by then moved to Observatory. I did so and he told me that he could remember the first and surname of every boy he had ever taught, and the surname of every boy who had been at the school when he was headmaster. He also mentioned to me the interest he had in the careers of certain of the old boys.

Another example of the interest of the Brothers in their scholars was shown by my class teacher, Brother Pius, in 1913, when I was in Standard 1. When, in 1948 – 35 years later – I was appointed King's Counsel, Brother Pius came to see me in my chambers to congratulate me.

Although Marist Brothers was, of course, a Catholic school, there were a number of Jewish boys. In fact I think the reason why my parents sent me to Marist Brothers was because two of my cousins and an uncle on my mother's side had been pupils at that school. Siegfried Raphaely, to whom I shall refer later, was one of the first matriculants at that school. He later played a prominent part in Jewish affairs. I cannot recall a single incident of anti-semitism during the whole of my schooldays. The Brothers fully respected the Jewish holy days and the consequent absence from school of Jewish boys on those holy days.[2] Jewish holidays were often used as an excuse by non-Jewish boys to absent themselves from school – in the mistaken belief that their absence would not be noticed. One such, Murphy by name, was to discover that the brothers had eagle eyes and sound memories. One day following a Jewish holiday came the question: 'Where were you yesterday Murphy?'

'Jewish holiday, brother.'

'Bend over boy.'

I was at school during the First World War, and I well remember the horror which filled my friends and me on reading the list of casualties published in *The Star*. I also recall the terrible flu epidemic and remember seeing the Twist Street School, situated on the north-western corner of Smit and Twist Streets, being used as a hospital. Fortunately none of our family died during that epidemic.

The playground of the school was known to us as the 'yard'. In it the inter-class soccer games were played. The cricket nets were there as well. I played soccer for my class, as goalkeeper. I never made the first team of the school at soccer, but I managed to play cricket for the school's first team. We used the lunch interval to play soccer or cricket at what was then the open Union Ground. The Brothers were all keen on sport and many of them coached us, particularly at cricket.

The Wanderers' Ground, later expropriated by the South African Railways in the 1940s, was just around the corner from where our family lived, and I spent a great deal of time watching the football or cricket matches played there. Indeed, every sport was played on that ground: rugby, soccer, cricket, tennis; and athletics and cycling. A hall at the Ground was used for dances – or, as they were sometimes called, balls. With the exception of certain professional cricketers who came with the English side to South Africa, all the sportsmen of those days were amateurs. I well recall two dressing rooms – one for the amateurs, who were called 'gentlemen', and the other for the professionals. One of the great professionals whom I saw playing was the famous J B Hobbs. In later years I saw there some of Australia's best bowlers, such as Gregory and MacDonald; and many other famous sportsmen.

When I was in the matriculation class, we experienced the miners' strike of 1922, which eventually became almost revolutionary in character. The white miners who went on strike (the black workers did not strike) were members of the then Labour Party. Martial law was declared, the army was called out, and there were heavy casualties – among both the defence force and the strikers. In addition, I well recall seeing a large number of people being marched to the Wanderers' Ground from their homes in Fordsburg and Vrededorp, where there had been considerable military activity. Tents were erected at the Ground and these people were housed there.

I remember following the newspaper reports of the case of one of the leaders of the miners' strike, a man called Taffy Long. He was charged with murdering one Marais, a storekeeper in Avenue Road, Fordsburg, not far from where my father and my grandfather carried on their business as produce merchants. A special court had been set up to try persons alleged to have committed crimes during the period of martial law. Originally Taffy Long was defended by a junior pro deo counsel. The judge presiding at the special court, Mr Justice Dove-Wilson, stated that he thought it unfortunate that a more senior counsel did not appear on behalf of the accused. As a result of this remark, the then leader of the Johannesburg Bar, Colonel Charles Frampton Stallard, KC, DSO, MC, acting *pro deo*, undertook the defence of Taffy Long. If anybody, as a matter of personal conviction, was opposed to the strikers and on the side of the mining houses it was Stallard; but in accordance with the high tradition of the Bar, he felt it was his duty to defend Taffy Long. His example was followed by other senior members of the Bar. Despite the defence put up by Stallard, however, Long was found guilty and sentenced to death. It was said at the time that he marched to the gallows singing 'The Red Flag'.

Another incident I recall from that time demonstrates the bravery of General Smuts, who was then prime minister and minister of defence. Parliament was in session when the strike occurred and General Smuts came up by car from Cape Town. Just outside Johannesburg the car had a puncture. Although the policeman accompanying General Smuts was much concerned for his safety, General Smuts sat on the side of the road, apparently fearless, until the puncture was repaired and they could proceed on their journey. It is not inappropriate to mention that General Smuts, himself a distinguished advocate, illegally issued orders for the deportation of some of the strike leaders. An interdict was obtained in the Supreme Court to restrain him from doing so, but by the time the interdict was to be served the deportees were already on the high seas.

At the general election in 1924, Smuts's South African Party was defeated and a pact government was formed from the coalition between the Labour Party (under the leadership of Mr Walter Madeley) and the National Party under General Hertzog. Hertzog, who in 1910 had been a cabinet minister with Smuts under General Botha in the first Union government, had broken away from Botha to form the National Party.

I matriculated in 1922 and managed to get a first class. We wrote what was known as the Cape matric in those days. Every Johannesburg student who gained a first-class pass and who wished to go to university was awarded a bursary for three years by the Johannesburg Municipal Council. Consequently I was the recipient of a bursary of £40 a year for three years.

My parents wanted me to study medicine. An uncle, whose first name was the same as mine, and to whom I was very close, dissuaded me from taking medicine on the basis that the life of a general practitioner was a miserable one. He was then a very busy general practitioner, but subsequently became a leading urologist in Johannesburg. He and his wife 'Dolly' – who was Fanny Beatrice Marks, youngest daughter of the famous pioneer and industrialist, Sammy Marks[3] – were all their lives invariably kind and helpful to me and my wife. In those days doctors specialised, as did my uncle, only after they had done a lengthy period of general practice, which involved visits to patients at their homes at all hours of the day and night. Today's young general practitioners seem rarely to visit their patients and seem to be getting closer and closer to the American system of requiring their patients to see them at their rooms, hospital or nursing home.

I decided to take law and applied for admission to the University of the Witwatersrand. The vice-chancellor and principal was the great Jan Hofmeyr, who was rightly regarded, certainly by my generation, as a genius. He had matriculated at the age of 12. He went to Oxford, accompanied by his mother, where he took a BA degree. As vice-chancellor and principal of the University of the Witwatersrand he interviewed every applicant. He asked me what I wanted to take and I told him law. He asked, 'What would be your first degree?' I told him I thought I would like to take a BCom. 'BCom,' said he; 'what on earth do you want to take that for?' I told him that I understood it would be very useful for somebody practising law to know something about accountancy. Hofmeyr replied 'BCom, that is not a university degree, that is bookkeeping.' He asked me to show him my matriculation certificate. He looked at it and said, 'You will take a BA, with Latin and Roman Law as your majors.' And so it was.

In case anyone is under the misapprehension that Hofmeyr was solely a classicist I should perhaps here mention something that was told to me by Dr Holloway, who had been secretary for finance under various ministers of finance. Dr Holloway, who himself was a very cultivated man and also a mathematician of the first rank, told me of the respect that he had for Hofmeyr when Hofmeyr was minister of finance. He told me of an incident when he had had to prepare a paper for submission to Hofmeyr, and in which there was an abstruse mathematical calculation. He gave the paper to Hofmeyr late one afternoon and Hofmeyr said he would take it home with him and see him the next day. Dr Holloway told me that he woke up in the middle of the night and realised that he had made an error in the mathematical calculation to which I have referred. He made up his mind to get into Hofmeyr's office first thing next morning to point out his error. To his astonishment as he walked into Hofmeyr's office, Hofmeyr said to him: 'Look here, Holloway, isn't that mathematical exercise of yours incorrect?'

As a speaker both in English and Afrikaans, Jan Hofmeyr was outstanding. When he became chancellor of the university, the graduation ceremony was always marked by a magnificent oration by him. It is the common practice of persons like cabinet ministers, who have to make important speeches, to prepare their speeches beforehand and have them typed out in order to ensure correct reporting by the newspapers. Many having to make this kind of speech hand a copy of the speech, prior to making it, to the newspaper. A friend of mine who was a reporter for the *Rand Daily Mail* told me of an occasion at which he was present when Hofmeyr delivered a speech. He, the reporter, had received a copy of the speech that Hofmeyr was going to deliver that night. It was a long speech and Hofmeyr made it without looking at his notes. According to what my friend told me, it was exactly the same – word for word – as the typed speech earlier handed to the press.

I have always felt that Alan Paton's biography of Hofmeyr does not do justice to Hofmeyr. What President De Klerk advocated, when the decision was made to hold a general election based on the universal franchise, is what Hofmeyr advocated years ago. His untimely death shortly after the National Party came into power in 1948 was a grievous loss to South Africa. He had been a member of General Smuts's cabinet, but on one occasion he resigned as a matter of principle when a Mr Fourie was made a senator to look after Coloured affairs because of his alleged knowledge of the Coloured people. Hofmeyr, like another minister (I think it was Mr F W Sturrock, who also resigned), regarded this appointment as a political one, devoid of any real merit. Of course, Hofmeyr's liberalism was anathema to many whites in this country and particularly to Afrikaners. One often wonders what would have happened if Hofmeyr's liberal policy had been the state of this country instead of the apartheid policies of Malan, Strydom, Verwoerd, Vorster and others.

I took a very ordinary BA LLB degree[4] and managed to play cricket for the university. We were then in the second league and during vacation time it was very often difficult to get a team together. I also played soccer for the university in what was then known as the Wednesday League. I was chairman of the Law

Students' Society and had great fun in what was called our Debating Society. We used to have a best speaker's prize and I had the good fortune to win it twice. I have donated both medals to my grandson, James Maisels, who lives in the United States, and who is apparently regarded as a fairly good speaker. He was awarded a Marshall scholarship to Balliol College, Oxford.

My lecturers in the BA course were Professor Haarhoff, a man of great culture and learning, for Latin; and in Roman Law, Oliver Schreiner – then at the Bar, but later to become one of the greatest judges before whom I had the privilege of appearing.

I started at university in 1923 and our law lectures were held in what was known as the Tin Temple, a temporary structure that had been in existence, despite its temporary nature, for some years. It was situated in what is now a park at the corner of Plein and Rissik Streets, Johannesburg. Some of the lectures, such as French and English, were given at the new university building in Milner Park, and chemistry was taught at what was known as the old School of Mines building, situated at the northern end of Eloff Street opposite the railway station.

A lecturer in our LLB class, Mr W H Ramsbottom, subsequently became a judge of the Transvaal Provincial Division, and then a judge of the Appellate Division. I shall refer later to his career and, of course, to that of Oliver Schreiner as well. Another lecturer (an attorney who had been a Scottish solicitor) was Colin Murray, a senior partner in a well known firm of attorneys called Steytler, Grimmer and Murray. This firm is regrettably no longer in existence. He lectured us in mercantile law, insolvency law and bills of exchange. He pronounced the word 'secondly' with the 'e' being pronounced as an 'i'.

Law lectures for both BA and LLB were held at the Tin Temple, either early in the morning or late in the afternoon – that is before all the legal offices opened or after they had closed. This being the case, it was obvious to me – and, of course, to many of the other students who had taken their BA at the same time as I did and were taking the LLB degree – that we should try and get employment in an attorney's office. (I should perhaps explain here that if one obtained an LLB degree it was not necessary to be articled if one wanted to become an attorney.) I then did the rounds.

The manager of the bank of which my father was a customer

introduced me to the bank's attorneys, a firm called Lindsay and Appleyard who used to get half of the Johannesburg Municipality's legal work. Judge Greenberg had been a clerk in that firm, and I hoped that I would be able to get a job there. Mr Lindsay saw me and asked me whether I intended to go to the Bar. When I replied that I hoped to do so, he said that he did not think it would serve any useful purpose for me to be employed in that firm as their practice was virtually wholly devoted to conveyancing. I then went to a firm called Pitts and Weston but I was not successful in getting a job. I finally went to my father's attorneys, Raphaely and Gratus. When I joined this firm, there was another partner, a Mr Liebson, a brother of the famous Sarah Gertrude Millin. He left the firm to practise in Pretoria shortly after I became a clerk there.

It was quite common in those days for students who wanted to be articled to pay a premium for the privilege of being articled. I did not want to be articled; but I received no salary at all for three months. After that period had elapsed I was bold enough to ask Mr Raphaely if he did not think I should receive some salary. He said he would think it over and I eventually was paid £5 a month. This was my salary until I obtained my LLB degree and was admitted as an attorney. I was then paid £20 a month plus one third of any of the fees earned from work that I was able to bring into the firm. It is not irrelevant to mention that the country was then in a state of depression. Be that as it may, after I had been appearing in court and doing the work of a qualified attorney, notary and conveyancer for 18 months I asked Mr Raphaely whether I had any prospects in the firm. In response, Mr Raphaely gave me a short answer. He said, 'No.' I thereupon decided to have my name removed from the Roll of Attorneys and after a lapse of six months to join the Bar; which I did on 3 March 1930.

Chapter Two

DAISY DE MELKER

In one of my first appearances in the magistrate's court my opponent was one of the characters of the Side Bar (as the attorneys' profession is known), Mr Emanuel Gluckman. He had a marvellous sense of humour. The case was one depending on the credibility of the plaintiff and his witnesses compared with the credibility of the defence. I was appearing for the plaintiff and had some independent witnesses whose evidence was very much in favour of the plaintiff's case and, of course, adverse to the defendant. In the course of my argument I used a strategy that is often employed in the courts and posed the question why an independent witness should give false evidence against the defendant, Mr Gluckman's clients. Mr Gluckman came up with a wonderful answer. In those days cinemas did not have 'trailers', but they showed slides. The United Building Society had a slide that pictured a house and had the words on it, 'Why pay rent?' Gluckman's answer to that was a very simple one. 'People do pay rent.' Just one of my less successful cases.

Members of the Bar were then accommodated in a building called Corporation Building (not the Corporation Building as it is now, but in a much earlier and cruder building that was subsequently pulled down and replaced by the building that now stands there). That part of the Corporation Building occupied by members of the Bar – and also by certain firms of attorneys – was a very different proposition to the premises they now occupy. Juniors like myself could be accommodated only in what I think would be called the 'second floor back'. Although a lift served the front of the building, which consisted of two storeys, there were no lifts leading to the part of the building where the juniors were located, which was known as 'The Island'. The rooms were very small and all I could manage to get into the room was a small desk, two chairs and a small bookcase. The rental was £2 a month.

Among the other occupants of The Island, when I joined it, were J G N Strauss, who later entered politics and who, after the death of General Smuts, became the leader of the United Party (having been a member of General Smuts's cabinet during the Second World War).

The ambition of all of us who occupied chambers in The Island was twofold. Firstly to be briefed, and secondly to move out of The Island into a decent office. Early in 1932 Dr Manfred Nathan, KC, was appointed president of the Income Tax Court. This did not necessitate his devoting his whole time to that court, and he invited me to share his chambers with him. This was a large room on the first floor facing south, but it fortunately had a fireplace.

Manfred Nathan was rather old fashioned in his way of life. He did not have a telephone at home and the telephone at his office was on my desk. Consequently whenever he wanted to make a call he would come to my desk to do so. As the junior I did not have many consultations, but somehow or other whenever I had one, this was an occasion for Manfred Nathan to telephone his plumber or some other tradesman in order to have something fixed up in his house in the Berea. He smoked strong Magaliesberg tobacco, kept the windows closed and used a spittoon.

It was, and is, the custom at the Bar for members freely to borrow a book that another member might have, provided he left a slip. Manfred Nathan gave me instructions that no one was allowed to borrow any of his books. One day he arrived at the chambers when a colleague had taken one of his books out of its shelf and was reading it in Manfred's room. When he left, Manfred told me I was not allowed to let anyone do that because the top of the binding of the book would become worn out if it was taken out too frequently.

I stayed in those chambers until another room on the same floor became available, which I occupied until I joined a group on the second floor. (At a later stage the Bar moved to His Majesty's Building, and this group, known then – and still known – as 836, moved to the eighth floor of His Majesty's, and subsequently, when the Bar moved again, to Innes Chambers. I remained a member of this group for almost 60 years.)

I was once asked to what I attributed my alleged success. My answer was through luck and hard work and indeed I was very lucky in my early days at the Bar – not that all my clients were so lucky.[5]

In the first trial in which I was briefed, I was to defend two miners charged with culpable homicide, it being alleged that through their negligence they had been responsible for the death of a Black miner. (In those days culpable homicide cases were invariably held in the Supreme Court. Nowadays they seem to be held almost entirely in the regional division of the magistrate's court.) There had been a preparatory examination in the magistrate's court lasting several days and there was quite a fair sized record.

As is customary at the Bar I went to introduce myself to the judge who was to preside over the trial. He was Mr Justice F E T Krause, who as an advocate had had an illustrious career at the Bar, specialising particularly in criminal work. He asked me how long I thought the trial would last. I said that I thought it would last two, or perhaps, three days. He told me that things ran differently in the Supreme Court – and so they did in this case.

There was a jury in the case and the crown prosecutor was a very able man, Mr Simons. He led his first witness, whom I cross-examined to no great effect. As he was about to call his second witness the judge, who had read the preparatory examination record, said to Simons: 'I suppose he will say the same as the first witness,' to which Simons said yes, he thought so, if he adhered to the evidence he had given at the preparatory examination.

The judge told him not to bother to call the witness. A few more witnesses were called and as I thought that no *prima-facie* case had been established against one of the accused, I asked the judge to withdraw the case against him from the jury and to acquit him. 'No, no,' said the judge, refusing my application, and adding very improperly; 'the sentence may be less than his fellow accused.' I then called my clients, the accused. They were cross-examined by the prosecuting counsel and the judge also did not refrain from asking them questions.

After I closed my case, as was the practice, the crown counsel addressed the jury. I said what I had to say and the judge summed up. The jury retired to consider their verdict. The time was now 12.50 pm (the trial having commenced at 10.00 am) on the same day. After five minutes the jury returned a verdict of 'not guilty'. Thereupon Judge Krause addressed the accused and told them that they were very lucky to be acquitted and that they should thank me for the defence I had put up on their behalf, making some complimentary remarks about the nature of that defence.

I need hardly say that the complimentary remarks were entirely unwarranted, but it so happened that there was a reporter from the *Rand Daily Mail* in court and the case was reported next morning, including the complimentary remarks that the judge had made about me. This might have been the cause of my getting briefed in criminal cases and, in particular, in the notorious case of Daisy De Melker.

I was briefed as junior in that case to the great Harry Morris, an outstanding advocate in the field of criminal law. Benjamin Bennett's biography of him is aptly entitled *Genius for the Defence*.[6] In a tribute to his memory before the other judges of the Transvaal Provincial Division and members of the Bar in the Witwatersrand Local Division on 12 October 1954,[7] Mr Justice Ramsbottom concluded: 'I shall, I trust, be pardoned if I use the words that were spoken of him at his graveside and that so well describe him. "He was a gallant defender of men." No finer epitaph could be written.'

Daisy De Melker was arrested in 1932 on a charge of murdering three men: her two previous husbands, William Alfred Cowle in January 1923, and Robert Sproat in November 1927, and a son Rhodes Cecil Cowle in March 1932, in all cases by poisoning. She was alleged to have murdered Cowle and Sproat by the use of strychnine, but in the case of her son Rhodes, by the use of arsenic.

A preparatory examination was held in Germiston and despite enquiries made by the police, they had been unable to find out where she had obtained the arsenic. The public prosecutor in the magistrate's court, Mr S Goetzche, thought it would be a good idea to have her photograph published in *The Star*.

It was seen by a chemist by the name of Spilkin, who had a pharmacy in Kenilworth, Johannesburg. He then went to consult his attorney, a Mr James Cranko, about what he should do. Cranko told him it was his duty to go to the police. He told the police, as indeed was proved to be the case, that Mrs De Melker had purchased arsenic from him on 23 February 1932. At that time she was living with her third husband (De Melker) and his daughter in a cottage at Simmer East in Germiston – within walking distance of a pharmacy. She had had to take a train and a tramcar to get to Spilkin's pharmacy in Kenilworth. Spilkin knew her as Mrs Cowle. Giving her name as Mrs Sproat, with the explanation that Cowle had died and she had remarried, she told him that she wanted the poison for a cat. She gave an address in Bertrams where she no longer resided. Mrs De Melker was required by law to sign a poison register kept by the pharmacist and she signed as 'D L Sproat'. Apparently she did not wait long to use the poison, but instead of using it on a cat, she poisoned her son ten or eleven days later on about 5 March 1932.

In those days the accused could elect to be tried either by a judge and jury, or by a judge sitting with assessors. Long before the trial it became clear that public opinion had convicted Mrs De Melker, and it was early manifest that this was not a case for a jury. The publication of the evidence given at the preparatory examination was entirely responsible for this state of affairs. The public were prepared to overlook the murder of a couple of husbands. The death of her son was unpardonable. Moreover, they appeared to agree with Mr Justice Avery: 'Of all forms of death by which human nature may be overcome the most detestable is that of poison.' Never before in this country had public feeling reached such a pitch of animosity against any accused. In every case of murder there is nearly always a section of the public that sympathises or sides with the accused. In this case there were no two opinions. Everyone was on the same side. The wits, and half-wits, vied with each other in the creation of conundrums, jokes and parodies mainly based on an assumption of her guilt. The very school children were engaged in composing parodies on 'A Bicycle Made for Two'. They all began with 'Daisy, Daisy' and ended with a prophecy relating to her fate.

One day during the case, Mrs De Melker's attorney, the late Mr Alec Wise of the firm Wright Rose-Innes & Wise of Germiston, brought her to consult with Harry Morris and me, in order to prepare her for the cross examination she would have to undergo in due course (if indeed it was decided that she should give evidence at all). Harry asked her a number of questions that, for reasons which were even then obvious, she had great difficulty in answering. The questioning was quite severe and Mrs De Melker was first visibly upset and then started crying. The consultation terminated and Alec Wise took her out of Morris's room but then returned and apologised to Harry asking him to excuse the conduct of Mrs De Melker as, he remarked, she was 'very highly strung'.

The rejoinder was swift and typical: 'Not as highly strung, I think, as she is going to be.'

The trial commenced on 17 October 1932 and lasted 30 court days, ending on 30 November 1932. It was before Mr Justice Greenberg sitting with two assessors, Messrs Graham and Stanford, both experienced magistrates. Mr Justice Greenberg, when he delivered his judgment, stated that although the responsibility for the verdict rested with him, that responsibility had been enormously lightened by the wholehearted co-operation and invaluable guidance and advice he had received from both these gentlemen at every stage of the long and arduous trial. It was said that, at that time, it was the longest trial of a European held in the Union. (Since 1932 there have been many criminal cases of far longer duration, for example the so-called 'treason trial' and the 'Delmas trial'.) The evidence and addresses concluded on 29 November. The crown prosecutor, Mr Cyril Jarvis – to whom Harry Morris rightly paid a compliment for the fair manner in which he had conducted the prosecution – had addressed the court for 13 and a half hours, Harry for 16 and a half hours, and I, on questions of law, for about an hour and a half. According to Harry Morris, the addresses of counsel were up to that time the longest ever delivered in any criminal trial in South Africa. Other statistics that Harry Morris gives in *The First Forty Years* are that the Crown called 59 and the defence called 14 witnesses, including the accused. The full judgment appears in *The First Forty Years,*[8] and an excellent account of the trial appears in Bennett's *Genius for the Defence*.

Queues formed outside the court at a very early hour every day during the trial. The courtroom was crowded to overflowing. Those who could not obtain accommodation in the morning waited at the doors and took the places of those who left during the luncheon interval. My own sister wanted to get into the court one day and asked the police orderly if he would let her in, explaining to him that she was my sister. He remarked to her with some disbelief that I seemed to have a lot of sisters.

At the conclusion of the day's proceedings the crowd rushed round the building to get a glimpse of the prisoner as she was being removed. On some of these occasions she was hooted. Mild demonstrations indicating public hostility were made in court. These, however, stopped for good when the demonstrators realised that by giving vent to their feelings they were jeopardising their accommodation. As in all such cases, the majority of the audience and all the demonstrators were women. Some of them did not miss a single sitting and they still speak of the trial as 'the finest entertainment they ever had'. I understand that someone has made a film about this trial, to be screened by the SABC. I shudder to think what it will be like.[9]

The Crown had to prove the cause of death of both husbands and, of course, of her son, Rhodes Cowle. With regard to the son, a post-mortem examination carried out at the instance of the police after they had exhumed his body, established clearly that the cause of death was arsenic poisoning. A post-mortem performed on Sproat gave cerebral haemorrhage as the cause of death. When his corpse and that of Cowle senior were exhumed, traces of strychnine were found in both corpses. Although Mrs De Melker had inherited over £4 000 from her second husband Sproat, she stood to inherit only £100 from a policy that her son had taken out on his life. She was consequently unable to engage the services of any forensic experts to assist her defence.

In order to prove that Cowle, Sproat and Mrs De Melker's son had died as a result of poisoning, the Crown called a large number of lay persons, including the son's fellow employee Webster and Webster's mother, who deposed to her son's symptoms after he had drunk some of the coffee in the flask. There were lay witnesses who had seen Cowle and Sproat shortly before they died.

The part that I played in this case was really an insignificant one. Leaving aside the research and its results, which I was able to furnish to my leader, I had to argue twice in the course of the case and to cross-examine one or two witnesses, really to no effect. The crown case had closed on a Friday and to my horror Harry Morris instructed me to apply for the discharge of the accused on counts one and two – the alleged murders of the husbands, on the following Monday. I spent a miserable weekend trying to think of something I could say in support of this application. An application made at that stage in a criminal case can succeed only if there has been no evidence before the court on which a reasonable person might convict the accused – not one on which a reasonable person *should* convict, but on which a reasonable person *might* convict. The judge listened to my argument, such as it was, with patience. In a most polite manner he refused the application, pointing out the law as I have stated it and adding that the test would, at the conclusion of the evidence and argument, be whether the Crown had proved beyond reasonable doubt that the accused was guilty of the crimes of which she was charged. In the course of the Crown's argument it was contended that the first and second counts could lend support to each other – that one may fill gaps in the other. This raised a question of law and I was asked by Harry to argue for our side. This I did; and after referring the court to South African and English authorities including the well known 'Brides in the Bath' case, the judge rejected the Crown's argument holding that the Crown had failed to prove, by independent evidence, the cause of death in either of these two counts.

Lest it be thought that my argument had anything to do with the acquittal of Mrs De Melker on the first and second counts, I hasten to state that the crown case failed because of Harry Morris's magnificent cross examination, particularly of the expert witnesses called for the Crown – Professor J M Watt, then Professor of Pharmacology at the University of the Witwatersrand, Mr T F Britten, a highly qualified senior government analyst, and the medical practitioners who had attended each of the three deceased. We had no experts to call and the acquittal on the first two counts depended on Harry Morris's being able to cast doubt upon the evidence of the expert witnesses, and on the evidence of certain of the lay witnesses.

Judgment commenced after all the arguments had been made and the evidence given. On the morning of the day after the evidence and addresses concluded, commencing at 9.00 am, Mr Justice Greenberg delivered his judgment, 65 pages in length. It seemed to me that he was hardly looking at any notes. His judgment was masterly in every respect. He dealt in detail with the evidence and the argument and gave full reasons for coming to his conclusion. Mr Bennett remarks in his book that queues formed outside court throughout the night before judgment was given. In his book, Mr Morris mentions that the courtroom was crammed to overflowing.

Harry Morris was not in fact in court on the day that judgment was given, when sentence was passed that Mrs De Melker be hanged. We had realised that whatever the prospects of success might be on the first two counts of killing her husbands, there was absolutely no prospect of success on the third charge, namely that of killing her son. The evidence – of the purchase of the arsenic from a pharmacy far away from where she lived, under a false name and for a false reason; that there were no cats causing trouble; that Mrs De Melker had on her own evidence given her son a flask of coffee and that a fellow employee of her son, one Webster, had drunk a portion of the coffee and was proved to have sustained some poisoning by arsenic (fortunately not lethal) – indeed provided obstacles that could not be overcome.

Leaving aside the fact of making due allowance for the strain to which she had been subjected, Mrs De Melker was a wholly unsatisfactory witness and added to the view we had taken of our chances of an acquittal on the first two counts.

Harry Morris went to see Judge Greenberg in chambers on the last day before the judge went into court, and asked him if there was any point in his being present when judgment was given. He had made a superhuman effort on behalf of his client. As Harry Morris puts it in his book, *The First Forty Years*, 'Daisy was not popular. Neither was I. During her trial she received threatening letters. So did I. She was told that if she were not hanged she would die. So was I. Her conviction appeared to be the only escape from death.' The physical, apart from the mental, strain both prior to and during the trial was terrific, leaving aside the enormous amount of preparation that was done before the trial commenced. Judge Greenberg, who fully recognised what Morris had been through, as an act of kindness told him that he need not be present in court. In his judgment the judge rightly complimented Harry on the defence that he had put up but, of course as I have already stated, an adverse verdict was inevitable.

I, however, was in court when judgment was given. I remember seeing Mrs Sarah Gertrude Millin, Mrs Ethel Hayman (the wife of a leading attorney) and another lady whose name I cannot recall, sitting opposite me in what was known as the jury box, listening to the whole judgment. Mrs Millin wrote a novel afterwards about this case entitled *Three Men Die*.

In giving his final judgment, Mr Justice Greenberg dealt with each count *seriatim*. He found that the Crown had failed to prove that Cowle or Sproat had died of strychnine poisoning and Mrs De Melker was found not guilty on these two counts. I recall hearing a murmur from outside the court because the news must have percolated to the people standing in the foyer. Relying on the overwhelming case against Mrs De Melker on the count of murdering her son, the judge found her guilty and sentenced her to death. Harry Morris went to see the then Minister of Justice, Mr Oswald Pirow, KC, in an attempt to obtain commutation of the sentence for her, but this was unsuccessful.

* * *

What did *not* emerge during the trial was how the police came to be alerted to the doings of Daisy De Melker. The answer to that question, in my own view, is to be found in two pieces of evidence. Her husband Sproat had a brother William, who was seven years younger than the deceased. In the evidence given by William Sproat at the trial, he spoke of his brother as having been a healthy man and stated that his brother had originally executed a will. According to his evidence, Mrs De Melker (then of course Mrs Sproat), told him that her husband had made a will in his mother's favour. This was in about June 1927. He said that he was summoned to Johannesburg one day to find his brother ill in bed. He also described his brother's condition. His brother, who seemed to be quite all right, told him that he (the deceased) had just been telling Bill Johnson that if he did not see the witness again, 'Daisy is to get everything, lock, stock and barrel.' He added, 'And I know, Will, you will see that she gets it.' His brother apparently recovered from the illness from which he was suffering at the time, but a short while after, William was again summoned to the deceased's house and he described in detail the condition in which the deceased was. On this occasion William Sproat said to Daisy that she need not worry about what would happen to her if her husband died; and that although her husband was too ill to write a will, he would make one when he got better. To which Daisy replied, 'He does not need to write a will, I have a will here. He only needs to sign it.' There was indeed a will prepared leaving everything to Daisy. He arranged for the will to be witnessed and another witness was found shortly after the deceased had signed the will. Sproat died a few days later. William Sproat mentioned that when he was informed that his brother had died he was then living in Pretoria. He immediately came to the deceased's house and saw the accused. He sympathised with her but she did not appear to him to be much upset. There was some discussion between him and Daisy about whether the doctor would give a death certificate. Whether such a certificate was obtained or not the witness did not know, but he found the accused's conduct very strange in that even before her husband's body was removed from the house, she had set about trying to let it and he was ashamed at that conduct. I need not, for the present purposes, deal with much of his further evidence in detail except a portion to which I shall now refer.

Some time after his brother had died he wrote a letter to his mother, who lived overseas, informing her of his brother's death – because up to that time his mother had merely been informed by cable that her son had died. In his letter to his mother he said that she did not have to worry about the widow as she was pretty well provided for, that she had two houses of her own and that there was quite a bit of money coming.

After a time, he received a letter from his mother, who said she could not understand his telling her that she was not to worry and she enclosed a letter written to her by the accused. The witness said he opened the enclosed letter and when he read it he was astounded. William Sproat recounted:

> It said, 'Dear Mother, no doubt you have heard by now about Robert's death. And what a big funeral he had.' Then she said that I [William] had got Robert to make out a will. Immediately after that she said that with my brother being ill for so long, all the money that had been saved had been spent on doctors and during the time my brother was ill several people used to come and see him and she had to give them a cup of tea and in these times every cup of tea counted.

Daisy had actually asked his mother whether the latter could afford to let her come over with her son Rhodes, 'because Bob [the deceased] had intended taking a trip across'. William Sproat said he had kept the letter. One can imagine his feelings. He went on to say that he thought that when Daisy came to visit he would have to tackle her and ask her whether she was in the habit of writing letters like that.

Daisy had come over to see him and his wife in Pretoria a short while later and she said that she was surprised and couldn't understand why she had not heard from him and his wife. Having made up his mind to deal with her, he taxed her with the contents of the letter, saying, 'Daisy, have you been in the habit of writing to my mother complaining of poverty?' According to him she tried to avoid the question, but he said, 'Daisy, I want a straightforward answer to a straightforward question.' She then said that perhaps Sproat's mother had misunderstood her, to which William had replied, 'My mother could not misunderstand.' He asked her whether she intended going overseas on holiday; and told her that if so, he did not want her to go and see his mother. In answer to Daisy's question as to why his mother would not want to see her, he said that his mother did not want to be bothered with her. The Sproats took Daisy to catch the train at the Pretoria station and when she wanted to shake hands with them he said, 'No Daisy, there are one or two things I want to tell you. I do not want to see you again or speak to you. Never put your foot in my home again.' She asked 'Why?' to which the witness replied, 'Because I have lost all faith in you.'

It will be recalled that Cowle died in March 1932. *The Sunday Times*, on 6 March, had a death notice and funeral notice. The death notice inserted by Daisy read: 'COWLE. Died at 19 Simmer East, Germiston on the 5th instant, Rhodes Cecil Cowle aged 20, son of Mrs De Melker and step-son of S C De Melker'. The funeral notice read 'Cowle, Rhodes Cecil aged 20 years, died on the 5th instant, the son of Mrs D L De Melker (Sproat). Deeply mourned. Cortege will leave Swift's Parlour, 223 Bree Street, at 3.30 pm today (Sunday) for the Cemetery. Friends kindly accept this intimation. John Swift Ltd Undertakers.'

It will be observed that the name Sproat appears in the funeral notice inserted by the undertakers, but not in the death notice inserted by Daisy. I have little doubt in my mind that it was seeing this notice, coupled with his brother's death and the extraordinary letter written by Daisy to his mother, which must have caused Sproat to raise with the police the question as to how two husbands and one son had died within a comparatively short period of time. Cowle had died in January 1923, Sproat in November 1927 and the son Cowle in March 1932.

* * *

As junior to Harry Morris, I was fortunate enough to be briefed in several cases, some of which I would like to mention.

Harry was briefed, and I as junior, to defend a man in Bethal who had had the misfortune of having his estate sequestrated and being prosecuted, *inter alia*, for having incurred debts without any reasonable expectation of being able to pay them. In the 1930s there were frequent prosecutions under the Insolvency Act of persons who had had the misfortune of having had their estates sequestrated. One of the favourite charges was that of incurring debts without reasonable expectation of being able to pay them. These were regarded as serious offences and those found guilty were invariably sent to jail.

In this case, one of the witnesses – who was plainly a creditor – was called to prove that the accused had incurred a debt with him. He was cross examined and after he came out of court he said to me, 'You know, when I went into the witness box I thought I was a creditor, now after what has happened to me as a result of Harry Morris's cross examination, I have begun to feel as if I was the debtor.' I mention this case not because of its particular importance, but as an example of Harry Morris's devastating powers of cross-examination.

I remember two local inhabitants saying to me, on either that occasion or a subsequent one when Harry Morris was briefed to defend an accused, 'Oh he [the accused] must be guilty – otherwise why did he get Harry Morris to defend him?' I must admit that I derived a certain amount of satisfaction a few weeks later when I saw the same two gentlemen going into Harry Morris's chambers to consult him on a certain matter. Were they guilty of some crime or other?

One of the most sensational cases in Harry Morris's career took place[10] in the mid-1930s. Two Johannesburg detectives were paid protection money by wealthy bottle store keepers who warred with the illicit liquor tsars whose territory bordered on theirs. As a result, men and women were jailed on perjured evidence, which in many cases was carefully rehearsed. (In passing I might mention that these two detectives employed a third person as a 'trap' in many cases, and he had no difficulty in giving perjured evidence. During the Second World War, in the course of my duties I had occasion to go to what was then Germiston Air Station. There I discovered that this informer was employed in the army pay corps. Needless to say I felt it my duty to tell his commanding officer something of this man's background.)

One of the victims of a false trap was the licensee of the Pretoria Bridge Bottle Store, a Mr Abelson. He was alleged to have sold liquor after hours. If ever there was an innocent man it was this one. He had an alibi, and had witnesses to support him, that at the time he was alleged to have been at the bottle store he was in fact in synagogue on the Jewish New Year's eve. He was convicted in the magistrate's court on the evidence of the two detectives and their trap informer. The magistrate accepted the evidence of the detectives and their trap despite the strong defence put up, based on the alibi. An appeal against the conviction failed. One of the judges who dismissed the appeal was Mr Justice Saul Solomon.

There was a fallout between the two detectives and one of them decided to get even with his accomplice, who was eventually prosecuted, and to inform the police of what the two of them had been up to for a long period. Judge Solomon again presided over this trial, in which the two detectives faced serious charges of perjury, of interfering with the course of justice, and of bribery. The accused elected to be tried by a judge and jury.

One of the persons summoned for jury service was a friend both of mine and of Harry Morris. The defence, as was the Crown in those days, was entitled to challenge three persons without giving any reason. I suggested to Harry that he should challenge our mutual friend who, in my opinion, was far too intelligent to be swayed by arguments that might not be of substance. Harry thought otherwise and as it turned out this man became the foreman of the jury and as the trial proceeded there seemed to be a rapport between him and the judge. I always had a feeling that the judge, when he realised that he had quite unwittingly been a party to confirming the guilt of an innocent person, had taken an immediate dislike, quite understandably, to the accused.

The trial was a long one. Harry Morris ran the whole defence virtually by himself. I don't think that I played any real part in the case. It was far too difficult for me to be of any real help. The trial ended on the eve of Passover and I remember going to my father's house after a verdict of guilty, which was inevitable, despite Harry Morris's efforts on behalf of the accused, and the two detectives were given a sentence of ten years' imprisonment.

Another case concerned a nursing sister,[11] one of the bravest women I have ever met. In defending a fellow nursing sister from being seriously assaulted by her husband, she shot the man and killed him. The evidence revealed that this man had been in the habit of visiting the nursing home where the two nursing sisters were employed and beating his wife. On many occasions prior to the killing the accused had been called on to help the unfortunate wife who was being battered and bruised to such an extent that she was even ashamed to appear before her patients or the public. Evidence revealed that on several occasions the man had threatened to kill his wife. I need hardly add that there was also evidence that the deceased was a heavy drinker and that there had been objections by patients of the nursing home to his conduct towards his wife.

When the accused heard that he was coming to visit his wife again, she was certain that he would assault his wife, as he usually did on these occasions. He had done so on so many occasions and with such brutality that she had made up her mind that if he assaulted his wife again in the same manner as before, she would kill him if necessary. She had a revolver, which she had loaded in anticipation of having to come to the rescue of her friend.

On the occasion of the killing she heard an uproar in the dining room and also heard the deceased threaten to kick his wife in addition to saying that he would shoot her. When she heard what was happening and saw the deceased assaulting his wife, she shot him. She described in her evidence that the deceased had a most malign expression on his face. He was holding a chair in his hands and she thought that he might hit his wife with it. According to her evidence she thought that this man's wife was in danger and she then and there shot him. She said openly in evidence, 'I fired deliberately at him.'[12]

What she said in evidence was what she had told us in consultation and I remember saying to her that although the law was that she was entitled to kill somebody who was trying to kill another person unlawfully, there was a danger that the jury might not believe her evidence and might find, for example, that her friend's life was not in any danger. Her attitude was one that I have never forgotten. She said: 'I intended to kill him and I am going to say so – and if that means that I may be found guilty, I am prepared to take the consequences.' She gave her evidence in a faultless manner. Harry Morris's address to the jury was, of course, as brilliant as ever. The jury retired and came back within ten minutes with a verdict of 'not guilty.'

One other case – probably the last of Harry Morris's famous cases – the defence of Delves Broughton in Nairobi in 1941 on a charge of murdering the Earl of Erroll, premier Earl of Scotland, I will relate a little later.

Chapter Three

A BUSY JUNIOR PRACTICE

One day not long after the De Melker case was finished – I was still in Manfred Nathan's chambers – an old friend of mine, Reuben Kahanowitz, walked in. He was then practising as an attorney in partnership with a well-known sportsman, Alf Reid, in Benoni. He asked me whether I would be prepared to go to Bloemfontein to argue an application for leave to appeal for a fee of 35 guineas. I was then 28, and as I had never been to the Appellate Division of the Supreme Court I would have been prepared to go there for nothing; and a fee of 35 guineas was certainly good compensation in those days. He then told me what the appeal was about. A man called Manasewitz, who practised as an attorney in Witbank, had been found guilty of fraud. In those days – the early 1930s – farmers could obtain loans from the Land Bank amounting to two thirds of the value of the cattle that they owned: eg, if the farmer had cattle valued at £1 500 he would get a loan of £1 000. Manasewitz and a local valuer thought of a way of getting greater loans for farmers and at the same time enriching themselves. Instead of valuing the cattle at £1 500, they were to be valued at £3 000, enabling the farmer to get a loan of £2 000. The extra money so received would then be shared by Manasewitz, his co-conspirator and the farmer. Fraud can only be said to be committed if there is prejudice or potential prejudice to the person defrauded. As the farmer in question probably never intended to repay the loan whether it was £1 000 or £2 000, he was apparently a willing accomplice. However, the fraud was discovered and Manasewitz was charged with fraud to the prejudice of the Department of Lands.

He was duly convicted and he appealed to the Transvaal Provincial Division against his conviction. This appeal was heard by Judge N J De Wet and Judge of Appeal Mr Justice Grindley Ferris. Judge De Wet had been a Minister of Justice and he was well aware of the workings of government. He took the view, with which his brother judge concurred, that it was not the Department of Lands that had suffered prejudice, but the Union government. The court, therefore, upheld the appeal and the conviction and sentence was set aside. The Attorney General of the Transvaal decided to re-indict Manasewitz, now alleging that fraud had been committed to the prejudice of the Union government. Manasewitz appeared before the magistrate in Witbank and his counsel took the point of *autrefois acquit* – arguing that Manasewitz had already been acquitted on this charge and could not be charged again on the same charge. The magistrate rejected this defence and found Manasewitz guilty.

Again there was an appeal. This time the court consisted of two of the most eminent judges I have ever appeared before, Judge Tindall and Greenberg. That court apparently considered itself bound by the previous decision of Judges De Wet and Grindley Ferris, which had decided that if there had been fraud it had been a fraud on the Union government. Consequently the court dismissed the appeal.

For a junior such as I to think that Tindall and Greenberg could ever be wrong was probably heresy. As if the fact that this was to be an application for leave to appeal against their judgment was not sufficiently daunting, to add to my dismay I was shown an 'opinion', written in his own handwriting by Advocate Philip Millin, in which he said that an application for leave to appeal was without merit, was bound to be dismissed and he was not prepared to argue it. However, I duly went to argue the appeal in Bloemfontein. The Chief Justice was Sir John Wessels, a great judge but well known for the hostile treatment that he meted out to counsel when not in agreement with a point being argued.

As this case was to be my first appearance before the court I decided to spend some time listening to another appeal being argued before mine was to be heard. The appeal court in Bloemfontein is one of the most beautiful courts I have ever seen. It is a large room, all panelled in stinkwood. The story is that the court was being built during the tenure of a previous Chief Justice, J A De Villiers, who being an expert on timber had insisted on this panelling. The members of the Bench were Chief Justice Wessels, Judges of Appeal Curlewis, Stratford, F W Beyers and Sir Etienne De Villiers. The judges, as in all cases, sat in order of seniority so that in this case Judge of Appeal Curlewis sat on the right of the Chief Justice, and to the right of Curlewis sat F W Beyers; to the left of the Chief Justice sat Stratford, and to his left sat Sir Etienne De Villiers, who was a junior Judge of Appeal.

The appeal I heard was in fact in the case of the Roodepoort–Maraisburg Town Council *v* Eastern Properties (Prop) Ltd. I recall that Jack Brink, one of the leading silks at the Johannesburg Bar, argued some point and Mr Justice Wessels said to him, 'Oh, Mr Brink, is that your point?' Brink – who had probably had a pretty rough time before then – said, 'Yes m'Lord, I have been trying to make that point for two days.' The heavens descended upon him as Wessels thundered, 'Mr Brink how dare you say such a thing? There has been far too much talking in this case already.' (As far as I could gather, Wessels had done most of the talking.) The next-senior judge, Judge of Appeal Curlewis, was customarily very polite, and added, 'No, Mr Brink, you mustn't say things like that. We always give counsel a proper hearing.' Judge of Appeal Stratford also expressed his disapproval of Brink's attitude, and on that unhappy note the appeal came to an end.

The case in which I was to argue was then called.[13] I confess that I cannot think of a single defended case or appeal or opposed application – and indeed some unopposed applications – when I was not nervous when starting to argue. In this case, my client was hardly one deserving of sympathy; and I was likely to get a rough time, particularly from Chief Justice Wessels. After what had happened to Brink, it can be imagined how nervous I felt. I began: 'M'Lord this is an application for leave to appeal.' Wessels said loudly, 'Leave, leave!' and turning to my opponent – W G Hoal, KC, Attorney General of the Orange Free State, who was appearing for the Crown – said, 'Oh, you don't oppose *leave* do you?' Hoal wanted to, but the manner in which these words were delivered indicated to me, and I am sure that Hoal felt the same way, that Wessels was going to dispose of this application in a summary manner.

I then commenced my argument.[14] I had, as anticipated, a very rough time from Chief Justice Wessels, so much so that by the time

I sat down I felt that I was the accused. As I sat down Judge Wessels said in a whisper to Judge Curlewis – heard by me and probably audible at the back of the court – 'You don't want to hear Hoal do you?' The significance of that question, of course, was that he, Wessels, had made up his mind to dismiss the application and did not feel it necessary to hear the Crown's argument in reply. Curlewis agreed with Wessels as did Stratford and Beyers.

When Wessels looked at Sir Etienne to find out whether he agreed as well, Sir Etienne indicated that he did not agree. He then did a thing that I have never seen since – and I gather from my colleagues that neither have they seen it in their experience of an appeal court. Sir Etienne got up and walked right across the court to where the Chief Justice was sitting and he and the Chief Justice had a discussion behind the chair. The Chief Justice's chair is a very high one and I did not hear what was said between them; but whatever was said, the result was that Hoal was called upon to argue. He had a smooth passage. I replied – I cannot remember what I said – but the court reserved judgment. The result came as a surprise to me. All the members of court, except Curlewis, who dissented, decided to give leave to appeal. The main judgment of those deciding to grant leave to appeal was that of De Villiers. He pointed out that unlike the judges in the Transvaal Provincial Division (Tindall and Greenberg), the Appellate Division was not bound by the previous decision of Judges N J De Wet and Grindley Ferris, which in his view was incorrect. The accused should have been found guilty on this charge, but having been found not guilty was entitled to the benefit of the plea of *autrefois acquit*. He was in jeopardy of having been found guilty on the first trial and first appeal. De Villiers's judgment – like all his judgments – was a model of clarity and logical reasoning.

The report of the case says that the appeal was then allowed. As I have already pointed out there was not an appeal at that stage, but an application for leave to appeal. Chief Justice Wessels said that the court could not finally decide the matter until the full record of the proceedings in the courts below was before the Appellate Division. Sir Etienne did not think so; and correctly in my opinion, because the point was one essentially of law and a sufficient portion of the record was before the court on the application. The appeal itself was heard the following year and the result was a foregone conclusion. It was a formality and the appeal was duly upheld.[15]

While I was still in Manfred Nathan's chambers, I was appointed arbitrator in a dispute between the attorney Emanuel Gluckman, whose wit I have already mentioned, and a client of his. I was probably appointed because I had had some experience myself in the magistrate's courts and the amount in dispute was small. The dispute was about the fees that Gluckman had charged in a matter conducted for his client in the magistrate's court. I found in favour of Gluckman; but his client, whose name I have forgotten, started a campaign of defamation against him. The result was that Gluckman sued him for damages in the Supreme Court. In this case, Gluckman was represented by Norman Rosenberg, then a leading junior at the Bar. Oliver Schreiner, also a leading junior, appeared for the defendant. I was subpoenaed and was called to give evidence by Gluckman's counsel about the client's conduct in the arbitration proceedings. He had behaved rather badly and it was thought that my evidence might increase the award of damages that would be made against Gluckman's former client. The trial came before the then Judge President, De Waal, who in referring to my evidence said that I was 'a barrister of standing.'

In fact I was not a barrister, and did not become one until many years later. I was an advocate and if the judge had said I was of two years' standing that would have been correct. I was neither a barrister nor of standing. Up to that stage – although Mrs De Melker was not lucky – I considered myself to have been very lucky. My practice in the early years was mainly confined to civil and criminal work in the magistrate's court, an occasional civil or criminal and pro deo trial in the supreme court and appeals to the provincial division in both civil and criminal matters.

Then along came what I thought was a case in which I was going to earn large fees. In those days the film industry in South Africa was largely controlled by a company known as African Films, the head of which was the well known I W Schlesinger. Metro Goldwyn Mayer (Metro) opened a large cinema at the corner of Von Brandis and Bree Streets, Johannesburg. This cinema had, of course, what was known as 'the first run' of all films produced by Metro, then a leading Hollywood producer of films. Metro had a local representative, a Mr Carl Sonin. Schlesinger apparently came to some arrangement with Sonin which resulted in films being shown at the Metro cinema for one week, as was the custom in those days, and would immediately thereafter be made available to Schlesinger's company and were shown at his cinemas – the Bijou and the Orpheum, around the corner from the Metro cinema.

Carl Sonin, however, had committed suicide, leaving a letter in which he made certain allegations against Schlesinger and his dealings with him. It so happened that Metro had at that time just lost a case in England against a Prince Yousopov, a relative of the Tzar of Russia. The prince had sued Metro for libel as a result of the manner in which he was depicted in a film produced and shown by Metro. The plaintiff's counsel, Sir Patrick Hastings, KC, was then one of the leading silks at the London Bar. Metro decided to brief Sir Patrick to act in proceedings in South Africa against Schlesinger and / or African Films, for damages that Metro claimed it had sustained as a result of the alleged conduct between Schlesinger and Sonin. Hastings, KC, briefed Rosenberg and Ramsbottom, both leading senior juniors in Johannesburg (if indeed they had not already taken silk – I am not sure of the exact date).

Schlesinger's attorney, the late Philip Friedland (of Edward Nathan and Friedland), acted for Schlesinger and his company and he briefed Mackeurtan, KC, Harry Morris, KC, Philip Millin, KC, and myself as junior. A difficult question of law being the admissibility and probative value of Sonin's letter, I was shown an 'opinion' that had been obtained on Schlesinger's behalf in the United States. This 'opinion' was very short, but attached to it was a long list of decisions in the courts of the United States. I thereupon decided to buy what was a leading authority of evidence – the one written by Professor Wigmore. The edition I bought was the second edition and as far as I know, apart from the Wigmore in the Bar Library, no other member had a copy of this monumental work. I can remember the cost, £35.

Although Sir Patrick was a barrister in England, he had to pass an examination in Roman Dutch law in order to be able to appear in a South African court. He wrote the examination twice and he was failed twice. Whether or not this resulted in the case being settled, the fact is that the case was then settled on terms of which I know nothing and all I was left with was my Wigmore. Although I acted as a junior to Philip Millin and Harry Morris in many cases subsequently, I never had the good fortune of ever appearing as a junior to Mackeurtan, who was a recognised legal giant in those days.

By the time of the Metro débâcle, I had acquired a fairly busy junior practice, and was briefed as junior and appeared on my own in the usual run of civil and criminal cases in the Supreme Court.

In those days, criminal trials were held before a judge and jury – unless the accused elected to be tried by a judge and assessors. Juries, in finding an accused guilty, very often made a recommendation to mercy which the judge would frequently consider (but not always, as he was not obliged) in determining the sentence. When I was a clerk in Mr Raphaely's office, an example of a case where a recommendation to mercy led to nothing was the notorious case of Rex *v* Nafte which came before Judge Saul Solomon and a jury in Bethal. No doubt Nafte elected to be tried by a judge and jury instead of a judge and assessors because the farmers in Bethal were not known for being liberal in the treatment of their labour. Nafte had beaten one of his employees to death and was charged with murder. The jury – composed of farmers in the Bethal district – could or should, in the opinion of many people, have found Nafte guilty of murder, but they found him guilty of the lesser crime of culpable homicide only, and brought in a recommendation to mercy on the ground that they thought that Nafte did not intend to kill the deceased. The evidence established that Nafte had caused the death of the deceased by a severe flogging, by breaking his breastbone with a stone and kicking in two of his ribs. The deceased died of shock caused by multiple injuries.[16] Judge Solomon sentenced Nafte to seven years' imprisonment and ten lashes. I recall that I was telephoned by Nafte's attorney, Maurice Porter, a friend of mine, who seemed shocked by the punishment imposed on Nafte and asked me to tell Mr Raphaely about it, which I did. Mr Raphaely's attitude was that Nafte was lucky not to have been found guilty of murder and he deserved a punishment more severe than that imposed on him by Judge Solomon.

I mention this case and the recommendation to mercy in contrast to a case in which I defended a Greek shopkeeper charged with attempted murder. In this case the jury put in a recommendation of severity, something quite unusual. It was alleged that the shopkeeper had attempted to kill a Black employee of his whom he had shot and wounded. The trial was before a judge and jury, the jury I think consisting entirely of Afrikaners. Judge Greenberg presided, and Walter Pollak, later to become one of the leading silks at the South African Bar, was prosecuting. (But for the fact that he was not a favourite of the National Party when it came into power in 1948, he should have been appointed to the Bench, finishing his career in the Appellate Division.) The evidence of the person who had been shot was very poor. The defence was that the accused had acted in self defence and proof of this picture emerged in the course of cross examination of the complainant. At the end of what was then a crown case (it would now be called a state case), if there is no evidence upon which a reasonable man *could* or *might* convict the accused, the judge was asked to withdraw the case from the jury and if he agreed he would direct the jury to bring in a verdict of not guilty. I applied for the discharge of my client at the end of the crown case and Judge Greenberg agreed with submissions I made. He thereupon instructed the jury to bring in a verdict of not guilty. The jury remained sitting for some time, apparently thinking to themselves that if there was any shooting of Blacks to be done, a sort of royal game, it should be done not by Greeks, but by Afrikaners. Eventually the foreman of the jury got up and pronounced the words which he was instructed to pronounce: 'Not guilty'.

EDITORS' NOTE: *Isie's sons recall that one of their greatest treats when growing up was to be taken out on a Saturday night to what was known as an 'early show' and thereafter for a mixed grill at a café.*

He frequently took them to a certain café in Orange Grove where he appeared to be on excellent terms with the proprietor. At the end of a meal there, he would call for the bill, to be told – with monotonous regularity – that no charge would be made. But he always insisted on paying the bill. With equal regularity the children asked their father why it was that the proprietor did not wish to be paid. They were told: 'shut up and mind your own business.' However, with the nagging persistency possessed perhaps only by teenagers, they finally extracted from him the infor-

mation that the café proprietor was the accused in a murder trial in which, it was alleged, he had shot dead an intruder, using 'excessive force'. Isie put on the accent of a Greek speaking English, and said that the proprietor had told him that he had 'sot the boy', but that, fortunately, the jury had believed that it had been in self defence; and thus the proprietor was delighted to throw in a few mixed grills against the low fees he had been charged.

Isie was always inclined to discretion and brevity in such matters, which was not only unsatisfactory to an inquisitive boy, but used also to infuriate his wife, who often said – with justification – that he told her nothing whatsoever about his cases. Perhaps a further example will illustrate this.

When his eldest son, Keith, was thirteen he had a Barmitzvah and received a number of beautiful and expensive presents. Perhaps the most lavish of these was a gold Schaefer pen and pencil set, accompanied by a card with best wishes from 'Mr S'. Keith had never heard of Mr S (and neither had his mother) – and he certainly did not attend. After constant nagging and questioning by both of them, somehow they managed to extract the information that he was someone for whom Isie had 'done a small favour'. They persisted with questions and were eventually told that he had defended Mr S, and the latter had gone to jail for six months.

'So what kind of a favour is that?' asked Keith.

'He should have got five years.'[17]

There was – and for all I know there may still be – a practice, when counsel is briefed to defend a person on circuit, that he is obliged to undertake what is known as a 'dock brief' on behalf of other persons who are to stand trial at the same circuit. On one occasion it was a Mr Pitt, a very skilled interpreter, who made the approach. The fee was three guineas irrespective of how long the case would last. The client whose defence I had to undertake was a young Black man charged with raping a Black woman. He was correctly found guilty by the jury who expressed the wish that the court should impose a severe sentence on the accused. I should mention that although all rape cases are serious, the complainant of this case really suffered no serious injury at all. Judge Greenberg was obviously somewhat surprised to hear the jury's recommendation and asked the jury why they had recommended a severe sentence. The foreman of the jury then said that they feared for the future of this country if this young Black (they did not use the word Black) could show no respect for the court by telling such lies and that he ought to be punished severely because of that. The judge thereupon asked the foreman of the jury whether perhaps it could not be said that the accused had told lies because he wanted to be acquitted and not because of any disrespect for the court or anybody else. The reply, in Afrikaans: '*O ja, ons het nie daaroor gedink nie.*' The judge thereupon sentenced this young man to what was more or less the standard punishment for that kind of crime committed by young men, namely six strokes with the cane.

Chapter Four

MARRIAGE, WAR AND 'WHITE MISCHIEF'

Perhaps I should now deal with a somewhat more important aspect of my life. Early in 1933, not long after the De Melker case had concluded, I met Muriel Freed who then lived in Durban. My friend Maurice Porter and I had decided to take a very popular trip in those days, to go by ship around the coast from Durban to Cape Town. On the day before the ship sailed, Maurice and I were walking in Durban when a car stopped at a traffic light. Maurice recognised the driver as Muriel, whom he had known for some time, and introduced me to her. We eventually became engaged and were married in Durban on the 28 June 1934.

Our elder son, Keith, was born on 1 October 1935, and our younger son, Jeffrey, on 18 October 1937. I well recall Keith's birth. My wife, as was the custom in those days, was confined at home and was in labour on the night of 30 September when I had a phone call from an attorney, one Henry Levy. He was an extremely able practitioner, especially in the field of company law. When he said he had to see me urgently that night and asked if I could come to his house, I explained that Muriel was in labour. He replied: 'What can you do about it?' My mother-in-law, who was in our house at the time, agreed with him. So I went to his house, the arrangement being that I would be telephoned when the child was born. Levy consulted me that night about a matter dealing with some mining rights, in the course of which he showed me a certain document. After I had been at Levy's house for about two hours we were having tea when the telephone rang and I was told that a son had been born. I then said to Levy, 'Well, I would like to go now.' To which he replied: 'What do you think you can do now?' About two years ago, Henry Levy having long since died, I was consulted by another firm of attorneys about a matter concerning the very document which Henry Levy had shown me that night. Probably because of the circumstances under which I had first seen the document, I was able to recall the matter about which I had been consulted.

A little more than a year after Jeffrey was born, at the end of 1938, Muriel and I took our first trip overseas, travelling by ship on the Holland Line, the fare for both of us being £45 first class return. We had a wonderful time in Europe at very little cost until the end of January 1939.

In May 1939, my mother died suddenly.

In September that year the Second World War broke out. It is not inappropriate to say that when South Africa entered the war in 1939 its defence force was in a shambles. Oswald Pirow, Minister of Defence up to the outbreak of the war, was strongly suspected of being unduly enchanted by Hitler and his philosophy. There was an added difficulty in that a number of officers in the permanent force, according to law, could be compelled to serve only within South Africa. Unless they agreed otherwise (and some senior officers did not) they could not be sent out of this country on active service. In addition, such officers and men – and, of course, persons joining the army or airforce for the first time subsequent to the outbreak of the war – could not be compelled to serve outside South Africa unless they had taken an oath undertaking to serve anywhere in the world if called upon to do so. This was known as 'the red oath'. All of us took it and we all wore a red flash on our shoulders to demonstrate this fact.

I may perhaps here mention that I met Pirow for the first time, at the robing room at the Supreme Court in Pretoria, just after he had retired from government – that is, at the time that Parliament decided to declare war against Germany, and the Smuts government came to power. When I was introduced to him, he said, 'Oh, I think I have heard of you.' To this I replied somewhat cheekily, 'I hope you won't mind my saying so, but I have heard of you as well.' One need hardly add that he was not the most popular figure in South Africa at that time, certainly as far as it concerned the English press, followers of Smuts and those who were anti-Hitler.

In April or May 1940, a colleague of mine at the Bar, Gordon Davis – who had won a DFC in the First World War – recruited various members of the Bar, including myself, for a unit known as the Air Intelligence Liaison Office (or AILO in short), and subsequently called the IOUs by us. Among those whom I remember were H C Nicholas (subsequently to become a Judge of Appeal), Bill McEwan (subsequently a judge of the Transvaal), Dennis Levy, Charlie Rosenthal and Ovi Measroch. Having failed my first medical examination I tried again, was accepted, and was made a staff sergeant. The others were either ordinary airmen or corporals. It is unnecessary to say anything about the usefulness of the work which this unit was supposed to do, save to say that it might possibly have been of some use when aeroplanes were first used in combat in the First World War, but by the time the Second World War came along, the *raison d'être* was not readily apparent.

We were all told by Gordon Davis that although we had joined 'in the ranks', as it were, we would soon be commissioned. This, I need hardly say, did not happen. We underwent some sort of minor military training at a camp in Waterkloof.

One day when we were paraded for some reason or other, an officer senior to Gordon Davis, a Major Schoeman, came to inspect us. With him was a young officer who had left the Bar because he had not been successful there (he was very successful after he left the Bar). We knew that he had had no military training and the fact that he was commissioned, and none of us was, rankled with us. We raised the matter with our officer in charge at Waterkloof, Captain Geoff Treadwall (the well known cricketer), as to how this man had been commissioned when all of us had been in exactly the same position as he when we had joined. Captain Treadwall, considering there was some merit in our complaint, reported the matter to Gordon Davis, who – I think – must have reported it to Major Schoeman. The result of all this was that we were paraded and it was suggested that we had been guilty of some offence, the nature of which I cannot recall, and that we could consider ourselves lucky not to be court martialled.

It was apparently realised in the airforce or army (we were never quite sure what we were in) that we were a lot of troublemakers; and we were almost immediately dispatched to East Africa in the SS *Dilwara*, a troopship formerly used by the British to take troops from England to India and possibly other parts of the world where there were British colonies. As an aside, I might perhaps mention that while boarding the train at Pretoria station on the way to

Durban for embarkation 'north', I saw two attorneys who had been struck off the roll for theft of trust monies, dressed as members of the Pay Corps!

The distinction between the way officers and other ranks were treated in the British Army became all too apparent to us. Our food was inedible and our sleeping quarters were cramped, while the officers, some of whom I knew, ate well and slept in luxury.

We ended up at an airfield in Nairobi with absolutely nothing to do. One day we were sitting at the aerodrome when my friend and colleague at the Pretoria Bar, Oscar Galgut, then a Captain, arrived at the aerodrome, saw me there and asked me what I was doing there. (Subsequently in civil life he enjoyed a long and distinguished career as Judge of Appeal. I replied: 'You tell me – I don't know.' Well, the next day I was transferred to Airforce Headquarters and after a few months was commissioned as a second lieutenant. All my colleagues who had joined the AILO were also commissioned, and some ended with ranks much higher than that of lieutenant. There were, of course, other members of the Bar who joined the army: Eddie Tobler, who joined the Transvaal Scottish; and some who did not return from the war, one of whom was Johnny Kneen. He was killed in a flying accident which I actually witnessed. He was being flown to Cairo in a very well fitted plane. It had, I believe, been the private plane of Howard Hughes, and Johnny Kneen had taken me to see the plane just before it took off from Nairobi Airport. It had been in the air for no more than a minute or two when it suddenly dived and hit the ground. Of course, everyone on board was killed. Johnny Kneen, in addition to being an extremely able junior at the Bar, had been a first class sportsman and played wing threequarter for Wits University – I have an idea he played for Transvaal as well. I had the melancholy task of being one of the pallbearers at his funeral. Another man who did not return was Adrian Hope, a senior junior at the Bar. When war broke out, he became a major in the ACF. He was killed while being parachuted into Yugoslavia to join the partisans.

In Nairobi, the only Intelligence work that I was called upon to do was to interrogate two Italian pilots shot down by the South African Airforce. They could speak no English and I could speak no Italian. There was no interpreter and consequently the interrogation could hardly be called a success. As far as I remember they were under the illusion that they had encountered a large number of enemy aircraft whereas, in fact, the pilot of a solitary South African plane had shot them down in combat. I spent some time in the 'Intelligence Room' at Air Headquarters, but do not recall being of any real value to anybody. I was then attached to the organisational side under a Major De Vos (subsequently Colonel), and struggled to learn something about organisation so far as the airforce was concerned.

There were RAF members at headquarters as well as South African officers and other ranks. The class distinction between the officers and other ranks in the RAF was strikingly apparent. There was certainly not the same situation in the South African Airforce. I recall that before I was commissioned, I was very friendly with a RAF warrant officer and we used to have a drink together occasionally. Once I was commissioned the friendship ceased, not from my part, but from his; he could not overcome the 'class situation' in which he had been brought up.

I had had an introduction from a senior at our Bar, Norman Rosenberg, KC, to Mr Lazaras Kaplan, an attorney who was practising in Nairobi. I called on him one day and he was kind enough to invite me to lunch and we became friends.

Early in 1941 the Earl of Erroll was murdered and the baronet Sir Delves Broughton was arrested on a charge of murdering him. Broughton's wife, Lady Diana Broughton, was a most beautiful and attractive woman, much younger than Sir Delves. She had been his mistress before they were married and the story, as I understood it, was that he had married her so that she could live with him in Kenya as his wife. Whether or not this was so was never clear to me, but what became public knowledge was that she was having a torrid love affair with the Earl of Erroll – a handsome, arrogant man who had apparently been divorced twice and was said to have had affairs with many women in Nairobi. He was, at the time, an Assistant Military Secretary for the Protectorates of Kenya. There had been a strange arrangement between Broughton and his wife Diana – apparently intended for her benefit – that if either of them fell in love with someone else, the other partner would agree to a divorce. There was also a marriage settlement under which Diana was to receive financial benefits as long as she stayed put.[18]

Broughton's attorney was Kaplan. He got in touch with me and asked me whether I would be prepared to accept a brief to defend Broughton. I said of course; but I had to get permission from the airforce to do so. My commanding officer was Brigadier Hector Daniel, and his staff officer was my friend Oscar Galgut. Brig Daniel, possibly influenced by my friend Oscar, was quite keen on my undertaking this defence and I, of course, was also keen to do so because apart from anything else army pay was not such as to enable one to live in luxury. When the war broke out there was a general meeting of the Bar and by an overwhelming majority the members decided that those who did not join the army or airforce would hold briefs for their colleagues on active service on the basis of sharing the fees equally. This arrangement did not last very long and we had no other income but our army pay. Brigadier Daniel told me that he would, of course, have to get confirmation from South Africa for his agreement to my accepting the brief, and after a lapse of some time a reply came, not entirely unexpected, that I was in Nairobi not to defend murderers, but to fight a war.

Before this message came through I had been introduced to Lady Diana, who invited Kaplan and myself to dinner at her house one night. The set in which Lady Diana moved was a pretty hard drinking one. I saw more empty champagne bottles in the yard of the house than I had ever seen in my life. Dinner was supposed to start at 7.30 pm but only started at about 10.30 pm, Kaplan and I meanwhile drinking vodka.[19] It was fashionable at the time to serve vodka and caviar before dinner; Lady Diana Broughton, however, omitted the caviar. By the time the dinner was served, Kaplan and I were close to being inebriated. I was never, for the rest of my life, able to stomach the taste of vodka.

Before sitting down to dinner we were taken around the house. It was of some importance that we should see the house and particularly the drainpipe down which at some stage – it seemed to have been suggested – Broughton had climbed in order to get out of his house and get to the spot where he was alleged to have shot and killed Erroll. This was some considerable distance, two and a half miles, from the house in which the Broughtons lived. Lady Diana took us into her bedroom, where I noticed what was to me a somewhat bizarre thing – next to the bed, on a small table, was a photograph of Erroll with his glengarry cap across it. By that time, of course, her husband had been arrested and was in prison awaiting trial.

On the night on which Erroll was killed he and Lady Diana had been seen dancing together. There had been a very strange dinner party before she went out dancing with Erroll that night. Apparently Delves Broughton had become reconciled to the fact that Diana wanted to be divorced from him so that she could marry Erroll. They were deeply in love with each other and he had, at that dinner, toasted them on their forthcoming marriage and said that he hoped that the union – between Erroll and Diana – would be blessed with a son and heir. Erroll's previous marriages had yielded only an heiress. Also present at this dinner party, which took place at the Muthaiga Club (one very much like the Johannesburg Country Club), was a woman, Lady June Carberry, a friend and confidante of Diana.

One Sunday not long afterwards, I was invited by Mr Stretton, Kaplan's partner, to have lunch with him at the Muthaiga Club. The other guests were Lord and Lady Carberry. Carberry, an Irish lord, used the title only when it suited him. Lady June had spent the night on which Erroll was murdered at the Broughtons' house and was clearly to be a material witness in the case, although I knew nothing of this prior to the lunch. We had a pleasant lunch and at the end of it Carberry said to me, 'Let's get down to business.' I had not the faintest idea what he wanted to talk to me about and he started off by saying, 'Well as you know, girls will be girls.' This did not seem to call for any comment from me. He then said, 'Look, I want you to tell me what Junie [his wife] should say in evidence.' I tried to explain to him that it was not part of counsel's work and duty to tell a witness what to say. Indeed it was highly improper for him to do so. It took a lot of convincing on my part before Carberry dropped the subject and we parted. Junie, as he called her, was an alcoholic and a member of the fast set in Kenya. What I subsequently read confirmed that she was a material witness in the case.

Broughton was to be tried by a judge and assessors. It was said at the time that no jury of white men (as they then were in Kenya) would ever have convicted Broughton or anyone else of murdering the Earl, as the latter was said to have slept with most of their wives.[20]

Once I had told Kaplan that I was not allowed to take the brief, he naturally sought other counsel and was fortunate indeed in obtaining the services of Harry Morris. I have read the accounts of the trial as given both by Harry Morris and by Benjamin Bennett,[21] and I must say, quite frankly, that Broughton was very lucky to have obtained Harry Morris as his counsel instead of me. Harry Morris's knowledge of firearms was of tremendous – if not vital – importance at the trial. There was, of course, a strong motive, so the Crown alleged, for Broughton to want to kill Erroll – who was as it were taking away his beautiful wife from him – but at the end of the day the question was whether it could be proved beyond reasonable doubt that Broughton had committed the crime. The crown prosecutor was Walter Harrigan, subsequently Sir Walter Harrigan. (When he left the courts of Appeal of Botswana, Lesotho and Swaziland many years later, I was invited to fill the vacancy on the Bench created by his retirement.) One of the serious difficulties facing the Crown was that Erroll was undoubtedly shot with a five-groove gun. No such weapon had ever been traced to Broughton's possession and the Crown's evidence – that the shots had been fired from a Colt that Broughton possessed – was destroyed in cross examination.

Strangely enough I had just finished writing this part of my memoirs when a friend of mine, who knew that I had been offered a brief in the Broughton case, brought me a copy of the well known English publication, *The Spectator*, dated 13 February 1993, in which there is an article entitled, 'Mischief, Murder and Multiple Adultery' by Simon Courtauld. He speaks of an interview he had had with a woman, Juanita Carberry, aged 67, who was then living in a London flat overlooking the Thames. In that article he refers to a book written by James Fox entitled *White Mischief*[22] in which the author tells of Juanita, then 15 years of age, having told him that Broughton had confessed to her four days after the killing of Erroll that he, Broughton, had killed him.

I myself had read this book, and had had my doubts as to whether what this woman told Mr Fox was correct. My doubts were not dispelled by the article written by Mr Simon Courtauld in which he states that he was told the same story by her recently. Again I do not doubt that Mr Courtauld has correctly recounted what he was told by her. But it seems to me unlikely that

Broughton made the confession in question. I had met Lady Broughton on other occasions such as the one of which I have written and I particularly remember talking to her at her house the day before I left for South Africa, having been recalled there. There was undoubtedly a strong motive for Broughton to have killed Erroll – but I was left with the impression, perhaps wrongly, that she, Lady Broughton, did not think that her husband had in fact killed Erroll. In addition, I find it difficult to reconcile the alleged confession with what Harry Morris wrote about this case in *The First Forty Years*. He ends his account of the case[23] by saying: '[Sir Delves] was a fine English gentleman. At least two persons must have taken part in this job. If Diana, Lady Broughton, had not told the police about the target practice at Nanyuki, this chapter could not have been written.' In *Genius for the Defence,* Mr Bennett gives what seems to be a fairly full account of the trial. Harry Morris returned to Johannesburg the day after he had argued for his client's acquittal. Counsel for the Crown, as was the English practice, addressed the jury after Harry Morris had concluded his address. Consequently Harry did not hear it – but, of course, he heard the verdict the day after the acquittal when he had arrived in Johannesburg.

Bennett (and I knew him and respected his reputation as a first class journalist and accurate reporter) says that the day after Harry Morris returned to Johannesburg he wrote to Broughton 'assuring him that he never doubted his innocence for a moment and he paid tribute to his honesty and sincerity, which had eased his onerous task'. I have known and had the good fortune to be associated with Harry Morris in many cases. In addition to his outstanding qualities as an advocate he was a pretty good judge of human nature. I simply cannot visualise Harry Morris writing what he did about Sir Delves Broughton, in his book; nor his writing a letter in the terms set out in Mr Bennett's book, had he not honestly believed in his client's innocence. However, when – as frequently happened – Morris was asked by members of the public whether Broughton, notwithstanding his acquittal, had actually done the deed, Morris would reply: 'You know, dammit, I forgot to ask him!'[24]

I myself could never believe that Broughton, who was alleged to have shinned down a drainpipe, gone two and a half miles across country and thereafter back up the drainpipe, was ever physically able to have done this. In my view the murder was committed by Lady Diana Broughton in conspiracy with June Carberry and the remark 'girls will be girls', made to me by Carberry at luncheon, was strongly indicative of this.

Of course the fast set, to which Erroll, the Carberrys and many others belonged, did not constitute, by any means, the bulk of the white population in Kenya. There were hard-working farmers and dedicated district commissioners: great hospitality was offered to the troops and received, of course, with gratitude by them.

On New Year's day 1941 I was ordered, as a junior officer, to join some senior officers and fly to Mombasa for a conference on board HMS *Dorchester*, at which plans were made for the invasion of Abyssinia (now known as Ethiopia) including, of course, Mogadishu, which is very much in the news today. At lunch time on that humid, hot day I was introduced in the junior officer's mess to what was apparently a favourite naval drink, 'pink gin'. The invasion took place shortly after that conference. The South Africans put the Italians to flight and, of course, a large number of prisoners were taken. It will be recalled that Abyssinia had been conquered by Mussolini as part of his attempt at colonial empire building and there is no doubt that the Italian occupation made, and left, good roads. The buildings that they put up were not of particularly great quality. After the invasion had taken place I was ordered, for some reason which I can no longer recall, to go to Harar, where it is said that the Queen of Sheba was born. Once the Italian occupation had come to an end, Emperor Haile Selassie returned to power. One day he sent his son, the Prince, whose name I cannot recall, to Harar and as he alighted from the plane holding an umbrella over his head, he was welcomed by a guard of honour consisting of South Africans. He was rather a short person and I wondered what was going through the minds of the men forming the guard of honour.[25]

When I left to return to Nairobi by air one of the other passengers in the plane was a British army officer. The plane had to stop on the way to be refuelled. We had left very early, and we South Africans had not had any breakfast and had omitted to take any food with us. The British officer, however, clearly much more experienced than we were, had with him a hamper of food and drink of which he partook heartily whilst we were waiting for the plane to be refuelled. It goes without saying that he did not offer any of us any part of his hamper.

One of the officers stationed in Nairobi was Major Miller, a famed airforce officer who had served in the First World War. He thought it would be a good idea to use pigeons as a means of communication. Among the men stationed at airforce headquarters was a pigeon fancier, who was sent back to South Africa to recruit (if that is the correct word) pigeons for this purpose. The idea of using pigeons did not prove a success. There were too many hawks about. The pigeon expert or fancier, who was a sergeant, was hospitalised for some unknown reason and I was instructed by Brigadier Daniel to visit him in order to find out what his trouble was. He appeared to have had a nervous breakdown and complained to me that he had been unfairly treated in not having been commissioned. I wondered then, and still wonder, whether he thought the pigeons would have had more respect for him if he had been an officer.

Chapter Five

COURTS MARTIAL, THE MIDDLE EAST AND TAKING SILK

On my return to South Africa I was posted to Airforce House in Pretoria to serve under Colonel Rod Douglas, who was head of the organisation and personnel section of the airforce. Col Douglas was not a member of the permanent force but had joined up when the war broke out. He found the pay section of the airforce in shambles. Wives were writing letters complaining they had not received the pay due to their husbands, which had to be sent to them while their husbands were away on active service. He thereupon hit upon an idea of recruiting young, able accountants from the civilian section; and thereafter, the pay section of the airforce was efficiently run and there were no more such complaints. I shall have occasion to refer to this aspect of the matter later.

After I had been at airforce headquarters for a short while I received a call from Colonel Charles Gardner, Judge Advocate to the Forces, formerly a silk practising in Grahamstown (after the war, he became a judge of the Eastern Districts Division of the Supreme Court). Colonel Gardner told me that he had been asked by another colonel, with whom he had served in the First World War, to defend him at a court martial for some offence which I cannot now recall. Colonel Gardner told me that he had informed his friend that in view of the fact that he was a Judge Advocate he could not possibly defend him. Consequently he asked me if I would undertake the defence at the court martial, which was to take place in Pietermaritzburg. I was then either a second lieutenant or a lieutenant. I went down to Pietermaritzburg and was taken into the tent where my prospective client was under close arrest. I told him that I had been asked by Colonel Gardner to defend him. He looked me up and down and told me that he did not require my services as he had engaged a Pietermaritzburg attorney to defend him. By that time I had been at the Bar over ten years and had had a fair practice and I thought to myself that possibly I was as good as the Pietermaritzburg attorney. However I bore my prospective client's refusal with as much courage as I could summon and went out of the tent. I then saw the officer who was to preside at the court martial and he asked me whether I was ready to go on. I told him what had happened and that I was going back to Pretoria. This officer then went into the tent and came out a short while later and told me that the prisoner, as he was called in the army, had changed his mind and asked for me to defend him. The court martial proceeded and at lunch time when the court adjourned I was invited to lunch at the Pietermaritzburg Club.

While having a pre-lunch drink at the bar of that club I saw Colonel Stallard. He was then Minister of Mines in the Smuts government; but when I had come to the Bar in 1930 he was the leader of the Bar. He had served in the First World War with distinction and had a DSO and an MC. I, of course, recognised Col Stallard, but did not for a moment think that he would remember me. I had never appeared in court either with him or against him although I had heard him – a most impressive and able advocate. The custom at the Bar is for a new member to call on the person senior to himself. There is also a custom that one does not call a senior 'mister' – thus when I had to introduce myself to Stallard I had to call him 'Stallard', not 'Mr Stallard'. Considering our respective positions this was a very difficult thing for me to do. It is a difficulty which many juniors experience even today when they have to introduce themselves to a senior. As to calling a senior colleague by his first name, this is still today unusual at the Bar, save among those who have become personal friends. In Professor Ellison Kahn's comprehensive work of legal anecdotes and portraits, *Law, Life and Laughter*, Stallard is of course referred to, and reference is made[26] to an article written by Mr Justice Schreiner about Stallard.[27] Schreiner wrote the following 'Stallard respected all juniors of the Bar as his brethren and sympathised with their difficulties.' To my amazement, undoubtedly in accordance with what Judge Schreiner has written about him, Stallard came right across, shook hands with me and enquired how I was getting on. I was astounded that he had even recognised or remembered me at all, and I recount this incident as indicative of the character of this outstanding leader of the Bar. To finish this episode I should perhaps say that luckily for me and for my client, the court martialled colonel, he was acquitted.

The fact that a person is a lawyer is something that becomes known fairly rapidly in the army. My advice was sought frequently on traffic offences and other trivia, and I was also asked from time to time to defend soldiers or officers who were being court martialled. I was also asked to sit as Judge Advocate in certain courts martial. There is one to which I should like to refer.

It was a British court martial at which I was asked to act as Judge Advocate. The court martial took place in a transit camp in Durban utilised by the British Army as a suitable place for men awaiting transfer to other zones of the war. The events leading up to this court martial arose as a result of the refusal of a large number of British soldiers to board a ship, one of three, which was due to sail to Singapore from Durban. (Ironically the men on the two ships that did sail arrived in Singapore only to be taken prisoners by the Japanese.) Prior to the relevant ship's departure there had been an inspection of its condition by senior officers. It was found to be lice-ridden and one of the officers was overheard saying that if he were ordered to go on that ship he would refuse. This statement became known to the men who had to sail on this ship. They refused to do so. There were so many men involved that they were split into two and two courts martial were held. Edgar Henochsberg, who was a silk, and was in the army, and who subsequently became a judge in Natal, was asked to act as Judge Advocate in one of the courts and I in the second one.

The role of a Judge Advocate is to advise the officers who sit in judgment as to the law applicable and, if he deems it necessary or desirable, to advise the prisoner or the person defending him, usually called the 'prisoners' friend', on questions of law or procedure. The men were charged with mutiny, without doubt one of the most serious of offences; and alternatively, with not being in a place where they should have been, an offence under the military code of discipline. The men were defended, not by a lawyer, but by a captain. He was thus the prisoners' friend. A major was called as one of the first witnesses to give evidence about the order given that the men sail on the ship in question and their failure to do so.

He was asked a question by the prisoners' friend, which he answered, and then the prisoners' friend said, 'Sir, may I ask you another question?' I thought it was time that I intervened, because it seemed to me that the captain had not the faintest idea of how to cross-examine. I thereupon asked the president of the court martial for a short adjournment and spoke to the prisoners' friend. I asked him why he was putting questions in that manner and he said, 'Well you can imagine what will happen to me in the mess tonight if I cross examine my senior officer.' I thereupon asked him what the facts were as far as he knew and he told me about the lice-ridden ship and of the remark by the senior officer to which I have referred above, as reported to the men. The case proceeded and I think I took over, as I was entitled but not obliged to, the cross-examination of the witnesses for the prosecution, bringing out the real reason for the men's refusal to sail on the ship. After evidence was given by one or two of the prisoners, argument was advanced both for and against the prisoners. As is the practice, the court was then cleared and the members of the court had to discuss their verdict; and, in the event of their finding the prisoners guilty, the sentence that should be imposed on them.

The procedure, and the correct procedure to determine the verdict of the court at a court martial, is to ask the most junior officer his view and then to canvass the views of the officers senior to him in order of seniority. The idea behind this procedure – which is, of course, a fair and proper one – is that the junior officer should not, in coming to his decision, be influenced by what a senior officer had decided. I should also add that whatever decision is come to by the court martial, if there is a finding of guilty, this decision is subject to review, in a camp of the kind that I have mentioned, by the senior officer in charge of the camp. After a lengthy discussion, the officers (and I think I played some part in advising them) came to the conclusion that the prisoners were not guilty of mutiny but were guilty on the alternate count, which was far less serious than that of mutiny. The officers were then asked, again in order of seniority, what they thought was the proper sentence. The sentence proposed by the most junior officer was double the maximum provided for in the military discipline code and after this was pointed out by me, as was my duty, sentences of imprisonment were imposed on all the accused. I cannot remember the number of years. After the case concluded, I was summoned by the officer commanding the camp, who had either to confirm or reject the decision of the court, and told him what had happened. He was a very gentle, humane and experienced officer. He asked me whether I thought, bearing in mind the circumstances in question, that it would be in order if he suspended all the sentences of imprisonment on the condition that the men went forward the next time they were ordered to do so. This, I thought, was an entirely appropriate sentence. And so it was.

In the mid-1940s I was ordered to join a squadron of the South African Airforce stationed north of Acre near Ramat Yochanan, a kibbutz named after General Smuts who was a great proponent of the idea of a Jewish state (and, of course, a strong supporter of the Zionist movement). This was my first visit to Palestine (a second visit came early in 1944).The squadron, which was to be called upon to perform certain missions, was stationed there in the belief that Turkey would join the war on the side of the Allies and not on the side of the Germans, with whom it had been allied in the First World War. As it happened Turkey did not join the war and this camp was disbanded.

Whilst stationed there I went with a fellow officer, Norman MacRobert, to Haifa, where we went to a restaurant to have some coffee. We were duly served but had no sugar and asked the waiter for it. He then told us that they did not have any sugar. Both MacRobert and I had forgotten that we, in the forces, had sugar and anything else that we required, but that sugar was not readily available to people living in Palestine. A stranger sitting at the next table to us heard what had happened. He got up, took out a small tin from his pocket, and offered us what was obviously the whole of his sugar ration. Of course we did not take any. I mention this incident because it was typical of the conduct of the Israelis, as they came to be known, toward members of the forces. If they were standing in a queue waiting for a bus and a soldier joined the queue, they would make way for him to allow him to stand in the front.

I was also sent to Cairo for some purpose or another. Cairo during the war was, of course, full of troops of various nationalities. I was billeted with an old French lady who could not speak English. Although I had taken French both at school and at university and was able to read it without much difficulty, I did not find it easy to converse with her – not that it was really necessary to do so. Naturally, in Cairo I was shown the magnificent mosques, the museum and the pyramids. I also visited somebody at the famous Shepherds Hotel, carpeted with oriental splendour, and I heard the Palestine Symphony Orchestra perform there at a concert. The concert hall was, of course, packed and I had been lucky to get a ticket. The overwhelming majority of the audience, as I could see it, consisted of men in the ranks of the British forces who appeared to have the score of the music that was being played.

Having accumulated some leave, I had the good fortune to obtain a seat in an RAF plane which was flying to Lydda, now known as Ben Gurion Airport, outside Tel Aviv. After lunch at the officer's club which was near the seafront, I decided to look for a shop in order to buy my wife a piece of jewellery. I did not know where the shops were and asked a British policeman if he could tell me where they were. He did so and I was about to depart when he said to me, 'Sir,' – I was then a major – 'may I give you a word of advice?' I of course answered in the affirmative. He said, 'You must be very careful here you know, the shops are all run by Jews.' I laughed and told him I thought he had got the wrong number. I mention this because it was the first and only incident of anti-semitism which I encountered during the whole of the four and a half years that I spent in the forces.

I met a former South African friend of mine then living in Tel Aviv, Ellie Kirshner. He had a sister living in Jerusalem and through her I met a man called Zvi Schwarz, the father-in-law of Moshe Dayan. As is probably well known, Dayan had been locked up, together with other members of what was known as the Haganah, a volunteer force whose job it was to protect the kibbutzim from attacks by the Arabs. He was court martialled for being in possession of a rifle – which he had of necessity carried for the purpose – and was sentenced to ten years' imprisonment in a dreadful jail in Acre.

Syria was then in the hands of the Vichy French. Mr Schwarz told me about the incident that led to Dayan's losing an eye while under attack from French detachments in the Iskenderun area. (Moshe Dayan himself describes the incident in his book, *The Story of my Life*.) The British had asked Dayan to join forces with some

Australians and with some of his colleagues in the Haganah, to invade Syria so that the British could oust the French troops and take control of Syria. In his book, Gen Dayan reports how in the operating theatre of Haifa Hospital, to which he was eventually moved, in response to his questions about his condition, the doctor had replied: 'Two things are certain. You have lost an eye and you will live. What is not clear is the condition of your head with so many bits of glass and metal imbedded in it.'[28] Gen Dayan, of course, became a world renowned figure. He was rewarded by the British for his services with payment of the sum of £25.

Jerusalem was in those days undivided. The Jews and Arabs lived side by side, particularly in what is now known as the walled portion of Jerusalem. It was occupied, after the War of Independence in 1948, by the Jordanians. The Jordanians never really had any title to that city at all. It formed part of the mandated territory of Palestine and the first time that the Jordanians ever took possession of the city was during the War of Independence. They remained in possession only because an armistice was declared during that war. People are inclined to forget that the Jordanians were driven out of Jerusalem during the Six-Day War, not because Israel had declared war on Jordan, but because the Jordanians, in the belief that Israel would be defeated by Egypt and Syria during that war, had started bombarding the so-called 'new' part of Jerusalem, largely occupied by the Jews. The Jordanian participation in that war was quite uncalled for. In fact a message was sent to the King of Jordan through the head of the United Nations Office (then stationed on the appropriately named 'Hill of Evil Counsel') that nothing would happen to Jordan if it kept out of the war. It was as a result of their defeat that the Israeli state, already established, took possession of the whole of Jerusalem. I can recall how prior to the Six-Day War one could see, from the rooms of the King David Hotel, Jordanian soldiers stationed on top of the walls, presumably guarding Jerusalem from attack.

But to return to my visit to Palestine during the Second World War: I was fortunate enough to be able to join a tour of South African soldiers of the Sixth Division, who were being taken by a guide to Bethlehem where Christ is said to have been born. There was, among the troops, a chaplain and the guide was Jewish.

When we came to the place in Bethlehem where Christ was said to have been born, the guide, respectfully and very properly, asked the chaplain, whom I think was an Anglican, if he would like to tell the Christian version of the birth of Christ. The chaplain asked the guide to do it which he did. I was not sufficiently aware of the facts of the New Testament to determine whether a good or proper account had been given. I was told by the chaplain that it had been, to quote his own words 'magnificently done'.

Jerusalem, in 1944 when I visited it for the first time, was not such a thickly populated or busy place as it is now. The sabbath eve is one I shall never forget because of the complete silence which overtook the city. I was taken by Mr Schwarz to visit a Jewish family that had lived in the Old City for many years. The house in which this family lived was built on top of another house. The occupants were, of course, strictly Orthodox Jews and I had a feeling that to some extent they and their two daughters were really living in the past. I wondered how the young people could adjust themselves to modern conditions. (Some years later, on a visit to what was then Israel – that is, after May 1949 – I asked Mr Schwarz what had happened to these two girls. He said, 'Oh, don't worry about them, I saw one of them yesterday. She is working at the income tax office.' They had obviously become fully integrated into the Israeli society, which was then, to a large extent, removed from the atmosphere in which they had been brought up.) I met during this visit, among many others whose friendship and hospitality I have not forgotten, a lawyer, Mr Olshang, subsequently to become the first Chief Justice of the Supreme Court of Israel after Israel became independent.

On expiry of my week's leave, I tried to get a seat on a plane back to Cairo, but without success, and was walking towards the railway station in Jerusalem to catch a train back to Cairo when I met a Major Chick Nathan, then Deputy Chief Censor of the British Army in the Middle East, and whom I knew before the war as an attorney practising on the West Rand. When I told him that I had tried to get a seat on a plane, he said, 'Leave it to me' – which I did; and he got me a seat on an Egyptian plane run by a company known as MISR Airways, naturally known to us as 'Miserable Airways'. The plane was a small De Haviland plane piloted by an overweight Egyptian. Fortunately we landed safely in Cairo – I heard subsequently that on the following day the same plane went down in the desert and the occupants were killed. From Cairo I went, via Malta, by air to Italy which by then had fallen into Allied hands. There I met my friend Colonel De Vos, under whom I had served in Nairobi, and he took me on a tour of Italy. We spent one night in Naples, where I went to the opera house and saw an Italian opera for the first time.

After I returned to Airforce House in Pretoria I learned for the first time that no squadron – or, in fact, any army unit – could be formed without what is known as an 'establishment' duly authorised by the finance authorities. Obviously, formation of any unit creates recruitment costs and expenditure on equipment and pay for officers and the ranks who are to serve in them. Colonel Douglas, as Director of Organisations in the airforce, had formed additional squadrons required for service (undoubtedly on instruction from the head of the airforce, General Venter). Somehow or another the necessary permission had not been obtained and large sums of money had been properly spent as required, but the expenditure had not been formally authorised. In this connection, I was visited by a school friend of mine, Geoffrey Madden, who was then in the office of the Auditor General. I thought the Auditor General had been quite satisfied with the explanation that I had given him, but I was quite wrong. Shortly afterwards a letter was received by the Director General of the Airforce, General Venter, that he had been surcharged some millions of pounds, that being the cost incurred as a result of the employment of various personnel without the necessary authorisation of 'establishment tables.' General Venter, naturally very alarmed at this, reported the matter to the Chief of General Staff (CGS).

I was instructed to draw up a memorandum setting out our reasons for having acted in an irregular manner, which I did. This was shown to the CGS, General Van Ryneveld, who said that he disagreed with one or two of the sentences in my memorandum and requested me to alter them. This I agreed to do, provided Colonel Frank Shaw, a leading King's Counsel at the Natal Bar – then a senior law officer in the Army – agreed with the CGS. He did not agree; and my memorandum remained unaltered. A letter was, in due course, received by General Venter signed, I think, by the

Minister of Finance or possibly the Secretary for Finance relieving him of the liability in question. I subsequently learned that if the total amount irregularly spent was a few hundred pounds, General Venter would have had to pay that sum of money; but the sums involved were so large as to make the demand for payment stupid.

While still at Airforce House, at about the end of July 1944, after D-Day and the successful progress of the Allied forces in France, I was summoned by General Beyers, Adjutant General of the Army. He told me he wished to appoint me as Judge Advocate to the Forces.[29] I would be promoted from the rank of major to that of colonel and I would be made a King's Counsel. I was certainly in no position to be made a KC, having been at the Bar only about ten years before going on active service.[30] I had to explain this to him and asked him whether the result of this appointment was that I would have to spend the rest of the war doing law in the army in South Africa. He replied, 'Yes, that would be the case' – whereupon I told him that if I had to do law I would like to be able to do so and earn a living again in my practice as an advocate. He did not know that apart from the army pay, people like myself who were advocates, had no other source of income – unless, of course, they had private means, which I did not have. General Beyers was quite surprised to hear this and said he thought it was quite unfair to keep people like myself in the army and that it was time that the Permanent Force officers learned to do their jobs. He said that he would speak to the head of the airforce, General Venter, on my behalf and suggest to him that I should be released. This he did, and a short while later this was confirmed by a telephone call from a major on his staff. I was released from the army at the end of September 1944.

During the war my chambers had, of course, been vacant, but my books were there and everything that I left behind before joining the army was still there when I returned. This was largely due to a faithful clerk of our group, Mr Tyndall. Luckily for me there was a number of firms of attorneys who had made up their mind not to brief advocates who did not join the forces, but to brief those who had returned to the Bar after active service. The result was that I was fairly busy from the time I returned to the Bar.

I should perhaps mention one case where I expected to get some work and did not. Shortly before I was due to retire from the airforce I was in synagogue on the Jewish New Year. Sitting behind me was an attorney from whom I used to get an occasional brief before the war. He asked me when I was coming out of the army, 'Because,' he said, 'we are waiting for you chaps to get out.' I told him that I was to be released at the end of the month. He received that information with pleasure, but sad (or perhaps not so sad) to relate, I never got another brief from him.

Before I recommence the tale of my life at the Bar I should mention that during the time that I was stationed in Pretoria I lived at the mess at Voortrekkerhoogte during the week and, naturally, went home at weekends to see my wife and family. During this period, there were two additions to our family. My wife had always wanted girls in addition to our two boys, and we were lucky enough to be able to arrange matters in this way.

Our elder daughter, Elizabeth, was born on 21 January 1945 in the first house that we had acquired after our marriage. Dr Joe Schwartz, an old school friend of mine (we had matriculated together), attended the confinement. Elizabeth, now married to Jesmond Blumenfeld, lives in Oxford, England. Our second daughter, Helen, was born on 6 November 1949 at our house in Young Avenue, Houghton. Helen, having spent many years in the United States and England, returned eventually to South Africa and is married to Benjamin Trisk. Luckily for us she lives in Johannesburg.

Two of the first briefs which I had were rather unusual applications, or rather, applications that had unusual results. In both I was briefed by Mr C Friedman of the well known firm Hayman, Godfrey and Sanderson.

The first concerned the descendants of a very wealthy man who had died in Johannesburg. He left no children but had nephews and nieces both in South Africa and in other parts of the world. Some of them had lived in Russia, and information as to their whereabouts resulted in a number of affidavits being filed by persons who were in a position to know the whereabouts of these people, that they had, in fact, perished in concentration camps set up by the Nazis. Consequently I was briefed to obtain an 'order' presuming that these people had died. Such an order can be granted only if there is strong evidence to justify it. The affidavits that these people were dead were, in fact, very strong and an order presuming death was granted by the court. Some years later a firm of attorneys in Johannesburg, who had acted for the Russian government before the Second World War, received a letter from the Russian government in which it was alleged that the persons whom it had been believed were dead were, in fact, alive. Enquiries were made by the Russian government on behalf of these persons as to whether they were not entitled to inheritances from a rich uncle whom they believed had died. This firm of attorneys communicated with the attorney acting for the executors of the estate of the deceased, advising him of the contents of this letter and making certain enquiries in connection therewith. In order to verify that the persons claiming the inheritances were, in fact, alive, it was necessary for the attorney, accompanied by one of the deceased's nephews who lived in South Africa, to go to Moscow, and they ascertained that three persons who had been presumed to be dead were indeed alive. One had survived the concentration camp at Auschwitz. The result was that steps were immediately taken to transmit the inheritances to these people. Permission was received from the South African government in order to do so. The monies had to be transmitted to a bank nominated by the Russian government, and they did eventually reach the beneficiaries. I have ascertained from the attorney who went to Moscow that one of those three persons has since emigrated to Israel.

The second application to court arose in the following manner. A British Palestinian policeman by the name of Neville Heath, being returned by ship from Palestine to England, jumped ship in Durban and masqueraded as a wing commander in the RAF. He also claimed to be the nephew of an earl and used first names which were of such a nature as to lead one to believe that he was a member of English aristocracy. He soon entered Durban society and, being a 'wing commander', was admitted to membership of exclusive clubs in Durban. He married an attractive young woman from one of the upper-class Durban families and a child was born of the marriage. He had no money at all, but by trickery he was able to obtain money from various persons. When it was discovered that he was, in fact, not a wing commander and that he had defrauded many people, he was sentenced to imprisonment. His wife was fortunate enough to obtain a divorce, but as he was the father of the child, he was, by law, its guardian. I was briefed to have his guardianship terminated and transferred to his wife. His wife's attorney wasted no time in getting this person deported to England. He did this by communicating the facts to the appropriate authorities in Pretoria. How fortunate his wife was in getting rid of this man was demonstrated shortly afterwards. In England he had successively married five women, all of whom he had murdered, and he was duly executed.[31]

Together with David Gould, I was briefed to appear at a preparatory examination as junior to Oswald Pirow, KC, to represent one Norbet Erleigh, then a well known director of companies and so called 'whiz kid' who had, together with his co-director Joseph Milne, been arrested on charges of fraud, theft and contravention of the Companies Act. The preparatory examination was a very long one. Erleigh used to think it proper to telephone me at all hours of the night to discuss a point or points that had occurred to him. None of these points was of any substance and the phone calls really became a burden. Erleigh and Milne were duly committed for trial, but Erleigh dispensed with the services of Pirow, Gould and myself and briefed another counsel to defend him at the trial. This seemingly stroke of bad luck turned out to be a piece of good fortune for me.

My practice had grown and I was reaching a stage at which I felt I might apply for silk. In those days, this of course meant applying to become a King's Counsel. Prior to South Africa's becoming a republic, George VI being King of this country, the title was King's Counsel. At the succession of Queen Elizabeth, the title became Queen's Counsel, and when South Africa became a republic those who successfully applied for silk became Senior Counsel. Those of us who were at the time Queen's Counsel were offered the opportunity of changing the letters QC to SC. None of us availed ourselves of this opportunity and there are still a few, very few, Queen's Counsel in practice.

Normally a member of the Bar who has become what is known as a senior junior applies for silk when he finds that his practice is such that he can no longer cope with the volume of work offered to him. The procedure in my days was to apply to the Chairman of the Bar Council who made enquiries into one's practice, the nature of the practice and, of course, the character and integrity of the applicant. If he thought that the applicant's case was a worthy one, he forwarded a recommendation to the Judge President of the Division of the Supreme Court in which the applicant was practising and, if the Judge President agreed with the recommendation, he forwarded it to the Minister of Justice, on whose approval, letters patent were issued. The term 'taking silk', when one is appointed as set out above, derives from the fact that one's stuff gown is discarded and one acquires a silk gown.

The grant of silk in those days carried with it the obligation of not appearing in court alone, but of having an accompanying briefed junior. In effect, this meant that the silk was briefed only in matters of importance and by persons, corporations and other bodies who could afford the expense of employing two counsel instead of one. Some years ago the practice for taking silk was slightly changed, in that the application is made to the senior members of the Bar Council and it is their recommendation that is forwarded to the Judge President.

One other change to the old procedure has been much more important. Upon taking silk it is no longer necessary for the silk to appear with a junior. He is entitled to accept briefs to appear by himself and this, of course, means that it is not so costly to employ Senior Counsel.

There are, however, many cases in which silks will not appear without a junior and, of course, there are many cases which necessitate the employment not merely of a silk, but also of a junior or juniors. These are usually cases in which the nature of the matter and the complexity of the law or the facts necessitate the employment of more than one counsel. In many cases, if not in most, the junior or juniors play a most important part in the trial or appeal. They prepare arguments, look up the authorities and very often cross-examine certain witnesses or take part in the final argument. In the 'Treason Trial' (to which I shall make reference later), there were two silks and six juniors briefed for the Crown (ie the prosecution) and for the defence there were two silks and eight juniors. This, of course, was an exceptionally long and difficult case, and certainly in that case the juniors played a very big part – not merely in the work preparatory to the trial (which was considerable), but also in the examination and cross examination of witnesses and in taking part in the argument on both sides.

In 1932 when Mr Justice Millin was Chairman of the Bar Council, I had been Secretary to that body. He had always been friendly to me, and indeed I had known him from the time that I was an attorney's clerk and took briefs to him, and, of course, at the Bar, before he became a judge. As I have mentioned, my practice had grown considerably. In 1946, three senior juniors who had not gone on active service applied for silk – which was rightly granted to them at the beginning of 1947. He spoke to me one day early in 1947 and asked me why I had not applied for silk as well, because he thought that my practice was comparable to that of three persons mentioned. I explained to him that I felt that I needed more experience in certain fields of the law and that there were also financial reasons for my not being able to risk taking silk. I should perhaps add here that it does not follow that because one takes silk that one is going to get more work or better work than one had as a junior. Be that as it may, I did apply for silk at the end of 1947 and this was granted to me in February 1948.

I was Chairman of the Bar Council on three occasions and the duty fell upon me to make the necessary recommendation for persons who wished to apply for silk. In one of the cases that I recommended, I had tried to dissuade the applicant from proceeding with the application for silk, not on the grounds that he was not a person of integrity, nor that he did not have a busy practice, but because I felt that he did not have the quality of work as a junior which justified his taking silk – and more importantly, perhaps because I did not think the attorneys who briefed him had what is known as 'silk work': the type of case in which it was desirable or necessary to brief a silk. He, however, was confident that he could carry silk and against my better judgment I recommended him. Unfortunately this was a disastrous step. From being a junior in a busy practice earning a fair amount, he was reduced to being a senior with virtually no practice at all.

Nowadays as I have stated above, it is no longer necessary for a silk to have a junior with him in court, and it is consequently to some extent less risky to take silk. There are many members of the Bar extremely able and with good practices who have never applied for silk for good and sufficient reasons. On the other hand there are certain of my erstwhile brethren who seem to be keen on taking silk because they think that the letters SC behind their name somehow improves their standing in society. However, the Bar Council is careful not to recommend the appointment of anybody for silk who, in their opinion, does not warrant it.

In my last year as a junior I appeared in the Appellate Division and was briefed in trials both criminal and civil in the Supreme Court. I shall tell a story of only one of those civil trials mainly because of certain answers given in cross examination. I was briefed by a very able attorney, Albert Livingstone, to appear for what was then a well known firm of estate agents, L K Jacobs & Co Ltd, in an action brought against one Webranchek, for commission which the plaintiff, Jacobs & Co, claimed was due as a result of its having been the effective cause of a sale of a property belonging to Mr Webranchek. The case came before Judge Roper. What happened as far as the plaintiff was concerned was a very simple thing. It, through one of its directors, a Mr Marcus, had procured a purchaser for a building owned by Mr Webranchek and an appointment was made on a Saturday for the deed of sale to be signed by the purchaser and Mr Webranchek. On Saturday afternoon another firm of estate agents, Seef & Co, who had had a mandate to sell the property in question but had not found a purchaser, somehow or another got hold of the purchaser that Marcus had found and persuaded Webranchek to sign the deed of sale to the purchaser who had been found, as I say, by Mr Marcus. That Mr Webranchek feared that he might be liable for commission to L K Jacobs & Co Ltd emerged clearly from the deed of sale which he entered into at the instance of Seef & Co, for it contained a clause in terms of which Seef & Co indemnified him against any claim for commission which might be made by L K Jacobs & Co Ltd in connection with the sale in question. There was plenty of material upon which one could cross examine Mr Webranchek. It was easy to demonstrate that he had acted in a dishonourable, if not dishonest, manner and had done so because Seef & Co were going to charge him half the commission which he would have had to pay to L K Jacobs & Co Ltd and he supposed he had saved himself approximately £500. In the course of cross examination I asked him, 'Mr Webranchek have you no ethics?' To which he answered, 'Ethics, I leave for the synagogue.' Any doubts there might have been of our success in that case disappeared, in my opinion, entirely when that answer was given, especially before a judge of the calibre and integrity of Judge Roper. The salesman at Seef & Co was also not a very satisfactory witness and I remember asking him a question which called for a plain answer, either 'yes' or 'no.' I said to him, 'Mr X what is your answer, yes or no?' He said, 'I cannot answer you until I have had a drink of water.' I gave him a glass of water to drink and after he had had his drink I repeated the question, 'Well Mr X, is your answer yes or no?' He answered, 'I don't know.' As indicated above, judgment was in favour of L K Jacobs & Co in amounts claimed with costs. Seef & Co, however, who had given an indemnity to which I have referred, decided to appeal against Judge Roper's decision in the Appellate Division. By the time this appeal was heard I had become a silk and it was my first appearance as a silk in the Appellate Division. My junior was Mr George Colman (who subsequently became a judge of the Supreme Court and who should, in my opinion, have ended his career as a member of the Court of Appeal). The appeal court had no difficulty in dismissing this appeal and in the judgment of the court, written by Judge of Appeal Van den Heever, I quote the following passage merely as an example of the felicitous manner of a judgment of this great judge (given both in English and Afrikaans) as given by him in the Court of Appeal, and prior to that in the Orange Free State Provincial Division:

> If we weigh up the causative value of plaintiff's efforts and those of Seef & Co the former preponderate, if one may use a simile, plaintiff designed and built a ship ready for launching; Seef & Co presided over the formalities at the celebrations and pressed the button at the slipway. Plaintiff said it is due to me that the vessel exists at all whereas the defendant, for his own ends, praises Seef & Co as the sole cause of its being afloat.[32]

Strangely enough the first brief I had as a silk, in February 1948, was to defend somebody – who and what the charge was I cannot now remember – in the High Court of Rhodesia before Mr Justice V A Lewis and a jury. I had as my junior Mr Bennie Goldin. He was my junior in a number of matters in which I was briefed subsequently in Rhodesia. He became a judge in Rhodesia, as it then was, and a member of the Court of Appeal when Rhodesia, as Zimbabwe, became independent. I then appeared in a matter before him. Because of the many years that I spent at the Bar, I have appeared before a number of judges both in the Provincial and Appellate Divisions who had from time to time acted as my juniors in certain matters.

Some time later in 1948, the notorious 'Bubbles' Schroeder case arose. Bubbles Schroeder was a young, attractive girl from Vereeniging who, because she found life in her home town dull, had come to Johannesburg, where she became essentially, young as she was, a *femme de nuit*. She was found dead one morning in a thicket at Melrose not far from the south side of the Wanderers Club. Two young men, whom I shall call 'X' and 'Y' respectively, were arrested on a charge of murdering her.

I was briefed to defend X at the preparatory examination. He was alleged to have been an accessory to the murder of Bubbles Schroeder. Before his arrest he had been questioned on many occasions for several days by police officers and one night, before he was arrested, he was brought to my house by his attorney, Victor Mansell. Y, also after having been interrogated for some days by the police, was arrested on a charge of murder. If ever there was a case when two innocent people were charged with a murder, this was it. A full account of the events leading up to the discovery of the body of the deceased and of the court proceedings that followed appears in Benjamin Bennett's *The Evil That Men Do*,[33] where he quotes the court proceedings as reported in *The Star* and the *Rand Daily Mail*. X, after his arrest, was admitted to bail in the sum of £500 and Y in the sum of £5 000. Y was defended by Maurice Franks, KC, and Cecil Margo. My junior was Melville Festenstein.

The senior police officer in charge of the case was Major Ulf Boberg (he later became Colonel Boberg and was frequently referred to in Joel Mervis's *Sunday Times* column, 'Passing Show', as 'Ulf, Ulf'). In cross examination, I asked Major Boberg whether X had not been questioned by the police on a number of occasions and whether he had not made verbal statements when required to do so. Verbally Major Boberg agreed that X had always been ready and available to answer questions, by day or by night, and that during all the questioning X had at all times been frank and acted like a perfectly normal person. I asked Boberg why X had been arrested. He said he had been arrested without a warrant on the allegation 'of being concerned in the murder of Miss Schroeder'.

The facts of the case were that Bubbles Schroeder had been at X's house and had left his house in a car driven by Y. A watchman at X's house had made a statement to that effect to the police. The watchman had been interviewed on several occasions on this aspect of the matter and he maintained that the young woman was alive when she left X's house in Y's car. The watchman was also interviewed by the police and made a statement after he left the service of X. I give the following extract of the cross examination:

BOBERG: Each time he [the watchman] was interviewed he said she [Miss Schroeder] left in Y's car alive.
MAISELS: I take it there is nothing to suggest that this is not the case?
BOBERG: There is evidence which could have made it possible that the watchman was not telling the truth.
MAISELS: What happened to that evidence?
BOBERG: He adhered to his statement even after he left the service of X. We now accept that Miss Schroeder must have been alive when she left the house.

This answer, of course, meant that there was absolutely no case against X. I pointed out that when the bail application was made in the Supreme Court there was no indication of what the case was against X, and that the crown prosecution had said that if he was permitted to make an ex parte statement, the highest he would put it was that X *may* (he emphasised 'may') have been an accessory after the fact. Boberg agreed with this.

I thereupon asked him: 'In what way was X an accessory after the fact?' Major Boberg looked at the magistrate, who remarked that, as it was a preparatory examination and not a summary trial, the witness should answer the question unless he could give any reason – of public policy or police investigation – why he should not. He had the right to claim protection.

BOBERG: I claim protection.
MAISELS: On what ground?
BOBERG: It may be concerned with police investigations.
MAISELS: We have now had the privilege of hearing a preparatory examination for 11 days. We know the list of crown witnesses. What police privilege and protection

are you claiming in this case?

(No answer.)

MAISELS: Are your investigations complete? What police privilege are you claiming – or is it because you cannot answer the question?

BOBERG: The investigations are complete. It may be public policy. I do not know my position.

MAISELS: What is the public policy when an accused person cannot be told what the case is against him?

BOBERG: All I can say is that the accused was arrested after consultations with the Senior Public Prosecutor and my senior officer in the police.

It is not surprising that I asked Boberg what X was doing in court. At the end of the evidence for the prosecution I applied for the discharge of X submitting that the charge against him was groundless. Not surprisingly, Mr Verschuur did not oppose the application and the magistrate discharged X.

The cross examination continued against Y. Mr Franks, too, having called certain evidence on behalf of Y, successfully applied for Y's discharge. Shortly after this case, I was on holiday with my family at Muizenberg. We were leaving the beach one morning when I saw someone with whom I wanted to speak. Getting out of the car I had a chat with a particularly inoffensive and mild looking young man. On my return to the car I was asked to whom I had been speaking. 'That,' I had to tell my family, 'is the noted and ferocious murderer Y.'[34]

I should mention that when the body of Bubbles Schroeder was discovered, it was found that lime had been placed in her mouth. She was lying on her back as though she had been carried over someone's shoulder then carefully laid out with the left leg across the other. Her frock was in place and the skirt well below her knees. Her shoes and coat were missing. It happened from time to time, when I was engaged in murder cases that captured public interest, that I would get anonymous letters. I received an anonymous letter after X and Y had been acquitted, in which the writer suggested that a certain tribe of Africans put lime in the mouth of a victim who had been murdered so that it should not speak evil of the murderer afterwards.

Chapter Six

FIGHTING VERWOERD AND FARM LABOUR

Looking back, I suppose the years 1950–1961, before I accepted an appointment to the Bench of Southern Rhodesia, were the busiest years of my career at the Bar. They included the so-called 'tobacco case' (the International Tobacco Company *vs* United Tobacco Company, which lasted almost a year subject to certain interruptions); the 'diamond case' (Consolidated Diamond Mines *vs* The Administrator of South West Africa and Others); the Central African Airways case against Vickers Armstrong (heard in Rhodesia); one I shall call the 'forced farm labour case'; three murder trials culminating in the defence of Pratt on a charge of attempted murder of the then prime minister, Dr H F Verwoerd; and what came to be known as the 'treason trial'.

Apart from the court work, I was chairman of the Johannesburg Bar Council in 1952, 1956, 1958 and 1960 until January 1961. I was also vice-chairman and acting chairman of the General Council of the Bar, 1954–1960.

Before dealing with the trials, appeals and applications in which I appeared, I should like to say something about matters with which the Bar was concerned. When the National Party came into power in 1948 it did two things. Firstly, it embarked upon a course of what is now called 'affirmative action' as far as judicial appointments were concerned, and secondly, it introduced legislation designed to remove 'Coloureds' from the voters' roll. It is strange, in the light of subsequent events, how from the late 1980s onwards the same National Party seemed to be concerned with obtaining as many 'colours' as possible in the National Party membership, the principle of universal franchise having been, at long last, recognised by the government of the day. The introduction of legislation known as the Introduction of Separate Representation of the

Voters Act led to a long constitutional struggle. The appeal court declared the Act unconstitutional, so another Act was passed to deal with the situation after an attempt to create Parliament as a court of law failed. This second Act did two things: it provided for an increased number of senators, so that the necessary two-thirds majority could be obtained to pass the required legislation; and, to make doubly sure, it appointed five additional judges to the Court of Appeal. The then leader of the opposition said, 'The new judges have been appointed in a manner which will result in making them a focal point of political controversy and this will undermine the respect in which the judiciary has always been held.' The majority of members of the Johannesburg Bar passed a resolution stating:

> We are forced to conclude that the Government has moved solely with the hope that it will obtain the decision it desires on the constitutional question from the new 11-Judge court. This conclusion is confirmed by the fact that there are several judges whose eminence, ability and experience are such that it is incredible that all of them should be passed over in any genuine attempt to strengthen the appeal court. Political consideration alone can account for their exclusion.[35]

The introduction in 1950 of the Suppression of Communism Act, amended in 1954, had met with strong objection from the Johannesburg Bar. The concept of persons being detained without trial or being banished or having general restrictions placed upon them once they were named as Communists, was something, of course, that no self respecting body of lawyers could stomach without protest. The Johannesburg Bar protested, of course, to no avail. I recall one of the senior silks at the Bar who was then nearly 90 years of age, George Angus Mulligan, making a public speech on a cold winter's day in front of the City Hall in Rissik Street, Johannesburg, in strong protest against this legislation.

Then, of course, there was the introduction of the Group Areas Act with its completely inhumane provisions, which resulted in persons being forced to move from homes or shops they had occupied for many years. One thinks of the Black people in every part of the country, of Cape Coloureds who were removed from 'District Six' and other suburbs of Cape Town, where they had been born and resided for years; of traders, particularly Indians, who were moved from homes that they occupied and, more particularly, were compelled to stop trading in places where they and, in some cases, their parents had traded for years. Whites could also – theoretically – be moved to assist in bringing about this grand piece of apartheid legislation, but the number of Whites who were moved was infinitesimal. In some cases the properties from which the Coloureds or Indians had been forced to moved were sold at ridiculously low prices to government officials. Corruption – of which so much is heard these days – was nothing new as far as the National Party was concerned during many years of its parliamentary control of this country.

Another practice, again of unbelievably inhumane proportions, was what I have called 'forced farm labour'. According to the law then in force – and I am talking particularly about the period from the 1950s and until comparatively recently – every 'Native' (the term then used for Africans), had to carry a pass on pain of being arrested if apprehended without it. (This kind of pass was known as a *dompas*.) Generally speaking, also, he was permitted to be employed only in certain areas, and was liable to be arrested if he perchance took up employment outside such areas. Some bright person in government conceived the idea of taking advantage of what were known as the 'pass laws' to provide farmers with cheap labour, by arresting natives who did not happen to be in possession of a pass and offering them the option of either being imprisoned for this 'offence' or agreeing to work as a farm labourer.

An attorney, Joel Carlson, determined to put an end to this savage practice. I was briefed in what I believe was the first of the cases brought as a result of Carlson's efforts. My junior was Mr George Bizos, and Mr Eloff of the Pretoria Bar, now Judge President of the Transvaal, was briefed by the government to oppose habeas corpus applications launched against farmers who had the Africans in their so-called employ. I recall one particular case where a Black municipal employee, who had been engaged in 'dirty work', was arrested by a policeman one day for failure to produce his pass. When arrested he explained to the policeman that his pass was at the hostel where he lived whilst employed by the municipality, and he could not carry it with him because of the nature of the 'dirty work' he had to perform. This did not satisfy the policeman, and he then gave the option of which I have spoken, either of going to jail or to work as a farm labourer. The practice was to get the person arrested to sign or make a thumbprint (many of them were illiterate) on a form which contained certain conditions which the signatory was obliged to accept.

In another similar case, we demanded to see the original document that was alleged in the affidavits filed by the police to have been signed or thumbprinted by the unfortunate labourer. In that case the police had not even bothered to get the African's 'signature'. Despite opposition by the police, all our habeas corpus applications succeeded, and on what is known as the 'return date' of the application, the Supreme Court had no difficulty in holding that the alleged agreements to serve, signed by the workers, were of no value, having been obtained under duress. There was a more or less common theme running through all the cases in which I was concerned: firstly, the arrest and, secondly, the conditions endured by the Africans who – allegedly willingly – undertook to work on the farm. The wages were derisory. The workers were clothed in sacks and locked up in compounds when they were not working in the fields.

I quote portions of a typical affidavit made by one of these labourers. I use the word 'typical' because with minor variations other labourers made similar affidavits which were corroborated by independent medical evidence and by a journalist who visited one of the farms where these persons were employed.

> When I arrived at the farm a European called me and took my reference book from me. He told me that I would get my reference book back when I finished there. He took the reference book of the others and certain other articles from them and told them the same thing that he had told me. The same European then told the boss boys to take us to the compound.
>
> The compound was a building with one entrance from the outside. We entered the building and the outside door was then locked behind us. When all the volunteers were in the building at night and over the weekends this door

was always locked and was guarded by boss boys or night watchmen.

That night I was given porridge and potatoes, no other food was given to me. I was able to drink water from a tap. I was given a number of mealie-meal bags for blankets and for my bed. The room was very dirty. The concrete floors were very dusty and were black and there were lice on and in the sacks given to us.

I soon found that the food consisted of porridge made out of No.3 mealiemeal. Occasionally potatoes were added to the porridge and very rarely we got beans as well. On Saturday we also received offal with our porridge, and also a small helping of brown sugar. We never received anything hot to drink. On two occasions while I was on the farm I received a portion of skimmed milk.

As lavatories we used half-drums. These drums stood in the passage-way and were emptied by us each day into a pit. They were usually emptied before breakfast. Some of the workers, however, did not always use the lavatories when they wished to urinate and our room smelled. Although we were locked in each night and over the weekends, we were nevertheless allowed to get water for ourselves but we were always guarded. At night a big light lit up the building. I think this was done to prevent us escaping.

We began work at 5 am. There was a break for lunch and we returned from the fields after sunset. Throughout the day we were guarded by boss boys while we worked. There was one boss boy on horseback. Some of the boss boys carried sticks and *kerries*. There was also a white man who carried a stick. We worked the whole of each day from Monday to Friday but on Saturday we knocked off at three o'clock in the afternoon. Although we knocked off on Saturday we were nevertheless kept under guard all the time, but some of the workers who had been there a long time were allowed to wander in the vicinity of the compound.

Last Saturday after I knocked off work the owner of the farm told me to wait for him as he was bringing me back to

> Johannesburg. I waited. He went to his shop which was on the farm and gave me a ten-shilling note and some half-crowns. He also gave me my reference book. Later that afternoon he brought me to Johannesburg and dropped me that evening at a certain house in Johannesburg.
>
> That night I was examined by a doctor and was given an injection and told to go regularly to the Alexandra Health Clinic.
>
> While I was on the farm I never saw a doctor or any inspector. I remember Daniel Mahloane. He was on the farm when I arrived. He was sick and had dropsy and wanted to leave the farm.

I should add that habeas corpus proceedings were invariably brought by the wife or mother of the labourer on information which she had received and the affidavit was only filed by the worker after habeas corpus had been granted.[36]

A notable case of this time was the '*affaire* Nokwe'. In March 1956 an African, Mr Duma Nokwe, was admitted as an advocate to the Supreme Court. As was customary for all persons admitted as advocates and who wished to practise in Johannesburg, he applied to join the Society of Advocates. I happened then to be chairman of the Bar Council. There was really no difficulty in his being admitted to the Society of Advocates despite the rumblings of a tiny minority of members, but the question was whether, in view of the provisions of the Group Areas Act, he would be permitted to occupy chambers in the buildings where all the members of the society had their chambers and where the Bar library and common room were. According to the Afrikaans paper *Die Transvaler*, of which Dr Verwoerd had been its first editor, a group of White advocates wanted to ensure that Nokwe would have the same privileges and the right to occupy chambers as any other member of the society. The 'Group' consisted of the overwhelming majority of the members of the Johannesburg Bar. There were, as I remember, three opponents, two of whom eventually became judges; the third, a man who had been a mining captain and had decided to take up law at rather a late stage in life, had obtained a degree at the University of Leyden in Holland during the time that Holland was occupied by the Nazis. It was always a matter of surprise to me that he, having seen what the Nazis had done, should have adopted this attitude towards Nokwe. He subsequently became a National Party member of the Provincial Council. Like one of the judges to whom I have referred, he is now dead. The Johannesburg Municipality and the owners of the building had no objection whatsoever to Nokwe's occupying chambers there, but it was necessary to obtain the permission of the then Minister of Native Affairs: one Hendrik Verwoerd (subsequently prime minister, 1958–1966). In a comprehensive article written in 1992 by Mr Pieter Paul of the Johannesburg Bar,[37] Mr Paul says – and correctly – that Dr Verwoerd is generally regarded as the chief architect of 'grand apartheid' in South Africa. He adds that in the words of State President F W De Klerk after the referendum of that time, 'the book of apartheid has now been closed'. In view of the law at that time, having obtained the views of the overwhelming majority of members of the Bar, I wrote a letter to Dr Verwoerd requesting permission for Nokwe to have chambers in His Majesty's Building. At a general meeting of the Bar held prior to my writing the letter, I had mentioned that I thought that there would really be no objection by Dr Verwoerd to our request; but a member of the Bar, one B J Vorster (subsequently to become prime minister and then state president of South Africa), said that he did not think that it was likely that Dr Verwoerd would give permission.

Well Vorster was right and I was wrong. Verwoerd turned down my application and I thereupon wrote a letter to the minister in which I endeavoured to explain why it was essential for any newcomer to the Bar to be in the same building as that occupied by all the members of the Society of Advocates, because in that way he would be able to consult with his fellow members, use the library, and generally, to put it in blunt terms, learn his trade. The mere fact that a person has obtained the necessary professional qualifications to be admitted to practice does not mean, by any means, that he is fully qualified to do so. One of the great and most important pieces of the Bar is the assistance which is readily given by a senior to any junior who requires help as to questions of law or procedure or ethics. It was simply unthinkable to the overwhelming majority of the Bar that Nokwe should be precluded from having the advantages which were necessary in order to enable him to make a living at the Bar.

Dr Verwoerd did not answer either letter himself, but took the step of answering through his private secretary. The secretary said, *inter alia*, that in pleading for Mr Nokwe the Bar Council was in fact only trying to protect the interests of certain of its members at Nokwe's expense because if Nokwe practised among his own people, wherever that might be, he would then take all the legal work of his people and the members of the Johannesburg Bar would lose work as a result of this. The *Rand Daily Mail* in an editorial said:

> To impute motives of self-interest to the Bar Council is a revelation of the way the Minister's mind works. To see 'leftist influences' in so responsible a body is to betray a way of thinking that may suit a street corner demagogue but never a Cabinet Minister. It is in fact an infamous suggestion, which implies that Dr Verwoerd has no real answer to the Bar Council and therefore hopes merely to cow them with abuse.

The Johannesburg Bar was not cowed by Dr Verwoerd. Nokwe was accommodated in His Majesty's Building. Accommodation was scarce and junior members very often had to share one room. George Bizos shared chambers with Nokwe.

My own personal connection with Nokwe arose when he was one of the accused in the treason trial, he having been arrested in 1956 and having to sit through a lengthy preparatory examination. I might here mention that as part of the defence in the treason trial itself, a part of my cross examination of Professor Murray, who was called by the Crown as an expert on Communism, consisted of a reference to the discriminatory legislation against Blacks, Coloureds and Indians, which had been enacted over the years – in many cases, long before the National Party came into power and which, of course, became worse from the time the National Party came into power in 1948. The object of the cross examination was to show the legitimate causes of complaint, not actuated by Communism or any other 'ism', that affected the lives of these persons. At lunchtime on the day that cross examination of Professor Murray on this aspect of the case took place, Nokwe came up to me and asked me whether I had notes on my cross examination. I said that I had and why did he ask me this question. 'Well,' he said,

'I would like to get those notes because I did not know things were quite so bad'. Like all the other accused in the case he was acquitted and regrettably died in exile a few years later. Nokwe had been a schoolteacher and it is sad to think of the number of Africans such as Nokwe who were deprived of ordinary human rights by the legislation of which I have written.

Dr Verwoerd was the unsuccessful plaintiff in the early 1940s in an action for damages for defamation that he brought against the Argus Company and Mr Paver, the editor of *The Star*. Mr Justice Millin, in giving judgment against Verwoerd, said:

> What they have proved is that the plaintiff caused to be published a large body of matter which was on the same general lines as matter coming to the Union in the Afrikaans transmissions from Zeesen and which was calculated to make the Germans look on *Die Transvaler* as a most useful adjunct to this propaganda service. The plaintiff cannot really deny this. He says it is not his fault. He appeals to the principles of free speech and a free press in a democratic country as justifying him, in writing as he did in support of his policy of neutrality and a separate peace between the Union and Germany as a means towards a republic in South Africa. He argues that if he had to consider whether what he said would be useful to the Germans the effect would be to silence him; and the law does not compel him to be silent. But the question in this case is not whether the plaintiff should be silenced. His legal right to publish what he did is not in question. The question is, whether when he exercises his legal right in the way he does, he is entitled to complain if it is said of him that what he writes supports Nazi propaganda and makes his paper a tool of the Nazis. On the evidence he is not entitled to complain. He did support Nazi propaganda, he did make his paper a tool of the Nazis in South Africa, and he knew it.[38]

At a public meeting held in Alberton, presided over by Mr J Ludorf (subsequently Mr Justice Ludorf) when Dr Verwoerd stood for Parliament, he was questioned by a brave member of the Bar, one

Harley Titren, as to what Mr Justice Millin had said about him. Dr Verwoerd's answer was that the judge was wrong, to which Titren responded, 'Well why don't you appeal?' This was not answered because the chairman decided that there should be no more questions and the plain fact is that Dr Verwoerd did not appeal because if he did he was bound to be unsuccessful.

Chapter Seven

MUNICIPAL VICES AND THE TOBACCO CASE

I mentioned earlier that one of the happy consequences of my being thrown out of the case against Erleigh was that I was briefed in matters in which some of my peers would have appeared had they not been involved in the Erleigh–Milne trial. It was for this reason, I think, that I was briefed for the appellant in the Appellate Division in a case heard in 1949: namely, Vanderbijl Park Health Committee and Others *v* Wilson and Others.[39] Other counsel had appeared in the courts below, but were probably not available for the appeal.

My junior in this case was Lem Goldsmid (who regrettably died far too young a few years ago), and appearing on the other side were Pirow, KC, and M Bliss. At a sitting of the Vereeniging Liquor Licensing Board in December 1947, Mr Wilson had applied for and was granted a Bottle Liquor Licence in respect of certain premises on a farm situated within the urban area of Vanderbijl Park. In those days, because of the restriction on the numbers that were permitted to be issued, the value of a liquor licence was far greater than it is today. The premises were owned by two brothers and consisted of a residence that – by reason of the provisions of Act 45 of 1945 – could be used only for residential purposes, unless written permission of the minister had been obtained for use for other purposes. No such permission was obtained. An application was launched in the Witwatersrand Local Division by the Vanderbijl Park Health Committee and certain others against Wilson, to whom the licence had been granted, and the two owners of the premises where the bottle store was to be situated, to set aside the decision of the Liquor Board.

The matter came before Judge Blackwell in the Witwatersrand Local Division of the Supreme Court. He came to the conclusion that the Board had acted in a grossly unreasonable manner in authorising the grant of the liquor licence in question, and he made an order setting aside the grant of the licence with costs against Wilson and the two brothers who owned the house. During the hearing of the case, the applicants invited the judge to view the site for himself and he did so in company with the attorneys on both sides. In his judgment he said 'The feeling of surprise that I had experienced on reading the papers and studying the maps and photographs, deepened into amazement as I stood on the site and surveyed the scene. It is in every sense a "bottle store out in the veld".'

Judge Blackwell's judgment was taken on appeal to the Transvaal Provincial Division and by a majority, Judges Malan and De Villiers, with Judge Lucas dissenting, the appeal was upheld and the judgment of Judge Blackwell reversed. The matter was then taken on appeal to the Appellate Division. The proposed bottle store was, as stated by Judge Blackwell , midway between two proposed 'native' townships. In those days the Liquor Act provided that no licence could be granted within half a mile of any 'native' location or village. Whilst the location or village had not yet been established, it was clear that such townships would be established. A plan that had been accepted by the Local Authority included these provisions. In those days, of course, the sale of intoxicating liquor to 'natives' was prohibited. The application for review of the Liquor Board's decision was opposed by Wilson and the two brothers. The Licensing Board was not represented in court, but it filed an affidavit stating that it opposed the application but left the conduct of the opposition in court in the hands of the other respondents. The respondent, Wilson, made an affidavit in which he attempted to justify the grant of the licence. In the face of the observations made by Judge Blackwell (as a result of his inspection *in loco* and as a result of the other evidence), it was plain that there was no basis upon which any reasonable person could have granted a liquor licence at the site.

In terms of Section 20(1)(a) of Act 30 of 1928, a court has power to set aside the proceedings of a Licensing Board if the 'Board ... exercised its powers in an arbitrary *mala fide* or grossly unreasonable manner'. The Court of Appeal had no difficulty in coming to the conclusion that the grant of the licence was a grossly unreasonable exercise of the Board's powers. In addition, having arrived at that conclusion, the court said it was not necessary to decide the question as to whether the premises could lawfully be used as a bottle store. It did however do so and held that the premises could not in any event be lawfully used for that purpose.

It is clear from the judgment of Chief Justice Watermeyer that one of the factors which led to his conclusion that the Licensing Board's action was grossly unreasonable, was the fact that the Board gave no reasons for its decision. I recall when I was arguing the matter the Chief Justice saying to me, 'What reasons did the Board have for granting this application?' to which I replied, I think somewhat cheekily, 'No doubt many.' It became apparent when Pirow started his argument in reply that he had not read his brief. In Bloemfontein in those days the favourite place to have lunch during the adjournment was Polley's Hotel. As my junior and I were going into the dining room, Pirow was on his way out, having apparently already had lunch. His junior told me after the appeal was heard that Pirow hadn't even read the 'Heads of Argument' which he, the junior, had prepared on their side before appearing in Bloemfontein. He may, of course, have appeared in the Transvaal Provincial Division and acquired some knowledge of the papers.

I referred earlier to the case that became known as the 'tobacco case'. This was an action instituted in 1953 by the International Tobacco Company SA Ltd (ITC) against United Tobacco Company (South) Ltd (UTC). A cigarette named 'Max' had been manufactured in South Africa since 1936 by ITC. The cigarettes were cheap (the cost in 1947 being 1s. 2d. for 20). 'Max' – of which 869 million were sold in 1947, sales increasing by 1949 to 987 million – was the main competitor of the cigarettes of UTC, which manufactured different brands in the same class. UTC sales of cigarettes of the same class in 1949 were 4 376 million. Towards the end of 1946 UTC decided to employ what were called 'Native propagandists' to advance the sale of its brands in the Transvaal, and various propagandists were so employed. The case against UTC was based upon an allegation that these propagandists warned the Blacks that if they smoked 'Max' cigarettes they would get TB. ITC's claim was for damages that it maintained it had suffered as a result of the drop in sales of 'Max' cigarettes, brought about by this propaganda.

I was briefed by UTC. I should perhaps mention that a fortnight after I had accepted a retainer from UTC, I was offered a brief on behalf of ITC, which, of course, I had to decline. The majority shareholder of ITC, if not the sole shareholder, was a Mr Wix, and I knew him personally. I don't think he ever forgave me for being on the other side. Leading counsel for UTC was the late B A Ettlinger, KC, the late Bram Fischer, QC. I and I Isaacs were briefed with Ettlinger. On the other side were N E Rosenberg, KC, the late H M Bloch, KC, George Colman and W G Trollip. A private detective was engaged by ITC to investigate the matter and although this person was a completely discredited witness, Judge Clayden came to the conclusion that UTC propagandists had indeed spread the message complained of, and that ITC was entitled to damages.

The case, with a few interruptions occasioned by vacation periods, lasted almost a year, with judgment being given slightly more than a year after the trial started. Apart from the lengthy cross-examination of the numerous witnesses called on both sides, there were many difficult questions of law. But the judge came to the conclusion that ITC had established its case, and he awarded damages in the sum of £572 241, with interest at the rate of 6% from the date of judgment to date of payment, and of course the plaintiff was in addition awarded the costs of the action, which must have been substantial. An appeal was immediately noted but was never heard for the simple reason that UTC bought out ITC.

On a more personal note I may be permitted to mention that during the course of that trial I was offered an appointment to the Bench of Southern Rhodesia. I explained that I could not be available until the tobacco case was finished. I should add that the directors of UTC felt that I was entitled to accept the appointment although it was offered during the course of the trial. Their attorney did not agree with them; and I myself thought it would be wrong to leave in the middle of what was clearly an important case to my clients in which I was playing quite a substantial part.

The Southern Rhodesian Government needed a judge urgently and could not wait until the tobacco case was over so they offered the appointment to a very good friend of mine, Anton Hathorn, QC, of the Natal Bar, who accepted it. When eventually, some years later, I did accept an appointment to that Bench, I had the great pleasure of having Anton as a fellow judge and of sitting with him. He resigned from the Rhodesian Bench in about 1965 for health reasons and was appointed a Judge of the Courts of Appeal of Botswana, Swaziland and Lesotho; which appointments, of course, were much less onerous than his position as a full-time judge in Rhodesia. I was appointed to those courts shortly after he was, but Anton and I never sat together on those courts because of his untimely death.

In the 1940s, when I was still a junior, the Licensing Committee of the Johannesburg City Council had decided to grant a licence for a butcher's shop in what was then the select residential area of Yeoville. Local residents were incensed at this decision and one of them, a Mr Bitcon, a prominent builder and mining man, decided to bring review proceedings against the City Council to set aside the decision of the Licensing Committee. The matter came before Judge Krause, who in the course of his judgment setting aside the Licensing Committee's decision, said it was sad to think that the affairs of the City of Johannesburg were in the hands of people like 'Z', who was the Chairman of the Licensing Committee.

Shortly after this judgment was given, the Administrator of the Transvaal ordered that an enquiry should be held into certain alleged irregularities in the City Council, as though anybody could think of such a thing happening in that august body. Among the persons questioned was Mr Z, and I was briefed to appear for him before the Commissioner, Mr John Murray, KC, then a leading silk at the Pretoria Bar. (After a spell on the Transvaal Bench, he subsequently became Sir John Murray, Chief Justice of Southern Rhodesia.) Philip Millin, KC, was briefed by the City Council to examine and, when necessary, to cross examine persons who were required to give evidence. Mr Z was one of these persons. The cross examination went something like this.

MILLIN: Mr Z are you the Mr Z who was the Chairman of the Licensing Committee which granted a Butchery Licence to the Y Company in Yeoville?

Z: Yes.

(Mr Z had rather a gruff voice and the 'Yes' was delivered loudly.)

MILLIN: Was this decision of yours taken on Review to the Supreme Court?

Z: Yes.

MILLIN: Did the court set aside the decision of your Committee?

Z: Yes.

MILLIN: In the course of giving judgment did the judge say of you that it was sad to think that the affairs of the City of Johannesburg were in the hands of persons like your self?

Z: Yes.

(Then came what I thought was an unnecessary question.)

MILLIN: Well, what do you have to say about that?

Z: That was the judge's opinion of me. You haven't asked me my opinion of the judge.

It is not difficult to imagine the laughter that this answer gave, so much so that Mr Murray disappeared under the table. He could not contain himself from laughing and the proceedings were then adjourned.

Later the cross examination became more heated and indeed Mr Z became so heated that he stood up, banged the table and shouted: 'Why am I being persecuted like this?' The hearing ended shortly after that outburst, and as we walked out of the Council Chamber I said to him, 'Mr Z why did you get so excited?' whereupon he gave me a wink.

Chapter Eight

BURNT STAMPS AND A RUSTED BOLT

Two unusual cases of the 1950s are worth recounting in some detail, particularly as neither of them was recorded in the law reports. The first was the case of Athineos *v* Lloyds, in which I was briefed with Dan Reichman for Lloyds. Mr Athineos had arrived in South Africa from Egypt some time after the First World War. He had flown in in his own aircraft and was possessed of £100 000. When he brought a claim against Lloyds it was for a loss he alleged he had sustained as a result of a fire in his house, on a small farm outside Brakpan. The most valuable items alleged to have been destroyed as a result of the fire were a collection of Greek stamps and a library consisting of beautifully bound and important books. It should perhaps be mentioned that although a policy had not yet been issued, he had received a cover note. His claim was, in those days at all events, a substantial one, somewhere in the neighbourhood of £80 000. Originally Athineos had briefed a silk at the Durban Bar to appear for him, but at the trial he appeared in person.

After the fire, the Lloyds assessor went out to the premises and brought back with him to Johannesburg a tin trunk containing burnt stamps. As is well known, a fire does not totally destroy paper and these stamps were recognised as ordinary used South African postage stamps of minimal value. The stamps which Athineos claimed had been destroyed in the fire were valuable Greek stamps – which curiously enough coincided almost exactly with the list of Greek stamps set out in the well known Stanley Gibbons catalogue. As for the books that had been destroyed, by some miracle books that contained pornographic pictures and articles and an old Rhodesian telephone directory, beautifully bound in leather, which were seen by the assessor, were not destroyed in the fire. The valuable books claimed to have been destroyed included, *inter alia*, a collection of Proust's *A la Recherche du Temps Perdu*, with three volumes missing.

Liability was repudiated on several grounds, including failure to disclose a history of fires previous to the one with which the present case was concerned, and a denial that the books and stamps that he alleged were destroyed were ever owned by him. In short the plea was that his claims were fraudulent and that there had been material nondisclosure of previous fire claims that had been met by various unsuspecting insurance companies.

It should perhaps be mentioned that shortly before the trial was due to commence, the office of the Lloyds assessor was burgled one night and certain papers relevant to Athineos's claim were stolen. There was little doubt as to who the culprit was; however, I decided, as a matter of tactics, not to commence cross-examination on that point but to use it after Athineos had been examined on matters to which it was thought he really had no answer.

On what may be called the stamp issue, as a result of some research done by the assessor, it was ascertained that shortly before the fire occurred, a job lot of stamps of a kind found by the assessor in the tin trunk, had been advertised for sale in a newspaper in Brakpan. I suggested that an expert be brought in from one of the well known British stamp firms who would be able to testify as to whether it was likely or not for a person to have a collection of Greek stamps such as was claimed by Athineos. This expert witness arrived and duly gave evidence. He said in his opinion it was almost impossible for anyone to have possessed a collection of Greek stamps such as the one that Athineos claimed had been destroyed in the fire. In fact, he put the chances of Athineos's possessing such a collection as being similar to that of a man winning the Irish sweepstake three years in succession.

I also advised that it was desirable to obtain information, if possible, from a book seller who in those days specialised in Johannesburg in the sale of foreign books and magazines, as to whether it was likely that Athineos could have had the said collection of Proust's works. The book seller was duly interviewed and produced a publication known as *BPC*, standing for *Book Prices Current*. This book records all sales of important books sold during any particular year. Again by a strange coincidence, it was established by reference to that book that there had been a recent sale in New York of Proust's works as mentioned above with exactly the same volumes missing as Athineos claimed were missing. Athineos was asked when he had acquired his collection of Proust's works. He said he had brought them with him when he arrived in South Africa some years prior to the fire, and it was thus clear that he was not the buyer of the Proust works set out in the *BPC*. He was asked in cross-examination if he had ever heard of the book called *BPC*. After a good deal of evasion on his part, he finally said he had heard of this publication and he eventually admitted that he had a copy of it. By that stage the case had turned into what might be called a cross-examiner's dream. Athineos admitted that it was a little strange that there should be the same books missing in his collection as were missing in the collection of books sold in New York; but he was not without resourcefulness. He pointed out that it happened that in a set of law reports certain numbers were frequently found missing. One need hardly say that the judge did not accept this explanation.

The broker who effected the insurance stated that he had not been told of Athineos's previous fires and that if he had, he would certainly not have issued a cover note. Information had, by the time of the trial, been received from other insurance companies which showed that Athineos had had a fire for which he made claims almost regularly every year over the five or six years prior to the issue of the cover note. Athineos claimed that he had disclosed his fire history to the Lloyd's broker. In support of his claim he produced a photocopy of a letter which he said he had shown to the broker and which showed on the face of it that he had disclosed his previous fires to African Guarantee. Athineos explained that the letter which he produced was a copy of an original letter which he kept after African Guarantee had refused to insure him. The original, so he said, had been destroyed in the fire. Investigation revealed that the photostat copy indeed bore a genuine stamp of the African Guarantee. This matter arose shortly before a weekend and it was suggested that over the weekend a test should be done by taking the attorney's letterhead and putting below it a separate piece of paper with something else written on it and that the two pieces of paper should be put into a photocopy machine. The result was one piece of paper containing both the letterhead and the writing of the separate piece of paper. When it was suggested to Athineos in cross-examination that that was exactly what he had done, he answered that he found the experiment 'interesting'.

In the light of the information which had become available and in the light of the burglary of the broker's office, it was decided not to leave the court during the tea and lunch intervals, sandwiches being brought in during the lunch hour. The reason for all this was of course a fear that Athineos would interfere with or steal or damage papers in my or the attorney's possession. Athineos, in his argument to the court, quoted from what appeared to be photocopies of pages from law reports. It was discovered after the trial that what Athineos had done was to have pages torn out of the law reports in the Supreme Court library and to have them photocopied.

Athineos was indeed a thoroughly dishonest person. After the evidence and argument had been concluded, judgment was reserved by Judge Williamson. A well known and very likeable *Rand Daily Mail* reporter who was present during the trial he came up to Dan Reichman when judgment was reserved and said 'Well he [the plaintiff] must get something.' 'Yes,' said Dan – 'six months.' Needless to say Judge Williamson found for Lloyds and Athineos's claims were dismissed with costs.

Undaunted, Athineos took the case on appeal to the Appellate Division, by which time I had been appointed to the Bench in Rhodesia. Margo, QC, was briefed to lead Dan Reichman. Athineos appeared in person. Dan Reichman was convinced that Athineos was armed with a revolver which he suspected he might well have used against him or both Margo and himself. One need hardly add to this saga that the Appellate Division had no difficulty in dismissing his appeal with costs.

The other case not recorded in the law reports was one of many actions in which I was fortunate to appear in the High Court of Rhodesia, as I did also in Northern Rhodesia. Cases in the Rhodesian courts were greatly sought after by South African counsel, as our earnings outside the country were not subject to South African income tax.

The case was that of Central African Airways *v* Vickers Armstrong, in which I was fortunate enough to have been briefed by Central African Airways (CAA) in an action brought against Vickers Armstrong Limited (VA) in the High Court of Southern Rhodesia, following an accident in the summer of 1950 in which a Vickers Viking airliner, belonging to Central African Airways and manufactured by Vickers Armstrong, broke up in the air above Tanganyika (now Tanzania). In the ensuing crash all on board – crew and passengers – were killed.

I must state at the outset that a major portion of what I have to write about this case was the product of C S Margo, QC, as he then was. As is well known, he was subsequently elevated to the Bench of the Transvaal Provincial Division, from which he has now retired. He is an acknowledged expert in aviation law and has presided over important commissions of enquiry into aircraft accidents. Claims were also made by relatives of persons who had been killed in the crash, but it was agreed between the parties that the outcome of the case brought by CAA against VA would govern the question of liability of VA to them for damages that they had sustained. VA was insured by Lloyds Underwriters and, of course, their defence was undertaken by the solicitors for Lloyds and counsel briefed by those solicitors.

The aircraft had been on a scheduled flight from Salisbury (now Harare) to Dar-es-Salaam. The wreckage was spread over a distance of several miles along the line of flight. Part of the centre section (ie, that portion of the primary structure of the aircraft to which the wings were attached) was found in thick bush about two miles short of where the main wreckage lay. Two of the bolts by means of which the wings were attached to the centre section were recovered. One, which was broken, was sent, together with other components of the wreckage, to the Royal Aircraft Establishment at Farnborough in England. The broken bolt was found to have failed in fatigue. It was also found that the bolt had not been cadmium-plated, which was a standard protection against corrosion in the state of the art at that time, although this was vigorously disputed by VA. Corrosion had occurred in the bolt to an extent which was unlikely to have occurred merely from the date of the crash until the wreckage was found.

Margo, QC, with B Goldin as his junior, had originally been briefed on behalf of CAA. It was decided later to bring in another Senior Counsel. An attempt was made by CAA's solicitors to obtain further information from the Royal Aircraft Establishment at Farnborough, but that authority took the view that it had no right to divulge information without an order of court and it declined to supply any further data.

An application was then made to the Southern Rhodesian High Court on behalf of CAA, for letters of request to the High Court in England whereby the Royal Aircraft Establishment witnesses would be subpoenaed to produce the necessary evidence before a commissioner in London. The application was granted.

Initially Sir Hartley Shawcross, QC, of the London Bar (later Lord Shawcross) accepted the brief on trial, but on leaving the London Bar to join the Board of Shell, he withdrew. I was then briefed to lead. I had no technical background in the field but I was taught what had to be understood by Margo, QC, who apparently knew everything that had to be known about aircraft and aircraft construction.

It should here be mentioned that CAA was not satisfied with the original discovery made by VA and further discovery was sought. The documents disclosed proved to be of great assistance to CAA. When counsel for CAA were in London to hear the evidence of the Royal Aircraft Establishment witnesses, in terms of the letters of request referred to above, the drawing of that part of the aircraft which contained the bolt (which CAA contended should have been cadmium-plated, but which VA contested), was specified in the drawing to be cadmium-plated.

It should be mentioned that the non-cadmium-plated bolts were found by an insurance assessor, James Risean, who is now unfortunately dead. His finding and retaining of the bolts was, of course, crucial to CAA's case.

To revert to the proceedings in London, the High Court there had appointed a well-known member of the London Bar to hear the evidence of the Farnborough witnesses. The witnesses had all been cautioned to say no more than was absolutely necessary and information was extracted from them with difficulty. They were called as CAA's witnesses and leading questions were out. One of these men, as far as I recall, was a Dr Walker, an authority on fatigue in aircraft structures who had solved the riddle of the three Comet crashes. However, no expert opinions were offered or obtainable from these witnesses, who limited themselves to the barest of bare facts, namely the examination of the bolt, the discovery of the fracture in fatigue and of the presence of corrosion in the bolt.

The London correspondents of CAA's attorneys were Hewitt, Woollacott & Chown, a well-known firm of solicitors. They were asked, in pursuance of the advice on evidence given by us, to obtain the services of an eminent aviation metallurgist, Professor Murphy, a former Principal of the Royal Aeronautical College at Cranfield. Professor Murphy was highly regarded on both sides of the Atlantic, but he had already been retained by VA. On being approached, however, he suggested that CAA might use the services of 'a promising young metallurgist' called E A G Liddiard of the Fulmer Research Institute. He turned out to be an excellent witness and although he was subjected to a vigorous cross-examination by H M Bloch, QC, of the Cape Bar, who was leading counsel for CAA, he remained unscathed.

In Johannesburg further preparations for trial were made and Professor Taverner of the Department of Metallurgy at the University of the Witwatersrand was consulted. He pointed out that particular protection against corrosion was required in the components of the primary structure of an aircraft if they were not able to be inspected at regular intervals. Such protection was all the more important where there was exposure to circumstances which exacerbate corrosion, such as high ambient temperatures, coastal conditions (with salt-laden air), increased frequency of reversals of stress consequent on operation of the aircraft in turbulent atmospheric conditions, differential electrolytic potential of different metals in contact with each other (in this case steel from the bolts and duralumin from the wing structure), and the presence of bolt holes – especially unevenly cut bolt holes – which act as stress-raisers. All these factors had been present in this case.

CAA called as its expert witnesses Mr Liddiard and Professor Taverner. Both of them easily survived cross-examination by Bloch, QC. The defendant produced a number of alleged internationally known experts, namely Professor Murphy, as well as the designer of the Viking Aircraft employed by VA and the designer of Afro York Aircraft. The defendant's case depended mainly on the evidence of Professor Murphy. His evidence in cross-examination was at the commencement offered with sublime confidence.

In answering a complaint by me – 'You have not answered my question' – the witness replied, 'Oh really? I thought I answered it rather well.' At the end of the morning, however, his confidence seemed to have faded. He asked to be allowed to be seated and took frequent gulps from the glass of water at his side, which required constant replenishment. My cross-examination, I having been duly instructed on the technical points by Margo, QC, was largely based on VA's own documents which were the subject of the late discovery. Professor Murphy was unable to deal with the inconsistencies between those documents and his testimony. At the end of his evidence, late one afternoon, the defendant's counsel rose to say that Professor Murphy had hoped to attend a very important conference in London the next day and he asked the court to excuse him from further attendance so that he could catch that evening's flight. The judge asked, 'Have you any objection Mr Maisels?' whereupon I replied, 'Not at all. In fact I am strongly in favour of it.'

The treatment meted out by me to Professor Murphy apparently created alarm and despondency on the part of some of the defendant's expert witnesses, one of whom, as stated above, was the designer of the aircraft. He, so it was said, was on the point of a nervous breakdown. It appears that he had left his hotel. In an effort to redress the position the defendant summoned, at short notice, an expert from the Boeing Aircraft Company in Seattle, USA, a Mr Butler, who was put into the witness box very shortly after his arrival in Salisbury. Indeed he was still wearing the thick, heavy tweed suit that was appropriate to the climate at the time in Seattle, but was wholly unsuitable for the hot summer conditions then prevailing in Salisbury.

Mr Butler gave evidence as best he could. He was cross-examined in a masterly fashion by Margo, QC, He was an engaging character. At one point during his cross-examination he was asked, 'Surely you are not going to be so bold as to give that answer?' He answered: 'Sir, permit me to assure you that I have all the intestinal fortitude necessary to say just that.' Towards the end of his cross-examination he advanced some odd theory which bordered on the ridiculous. Margo asked him how he dared put forward that theory, to which he replied, 'Oh well, I thought I would try it on.'

The expert witness from the A V Roe Factory in England was called and his evidence was also demolished by Margo without any difficulties.

It should be mentioned that after certain of the defendant's witnesses had been cross examined, Bloch, QC, was offered an acting judicial appointment in the Cape Provincial Division which he accepted, leaving the trial in the capable hands of John Lewis, QC, (later Mr Justice Lewis) and Michael May. Attempts had been made on behalf of the plaintiff to achieve a settlement and after Bloch left, these attempts were renewed – but to no avail. The solicitor for the defendant who had been brought out from England could not be persuaded that the matter should be settled. We were always aware of the fact that the case was a difficult one and that was why attempts were made to settle.

The designer of the Vickers Viscount aircraft, whose name cannot be recalled, apparently recovered from his breakdown and he gave evidence. He testified that the aircraft had been developed from a wartime version used in operations and that in practice no special precautions against corrosion had formerly been regarded as necessary. A covering of zinc-chromate, used in ships, was considered adequate. He had to admit, however, that wartime aircraft were built for short lives whereas airliners were required for operation for a period of many years. Despite the fact that it was demonstrated to him that cadmium-plating of the bolts in question was specified in the drawings made for the aircraft, once it was to be used as a civil airliner, he persisted in stating that it was not necessary to have the bolts cadmium plated. He was a sorry figure in the witness box.

After all the evidence the defendant's case was closed. I commenced argument on behalf of CAA. I argued until the court adjourned for tea whereupon to my astonishment, VA's counsel surrendered on behalf of the defendant and agreed to pay, with all costs, the damages claimed by CAA. To round off the story it should be mentioned that the case lasted about six weeks and needless to say we worked virtually every night during the trial until the early hours of the morning.

I may be permitted to digress at this point to relate something of the background to admission to the courts of Northern Rhodesia. [40] In order to be admitted to appear in those courts, I had first to be admitted to one of the Inns of Court in London. Owing to my being a Queen's Counsel in South Africa, I did not have to sit an examination. However, I was required to undergo the somewhat arduous procedure of having to 'eat dinners' (literally nine) at the inn for a certain period of time, and thereafter pay a fee for the admission. After staying in London for approximately three weeks for this purpose, at what I considered unnecessary expense, and eating the dinners, which I regarded as a waste of time, I completed the course and went in to see the treasurer of the inn to pay the admission fee.

I was inclined to feel that the treasurer displayed unusual and uncalled for familiarity when he asked me if I was joining the inn for the honour of so doing, or whether I had some ulterior motive. I replied that, although I was of course honoured to become a member of the inn, the treasurer was correct in his surmise, because the reason for my application was that I wished to practise in the then colonial territory of Northern Rhodesia. I duly paid the fee of £200, not refraining from remarking to the treasurer that I found it 'exorbitant'.

On leaving the office of the treasurer, however, I remarked to an acquaintance that I thought that the treasurer employed by the inn was rather impertinent. My colleague was surprised to hear this, and asked me whether I meant the treasurer of the inn which I had just visited. 'Of course;' I replied, 'that is the man.' To my horror, the other barrister pointed out that the treasurer of the inn in question was not a paid employee – the appointment was an honorary one and was at that time occupied by Lord Justice Ormerod, a 'law lord' who adjudicated in the Court of Appeal and the House of Lords. I was suitably chastened and considerably embarrassed by my *faux pas* and impertinence to such an eminent judge.

Chapter Nine

MURDER AND MADNESS

In dealing, briefly, with the three murder cases with which I was concerned in the 1950s, I do not propose giving the names of the persons in two of those cases, for the reason that even if they are not still alive, they may have relatives or descendants who may be hurt by mention of the fact that the persons in question were charged with murder, albeit they were acquitted.

I might perhaps mention that I have heard the death sentence passed only twice in the whole of my career. The first, of course, was in the Daisy De Melker case. The second time was when I myself had to impose it. I was then on the Court of Appeal in Botswana and there was at the time no High Court Judge available to hear trials, the Chief Justice having departed somewhat hurriedly. I agreed to act as Chief Judge until a new appointment was made. A Tswana was convicted on seven counts of murder. Prior to sentencing him I summoned his counsel in chambers and had enquiries made as to whether he was possibly insane at the time the crimes were committed, but there was no evidence to show this. This man had gone on the rampage and simply murdered seven innocent people for no apparent reason. I could find no extenuating circumstances and was therefore obliged to impose the death sentence.

'A', apparently a happily married young man, was charged with the murder of his wife. She was found dead in a bath of water, and the crown case was that her husband, the accused, had strangled her and thereby caused her death. The senior police officer in charge of the case was again Colonel Ulf Boberg. The defence was that she had not died as a result of strangulation, nor of any unlawful action on the part of her husband, but from another cause or causes (with which I need not deal). A post-mortem on the deceased was performed by the district surgeon, a man of undoubted integrity. There was a mark on the throat of the deceased and this was said to have been left there by the person who had allegedly murdered her by strangulation. If she was indeed murdered it was clear that the husband was responsible for her death. The trial lasted ten days, the judge being Mr Justice Millin with two assessors, William Currie and Felix Landau, members of the Bar. (The latter, son of the late Chief Rabbi, left the Bar and emigrated to Israel on ideological grounds, giving up a good junior practice at the Johannesburg Bar. He finally became Judge President of the District Court of Jerusalem, a post equivalent to that of Judge President of the Transvaal Provincial Division. On reaching the age limit he retired from that position and continued to live in Jerusalem where my wife and I recently spent a few happy days with him.)

The deceased's parents were, in my opinion, rightly convinced of her husband's innocence and they provided the funds for the defence. I was fortunate enough to have the expert advice and evidence of three persons eminent in their field. The first was Dr Hillel Shapiro, a forensic medicine expert with whom I have worked in the course of my practice on many occasions. The second was Professor O Gordon, a distinguished pathologist formerly employed by the government, and the third was Dr Andrew Watt, a leading neurologist. They supplied me with a battery of questions which I was able to put to the district surgeon and, of course, they gave evidence as well. They were of the opinion that the mark on the deceased's throat was caused not ante-mortem, but post-mortem as a result of the manner in which the post-mortem was conducted. In fairness to the district surgeon I should add that he performed his post-mortem, in this case as in others, in the manner in which he had been taught by a Professor MacIntosh at the University of the Witwatersrand.

I may mention that in order to witness how – in the opinion of the medical men advising and assisting me – a post-mortem should be performed, particularly insofar as the neck is concerned, I was persuaded to go to the anatomy laboratory at the university in their company. We were greeted with the news that we were 'in luck's way' because a fresh 'stiff ' (a corpse) had just been brought in. I then watched Professor Gordon removing the skin of the neck in much the same way as one would remove, as delicately as possible, the skin from a ripe peach.

One of the answers given by Professor Gordon to the crown prosecutor, P S Claasen, merits special reference in my opinion:

> CLAASEN: You say this post-mortem was performed in an improper manner.
>
> GORDON: Yes.
>
> CLAASEN: But Professor MacIntosh has performed ten thousand post-mortems in this way.
>
> GORDON *(turning and addressing a question to the judge)*: Am I supposed to comment on this? *(The judge replies in the affirmative.)* Well I am afraid this only shows that he has done it wrong ten thousand times.

In the middle of the defence case, Claasen approached me and stated that he wanted to withdraw the charge against my client. He asked whether I would have any objection to the district surgeon going back into the witness box to explain the error that he had made. I naturally agreed that he could do so. After that was done I called the accused as a witness and asked him one simple question: 'Did you kill your wife?' He answered in the negative. The crown prosecutor properly asked no questions. 'A' was therefore found not guilty and was discharged. As far as I can gather this was the last criminal case in which Mr Justice Millin sat.

Just before Easter in April 1952, one of the assessors, William Currie, died and news of his death appeared in the newspapers. It was then the custom that if a member of the Bar died, at the next court day after his death there would be a ceremony in court over which the senior judge would preside and all other judges in Johannesburg would be on the Bench. Members of the Bar would also attend. The presiding judge would then normally pay tribute to the deceased, and the senior member of the Bar present would add a tribute, and, of course, express condolences to the bereaved. In 1952 I was Chairman of the Bar Council and on Easter Monday I telephoned Judge Millin, who was the senior judge on duty and who would ordinarily preside at such a ceremony. I asked him whether he knew that Currie had died. He said he had not read it in the newspapers and had not known that it had happened. I asked him whether we could have the usual ceremony (which would be on the day after Easter Monday). He, of course, agreed. After this conversation I went to my chambers. On my return home my wife told me that she had had a telephone call from Mrs Millin, who said that the judge was not well and asked whether it would not be possible to arrange for another judge to preside over the proceedings. My wife said that she was sure that there would be no difficulty, and that as soon as I came back from chambers I would telephone her. Mrs Millin asked instead that my wife should do so, giving as a reason for this that if I telephoned and her husband answered the phone, I would have to explain to him why it was advisable for another judge to preside. My wife did telephone her, and told her that I would make the necessary arrangements; but Mrs Millin said that their doctor (who happened to be ours as well), had been to see the judge that morning and he thought there was no reason why he should not preside in court the next day.

The court duly assembled with Mr Justice Millin presiding and he made a gracious tribute to Currie in the course of which he mentioned that he and Currie had obtained their law degrees in the same year and that they were old friends. The judge concluded his address and as was the custom called on the senior member of the Bar to address him. The senior member present that day was G A Mulligan, KC, and after the judge had uttered the words, 'Yes, Mr Mulligan', he collapsed and had to be carried out of court by two judges. He was found to be dead. The judge's registrar or one of the judges telephoned Mrs Millin to tell her what had happened and she came down to the court immediately. I stood outside the judges' corridor with Fritz Adler, a member of the Bar and an old friend of the Judge Millin's, and saw her arriving. She obviously went in to the judge's chambers where he was lying dead. Then happened – to use a euphemism – an unpleasant thing, which shook me. No doubt due to her distressed condition, when she came out of the judges' corridor and saw Adler and myself standing there, she pointed her finger at me and said: 'You – you are responsible for Philip's death.' I did not see her again for some time after that. In fact as far as I can remember I saw her some nine years later, after I had become a judge in Rhodesia, and happened to meet her at the Johannesburg Country Club. She came up to me as though nothing had happened and discussed Roy Welensky (then prime minister of the Federation of Rhodesia, Northern Rhodesia and Nyasaland).

Mrs Millin was, of course, a highly gifted novelist but somewhat eccentric. After her husband's death she donated a sum of money to the Law Faculty of the University of the Witwatersrand to be utilised in giving prizes to the best graduates in certain of the subjects. It so happened that for two successive years the university authorities did not think there was a graduate deserving of the Millin Prize. Despite this explanation having been given to Mrs Millin, she apparently did not accept it and revoked the promise to give her late husband's Law Library to the university, willing it to the Johannesburg Bar. She stipulated that the judge's desk and the things that were on his desk when he died should be in the room where his books were kept and this stipulation was, of course, honoured by the Johannesburg Bar. Most of the library consisted of English Law Reports. These are issued every year and the Bar Library has kept the Millin Library up to date.

The next murder case with which I was concerned was that of an inoffensive-looking young man who had shot his wife and killed her. I will refer to him as 'B'. He was very young when they had married, and his wife – so the evidence revealed – had had an Italian waiter as a lover and apparently did not think that her marriage should interfere with this relationship. After a short while she left her husband and divorce proceedings were instituted. The couple had received some monies as wedding presents and these monies had been deposited in a building society in their joint names against the day when they would have saved enough money to enable them to buy a house. After his wife deserted him B thought that he had better find out what the state of the building society account was. To his horror he ascertained that there was no more money left there and he believed that his wife had given the money to her lover so that he could pay for a trip overseas on which she had planned to join him. This discovery was too much for B, and one Friday evening he went to his next door neighbour and borrowed a revolver. Armed with it he spent the whole night looking for her and in order to keep awake took a certain drug which he bought from an emergency pharmacy. It finally occurred to him early in the morning that his wife might be with the attorney who was acting for her in the divorce proceedings. He thereupon went to his office and – lo and behold – there was the wife and the attorney. Some words passed between B and his wife and he took out the revolver and shot her.[41] She died almost instantaneously.

The defence was that, by reason of the drugs that B had taken during the night, his mind was disturbed and that at the time of the shooting he was temporarily insane. The case came before Judge Dowling and a jury. One of the newspapers suggested – quite unfairly and unjustly – that I had thought up this defence relying on what I had read in a popular American novel of that time, *Anatomy of a Murder*, in which a plea of temporary insanity in a homicide case had been successful. In fact I had not read the book at the time of the trial in question. It was my unpleasant duty to bring out the circumstances relating to the life of the young wife who had been killed and I specially recall, with sadness, her father giving evidence and coming up to me in court after he had left the witness box and saying, 'My daughter was a good girl.'

The law at that time (this was before South Africa became a republic) provided that if it was found that an accused person had committed a crime whilst temporarily insane, the verdict would be 'guilty, but insane.' The judge would then order the person who had been found guilty to be detained at the pleasure of the governor general. Nowadays the law has been altered and – more logically in the type of case I refer to – the verdict is 'not guilty by reason of insanity'. The sentence is the same, namely that the accused be then ordered to be detained at the pleasure of the president.

The judge correctly directed the jury, in B's case, that the jury could find him 'guilty' or 'guilty, but insane' at the time of the commission of the crime. B cut a particularly pathetic figure in the court and the jury apparently felt so sorry for him that after they had retired to consider their verdict, they returned to court and the foreman enquired of the judge whether they could find B not guilty entirely. The judge nearly fell off the Bench and said, 'No'; whereupon they said, 'Guilty, but insane.' The judge then ordered, of course, that B be detained at the governor general's pleasure.

It is just possible that B was not merely temporarily insane, but that his insanity was of a more permanent nature. I say this because, after the trial, I received a letter from him written from

Sterkfontein where he was detained, in which he said that he had never enjoyed anything more in his life than hearing my address to the jury.

Being Chairman of the Bar Council carried with it certain perks. One of the perks I had during my term of office during 1956 was to defend a colleague on a charge of murder. As he has no living relatives I shall, in this case, depart from my practice of not mentioning the name of the alleged murderer. He was one Philip Manners. An attorney who was a friend of Manners had decided to augment his income by indulging in a fraudulent practice. It was in the days when persons who wished to import certain goods into the country had to obtain an import permit. These permits were issued by officials in Pretoria and the attorney's *modus operandi* was to tell a client who wished to obtain a permit that he was able, because of the influence that he had with officials in Pretoria, to obtain a permit for the client provided, of course, that the client gave him a certain sum of money which was to be disbursed to the official who issued the permits. Corruption was not unknown even in those days. It was discovered that the attorney apparently found it too much trouble to go to Pretoria so he would simply pocket the money that was to be used as a bribe and explain to the client that although he had given the money to the official, the application for a permit had not been successful. The attorney was tried, found guilty of fraud, and sentenced to a term of imprisonment.

He was married and there were small children of the marriage. Manners was asked to act *in loco parentis* whilst the attorney languished in jail. The wife of the attorney had meanwhile taken herself a lover, one Brown. Late one Saturday afternoon Manners was in his chambers when the phone rang. It was the attorney's wife, asking him to come to the flat in which she was living as – to quote Manners – she said, 'Phil, for God's sake, get the police, he is going to kill my children!' On leaving his chambers to go to the flat he picked up his pistol. He was not conscious of the fact that the pistol was loaded, having loaded it some days previously. When manners arrived at the flat, Brown threatened to kill him. I cannot say what actually took place, but it ended up with Manners shooting Brown in what Manners said was self-defence.

I had a consultation with Manners at which Dr Shapiro was present, the purpose of the consultation being to ascertain whether the deceased, Brown, could have been shot in the way in which Manners described it. I found, after a little while, that although I was supposed to be conducting the consultation, Manners was in fact doing so. I had to remind him that he was the accused and not counsel. A preparatory examination was held, as was the custom in those days, after Manners had been arrested on a charge of murder. I was briefed to appear at the preparatory examination, and the day before it was due to start Manners came to see me and asked me whether I would mind if the preparatory examination would not start at the appointed hour of 9.30 am, but at 11.30 am. He explained to me that he had a little brief himself and was anxious to dispose of that matter first. I said I thought that he would have to give up that brief.

After the preparatory examination was concluded, the Attorney General decided that Manners should be tried in the Supreme Court on the lesser charge of culpable homicide. Manners being a member of the Bar, I naturally enquired from him whether he would like to be tried by a judge and assessors or by a judge and jury. I thought that Manners had told me the truth and that he should take a judge and assessors, but he elected to have a jury. The case proceeded in the normal way in the Supreme Court and, after the case had been going on for a couple of days, the jury retired at about 11.15 am to consider its verdict. The jury had not returned by 1.00 pm – lunch time – whereupon I went to see the judge and asked him whether I should wait in court until the jury returned. He told me that he did not know why the jury were out so long as he would have found Manners 'not guilty', and said I should go and have some lunch; if the jury had reached a decision before 2.00 pm he would tell them to wait. My junior, Charlie Rosenthal, and I invited Manners to join us at lunch at a little café across the road from the court. It was not known particularly for its hygiene but, as arranged, my junior and I joined Manners at the café. He was then enjoying a plate of soup the sight of which was enough to sicken me and followed this by a hearty steak. I had tea and toast and became physically ill because I thought that the jury, having retired for so long, might quite easily bring in a verdict of 'guilty'.

We went back to court after Manners had finished his hearty

meal and luckily for him the jury returned a verdict of 'not guilty', seven to two. My junior and I went back to chambers. Manners came to thank me and ask me whether I didn't think it would be a good idea to have cake in the common room that afternoon. I said, somewhat cruelly I think, that I did not think that there was a precedent for this sort of thing. I should mention that Manners was apparently quite a prominent Freemason. Prior to the trial I was stopped in the street by quite a few prominent people who were Freemasons to enquire what I thought was going to happen in Manners's trial. They apparently assumed that I was 'on the square' (a term they used when speaking to me and which I believe has some meaning in Freemasonry). As I was never a freemason I did not, and still do not, know what that means.

On Sunday 25 July 1955, an order was issued on the officer commanding the South African Police. In issuing the order (in a form known as a rule *nisi*), Judge Blackwell said, 'This is not a police state yet.' The order called upon the officer commanding the South African Police to

> show cause the same evening why the officer or officers in charge of the members of the South African Police Force presently on duty in relation to a conference being held at the Trades Hall, Kerk Street, Johannesburg, should not be ordered to remove all members of the police force immediately from the Trades Hall and to refrain from any illegal interference with the petitioners [Advocate Wolpe and another person], or delegates or members of the said conference, or persons invited thereto, or the lawful proceedings of the conference.

What had happened was that there was a meeting of a body known as the South African Congress of Democrats in the hall, Wolpe being the national president of that organisation. The rule *nisi* was to operate as an interim interdict, and the return day was extended from time to time until the matter came before Judge President Rumpff in September of that year.

I did not appear in the original application before Judge Blackwell but was briefed, together with L Lazar and Jack Unterhalter, to appear for the applicants. My opponents were J F

Ludorf, QC, and with him P M Cillie. Both of these persons subsequently became judges, P M Cillie becoming Judge President of the Transvaal and for a short while a Judge of Appeal.

Judge President Rumpff, after hearing argument, ordered that oral evidence had to be given. The matter was postponed to a date to be fixed by the registrar. On that fixed date Ludorf decided not to call any witnesses and the respondents were ordered to pay the costs. Ludorf 's appearance in the case between the South African Police and Advocate Wolpe led subsequently to an application made for his recusal in what was known as the 'treason trial', which will be dealt with in some detail later.[42]

On Easter Saturday 1960, Dr Verwoerd, then prime minister of South Africa, opened the Rand Easter Show at Milner Park, the old Showgrounds. As is well known, he was shot by David Pratt. It was a miracle that the shots did not prove fatal. Loyal supporters thought that the Almighty had intervened to save Verwoerd's life. Cynics may say that if that was so why did the Almighty not intervene when he was later assassinated by a man called Tsafendas.

I was retained by a firm of attorneys, Dryden & Myburgh (no longer in existence), to act for Pratt in the trial that would inevitably take place. In fact I was briefed before it was known that Dr Verwoerd would survive the wounds inflicted on him. The trial was set down for 13 September 1960.

Pratt was duly indicted on the charge of attempting to murder Dr Verwoerd on 9 April 1960. There was a preparatory examination at which I appeared but asked no questions. Pratt was, of course, committed for trial, but before it took place I had managed to obtain evidence which indicated quite clearly, in my opinion, that Pratt was mentally disordered. The law as I understood it was that if it appears that a person charged or to be charged with a crime is mentally disordered, an enquiry must be held into his mental condition before he is tried.[43] There was a mass of medical evidence to establish that he was mentally disordered and in addition he was an epileptic. He was, therefore, by definition of the Mental Disorders Act of 1916 as amended by Act 37 of 1957, a mentally disordered person.

About a fortnight before the date fixed for the trial – although Dryden & Myburgh had, as far as I could see, done everything to collect evidence and make all necessary arrangements for the case – Pratt decided to jettison this firm and engaged another attorney, Benno Tennet. To me this seemed an extraordinary decision. The first I knew about it was when Tennet – as far as I knew, totally inexperienced in this type of case – telephoned me at my home one Saturday afternoon to inform me that he was now Pratt's attorney and that the *Sunday Times* wanted to take a photograph of him and myself together. I declined the invitation. Frank Ninow, a competent junior who died far too young, was briefed with me, but when Tennet entered upon the scene he added Leslie Lawrence, SC, to the counsel already briefed. I do not, of course, put Lawrence in the same category as Tennet. He was an experienced advocate, and was, together with Ninow, of assistance.

Reading recently through newspaper reports found for me by my researcher, I was reminded of something quite absurd told to me by Mr R W Rein, then Attorney General for the Eastern Cape, who was assigned to prosecute for the Crown in the Pratt case. The report of the first day's proceedings in the *Rand Daily Mail* relates that:

> Mr Rein said that he was empowered to state that the shooting of the Prime Minister was not disputed. 'I also wish to state that neither the accused nor his wife, Mrs Sarah Leonarda Pratt, has ever met the Prime Minister and that neither of them had ever had any dealings with the Prime Minister of any nature whatever.' Mr Rein said that he understood from the defence that a special application would be made to the court and he, therefore, wished to say no more.

Prior to the trial I had been to see Rein to tell him my intention to apply to the court to have Pratt declared mentally disordered. This would avoid the necessity of having a trial for attempted murder take place, with the inevitable finding that the accused was 'guilty but insane'. Rein said he would agree to my adopting that course, but said there was a rumour in Pretoria that Dr Verwoerd had had an affair with Mrs Pratt. I recall laughing at the absurdity of this rumour. He wanted me to give him an undertaking not to raise this fairytale – to which, of course, I agreed.

Pratt's second wife, a Hollander, had left him some time before

April 1960 and gone back to Holland, taking with her the children born of that marriage. I interviewed her a week before the trial was due to start and she agreed to give evidence of Pratt's behaviour, particularly his habit of sitting down at the piano on a certain night each month and playing one chord right through the night. He was indeed a classic lunatic. In view of her undertaking I agreed not to have her subpoenaed. Her attorney, whose name I cannot now recall, was present at this discussion, but despite her undertaking she immediately flew back to Holland. For this reason, a few days before the trial, a daughter of Pratt by his first marriage had to make an application to have a *curator ad litem* appointed for Pratt, to investigate his mental condition.[44]

On the Sunday before the trial, Pratt contrived to speak to me alone at the prison. Handing the warder half a crown, Pratt commissioned him to procure a copy of the *Sunday Times*, and then indicated that my colleagues should wait outside the interview room. With urgent confidentiality he proposed that, at the trial, I should create a diversion during my opening address, upon which he would leap from the dock and escape through an open window. A car would be waiting outside to carry him to Lanseria airport, from where, he said, he had chartered a plane to Swaziland. Needless to say, I found myself unable to accommodate Pratt's ingenious plan. I duly made my application, and led evidence of a number of lay witnesses who knew Pratt.

On the first day, Pratt made various interruptions from the dock and certainly behaved in a strange manner. The first day was certainly for me a very trying day and to cap it all the court sat rather longer hours than usual. When the court adjourned, Tennet came up to me and started making what he thought was a joke. I then told Lawrence that unless he kept Tennet away from me for the rest of the case I would walk out.

I may mention that on the second day just before lunch, Pratt stood up in the dock and said: 'I was shooting at the epitome of apartheid rather than Dr Verwoerd.' After the lay evidence and medical evidence had been concluded, I closed the defence case, having no intention of putting Pratt in the witness box.

Without my concurrence, Pratt said he wished to give evidence under oath from the witness box and Judge President Rumpff agreed that he could do so. Here I shall quote the *Rand Daily Mail* report of 14 September 1960, because as far as I can recall it is probably more complete than the report in *The Star* or *Die Transvaler*. The court was quiet for nearly an hour as Pratt spoke clearly and ended with an indictment of apartheid, calling it 'the slimy snake that is gripping the throat of South Africa'. He showed signs of emotion when he threw up his arms and spoke of the country's 'glittering future once the simple initial plunge is taken and Nationalism is thrown out'. He said that after he had shot the prime minister he had enjoyed his best night's sleep in six years on blankets and without a mattress in a cell. He described his urge to impart a message to the country and told of three suicide attempts which were averted at the last moment each time by his coming to the realisation that he must give a message. He said that when he had come to the Rand Easter Show he had had no fixed intention of shooting Verwoerd, but he felt a violent urge 'to shoot apartheid', which he regarded as preventing South Africa from taking 'its rightful place amongst the nations'. His message for every person of every colour in South Africa, which he accepted with deep humility he was allowed to give, was for 'each person to play his part if we are to build South Africa into what I know can be built'. The country would have to stop this policy of world isolation which would 'carry it into the depths of the wilderness and never to the promised land.' He then walked back to the dock and listened without showing any signs of emotion as the judge decided to send him to Weskoppies (an institution for mentally disturbed persons) for observation for a period of 14 days.

On the resumption of the hearing on 26 September, further medical evidence was given and Judge President Rumpff made an order in terms of the relevant legislation, committing Pratt to the Pretoria jail pending the signification of the governor general's decision. In fact I learnt afterwards that Pratt was sent to a prison in Bloemfontein where insane persons who are considered dangerous are kept. He committed suicide a few months after he had been detained.[45]

During the trial he had certainly behaved in a most extraordinary fashion with gestures and other interruptions to which I have not referred. I should mention that letters written by Pratt before he shot Verwoerd indicated that at various times he contemplated committing suicide. If I may say so with respect, the judge president conducted the proceedings in an exemplary fashion. When Pratt was giving evidence he stared, as a reporter of the *Rand Daily Mail* says, almost fixedly at papers in front of him, not once interjecting. In addition, once Pratt had finished saying what he wanted to say, the judge said to Rein: 'Mr Rein you don't want to ask any questions do you?'

There is, however, one passage in the judgment, which in the light of what Pratt did say in the course of giving evidence, may not be correct. The judgment reads:

> I do not wish to deal in detail with the speech Pratt made when he gave evidence. The manner in which he made his speech, his demeanour and the explanation of his motives for the attack on the prime minister give one the impression that the balance of his mind has been affected.

There can be no doubt that Pratt's demeanour and interjections during the course of the case were not those of a sane person, but in the light of subsequent events the question may be asked as to whether 'the explanation of his motives for his attack on the Prime Minister give one the impression that the balance of his mind had been disturbed.' I may be permitted to observe that South Africa has had to pay, and will continue to have to pay, a high price for the actions of Dr Verwoerd, one of the chief architects of the apartheid policy which has bedevilled this country and the people who live in it.

To end this account on a somewhat lighter note, I would like to mention some of the contents of a letter written on Sunday 10 April 1960 – the day after the shooting of Verwoerd – by a nephew of Pratt to his mother, Pratt's sister. It is the kind of letter that a boy at boarding school would send to his parents every week. The boy had spent the weekend on leave from his boarding school – Michaelhouse – and had been with his uncle much of the time.

He starts off the letter by saying that he went to a hotel in Bremersdorp where he met a man and his wife who knew his father. He suggested to his mother that she might go there and wait for him until 22 April 'as it is a much nicer hotel although a little further away from the centre of town.' The letter then goes on to say that he had gone to the Show and that there was a lot to see.

He described the cattle and the other exhibits which he said were 'extra good'. The following sentence then appears: 'Of course the climax to the Show came when Uncle David had a go at Verwoerd.' He then goes on to talk about what he and his uncle had done and how he and his uncle were full of jokes; and of how he had seen his Uncle David on the stand and went to talk to him. He said he later went off to another part of the stand to join a friend 'whom you will meet at the farm'. He then describes that Verwoerd finished his speech and the judging of the champions began. Just before the final animal was judged, the letter continues, he saw Uncle David walking into the arena and standing and joking with some of the exhibitors. He said the animals started leaving the arena and he suddenly heard two bangs going off like crackers. He says he jumped up and saw Dr Verwoerd collapsing. He said he had a horrible feeling that it was Uncle David who had shot Verwoerd although he didn't know at that stage who had done it. He said that he went to see another uncle of his who was at the Show but he couldn't stay long because 'we had to be in Springs at 6.00 pm'. He then described how well his other uncle had looked and that he was in a very jovial mood. He came to the conclusion that Uncle David had shot Dr Verwoerd in a moment of blind insanity. He said he felt very upset and then mentions certain other matters of no consequence, ending his letter by saying: 'I must run now but keep happy and I am looking forward to see you soon.'

Chapter Ten

THE SOUTH WEST AFRICA DIAMOND CASE

Early in January 1957 an old friend of mine, John Turnbull, then the senior partner of Webber, Wentzel, Hofmeyr, Turnbull & Co (now known as Webber Wentzel), briefed me in a matter that he said was of great importance to his clients. He stressed that he did not want an opinion from me, but my instructions were to fight a case to be brought in the High Court of South West Africa (now Namibia) by his clients Consolidated Diamond Mines of South West Africa Ltd.

As is well known, up to 1914 South West Africa was a German Protectorate, but by the Peace Treaty of Versailles the Union of South Africa was entrusted with a sea mandate over South West Africa in terms of which the Union was empowered to administer it as an integral part of this territory. When the Union vested the government of South West Africa in an administrator, Roman-Dutch law superseded German law as the law of the protectorate.

In October 1919, the Anglo American Corporation (Anglo), of which the late Sir Ernest Oppenheimer was chairman, wrote to the Minister of Mines of the Union of South Africa informing him that it was intended to amalgamate various German mining companies operating in South West Africa, including the German Diamond Company, and to form a new company, to be known as the Consolidated Diamond Mines of South West Africa Ltd, to acquire their assets. Anglo asked the Minister of Mines for an assurance that the Union government, as successors of the German government, would recognise the new company's titles. The Union government had no objection to this scheme and gave Anglo the assurance that the Union government would recognise, in the same manner as the German government had done, the title of the various German companies for which amalgamation was proposed, including the German Diamond Company.[46]

Immediately after the formation of Consolidated Diamond Mines of South West Africa Ltd (CDM) on 9 February 1920, it acquired the assets of several amalgamated German companies operating in South West Africa.

It appears that in 1923 CDM had, by an agreement entered into at that time with the Administrator of South West Africa, acquired exclusive valuable prospecting and mining rights over an area of some 10 000 miles of the west coast of South West Africa, known as the Sperrgebiet (literally meaning 'a restricted area'). The agreement, called the Halbscheid Agreement, provided that the exclusive rights were to be for a period of at least 50 years. At the time of the hearing of the litigation this period had been extended to the year 2001.

The prospecting and mining rights in question were in respect of all minerals, including diamonds and precious stones, but excluding minerals in respect of which rights had been lawfully acquired by any other persons prior to 15 January 1923, and which rights had not since lapsed or been abandoned. I should explain that '*Halbscheid*' translated into English means 'half-share' and the agreement between the administrator and CDM provided that the government would obtain half the profits made as a result of the mining operations which were carried out by CDM. (The Halbscheid Agreement is quoted in full in the Appellate Division Report.[47])

By General Notice 5 of 1957,[48] the then administrator (purporting to act in terms of Section 58 of the Mines and Minerals Ordinance No. 26 of 1954, as amended) granted to a company known as Suidwes-Afrika Prospekteerders (Edms) Bpk the exclusive right to prospect or mine for all minerals in any area described as being

> from a point on the high water mark of the Atlantic Ocean on the northern bank of the Orange River, thence in a northerly direction along the high water mark directly opposite Dias Point, thence due west into the sea to a point 800 yards west of the high water mark of the said Ocean, thence in a southerly direction parallel to the high water mark of the said ocean and 800 yards from it to a point due

west of the point of beginning, thence due east to the point of beginning.

The rights given to Suidwes-Afrika Prospekteerders, as contained in Government Notice 5 of 1957, were valid as from 1 January 1957 up to and including 31 December 1997.

CDM had protested against the grant of these rights, maintaining that the area in question formed part of the Sperrgebiet, but its representations were rejected by the administrator and consequently the decision was taken to bring proceedings, the case eventually ending up in the Appellate Division.[49]

That portion of the Sperrgebiet relevant to the litigation was its western boundary, stated to be 'west by the Atlantic Ocean'. The dispute between CDM and the first and second respondents was whether the extent of the right granted to CDM under the Halbscheid Agreement included the foreshore between the high and low water marks. It was CDM's contention that the rights included the foreshore between the high and low water marks; the respondents, of course, contending that the rights granted to CDM did not include the foreshore between the high and low water marks but ended – as far as the western boundary was concerned – at the high water mark.

As Chief Justice Fagan in his judgment stated,[50] the issue was whether the Sperrgebiet included the foreshore between the high and low water marks. Our research in the Windhoek archives revealed that in the 19th century it was believed that diamonds discovered in South West Africa came either from pipes in the sea or were alluvial (having been washed down by rivers from the interior). It should at once be stated that as far as Sir Ernest Oppenheimer was concerned, he was not worried about somebody having rights to mine a small portion of the foreshore or out to sea. He was concerned that if the rights given to the second respondent in 1957 were exercised, the Sperrgebiet, instead of being, as its name indicates, a 'closed area' would become an open area. The strict control over entry and departure of persons which had been exercised by CDM (and which were exercised at the time of the litigation), would be negated. If an army of guards were to be employed to ensure that persons operating the small area granted to the second respondent in 1957 did not enter the area which had hitherto been closed, *sed quis custodiet custodes ipsos*. On the only occasion that I met Sir Ernest Oppenheimer (he died before judgment had been given in the proceedings in South West Africa), it was made plain to me that that was what he feared – to put it bluntly, that if the grant of rights to the second respondent was valid, the closed area would become an open area.

Although Professor Hahlo, in his learned and helpful article on the case, entitled 'The great South West African diamond case',[51] says that the case was fought over the right to mine for diamonds in the area set out in Government Notice 5 of 1957, and the court was called upon merely to decide whether or not the western boundary described as the Atlantic Ocean included the foreshore as part of the Sperrgebiet, the real question that exercised the mind of CDM was this security question.

Insofar as the use of the foreshore for mining was concerned, CDM used it in connection with those operations and no one appeared to have doubted that CDM's rights included the foreshore. We obtained affidavits from former administrators as well as mining inspectors and police officers of high rank who had been stationed in South West Africa at different times, that the foreshore had been considered as part of the Sperrgebiet.

Despite the stringent steps that were taken to prevent unlawful entry into the Sperrgebiet (there had in fact been prosecutions of persons who had done so), an employee of CDM stole a large quantity of diamonds and concealed them in a brass container, which he buried under a stone near Chamois Bay. He then resigned from his employment and went to Cape Town, where he chartered a private aeroplane to take him to Lüderitz. On the return flight he proposed to the pilot that they land at the beach at Chamois Bay and collect the diamonds, offering to pay the pilot £3 000. The pilot agreed and landed on the beach, but the wheels of the aircraft became bogged in the sand and the plane could not take off again. Both the pilot and the former employee, if they were not to starve in the desert, had no choice but to give themselves up at the nearest CDM camp. They were arrested and duly charged and convicted, one of the charges being that they were in the prohibited area. According to Professor Hahlo,[52] this case caused lawyers and laymen to ask themselves whether the beach between the high and low water mark formed part of the Sperrgebiet.

Although – at the time the rights were given to the second respondents – there had been no serious attempt, as far as I can recollect, to mine diamonds in the sea, this has subsequently been done successfully, starting with a man called Collins; others have since followed in areas south of the Orange River. (It is interesting to note that the Cape Colony, well before the German Protectorate of which I have written, had taken possession of Walvis Bay, then known as Wallfish Bay and the control of that Bay has been the subject of a dispute between the Namibian Government and the South African Government.)

In the proceedings that were eventually launched in the High Court of South West Africa, CDM was the applicant, the Administrator of South West Africa (the administrator) the first respondent, and Suidwes-Afrika Prospekteerders, having obtained the rights disputed by CDM, was the second respondent. My juniors were Blen Franklin, who subsequently became a judge of the Transvaal Provincial Division, and Hans Berker, a South West African of German descent who subsequently became Chief Justice of Namibia. Regrettably both Blen and Hans are now dead, as is John Turnbull. Present in South West Africa with Franklin, Berker and myself, were our attorney Carveth Geach and Professors Hahlo and Kahn-Freund. I need hardly say that the assistance given to us by these persons was invaluable.

We had been given a copy of the Halbscheid Agreement by Turnbull. The very lengthy preamble of the agreement contains much of the history leading up to the agreement between the administrator and CDM. It seemed to us that it was necessary to ascertain what rights were held by the predecessors of CDM, what litigation and judgments had been given in connection with the Sperrgebiet and what laws, if any, had been passed by the German government in connection therewith. To do this it was necessary to go back to the early 1880s and to endeavour to trace the history as well as the rights of the public to the use of the seashore from that time.

Mr Carveth Geach, then a junior partner of Webber Wentzel (who has since retired as the senior partner of that firm), together with Mr John Rudd, an official in Anglo American or De Beers (I am not certain which company), were placed at our disposal, and they were assigned to go to the archives in Windhoek – and in any other place that they might find necessary, to obtain the information we required – and go through all documentation, letters and judgments of court that had been given from the time the Treaty of Protection and Amity was signed. I should immediately state that they did a thorough piece of work which turned out to be of great assistance to us in the arguments that were put before the court.

In addition we thought it necessary to endeavour to obtain the services of academics of standing to research what was for my colleagues and myself an esoteric subject – the law of the seashore. We were fortunate in obtaining the services of Professor H R Hahlo, then Professor of Law and head of the Department of Law of the University of the Witwatersrand, and of Professor J E Scholtens, Professor of Roman Law at same university. Prof Hahlo, in his article,[53] graciously recorded his indebtedness to Prof Scholtens for his invaluable assistance with the historical research for the article. Prof Hahlo also stated in his article that the case 'would go down in the annals of legal history as one of South Africa's great civil cases. Its nearest equivalent in modern times is in the "American tidelands" litigation.' Whether this is correct is open to question: but as far as I was concerned it involved the longest hearing of an application and of an appeal in the whole of my career at the Bar.

The argument in South West Africa took place in mid-summer. It lasted two or three weeks. With the agreement of counsel appearing on the other side, we approached the court to suggest different sitting hours. The normal court hours were 10.00 am to 1.00 pm, an adjournment of hour or an hour and a half, and resumption of argument until 4.30 pm. There was no airconditioning in the court and we suggested that the court should sit from 8.30 am until 1.30 pm – the normal court day of five hours. The court acceded to this request. We found it particularly useful because in the afternoons we could return to consideration of our argument and of our reply to the respondents' arguments.

The argument in the Appellate Division took two weeks. The court consisted of Chief Justice Fagan, and Judges of Appeal Schreiner, Steyn, Malan and Acting Judge of Appeal Hall. In the first week, commencing on 19 May 1958, we sat, as is customary in the appeal court, for only four days, leaving Wednesday of that week open. We obtained permission from the Chief Justice to work in the appeal court at night because of the quite enormous number of authorities that had to be consulted. In the second week we sat not only every day from 26 to 30 May, but also at night. The court would sit until late in the afternoon and resume hearings at 8.00 pm, continuing until about 10.30 or 11.00 pm.

Until 1914, while South West Africa was a German protectorate, German law had applied to South West Africa. It became obvious from certain papers that were handed to us that it would be necessary to research thoroughly both the events from 1884 to 1914 and also, of course, the German law (until 1914 the governing law of the territory) and the Roman-Dutch law (after 1918 the common law of the country).

We were anxious to obtain expert opinion on the German law relating to the seashore and particularly to the rights that might be given to private persons on the seashore. I asked Professor Dennis Cowen, who had apparently been consulted about this matter prior to our being briefed by Mr Turnbull, whether he was able to recommend anybody who might be of assistance to us on German law. He thought we should try to enlist the services of Professor Kahn-Freund, a most distinguished lawyer, and at that time a Professor at London University, who had formerly been a judge in Germany and had been a refugee from Hitler. About this time, I had to go to London in connection with the Central African Airways case (mentioned in a previous chapter), and during my stay in London was able to arrange a meeting with Professor Kahn-Freund. He was indeed of tremendous assistance to us, and found us German authorities, which are referred to in the judgment of Chief Justice Fagan.[54]

Professor Kahn-Freund referred us in particular to a case of *In re* A Prussian Fiscus *v* The Town of Kolberg. The facts of this case were that in 1488 the Bishop of Camin had granted the town of Kolberg in Prussia ownership of a portion of the seashore of the Baltic Sea. The state contended that with the introduction of the common law, the town of Kolberg had become divested of its ownership in the seashore, but the Rechsgericht, confirming the decision of the lower courts, held otherwise. 'If … a separate private property to the beach was established in favour of the Municipality Kolberg by feudal privilege, and if this still existed at the time of the introduction of the common law as a well-acquired right, then this remained in force even after this time'. The importance of this case was that in effect German law was the same as the Roman-Dutch law.

It has to be borne in mind, as pointed out by Judge of Appeal Schreiner in his judgment concurring with that of the Chief Justice in the Appellate Division,[55] that in the absence of legislative authority the executive cannot legally grant ownership of part of the foreshore. (However, grants of rights less than ownership must be approached from a different angle.) To grant a private person ownership of the foreshore is to empower him to exclude the public and so prevent them from exercising their common law rights for bathing, fishing and the like. Thus we held that in Roman-Dutch law and under German law there was full power to include the foreshore in the Halbscheid Agreement.

Hans Berker dealt with our argument on the German law and referred to the authorities that appeared eventually in the judgment of Chief Justice Fagan.

Chief Justice Fagan, when he reviewed the early history of the Sperrgebiet,[56] fortunately for us took the same view as ours: that it was necessary to go back further into history – that is, before the first mention of the Halbscheid Agreement in the German Ordinance of 22 September 1908. A problem that we had to overcome was that although there was a certain amount of documentation in support of our case, it would be difficult to prove this documentation in the ordinary way in which it should be proved in a court of law. Chief Justice Fagan took the view that the early history of the Sperrgebiet was a matter of historical knowledge of which the court might probably have informed itself and taken judicial cognisance.[57] We took the view that we would proceed by way of application, annexing the relevant documents and taking a chance that the respondents would not deny the facts set out in these documents. Indeed, we saw no other way of proceeding with the matter. In the result, our view was fortunately found to be correct in that the respondents did not deny the facts set out in the voluminous documentation attached to our founding affidavit – although they disputed certain inferences and certain conclusions of law.[58]

Although the issue before the court both in South West Africa and the Appellate Division was whether the Sperrgebiet included the foreshore between the high and low water marks, the history – as contained in the preamble and found in the documentation over the period from the early 1880s – proved to be of great assistance to our side. This appears from the whole of the judgment of Chief Justice Fagan and also from the short concurring judgment of Judge of Appeal Schreiner.[59]

The research had revealed that one Lüderitz (after whom Lüderitz Bay is named), a German merchant from Bremen, explored the coast of South West Africa and bought vast tracts of land from various indigenous chieftains. The first contract was with a 'Captain Josef Fredricks' in May 1883. In terms of this contract, Lüderitz purchased the bay of Angra Pequena (now known as Lüderitz Bay), and the adjoining territory in an extension of five miles in all directions, from Fredricks, who is described as a 'Hottentot chieftain of Bethany'. For this, Fredricks received £100 sterling in gold and two hundred rifles. Another contract was entered into in August 1883 in terms of which Fredricks 'sold and surrendered to Lüderitz the whole coast from the Groot or Orange River to the 26th degree of southern latitude inclusive of all harbours and bays as well as the hinterland to an extent of twenty geographical miles inland.' The price was £500 sterling in gold and 60 Wesley-Richards rifles.

Shortly thereafter Lüderitz asked for the protection of the German empire and not surprisingly the Lüderitz acquisitions were in fact taken under the protection of Germany. A Treaty of Protection and Amity was entered into between the German Emperor and Josef Fredricks on 28 October 1884. Lüderitz ceded the rights he had obtained under the agreement, which were recognised in the Treaty of Protection and Amity, to a company known as the Deutsche Kolonial Gesellschaft. He received two hundred thousand marks in cash and three hundred thousand marks in shares for all the rights he had acquired. Deutsche Kolonial Gesellschaft had, in turn, assigned and ceded the rights which it had obtained to the German Diamond Company.

The relevant portions of the Treaty of Protection and Amity of 1884, for the purposes of the case, were Articles 4, 5, 6 and 7 which provided as follows:-

Above: The young Isie Maisels (seated at extreme left) is seen here as Chairman of the Law Students Society Committee in 1927. Two of his fellow members, Willie Oshry (second from left, back row) and Arthur Suzman (seated extreme right) rose to become prominent QCs with substantial practices at the Johannesburg Bar.

Left: Isie around the time he became a Queen's Counsel. He was already an established advocate with a formidable reputation, but was still to reach the height of his powers.

Above: Muriel Maisels was always recognised as a beauty. This picture (taken in 1934, the year she married Isie), also captures her gentleness and sweet nature.

Right: Muriel Maisels with her son, Keith.

This photograph was taken during the war years. Standing, (right), in a dark uniform is Cecil Margo, (subsequently Mr Justice Margo) and seated (right) are Isie's commanding officer Colonel Koos de Vos and his wife Nolene. Muriel is seated to the left, behind Isie.

'Interrogation' of Italian prisoners of war.

On the occasion of the United Hebrew Congregation's jubilee in 1947, Isie in his role as president welcomes General Jan Smuts to the celebrations. From left are the then Chief Rabbi of South Africa, Rabbi L I Rabinowitz and next to him is the then Minister of Health, Dr Henry Gluckman.

Bram Fischer (left), an advocate of outstanding ability, with a young Sydney Kentridge and his wife Felicia.

A.J. Lutuli.P/B.,
P.O. Groutville,
Natal.

15th November, 1960.

Mr. I.A. Maisels, Q.C.,
JOHANNESBURG.

Dear Mr. Maisels,

This communication is intended for the Treason Trial Defence Team through you as leader.

You are now entering the last stage of this mammoth and marathon case which no doubt is destined to make legal history in South Africa. I wish to merely express my deepest appreciation and admiration for the way you and your team have given yourself to this case and handling it most masterly and devotedly.

Whatever the result, responsible African opinion will always hold you in high esteem and feel indebted to you for your magnificent performance which has been a big challenge to the Crown and the Government. What would have happened to us without you! I just wish humbly to express these sentiments.

On a personal plane, I feel honoured to have had the opportunity of knowing you all and establishing bonds of personal contact and friendship.

Things being what they are in our land you may find yourselves handling more and more political cases, for we are determined to carry on our struggle until victory is won.

I pray that your team may not be banned. Speaking as layman, I say it is a brilliant team that would match any legal team anywhere. You and your colleagues have virtually taught the Crown its case.

Best wishes to you all and greetings to each one of you.

Tell Mr. Parkington, your energetic, most alert and fiery instructing attorney, that I would still like to face Mr. Trengove in the next political case.

Yours most sincerely,

This letter from Albert Luthuli speaks volumes for the regard in which the entire treason trial defence team were held by the leadership of the African National Congress.

Triumphantly held aloft by some of the treason trial accused and their colleagues, Isie is carried from the court after the not guilty verdict was announced on 29 March 1961. Note that he has emerged from the 'Non-European Only' entrance.

Opposite page
This is the letter written to Isie and signed by all the treason trial accused when they heard that he had accepted an appointment to the Southern Rhodesian Bench. The family did not know of the letter until it was found, published in full, in Helen Joseph's diary of the treason trial, If This Be Treason. *By that time more than 30 years had elapsed since he had received it.*

22nd February 1961

1/c Mr I. A. Maisels, Q.C.

We, the accused in the Treason Trial, want to express our congratulations on the high honour which has been conferred upon you in your appointment as a Judge of the High Court in Rhodesia, an honour which should have been conferred upon you long ago in your own country. It is indeed a further measure of South Africa's shameful discrimination against all who oppose the vicious policies of the present Government that this recognition of your unsurpassed contribution to our system of law should have to be made by another country.

Throughout the long dreary years of our trial we have been proud to have been defended by you, not only because we know that in you we have had the best defence that this land could supply, but we have been proud because we know of the magnificent legal battles that you have fought to preserve the rule of law, to prevent it from being whittled away by the unscrupulous machinations of the Government.

Our joy and pride in your appointment cannot but be fraught with sadness at your departure from South Africa; we look a little enviously at Southern Rhodesia who will gain this addition to her legal ranks, who will gain the services of our most illustrious lawyer; but we will say here and now that in the free South Africa to come, we shall welcome you back with open arms - we are only lending you to Rhodesia.

You take with you our most sincere good wishes and our deep appreciation of the contribution which you have made to our struggle for justice in South Africa, and our appreciation of your confidence in us and the confidence which you have given to us throughout our trial. Words must be inadequate to express our feelings and our pride in you. We can only repeat, "We are proud of you and we shall wait for you one day to come back to a South Africa which will honour you as you should be honoured."

F. Adam
[illegible]
[illegible]
[illegible]
W. M. Sisulu
Helen Joseph
A. M. Kathrada
[illegible]
Stanley Lollan
N. Mandela
[illegible]
Leslie Massina
[illegible]
[illegible]
[illegible]
[illegible]
J. Kampeni

[illegible]
S. P. Mkalipi
[illegible]
S. Tyiki
G. Sibande
P. Nene
P. K. Selepe
E. P. Moretsele
L. Ngoyi
P. Mathole
J. Molefi
J. Nkadimeng

Always an imposing figure in Court, this picture shows Isie in Judge's regalia, including the full-bottomed horse-hair wig, worn at that time in Southern Rhodesia.

Opposite page
Isie returned to the Bar after his term on the Southern Rhodesian Bench and seven years as an executive director of the OK Bazaars. He defended a prominent Cape Town businessman, who bludgeoned his wife to death, and is shown here on his way to the Supreme Court during the trial

In 1969 Edmond de Rothschild, one of the leaders of world Jewry, visited South Africa as President of the Israel United Appeal. From far left is Yitzchak Unna (Israel's Consul to South Africa), Rothschild, Isie (then South African chairman of both the appeal and the Zionist Federation), and Sam Cohen (founder of the OK Bazaars).

Isie was awarded an Honory LL D by the University of the Witwatersrand in 1978. He is seen here with Muriel and his son Keith.

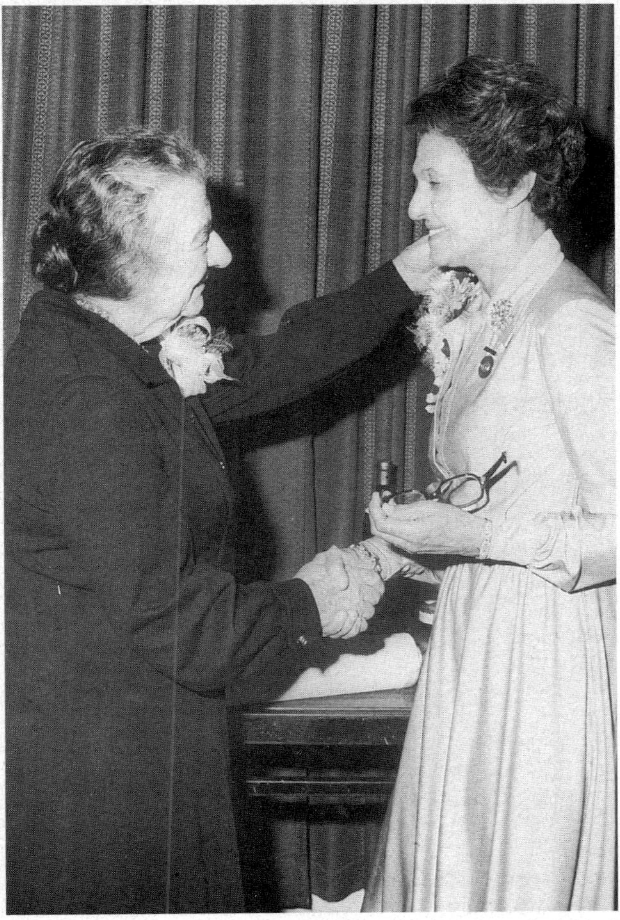

Above: In July 1980 the Johannesburg Bar celebrated the 90th birthday of Higgy Isaacs, QC (at centre). Isie spoke on the Bar's behalf. Bill Schreiner, SC, son of Mr Justice Oliver Schreiner, looks on.

Left: Muriel Maisels was a lifelong Zionist. Here as President of the South African Women's Zionist Organisation she is warmly welcomed in Israel by the Prime Minister Golda Meir.

81/143299

D220/82: NELSON MANDELA.

Pollsmoor Maximum Prison,
Private Bag X 4, TOKAI, 7966.
26 11 85.

CENSOR
CENSORED

DATUM/DATE 85 · 11 · 27

Dear Mr Maisels,
I was happy to hear from George that you recently celebrated your 80th Birthday. That reminded me of a remark made to you by Mr Oswald Pirow in the course of his address to the Special Court during the Treason Trial. He had made a statement which you apparently did not like and, as you rose to object, he said: "Please take it easy, Issy!" or words to that effect.

It would seem to me that on this occasion, at least, you heeded the advice of your controversial colleague; that throughout these past 25 years you took things easy and forgot about advancing age and retirement. Please accept our warmest congratulations on this magnificent achievement. May life continue to be sweet and your happiness complete. Again, congratulations and regards to your family and to the members of the Johannesburg Bar.

Sincerely,
NRMandela

On the occasion of his 80th birthday, Isie received this wonderful letter from his most celebrated client, Nelson Mandela, who was then incarcerated in Pollsmoor Prison.

When Muriel and Isie celebrated their golden wedding anniversary in 1984, Jeffrey paid them a visit with all his children. (Left to right) Gabriella, Muriel, James, Lisa, Isie, Carol (Jeffrey's wife), Amanda and Jeffrey.

A family photograph taken in 1990 when Isie and Muriel were holidaying in Cape Town. (Left to right) Lisa (Jeffrey's daughter), Muriel, Helen, James (Lisa's brother), Isie and Elizabeth (Isie's eldest daughter). Standing in front of the group is Elizabeth's daughter Rebecca.

BRICK COURT CHAMBERS

15/19 DEVEREUX COURT, LONDON WC2R 3JJ

TEL: 071-583 0777 FAX: 071-583 9401 TELEX: 892687 1BRICK G LDE: 302

17 November 1992

S. Burger S.C.,
Chairman,
Johannesburg Bar Council,
1st Floor,
Schreiner Chambers,
94 Pritchard Street,
Johannesburg 2001,
South Africa

Dear Schalk,

Thank you very much for your invitation to the dinner on 19th November in honour of Issy Maisels. It is extraordinary to think that Issy is retiring. It is hard to think of the Johannesburg Bar without his presence.

I am extremely sorry that I shall not be in Johannesburg and that I shall therefore miss the dinner. I very much wish I could have been there. Issy was undoubtedly the greatest advocate I have seen in action in court in any jurisdiction in which I have practised. I am glad that the Bar is honouring him. Please give my very good wishes to him and to the Johannesburg Bar.

Yours sincerely,

Sydney

Sydney Kentridge Q.C.

When Isie retired from the Bar, a gala dinner, which happened to coincide with Isie's 87th birthday, was held in his honour by the Johannesburg Bar Council. Letters of congratulation were received from every quarter, including Nelson Mandela, F W de Klerk, Mangosuthu Buthelezi, Chief Justice M Corbett and this fine tribute from Sydney Kentridge, QC.

Three Maisels generations: Isie (centre), Jeffrey, Isie's younger son (on left) holding Simon Trisk (Helen's son), and James, Jeffrey's son (on right).

Isie's 88th birthday. He took great pleasure in having his youngest grandson Simon on his lap when Muriel presented him with his cake.

Isie had great admiration for Walter Sisulu and his achievements. When Sisulu heard that Isie had been unwell in 1993, he paid him a visit.

Just prior to the 1994 election Nelson Mandela, accompanied by the present Deputy Minister of Finance, Gill Marcus (extreme right) came to dinner. He is seen here with Isie, Muriel, Helen and the Israeli Ambassador Mr Alon Leal and his wife.

Art.4. The Captain has by contracts of purchase of 1st May and 25th August, 1883, ceded the littoral of his country, situated between the 26th degree south latitude and the Orange River and extending twenty miles inland, to the German subject F A E Lüderitz in Bremen, together with all rights attached to it.

Art.5. His Majesty the German Emperor recognises this territorial cession; places the respective territory under the protection of the German Empire and assumes supremacy over it.

Art.6. The Captain in regard to the remaining part of his realm conveys once and for all to the above-named Mr F A E Lüderitz, respectively to a company to be formed by him, the exclusive right to construct and administer the roads, railways and telegraphs; to dig and work mines, and in general to carry out all public works, against the annual payment of a sum of £60 (sixty pounds sterling).

Art.7. His Majesty the German Emperor assumes the surveillance over, and the protection of the relationship arising from article 6 between the Captain and the German subject F A E Lüderitz and the company to be formed by him, respectively.

As Professor Hahlo rightly pointed out, the two 1883 contracts, together with the Treaty of Protection and Amity of 1884, form the contractual trinity on which Lüderitz's exclusive mining rights in South West Africa were founded and are the first links in the chain of title on which CDM relied.

The Halbscheid Agreement refers to the 'territory known as the Sperrgebiet defined in Proclamation 11 of 1920'. The preamble to the Halbscheid Agreement called for a re-proclamation of the boundaries of the Sperrgebiet so as expressly to include the farm Marmora and the railway strip. This came into effect with Proclamation 35 of 1922, dated 1 December 1922, and was promulgated on 5 December 1922, these dates both falling between the signing of the Halbscheid Agreement by CDM and the signing by the administrator.

The proclamation giving effect to the Halbscheid Agreement

provided that 'the territory known as the Sperrgebiet defined in Proclamation 11 of 1920 shall include …'. It therefore became necessary for the court to consider the terms of Proclamation 11 of 1920, which was described as being of crucial importance in the case.[60] It reads:

> Whereas it is desirable to define more accurately the dimensions of the territory known as the Sperrgebiet, referred to in the Ordinance of the German Imperial Colonial Office of the 22nd September, 1908,
>
> Now therefore, under and by virtue of the powers in me vested, I do hereby declare, proclaim and make known that the territory described in the Ordinance as bordered:
>
> In the north by the 26th degree southern latitude;
>
> In the south by the northern bank of the Orange River;
>
> In the west by the Atlantic Ocean; and
>
> In the east by the line running at a distance of one hundred kilometres from the seashore and parallel thereto, is delimited as follows :
>
> Eastern boundary. Commencing in the north-east at the beacon 1, 100 kilometres from the coast on the 26 deg. southern latitude, then southwards through the beacons 2, 3, 4, 5, 6, 7, 8, 9, to the beacon 10 in the north bank of the Orange River.
>
> Southern boundary. Thence westwards along the north bank of the Orange River to the Atlantic *coast line*.
>
> Western Boundary. Thence northwards along the Atlantic *coast line* to the beacon 11 on the seashore on the 26 deg. southern latitude.
>
> Northern Boundary. Thence eastwards along the 26 deg. southern latitude to the point of origin at beacon 1,
>
> as shewn on the plan of the Sperrgebiet filed in the office of the Inspector of Mines at Windhuk and Lüderitzbucht. *[The italics are mine.]*

On conclusion of our argument, D P de Villiers, QC, commenced his argument for the Administration. He had with him G Lowen, QC, G van R Muller, QC, and C J Mouton for the administrator. A word about these counsel. De Villiers, popularly known as *'lang*

Dawid' was a leading silk at the Cape Bar and became an Acting Judge – he would, I believe, had he not decided to leave the profession and become managing director of Nasionale Pers, in all probability have ended up in the Appellate Division; although he did return to practise at the Cape Bar. George Lowen, as he was known by us, was a refugee from Hitler who had practised as a lawyer in Berlin and came to South Africa after a short spell in France. When first in South Africa he had to get a job as a garage superintendent whilst he wrote his LLB examination. He came to the Bar, was a tremendous worker, built up a big practice and became a silk. He died a few years ago. Muller ended up as a Judge of Appeal and I believe that Mouton became a judge in South West Africa. G P Van Rhyn, QC, and E A Grosskopf appeared for the second respondent. Grosskopf subsequently became a judge in the Cape Provincial Division and is now a Judge of Appeal. Van Rhyn became a judge in Griqualand West, Chief Justice of Venda and subsequently Judge President of the Northern Cape Division of the Supreme Court.

On the respondents' side both Muller and Lowen took part in the argument, the latter, of course, dealing with the German law. It was the contention of the respondents that the definition as given in Proclamation 11 of 1920 diminished the rights granted to CDM in respect of the Sperrgebiet; or to put it another way, limited the area of the Sperrgebiet. Unfortunately I do not have the judgment of the South West Africa court, but the Appellate Division of the court gives the ratio of the conclusion reached at the South West Africa court in a judgment delivered by Judge President Claassen and concurred in by Judge Diemont.[61] There is no doubt that that court correctly decided that Roman-Dutch law (as existing in the Province of the Cape of Good Hope) came into force in South West Africa on 1 January 1920, by Proclamation 21 of 1919.

I have referred to the wording of Proclamation 11 of 1920 and particularly to the words italicised by myself. The issue turned on the construing of the words 'coast' and 'coast line', particularly as used in the description of the western boundary. It will be recalled that the German Imperial Colonial Office ordinance of 22 September 1908 proclaimed the boundaries of the Sperrgebiet *inter alia* 'in the west by the Atlantic Ocean', whereas the western boundary was differently described in Proclamation 11 of 1920.

Judge President Claassen thereupon examined precedents for the interpretation of similar words in South African cases referring to a number of them[62] and Chief Justice Fagan then quotes the conclusion of the judgment, which reads:

> First Respondent's counsel, Mr De Villiers, contended that in any description of a piece of land, if the land is said to be bounded on the seaward side by the 'sea coast' or 'sea shore', then provided the coast or shore is defined in the particular legal system applicable as lying between a line on the landward side and a line on the seaward side, the line on the landward side of the coast or shore must be the boundary described.

In support of this contention he relied on the South African cases to which I have referred. It seems to me that this contention is well founded. In South African Law, land described as being bounded by the coast or the shore extends to, but not beyond the high water line. To hold otherwise would be to ignore this considerable volume of precedent founded on well accepted principles of Roman-Dutch law.

We had argued both in South West Africa and in the Court of Appeal that it was wrong for the court to place reliance on the way in which the terms 'from the coast' or 'to the coast line' and 'along the coast line' had, by judicial interpretation, gained the well accepted meaning in the Roman-Dutch common law. We submitted that the presumption that the legislature used words in the sense in which they had been judicially interpreted could only be applied when the previous judicial interpretation is not only well stated and recognised, but in addition only if the reference is to the same subject matter and for the same purpose and for the same object. Chief Justice Fagan quoted a large number of authorities on this aspect of the matter.[63] This argument seems to have prevailed in the Court of Appeal. Chief Justice Fagan, in dealing with the portion of the judgment in the South West Africa High Court said:

> Legal systems lay down legal principles. Since words have to be read in their context and in their application to the subject matter to which they relate, legal principles which

> affect that subject matter may well affect the meaning of the words used in relation to it. Decisions of our courts are therefore useful precedents in the enunciation of legal principles and as guides in the application of those principles to particular facts and circumstances. When we find in a judgment statements which attach meanings to particular words or phrases, we must remember that the judge is dealing with those words or phrases in the context in which they occur and with reference to the subject matter to which they relate. Beyond that, a statement as to the meaning of a word or phrase would merely be *obiter dictum*. I should be loathe to read a judge's elucidation of a word with no specialised legal meanings as intending to lay down as a matter of law what that word means independently of the context in which he is dealing with it, for defining the meaning of words as such is not a judge's function, but that of a philologist. A judge's statement on the meaning of such a word can be no more than an expression of his opinion on a matter outside his domain of special knowledge, which is that of law, not of language.[64]

We were successful: the appeal was allowed by a majority of three to two and the judgment of the South West African court was set aside. The main judgment, delivered by Chief Justice Fagan, was concurred with in a short judgment by Judge of Appeal Schreiner, with whom Judge of Appeal Malan simply concurred. A dissenting judgment was written by Judge of Appeal Steyn and with him Acting Judge of Appeal Hall simply concurred.

The relief which we sought and was granted to us reads:

> an order is granted declaring that the applicant, the Consolidated Diamond Mines of South West Africa, Limited, is vested with the sole and exclusive right, subject to any mining ordinance from time to time in force, to prospect, peg and mine for and in respect of all minerals (including diamonds and precious stones, but excluding only such minerals in respect of which rights had been lawfully acquired by any other person prior to the 15th January, 1923, and which rights have not since lapsed or

> been abandoned), within the area known as the Sperrgebiet, and that such area specifically includes the area between the high-water mark and the low-water mark of the Atlantic Ocean, and which is bounded in the north by the 26th degree of southern latitude and in the south by the north bank of the Orange River.

I need hardly add, of course, that the respondents were jointly and severally ordered to pay the costs of the proceedings both in South West Africa and in the Appellate Division.

In the course of litigation, a couple of incidents occurred which do not, of course, appear in the reports. From the Thursday morning on which the respondents' argument began, certain members of the court put the normal sort of questions put by judges when they have difficulty with an argument presented to them. On the following Tuesday morning, to our astonishment, De Villiers stated that he wished to say something before he recommenced his argument. He then proceeded to say (because of something that the judges had found in the papers or had heard outside the court) that he and his colleagues felt that he was not getting a fair hearing. He ought to have been rebuked and probably would have been rebuked by another presiding judge.

To say that our side was astounded and could see no justification for De Villiers's remarks puts it at its lowest. Judge of Appeal Schreiner said nothing but merely looked straight ahead. Judge of Appeal Steyn looked startled. I cannot remember what Acting Judge of Appeal Hall's reaction was.

Chief Justice Fagan, however, was nature's gentleman, and instead of taking serious objection to what De Villiers had said merely stated that De Villiers was quite wrong in making his statement. All that the members of the court had done was to ask questions based upon certain difficulties they had with the argument, which counsel would be able to answer so that the difficulty might be removed. In other words what he was saying to De Villiers was that all that had happened was what usually occurs in any matter before the Appellate Division. When Chief Justice Fagan had said what he had to say, instead of De Villiers's merely saying, 'As your Lordship pleases,' he in my opinion compounded his offence by saying: 'We have no hesitation in accepting your Lordship's explanation.' This appeared to be too much for Judge of Appeal Malan. He leaned back in his chair and said 'Well, Mr De Villiers, speaking for myself, I have been sitting here for days waiting to hear some argument of substance from you. Thus far I have heard none.' On that unhappy note this incident concluded.

A well known attorney in Bloemfontein, the late Mr F S Weber, who had been attending hearings of the Appellate Division since its inception in 1910, came up to me at the tea interval and said, 'Have I written this down correctly?' and he showed me what he had recorded because he said he couldn't believe that such a thing could ever be said in the appeal court.

The first respondent's argument having ended on Thursday afternoon in the second week, the court called upon Van Rhyn to argue. To our astonishment and to the Chief Justice's obvious, but quite unusual, irritation, Van Rhyn asked whether he could commence his argument the next morning. The Chief Justice asked him why – in view of the fact that he had appeared in South West Africa and had been present during the whole of the argument both on our side and on the first respondent's side – he wanted time before he commenced his argument, whereupon Van Rhyn stood quietly for a few seconds then merely said that he adopted the argument of the first respondent.

Another episode that I recall concerns Acting Judge of Appeal Hall. He was known as 'Foxy' Hall, a soubriquet illustrated by the following incident. One night during the first week of argument, when we were permitted to work at night in the court, the Chief Justice emerged from his chambers in his shirt sleeves, apparently working on the case as was the custom of the judges in the Appellate Division in those days, and said: 'If a judge does not sit every day he cannot take part in the judgment, can he?' None of us was, of course, able to answer this question but on looking up the relevant statute we found out that this was indeed the case.

A few days after this incident occurred I was walking down to the hotel where I was staying and Hall walked down with me. He said to me, 'What do you think of the Chief?' I think I replied: 'I don't know what you mean' – and indeed I did not know what he was referring to. He said, 'I wasn't feeling well and wanted to stay in bed one day last week and the Chief told me that if I was absent from the hearing for one day I could not take part in the judgment.'

To this I replied: 'Well this is what the statute says, isn't it?' to which he replied: 'Well what can anybody do about it if we don't follow this statute?'

I may mention that during the second week Hall fell asleep one night and Judge of Appeal Steyn, who was sitting next to him, to our great joy, prodded him in the ribs to wake him up. Hall, born in England, had come to South Africa after completing his schooling in England. In the 1948 general election he stood on the same platform as Eben Dönges, the candidate for the National Party in Worcester. When the National Party won that election, Dönges became a cabinet minister. It is difficult to believe that it was purely coincidental that Hall was made a judge of the Cape Provincial Division in 1949, nor that he was one of the judges used to pack the Appellate Division decision when the appeal court was enlarged to deal afresh with the question of the removal of the 'Coloureds' from the parliamentary roll.

Chapter Eleven

RACE AND RAPE

Until May 1948 (when the National Party became the governing party of South Africa), I used to get briefs from time to time from the Assistant Government Attorney in Johannesburg, Mr Durham. (His grandson, who looked exactly like him, used to brief me years later when he was a partner at Werksmans.) After 1948 until I ceased practice, I received only two briefs from the Government Attorney and that was in the 1950s.

The first brief was to appear for the government in an arbitration set up to determine the value of land that the government wished to acquire for purposes of establishing a group area for Indians in an area that I believe is now known as Lenasia. I made it clear to the Government Attorney briefing me that I was able to appear only for one day because of my commitments to the accused in the Treason Trial. He agreed to this – not surprisingly – because of the fact that George Colman was my junior. I suppose I was briefed in this matter because I had been appearing for Indians before tribunals set up under the Group Areas Act.

The second brief was a strange one. I was telephoned one day by Mr Simons, the same gentleman who prosecuted in the first criminal trial in which I appeared (*see* Chapter 2), who was then a government law advisor. He asked me whether I would accept a brief to appear for the government in a criminal appeal in the Appellate Division. I said to him, 'Why – what cabinet minister has committed rape?' He replied that it wasn't a cabinet minister whose appeal would have to be argued, but that of a Coloured man who had been found guilty of rape by Judge Reynolds in the Eastern Districts court, and sentenced to death. As far as I can recall this is the only rape case in which I was ever briefed.

I understood from Simons that the usual procedure was that when the death sentence had been imposed, the matter was considered by the government law advisors who gave their advice to the cabinet as to whether, in their opinion, the sentence should be carried out or commuted to a term of imprisonment.

The rape was allegedly committed by the Coloured man on a White woman on the coast near Jeffreys Bay. The accused's defence at the trial was a plain denial of his having had anything to do with the complainant, let alone raping her. Simons told me that on his reading the record of evidence, he had an unhappy feeling that although the accused's defence was probably untrue, that in fact he had not raped the complainant and he had consequently reported to the cabinet that, in his opinion, the sentence of death should not be confirmed.

The complainant lived in the Orange Free State and the Minister of Justice was none other than C R Swart. The cabinet had then adopted the somewhat unusual procedure of deciding that if the accused obtained leave to appeal, the government would put up the necessary fees required to brief counsel to argue the appeal. Leave to appeal was granted and Simons asked me to accept the brief with Charles Theron as my junior. (Theron subsequently became a judge of the Transvaal Provincial Division).

In those days of race madness, it was a criminal offence for a person of one race to have intercourse with a person of another race – if, for example, a White man had intercourse with a Black woman he committed an offence; and if he were tried, the woman, if she gave evidence, would be treated as an accomplice. Thus, if in the present case the Coloured man had admitted that he had had intercourse with the complainant, who was White, he would have rendered himself guilty under the statute forbidding that kind of conduct.

Certain material facts enabled the appeal to be argued. The complainant alleged that she had been raped three times in one afternoon. There was no sign of any injury on her part and her description of the accused's conduct during the alleged rape incidents and her reaction to it was, in my view, unlikely. The only corroboration, if it could be called corroboration, of her evidence lay in the fact that she did not come back to the hotel where she was staying until it was almost dark, so much so that some persons staying in the hotel went out to look for her. They saw her approaching them and she was merely carrying her panties in her hand, but there was no evidence that she showed any signs of distress.

The mere fact that an accused person tells lies in his evidence does not necessarily result in his conviction. It is a factor which could be taken into account in determining whether or not the case against him has been proved beyond reasonable doubt. This is a well recognised principle of our law. Hence, although the accused's evidence in this case was plainly false, the falsity could be reasonably explained on the basis that he was afraid to admit having had intercourse with the woman, with the consequent punishment which would be meted out to him.

The court constituted to hear that appeal consisted of Chief Justice Centlivres, with Judges of Appeal Greenberg and Schreiner – probably as strong a Bench as could be obtained at any time. My argument before that court lasted until about 6.00 pm, when the court reserved judgment. Theron took the view that we would succeed. I was not so optimistic.

Whilst I was arguing I had a feeling that someone was standing behind me, an unusual event in the Court of Appeal. I turned around and saw standing in the doorway, which is the side entrance to the court, Judge of Appeal Van den Heever listening to the argument.

As I had come down by car it was too late, after the court adjourned, to go back to Johannesburg and I decided to spend the night at the Bloemfontein Club. Whilst I was having dinner, Judge Van den Heever came up to me and asked me what had happened and how I had come to be briefed in the matter. I told him that judgment had been reserved and explained to him what Simons had told me about the cabinet's decision. Judge Van den Heever had been Secretary for Justice and he knew the procedure which follows upon the passing of the death sentence, as told to me by Simons. 'Yes,' Judge Van den Heever then said, 'I am the person who gave leave to appeal and I knew that they were passing the buck to us [meaning the appeal court].'

The appeal was in fact allowed in its entirety by Judge of Appeal Greenberg in a lengthy and – as usual, impeccably argued – judgment, concurred in by Judge of Appeal Centlivres. Judge of Appeal Schreiner agreed that there should not have been a conviction for rape, but he thought that the appellant was guilty of attempted rape and should have received a short sentence, which he set out.

Chapter Twelve

THE TREASON TRIAL 1956–1961

In May 1956, the Minister of Justice, Mr C R Swart (subsequently the first President of the Republic of South Africa), announced in Parliament that charges of treason were being prepared against some 200 persons. On 5 December 1956, in dawn swoops throughout South Africa, 140 people of all races were arrested on the charge of treason. On 12 December, 16 more were arrested and on 19 December a preparatory examination began. This was the beginning of a trial which was to attract international attention as one of the largest political trials ever held.[65]

I was briefed, together with Vernon Berrangé, to appear for the accused at commencement of the examination. It took place in the Johannesburg Drill Hall, which had been converted into a huge court.

Outside the Drill Hall on the very first day there was rioting and guns were fired by the police. In terms of the examination, however, nothing really happened on the first day except that loudspeakers were installed so that the accused could hear what was being said by Mr J C van Niekerk, appearing for the Crown. (The preparatory examination and trial took place before South Africa became an independent republic and consequently the counsel appearing for the prosecution were referred to as 'counsel for the Crown' and the prosecution case was referred to as 'the crown case'.) But on the second day, to our horror, the accused were put in a cage of tubular scaffolding and wire netting – on which some of the accused had already hung notices reading 'DO NOT FEED'. This was something, of course, which could not be tolerated, and speaking for my colleagues and myself I told the magistrate who was presiding, a Mr Wessels, that we would walk out unless the cage was removed. It was removed overnight.

I took no further part in the preparatory examination, but was briefed to appear before Judge Dowling on 21 December 1956 to apply for bail on behalf of the accused, which was granted. The accused were of all races, that is, using South African terminology, Natives (currently termed Blacks), Indians, Coloured people and Europeans (currently termed Whites). The Crown did not oppose bail but suggested that bail should be given in recognisances of £1 000 for each European and £500 for each non-European. The total would have come to about £86 000, and as the overwhelming majority of the accused were impecunious, and the defence fund that had been set up had very little money at its disposal, this would have meant that the accused would have remained in custody. Eventually the court granted bail, fixing the recognisances at £250 for Europeans, £100 for Indians and £50 for Coloured people and Natives.

It should here be mentioned that there was a remarkable show of understanding by the chief magistrate and ten other magistrates who sat until late on the night of 21 December to enable the requisite recognisances to be given. Among people who 'stood bail' for the accused were the late Dr Ellen Hellman, the distinguished anthropologist, and the late Walter Pollak, QC, one of the leading members of the Bar, and a great lawyer. He eventually left south Africa, but he should long before that have been appointed to the Supreme Court and eventually to the Appellate Division. However, the fact is that – from the time that that government came into power in 1948 – appointments to the Bench were to a large extent made, not on the merits of the appointee, but on his political beliefs; and more particularly, if he was an Afrikaner.

Vernon Berrangé and John Coaker appeared for the accused during the whole of the preparatory examination, which concluded only in January 1958 – over a year from the time it commenced.

The basis of the case was that the African National Congress (ANC) was the main organisation in a conspiracy to commit treason. Despite this, strangely enough, its president (the late Chief Albert Luthuli) and his second in command (the late Oliver Tambo), who were among those arrested and, of course, among the accused at the preparatory examination, were not committed for trial. The reason for this was not at all clear to us, the counsel and attorney. I should perhaps mention that Mr Tambo was himself an attorney, and had practised in partnership with Mr Nelson Mandela – who was also among the accused, and was committed for trial. (The treason trial is often referred to as the trial in which Mandela was acquitted, as opposed to what was called the 'Rivonia trial', some years after the treason trial, when Mandela and others were convicted and Mandela was sentenced to life imprisonment.) In all, 92 people were committed for trial and were indicted. How this selection was made remained a mystery to the defence.

Speeches were made in Parliament that the persons subsequently arrested had plotted to poison water supplies and to bomb power stations. Berrangé, in his opening address at the preparatory examination, accused the security police of creating 'a fantastic atmosphere of treason around everything that the accused had worked for'. Berrangé said that the security police had done this by endeavouring to intimidate the public at open and legitimate meetings, by conducting mass raids and countrywide searches, and by flourishing stenguns, fixed bayonets and truncheons.

It is not irrelevant to mention that those arrested lived in different parts of the country and their arrests were coupled with searches and seizure of documents in a series of simultaneous raids which commenced at 4.00 am. The raids were not confined to those eventually arrested – a number of raids on the homes of others who were not arrested took place. Among the 140 originally arrested on 5 December 1956, some were flown from all parts of the country to Johannesburg by military aircraft on the same day. Of the total of 156 persons arrested, 105 were Africans, 23 Europeans, 21 Indians and 7 Coloured people. Of these, 138 were men and 18 were women.

The late Gerald Gardiner attended the opening of the preparatory examination and stayed for about ten days, until he was denounced in a public statement by Mr Eric Louw, then Foreign Minister, to the effect that South Africa could run its own business and did not need interference from troublemakers from England. Gerald Gardiner then left, but followed the proceedings as reported in the press both in South Africa and England. (*En passant* I may mention that in my opinion it would be difficult to think of any person less fitted for the post of foreign minister than Mr Eric Louw who, in addition to his other distasteful qualities, was a notorious anti-semite.) Gerald Gardiner had attended the preparatory examination on behalf of *inter alios* the General Council of the Bar of England and Wales and the International Commission of Jurists. I have relied for some of the facts set out above on an article he published at that time.[66] He was then one of the leading silks at the English Bar. He was a bencher of the Inner Temple and a member of the Executive Committee of the English Bar Council, and he subsequently became Lord Chancellor. His eminence in the profession was, I think, universally recognised. He wrote that the treason trial was 'unique in legal history'. At the end of the article he suggested that those who support the rule of law should be aware of what is happening in South Africa and 'should support the treason trial defence fund which will at least enable the accused to obtain adequate support and legal assistance in a trial unique in the number of the accused, in the weight of the documents, in the length of the proceedings and, not least, in the extraordinary width of the laws applicable.' As Gerald Gardiner points out in his article:

> In England by treason is meant, without giving a textual definition, either compassing the death of the Sovereign, or making war against the Sovereign within or without the realm, or aiding the King's enemies. But high treason in South Africa means something quite different. It is a Roman-Dutch common law offence. It is defined in the leading South African textbook by Gardiner and Lansdown as follows: 'High Treason is committed by those who with a hostile intention disturb, impair or endanger the independence or safety of the state, or attempt to actively prepare to do so.' Treason is punishable with death. Sedition, which is not a capital offence, is constituted of the same elements, except that there is not need to prove the hostile intention. High treason may also be committed by suppressing information. The South African definition of high treason is therefore very much wider than the definition of treason in England.[67]

The definition given by Gardiner and Lansdown,[68] referred to above was adopted by Judge Rumpff in the special court at page

18 of his 'Reasons for Judgment' which, like those of other members of court, were handed to the Registrar of the Court some months after the accused were acquitted.

In the United States Constitution there is a rigid definition of treason which reads:

> Treason against the United States shall consist only in levying war against them, or in adhering to their enemies, giving them aid and comfort.

As far as I am aware the trial under discussion is the only one in which high treason has been alleged to have been committed when there is no war or rebellion insofar as South Africa is concerned. In the Anglo Boer War there were a number of British subjects, citizens of the Cape Colony, who joined the Boer forces in the unjust war levied against the Republics of the Transvaal and Orange Free State by Great Britain, who were convicted of treason. There were also persons convicted in 1914 who started a rebellion particularly in the Orange Free State. Those persons claimed that they had not committed treason, but had merely taken part in *''n gewapende protes'*. They were convicted of treason but were sentenced only to short terms of imprisonment.

The last case of treason which I can recall was that in which Robey Leibrandt was convicted of treason and sentenced to death during the Second World War. He was actively engaged in spying on behalf of Germany with whom South Africa was at war. The death sentence, however, was commuted by the Smuts government to one of imprisonment. One of the first acts of the National Party government when it came to power in 1948 was to release Leibrandt from prison where he had been incarcerated for a very short period.

One further word about some of those who were originally arrested. They included in their number Professor Z K Matthews, academically the most distinguished African of the time, who was Acting Rector of the Fort Hare University College. He was told by the government that he would be made permanent head of Fort Hare if he gave up his membership of the ANC – which he refused to do. Others were Advocate Joe Slovo; Mr Duma Nokwe, one of the country's two African members of the Bar; and a number of prominent members of the Christian community, among them a Methodist minister. Professor Matthews incidentally was one of those committed for trial, but like many others committed for trial, he was never called upon to plead and the indictments against him and a number of other persons were withdrawn and they were acquitted. I shall later make particular reference to Professor Matthews, Chief Luthuli and Mr Mandela.

Before I deal with the evidence and the judgments given in the case, I should say something about the counsel who appeared for the Crown and those who appeared for the defence. Oswald Pirow, QC, who led for the Crown until he died on 11 October 1959, had been Minister of Defence in the government until the outbreak of the war (when the Hertzog–Smuts alliance broke up). He had been, before he entered politics, an advocate at the Pretoria Bar, with a substantial practice. He was suspected of having Nazi sympathies and, when he left the cabinet, formed a political party called 'The New Order', which opposed South Africa's entering the war against Germany. Although a fair opponent, he could not, I think, be accused of over exerting himself in any matter in which he was briefed after he ceased to be Minister of Defence and returned to the Bar. I do not know what went on behind the scenes, but apart from making the opening address on behalf of the Crown and occasionally making a comment when somebody on our side was arguing, he played no part in the trial proceedings.

Our view of the crown case, as framed by the second indictment, was stated by me as: 'Let's throw in everything the police have been able to find and see what comes out at the end.' We denied, of course, that there was any conspiracy and certainly not one motivated by hostile intent.

Pirow had stated, relying on a judgment given in the Appellate Division, that 'no middle ground exists between the ballot box and treason.' We maintained that the activities of the accused were characteristic of extra-parliamentary and non-violent movements in countries that excluded a large section of the population from the political process.[69] In addition, the grab-bag nature of the arrests, the failure to put on trial major leaders such as Chief Luthuli and Oliver Tambo, and the presence of minor personalities among the 30 accused, we submitted, suggested that no conspiracy existed. Pirow in his opening address said that the accused were 'inspired by Communist fanaticism, Bantu nationalism and racial hatred in various degrees.' We had, in anticipation of this kind of allegation being made, gone back over many years to show that as a result of a long history of legislation designed to discriminate against various sections of the non-White population, particularly the Africans, that the accused were not 'inspired by Communist fanaticism,' but wished to change, in a non-violent manner, what I shall conveniently call 'apartheid legislation' (institutionalised when the National Party came into power in 1948).

In the course of cross-examination of the Crown's star witness Professor Murray (during November 1959), I recall that when I went through various legislative acts of the kind I have mentioned, the presiding judge, Judge Rumpff, interrupted to ask me whether I was not treading on dangerous ground – in that I might be establishing a motive on the part of the accused to overthrow the state. I endeavoured to explain to him why I was cross-examining on these lines and that so far from desiring to overthrow the state by violence, the policy of the ANC was designed merely to bring about, in a peaceful manner, a change in the total supremacy of the Whites in government; so as to have a share in the government of the country by all its people. I will, at a later stage, endeavour to illustrate this by reference to the comprehensive judgment of Judge Bekker, in which he gives his reasons for acquitting the accused (*see* p160).

The next senior counsel on the Crown's side, Mr J de Vos, QC, became leader of the Crown side after Pirow's death. He dealt with the Communist aspect of the case and really entered upon the scene for the first time when Professor Andrew Murray was called to give evidence. He got off to a false start. After taking Professor Murray through his academic qualifications and establishing that he had read the documents which recorded the policy, particularly of the ANC, and the records of speeches upon which the Crown would rely, he said to Professor Murray, 'You have prepared a report.' At this stage I was halfway on to my feet to object to Murray's giving evidence in this way, when Judge Rumpff showed his extreme displeasure with De Vos for this attempt to present the evidence of the witness in the form of a written report – such as one that is often made by a medical practitioner giving the results of a post-mortem examination. When he told De Vos that he would not allow Professor Murray's report to be handed in, De Vos asked for the matter to stand down until the next day because he had not appreciated that Professor Murray's evidence would have to be led in the usual manner in which a witness is called to give evidence. This evoked a further sharp reprimand of De Vos, Judge Rumpff asking him what he had been doing for the months before Murray was called to give evidence. This was in October 1959, the proceedings having opened in Pretoria on 1 August 1958.

As will become clear later, the trial was from time to time adjourned for certain reasons, one of them being the declaration of a state of emergency on 30 March 1960. The accused were confined to jail during the state of emergency, and were released only on 31 August 1960. For some mysterious reason, De Vos asked the next day for the re-arrest of all the accused. (They had been on bail since the application was made – as far back as December 1956 – and after the first indictment was withdrawn (*see* p142) were now appearing on summons.) The wrath of the judge president descended upon De Vos, and his quite ridiculous application was rejected out of hand by the court.

At the end of all the evidence De Vos argued the Communist aspect of the case for about a day, during which time he was heckled by the court. Tony O'Dowd then demolished his argument in a short address lasting a few hours. Needless to say the Crown failed to establish that the accused intended to establish a Communist state.

Mr J C Van Niekerk, next in seniority on the Crown side, was on the staff of the Attorney General, as were J H Liebenberg, M O Barker and C N van der Walt. Van Niekerk was a man of character, who had practised at the Johannesburg Bar after retiring from the civil service. He had the thankless task of reading into the record documents found in the possession of the accused, or of their alleged co-conspirators, upon which the Crown would rely. I was amused when he read the words 'woe unto us' that appeared in one of the documents. He pronounced the word 'woe' as 'whoa!' – as though stopping a horse. Having been a crown prosecutor for many years he knew a great deal about police methods and their treatment of suspects. Once, he was defending someone who alleged that he had been assaulted by the police and that he had made a statement under duress. Van Niekerk had cross-examined the policeman who was alleged to have assaulted the defendant, and the policeman, a member of the Brixton Murder and Robbery Squad, denied that he had assaulted the accused and went on to say that he had never assaulted a suspect. This caused Van Niekerk to say (I am giving the English version of it): 'You dare to tell *me* that you have never assaulted a suspect?'

The other members of the Attorney General's staff, J H Liebenberg, M O Barker and C N van der Walt, played a minor part in the case, but Gus Hoexter and John Trengove really carried the burden of the crown case: in leading the witnesses, in cross-examination of the witnesses called for the defence, and also in arguing the crown case. Both Trengove and Hoexter were then members of the Pretoria Bar. Trengove later became a judge in the Transvaal Provincial Division and subsequently in the Appellate Division (from which he has since retired). Gus Hoexter became a judge in the Natal Provincial Division and subsequently a member of the Appellate Division (as his distinguished father had been). He is still a member of that court.

On our side, the late Bram Fischer (who was an avowed Communist) was the next senior person to me. Bram Fischer's grandfather had been administrator of the Orange Free State, and his father had been the Judge President of the Orange Free State Provincial Division. Bram himself was a Rhodes scholar and an extremely able, popular and distinguished member of the Johannesburg Bar. Despite his belief in Communism, which was well known, he was briefed in many important matters by the mining houses, and he generally had a first class practice at the Bar. I shall always remember him as a friend and as a man of courage who had a charming personality. His belief in Communism, I always thought and still think, was based on his sympathy for the position of the Africans in South Africa and it was that which made him turn to Communism.

Bram was arrested on some charge in about 1963. He had been briefed to appear on behalf of a mining house in an appeal from the Federal Supreme Court (that is, the Supreme Court of the then Federation of Rhodesia, Northern Rhodesia and Nyasaland as they were then known) to the Privy Council in London. As he was on bail he made an application for permission to leave the country in order to argue this appeal and undertook to return when the appeal was concluded. He did return and he was brought before the court again. On this occasion he decided to estreat bail and go into hiding. He did not attempt, nor did he wish, to leave South Africa, but he thought he could continue his political work for the cause which he had chosen in South Africa.

It so happened that on Christmas Day 1964 (before he went underground) Bram came to visit my wife and myself, at the rented house where we were then living. Bram knew that he would be sentenced to imprisonment (or for all I knew he might already have contemplated escaping trial) and asked us whether we would not like to occupy his house. We had visited each other for many years, but apart from the fact that we had already obtained other accommodation, neither my wife nor I could visualise living in Bram's house if he was in jail. When he said goodbye I had a nasty feeling that we would never see him again – and that turned out to be the case.

He was eventually arrested and imprisoned for life. He was allowed two visits each month by members of his family. His wife (a niece of the wife of General Smuts), who had shared his political beliefs, had died in a motor accident. He had two daughters and a son, but his son died while he was in prison. The police would not allow him to attend his son's funeral.

On one occasion, his daughters – who used to visit him regularly – were going away on holiday and he expressed the wish that Sydney Kentridge and I should visit him. We went together to the Pretoria Central Prison where he was imprisoned, on one of the days when visitors were allowed. An insolent prison officer, his hands in his pockets, demanded to know why we were there. We told him that we had come to see Bram, as we understood that he was allowed visitors on that particular day. He told us that we would not be given permission to see Bram. I asked him on whose orders he was acting and he mentioned the name of the senior officer in charge of the prison. When I asked where this man was, we were told that his whereabouts were unknown, but that he lived at a particular address which was given to us. I asked if we could telephone him from the prison. This was refused. We then left the prison, went to a grocery shop nearby, and telephoned the person whose permission we had to get, but there was no reply. I subsequently wrote a letter to the appropriate senior official in the civil service complaining about the refusal to allow us to see Bram, but received no reply. I mentioned the matter to my old friend Oscar Galgut, then Mr Justice Galgut, and he undertook to pursue the matter for us. His efforts met with no success.

Shortly before he died of cancer Bram was given permission to live in his brother's house in Bloemfontein. It was then known to the Minister of Justice that Bram's life would soon come to an end. His brother's house, however, was treated as a prison. Mr Justice Nick de Villiers, then a judge of the Orange Free State Provincial Division and an old friend of Bram's, went to see him when he was in the house in Bloemfontein. He was stopped at the door by a policeman who told him that Bram was still a prisoner; whereupon the judge informed the policeman that he was a judge and as such entitled to enter any prison when he wished to. He was then allowed in. When Bram died, a few of us, including my friends Arthur Chaskalson and George Bizos, Helen Joseph and a number of Africans, flew down to the cremation. Apart from Lewis Dison, a former member of our Bar, then practising at the Cape Bar, a Free State attorney, Louis Israel, and those of us who came from Johannesburg, there were no other White persons present. Arthur Chaskalson delivered a moving address.

Counsel on our side, besides Bram Fischer, included H C Nicholas, Rex Welsh, Sydney Kentridge, A P O'Dowd, J F Coaker, Victor Berrangé, Chris Plewman and David Osborn.

H C Nicholas, who took silk not long after the trial concluded, was appointed a judge in the Transvaal Provincial Division and then a judge in the Court of Appeal. He has reached retiring age, but continues to act as a Judge of Appeal.

Rex Welsh became the leader of the Bar in Johannesburg after my resignation in 1992. He died in 1994. To describe him as a top lawyer is an understatement. He was without doubt one of the greatest lawyers that I have encountered in the whole of my legal career. (Included in the term 'lawyers', I naturally refer not only to members of the Bar, but to members of the Bench.) He should, like Walter Pollak, have had a seat on the Bench of the Appellate Division. The Government's failure to appoint him is unforgivable.

As for Sydney Kentridge he has all the qualities of a top lawyer. Apart from a profound knowledge of the law, he is a master of cross-examination. His admirable manner, as well as the substance of the arguments he delivers so incisively before the courts, are rightly highly regarded by all the judges before whom he appears. He is truly 'a clever man' and a great lawyer. After taking silk in South Africa he decided, some years ago, to leave the country and to commence practice at the Bar in England. He had to start there as a junior, but within a very short time was made a Queen's Counsel in England. He was appointed by the Queen to the Bench of one of the courts in the Channel Islands from which he was recently obliged to retire on reaching the age of seventy. I have no doubt that had he started practice in England a few years earlier, he would have been appointed to the Bench in England. He is without doubt one of the leading silks at the English Bar. He regularly appears in cases of great importance in the Court of Appeal and the House of Lords. His practice is not confined to appearances in the courts of England. He has appeared in other parts of the Commonwealth and, recently, in Namibia. Since he started practising in England he has, from time to time, been briefed to appear in South Africa. To describe him as a brilliant advocate and lawyer is probably an understatement.

An anecdote about Sydney Kentridge, though it is on a somewhat different note, bears recording here. There is a society, which has members in both England and the United States of America, that propagates the view that the Earl of Oxford wrote the plays which have been attributed to William Shakespeare. There was recently in England a serious debate before two law lords, which excited a great deal of popular interest, as to who did write the famous plays. Sydney Kentridge won this debate in the same manner as he has successfully won cases for many clients over the years, the law lords finding, as he had argued, that William Shakespeare wrote the plays attributed to him.

Tony O'Dowd, whose demolition of De Vos's arguments on Communism I have mentioned, left South Africa shortly after the trial was concluded. That he was a first class lawyer cannot be questioned, but I am told that when he was consulted on a matter by an attorney alone, or by an attorney accompanied by his client, O'Dowd would sit and listen to what was being said and maintain an absolute silence. He would, however, write a first class opinion; and in fairness to him I should say that not only was the substance of his argument in the treason trial outstanding, but his manner of addressing the court was impeccable.

John Coaker who had a busy practice as a junior, took silk and had a good practice. He unfortunately died some years ago.

Victor Berrangé, who was an elegant dresser, was alleged to have been a Communist. I do not know whether he was or not. All I do know about him is that no one could cross-examine policemen as effectively as he could. During the trial he was given the task of cross-examining various policemen who had given evidence of speeches that they had heard, at meetings of the ANC attended by them and which they had recorded in longhand. Suffice it to say that the evidence of what I shall call 'longhand reporters' was held by the three judges as being so unreliable that no credence could be given to their evidence. Berrangé decided some years after the trial to live in Swaziland, where he farmed and occasionally appeared as an advocate before the Court of Appeal. On one of these occasions he actually appeared for the Crown (a most unusual role for him), which was the respondent in a case in which the appellant had been found guilty and sentenced to death. The evidence was of such a nature that the conviction could not possibly be allowed to stand. He permitted himself to say that if he had conducted the prosecution in the court below, the Crown would have succeeded in the appeal.

Chris Plewman in due course took silk and after a highly successful practice at the Bar was persuaded to accept an appointment on the Bench. He did this despite the fact that, as with H C Nicholas, his acceptance of the appointment entailed considerable financial sacrifice.

As for David Osborn, he took silk and has been for some years now one of the busiest silks at the Johannesburg Bar. I hope I will not be accused of being immodest if I say that our side was probably the strongest that has ever appeared for the defence in South Africa, to my knowledge – and I talk now not merely of the number of counsel on our side, but of their quality as well. Added to counsel there was Michael Parkington (to whom I shall refer later). I think it is fair to say that the accused were fortunate in having our side to defend them. I must also add that as a matter of principle all of us charged minimal fees.

To revert for a moment to David Osborn and John Coaker. They undertook the most onerous task of perusing all the voluminous documentation (including notes of the hundreds of speeches made), and of creating an index that enabled us to point out who it was said or wrote something, or in whose possession some document had been found – which was regarded by the Crown, at all events, as of some importance. Together with Chris Plewman, they also undertook the task of compiling a list of all the legislation promulgated over the years, intended to show unequal treatment of Africans, Indians or Coloureds.

There were, of course, difficult questions of law that had to be considered prior to and during the trial. Here the work of Rex Welsh and H C ('Nick') Nicholas , as was to be expected, proved thorough and invaluable.

I would like to add that every member on our side made a substantial contribution to the defence. We worked together as a team. The early discussions on certain legal points of law took place in my chambers, but Parkington took the view that it would be much better if we all worked together in a building in Twist Street, Hillbrow, in which he had hired an entire floor to accommodate us. This proved to be a most helpful way of working on the case. It ensured that there was a constant exchange of views and, where necessary, assistance could be given by anyone working on a particular aspect of the case. This team spirit prevailed during the whole of the lengthy trial and every one of us played a part both before and during the trial.

The treason trial was a most unusual one in that it moved through three distinct phases. The first was the preparatory examination, which began in December 1956 and ended in January 1958. Thereafter the indictment known as 'the first indictment' was drawn by the Crown, in which 92 of the 156 people arraigned in the preparatory examination stood trial, commencing on 1 August 1958. As will be seen, the Crown withdrew this indictment in mid-October, and all the accused were free to go. However, the charges were reformulated and a 'second indictment' was served against 30 of those originally charged. Thus, in its final form, the trial began in defence of the accused against the charges raised in the second indictment. This trial began on 4 August 1959.

The trial took place in Pretoria in an old synagogue which had been converted into a court for the purposes of the trial. The fact that the trial was held in Pretoria imposed upon the accused a further burden. A large number of them lived in or around

Johannesburg and it seems obvious that the government wanted to have the scene of the trial removed from Johannesburg for fear of demonstrations that might be made there. Some of the hardships that had daily to be overcome by the accused, during what turned out to be a trial of inordinate length, are described in a short book written by Helen Joseph (recently deceased and herself a 'treason trialist'), entitled *If This Be Treason*.[70] She was a remarkable woman – remarkable for her courage, character and bravery, a devout Christian and by no means a Communist.

A special court was constituted in terms of Section 112 of Act 56 of 1955, composed of Judge Rumpff, Judge Kennedy and Judge Ludorf. Ludorf's appearance, during the previous year, in the case between the South African Police and Advocate Wolpe, national president of the South African Congress of Democrats (*see* Chapter 9), led to an application made for Ludorf's recusal in the treason trial. As stated, the case against the accused in the treason trial was that they and certain organisations of which they were members had conspired at various times and places to overthrow the government. One of the 'acts of conspiracy' relied upon by the Crown in the treason trial was said to have occurred at the meeting at the Trades Hall which led to the aforementioned case.

At the time that the treason trial took place, Ludorf had been elevated to the Bench, and was thus in a position to be selected by the Minister of Justice, C R Swart, to form part of the special court delegated to sit in the treason trial. I applied for Ludorf to recuse himself from sitting because of the fact that he had acted for the police in Wolpe's case (although Wolpe was not an accused in that trial); and Judge Ludorf was obliged to recuse himself.

When I asked for Judge Ludorf and Judge Rumpff to recuse themselves at the outset of the proceedings in 1958, Judge Rumpff had called on the Crown to make whatever submissions they would like on this issue. Pirow, who was then leader for the Crown stated (quite correctly in my view) that he would say nothing on this matter, it being a matter for decision solely by the judge whose recusal was being sought.

However, when Pirow had dropped out of the case and the leader of the prosecution was De Vos, it was thought proper to say that we, in applying a second time (in September 1960, as will be seen) for Judge Rumpff to recuse himself, had indulged in a scandalous attack on the conduct of the Presiding Judge in a deliberate manner and brought the court over which he presided into public contempt, and to intimidate him and interfere with the lawful process of the court and the due course of justice. This, of course, is absolute nonsense.

Mr Joel Mervis, in his quite remarkable book *The Fourth Estate* [71] (in many respects a history of the times covered by the book), deals with the question of the recusal of Judge Ludorf. A Bill to validate the appointment of the special court to hear the treason trial was debated in Parliament. According to Mr Mervis's account, United Party members used the debate to taunt the Minister of Justice, Mr C R Swart, about the appointment of the three judges to the special court. Their line of attack was to ask, 'Who appointed the judges?' The South African Press Association reported that Swart stated that he had 'consulted Mr Justice Rumpff. The judge had recommended the two other judges who had been appointed.' *Die Burger* and *Die Transvaler* – which, if not government papers, were certainly not unfriendly to the government – reported that Swart 'appointed Mr Justice Rumpff as chairman and asked him to recommend the two other judges.' The *Argus* reported Swart as saying 'he had consulted Mr Justice Rumpff about the appointment of the two other judges. The two other judges appointed were those recommended by Mr Justice Rumpff.' (The two other judges being Ludorf and Kennedy). When I argued for the recusal of Judge Ludorf, I argued, quite wrongly I believe, that as Judge Rumpff had recommended Ludorf, Rumpff should also have recused himself.

This argument took place on the first day that the treason trial commenced. I told Judge Rumpff that I was relying on the newspaper reports, and he enquired whether I had the Hansard report. I told him, as was the fact, that it was not yet available. Judge Rumpff asked me to see him in chambers on the following morning (a Saturday). At this interview Rumpff told me that he had not recommended either of the other judges. He said that what had happened was that Judge President Maritz had apparently named him as president of the special court. Swart came to see him and told him that he, Swart, had decided to appoint Judge Ludorf and Judge Kennedy as the other members of the court, and enquired whether he, Rumpff, had any objection to sitting with those persons. Rumpff told me that his answer was clearly one that would be expected of him, namely that he had no objection to either of those judges. In addition Rumpff told me that he did not even know Judge Kennedy. As Judge Rumpff was undoubtedly telling the truth, it would seem to follow that Swart, who at that time was Acting Prime Minister as well as Minister of Justice, had told the House of Assembly an untruth.

It may not be inappropriate at this stage to say that among a pretty poor bunch of Ministers of Justice who were appointed from 1948 onwards, Swart was one of the worst. (He had some rivals, of course.[72])The *Sunday Express*, of which Mr Mervis was editor at that time, came to the conclusion that Swart hadn't told the truth in Parliament, and in large headlines on the front page said: 'Swart didn't tell the truth'. In the report the paper went further: 'not only was Mr Swart not speaking the truth, but he must have known that he was not speaking the truth.' Senator Leslie Rubin challenged Swart to sue the *Sunday Express* for libel. In addition I discussed the matter with Pirow, who was leading for the prosecution, and he said that of course Swart would sue the *Sunday Express*. I said in my opinion he would not, because the *Sunday Express* had merely told the truth.

In the debate on the Bill, which had gone to the Senate after the debate in the House of Assembly, certain remarks made by Senator Johannes, a former magistrate, gave confirmation of everything the paper had been claiming. (A number of senators had been previously appointed so as to obtain the majority necessary to enable a resolution – to remove Coloured people from the Roll – to be passed in both Houses of Parliament. Senator Johannes was one of those so appointed.) According to Hansard, Senator Johannes said: 'In view of the fact that the Hon the Minister of Justice told this House that the Judge President of the Transvaal Provincial Division, Mr Justice Maritz, recommended the appointment of Mr Justice Rumpff as President of this special court and that Mr Justice Rumpff recommended the appointment of Mr Justice Ludorf and Mr Justice Kennedy, the country as a whole will feel satisfied that the court that is being created will be the best court for the trial of anyone who is charged with the crime of high treason. Hon. Senators: Hear, hear.'

In refusing the application to recuse himself, Judge Rumpff stated in court that he had never recommended the appointment of his two colleagues and would never have had the audacity to do so. He thus correctly refused to recuse himself. Judge Ludorf, correctly, did recuse himself. His place was taken by Judge Bekker. Judge Kennedy was a judge of the Natal Provincial Division and Judge Bekker was a judge of the Transvaal Provincial Division.

The proceedings commenced on 1 August 1958. The names of the counsel who appeared for the Crown and for the accused are given at this point in the notes.[73]

The indictment (that is, the first indictment, as explained on p142) served on the accused was a formidable document. Prior to the commencement of the trial we had requested certain further particulars. We applied to quash the indictment and in the alternative, if our application to quash was unsuccessful, for certain further particulars that had not already been furnished, and which we thought were necessary. The argument of this application, together with the arguments of counsel for the Crown, lasted from 11 August to 27 August, and was an extremely difficult one. In addition to the charge of high treason brought against the accused there were two alternative counts on contravention of the Suppression of Communism Act. Our application to quash the indictment on the charge of high treason failed. The alternative application made by us to request the state to furnish certain further particulars to the charge of high treason was successful. An application to quash one of the charges under the Suppression of Communism Act succeeded and with regard to the remaining one, further particulars were ordered to be given.

I should say at this point that although I was the senior counsel on our side, the real captain, planner and organiser of the defence was our attorney, Michael Parkington, then a partner in the firm of Albert Livingston. He was a man of extraordinary ability, strongly anti-Communist (I emphasise this fact because it was part of the crown case that the accused were conspiring to form a Communist state). He devoted his considerable talents full time in the defence of the accused. When I talk of his planning the defence, I obviously include his grip and understanding not only of the legal issues, but also of the factual issues that arose prior to and during the trial. If it could be said of anybody that he devoted himself entirely to the defence of the accused, it certainly could be said of him. A man of many parts and interests, he left South Africa some years ago to live in London, where he died in 1994. He was co-author with Mr A P O'Dowd of the latest editions of the leading work, *McGillivray on Insurance*.

On the lighter side I might mention that the Boulevard Hotel is across the road from the old synagogue and Parkington made arrangements for a waiter from the hotel to bring him a gin and water before lunch every day. One of the judges remarked to me that he did not mind Parkington having his drink, but he wished he wouldn't smack his lips afterwards. Michael Parkington was a man of undoubted ability and I am quite sure that without his guidance and assistance, our side would not have been able to achieve the satisfactory outcome of that trial.

The case against all the accused on the charge of high treason was that they had joined in a conspiracy to overthrow the state by violence and to establish a Communist state. I have deliberately not mentioned all the alternative deeds to which the accused and their co-conspirators were alleged to have been parties. Instead, I have confined myself merely to what, in the end, turned out to be the case against the accused, namely that they were parties to a conspiracy, entered into at various times during the period 1952–1956, to overthrow the state by violence and to replace it by a Communist state. In the course of our argument we objected to the general reference by the Crown (in its 'Summary of Facts' served on the accused), to the Record of the preparatory examination. In the course of the argument the Crown asked for and was allowed an amendment of certain further particulars furnished to our side to be substituted by the following:

> The Crown intends to prove the existence of the conspiracy and the participation therein of the accused and co-conspirators by way of inference from the facts set out in the 'Summary of Facts' in sub-paras (1) to (15) hereunder, which said facts are more fully set out in the preparatory examination record and in the statements of a certain Bochenski, copies whereof have been served on the accused.

We strongly criticised this answer. The court held that there was substance in our criticism. The court said:

> In view of the large number of accused and the size of the Record (41 volumes of about 200 pages each) this reference, not being limited in any way to the 'Summary of Facts', was wholly inadequate.

The court pointed out that although the Crown had given the accused a 'Summary of Facts', it stated in paragraph 14 of that summary that it would also rely on: 'the facts set out in Schedule II and on the speeches made and resolutions adopted at each of the said meetings, particulars of which are set out in the preparatory examination record', and in the statement of a certain Bochenski, copies whereof had been served on the accused. Bochenski, a member of the Order of Dominicans, was a professor at the Swiss University of Fribourg. He was present at the opening of the trial in August 1956, and departed after about ten days without ever being called to give evidence. We never asked, nor were we told, why he was not called. Professor Bochenski, according to information which I have since obtained, was a well known expert on 'sovietology'. His works on dialectic – *Materialism, Marxism, Leninism*, etc, – are standard works of international reputation. Schedule II, it was pointed out by the court, was a typed book of 37 pages with five columns on each page.

The Crown sought to prove that the policy of the ANC was one of violence. The ANC was the dominant party of what became known as the Congress Alliance, consisting of the ANC, the African Indian Congress and two organisations, formed in about 1954, the South African Coloured People's Organisation and the South African Congress of Democrats. These latter two organisations each had only a few hundred members, whereas the ANC had, it was claimed, 100 000.

Thus, as stated by the court, in order reasonably to understand what the charge against him or her was, each accused was expected to study the evidence given at the preparatory examination, concerning the speeches and resolutions at 540 meetings. In addition, the 'Summary of Facts' said that the accused and alleged co-conspirators, whose names were given in Schedule I to the indictment, were in possession of documents handed in at the preparatory examination, numbering some 9 000. The court proceeded:

> It seems to us that the accused will not be in a position to prepare their case unless the Crown particularises the speeches and documents upon which it relies. It is a well known principle in our law that an accused person is entitled to such particulars as he properly requires for the purpose of preparing his case before he is called upon to plead and enter upon his defence, and he is entitled to such particulars even if it entails a disclosure of Crown evidence.

Consequently, the Crown was ordered to indicate – from each speech, document or resolution (or portions, if relying on portions only) referred to in Schedules I and II, and in certain paragraphs of the 'Summary of Facts' – the existence of the conspiracy, and the adherence to the conspiracy of each accused it sought to be inferred from these many thousands of pages. In addition the court ordered the Crown to inform each of the accused in respect of which overt act committed by a co-accused he was not to be held liable. The court indicated that it would have quashed the indictment but for the fact that to have done so would have operated to the prejudice and inconvenience of the accused in addition to what they had already suffered.

The arguments on the quashing of the first indictment and the request for further particulars ended, as stated above, on 27 August 1958 and the 'Reasons for Judgment'[74] were handed down on 15 September.

It seemed to our side that the Crown would have difficulty in reducing the indictment and the documentation to some reasonable size, or to give the particulars set out above, in order to comply with the court's order. In this we were right, for on 13 October the indictment was withdrawn by Pirow, the leader of the prosecution. Some of the accused did not understand the effect thereof. In fact one of them, Accused No 7, Mr Alfred Hutchinson, asked a policeman what this meant and when the policeman told him (needless to say not using the *ipsissima verba*) to 'go away', he took him literally and was never seen again. Hutchinson wrote a book, which, many years after the treason trial, I happened to open, to see, on the first page, my name mentioned and an account of what had happened to Hutchinson when the policeman had told him to go away. Hutchinson was then, I think, in Ghana.

A new indictment (the second) was served on us in January 1959 but the number of the accused was now reduced to 30 from the original 92. We could understand the necessity for reducing the number of the accused being tried together to 30. The whole concept of a mass trial was absurd. When I say that the number was reduced to 30, the idea was that the remaining 62 persons would be tried at a later date. Again we did not know on what basis the first 30 were selected.

Judge Rumpff pointed out that this second indictment differed from the first mainly in that it specifically alleged that the accused intended to overthrow the state by violence. It covers the same period of four years and alleges, *inter alia,* a conspiracy by at least 159 persons including the 30 accused. Judge Rumpff summarised the task which the prosecution set itself as being:

> to prove that over the period of the indictment the organisations that it had cited in the indictment had a policy to overthrow the state by violence, and that each of the accused and each of the co-conspirators actively supported that policy. The particulars supplied by the prosecution indicated that the court would be asked to return a finding that such was the policy mainly by way of inference from what had been published in thousands of documents consisting of bulletins, newspapers, minutes of meetings and other publications, and from what had been said in hundreds of speeches, allegedly made by the accused and others, over a period of at least four years, from 1952 to 1956. In addition, the court would be asked, also by way of inference from all the facts, to find that the organisations had a policy of propagating Communism, inherent in which is the theory of violent revolution, and that each of the accused with knowledge thereof supported that policy and intended thereby to achieve a violent overthrow of the state.

I might add that during the course of the concluding argument by the prosecution, Judge Bekker put it to Trengove that the Crown's case was 'wedded to violence' and Trengove admitted that this was indeed the position.

I should also mention that the second indictment differed from the first indictment in that the first indictment attached much importance to a document known as the Freedom Charter, a copy of which was annexed to the first indictment. Although it is mentioned in Part B of the second indictment, it turned out to be a damp squib as far as the Crown was concerned. Professor Andrew Murray of the University of Cape Town was called by the Crown as an expert witness in political science.[75] Professor Murray's definition of Marxism and Leninism was not challenged by us. What was challenged by us was his attempt to find signs of Communism in speeches made by the accused or their alleged co-conspirators, and in documents found in the possession of the accused and their alleged co-conspirators. Professor Murray stated in his evidence that there was nothing in the Freedom Charter which was not consonant with Communism. He conceded, however, that each of the demands taken separately were not necessarily Communist and could be bourgeois socialist, rather than Communist socialist.[76]

It has been suggested that the 30 trialists in the second indictment were the authors of the more inflammatory documents, and the speakers on occasions when violence was promulgated.

There were no alternative charges. I asked Pirow why it was that the alternative charges had been dropped. He gave me an answer that 'if a person is charged with high treason, we don't charge him in the alternative with a parking offence'. I don't think that this was the real reason why the alternative charges were dropped. One of the charges under the Suppression of Communism Act had been quashed and it was really quite impossible to frame a proper charge against the accused under the Act. The accused *could* be joined together in the charge of conspiracy. Yet they were alleged to have joined the conspiracy at different times during the period 1 October 1952 to 13 December 1956 – the court having come to that conclusion relying on a decision in the Appellate Division given by Judge of Appeal Schreiner in Rex *v* Heyne and Others.[77]

However, it had to be asked whether the accused could possibly be associated on the remaining charge under the Suppression of Communism Act. The answer was that it was not possible. Needless to say we attacked this indictment as well and applied to have it quashed.

Another application for particulars was made in March 1959.

Although we were unsuccessful, the court thought it fit to reserve questions of law for the consideration of the Appellate Division and postponed the trial. Our appeal to the Appellate Division failed for the simple reason that, upholding an objection *in limine* by counsel for the Crown, the Court of Appeal had no jurisdiction at that stage of the proceedings to decide the questions of law reserved. The point taken was that the Court of Appeal could decide questions of law only on points reserved after the trial had been concluded.[78]

In the result, the trial itself commenced on 4 August 1959. All the accused pleaded not guilty, and Pirow, QC, made his opening address. He stated that the case to be presented by the Crown was an intricate one. He said:

> The Crown will seek to bring within the scope of a single prosecution the developments of some four years or more, covering the entire country and requiring frequent reference to events in other countries; involving a score of organisations, many individuals, innumerable events, and last but not least, an excursion into the complex phenomenon known as Communism.

He then quoted the accepted definition of high treason to which I have referred above. He pointed out:

> In our system of law, as in the legal systems of most communities, it is not criminal to seek political reform. Constitutional changes, however radical and far-reaching, may be lawfully sought. But they must be sought by legitimate and constitutional means only. When the methods become unlawful and unconstitutional the individual using them commits High Treason.

We did not, of course agree with the last portion of that statement. He proceeded:

> The gist of the Crown's case of High Treason is that the Accused, acting in concert, and through the instrumentality of their organisations, prepared to subvert – and subvert

the existing state – with a state founded on principles differing fundamentally from those on which the present state is constituted.

In concluding his opening address, he said that the Crown proposed to arrive at the following overall picture:

1. That there existed over the period of the indictment, and for some time before, a countrywide conspiracy between the accused, the co-conspirators and persons to the Crown unknown, to overthrow the state by violence and to substitute for it another form of state.

2. This conspiracy had its origin in the so-called liberatory movement, an international Communist-inspired and supported movement pledged to overthrow by violence all governments in non-Communist countries where sections of the population did not have equal political and economic rights.

3. The liberatory movement had its counterpart in South Africa where it sought to obtain its objects, *inter alia*, by the Communist method of stirring up trouble in disputes of national and local importance. It was inspired by Communist fanaticism, Bantu nationalism and racial hatred in various degrees.

4. In June, 1955, the liberatory movement led to the holding of the Congress of People which formulated as a programme of action its less culpable objects.

5. All the organisations unequivocally and emphatically supported the Liberation Movement, but the most blatantly violent speeches were made by members of the African National Congress.

6. In conclusion, the accused participated fully in the activities of their respective associations and associated themselves with the attitude of the said association in addition

> to committing the overt acts with which they are charged in the indictment.

Vernon Berrangé, who led the defence case at the preparatory examination, did so on the basis that the accused had been brought to trial 'as the victims of political kite-flying on the part of those responsible for the prosecution.' He denounced the proceedings at this point as politically motivated and demanded that the law be interpreted in the framework of 'democracy' rather than 'fascism'. He added that:

> the defence would endeavour to show that the prosecution was for the purpose of testing a political affiliation in order to ascertain how far the originators thereof, ie, the prosecution, can go in their endeavours to stifle free speech and criticism of the government, whereas all 30 accused believed in their definition of the oft-misused word 'democracy'.[79]

By the time we rendered the opening of the crown case in August 1959, we differed from Berrangé's line of argument in that, although the trial was clearly a political one, we had decided to fight the case on the facts and law applicable in much the same way as we would act in a non-political case. We made a short statement explaining the basis of our case. It read:

> It has already become apparent during the preliminary stages of this case that the central issue is the issue of violence. While no admissions are made in regard to any of the Crown's allegations, the defence case will be that it was not the policy of the African National Congress or any of the other organisations mentioned in the indictment to use violence against the state. On the contrary, the defence will show that all these organisations had deliberately decided to avoid every form of violence, and to pursue their ends by peaceful means only. The defence will rely for its contentions as to the policies of these organisations upon their constitutions, the resolutions taken by them at their conferences and the pronouncements of their responsible nation-

> al leaders. If necessary these leaders will be called as witnesses for the defence. The defence will place before this court the material relating to these organisations from which their policies might normally be expected to be deduced. In its indictment the Crown has relied upon certain speeches, most of them by persons of minor importance, which may seem to suggest the existence of a policy of violence. Insofar as such speeches were in fact made in the terms alleged, the defence will say that they may have represented the notions of individuals and not the policy of the organisations.[80]

We did, however, make certain admissions, as follows:

> The defence admits:
> 1. That during 1952 the ANC (African National Congress) [81] and SAIC (South African Indian Congress) decided to conduct a campaign for the Defiance of Unjust Laws, and did conduct a campaign, involving the deliberate contravention of certain laws by the way of protest and in order to bring about political and social changes in South Africa.
>
> 2. That between March 1954 and July 1955, the ANC, SAIC, SACOD (South African Congress of Democrats) , and SACPO (South African Coloured People's Organisation) were represented upon the National Action Council for the COP (Congress of People) and supported the organisation of this COP.
>
> 3. That the campaign for the COP, supported by the abovementioned organisations, involved the collection of demands for inclusion in the Freedom Charter, and culminated on 26 June 1955, in the adoption of the Freedom Charter by the COP in Kliptown.
>
> 4. That after July 1955, the ANC, SAIC, SACOD, SACPO and SACTU (South African Congress of Trade Unions) were represented upon the National Consultative Committee and supported the publication and popularisa-

tion of the Freedom Charter.

5. That the ANC, SAIC, SACOD, SACPO, SACTU and FSAW (Federation of South African Women) were opposed to the enactment and/or provisions of the Group Areas Act, the Bantu Education Act and Natives Resettlement Act and the laws relating to the carrying of passes by Africans.

6. That during the years 1954, 1955 and 1956, the ANC conducted campaigns against the Bantu Education Act, the Natives Resettlement Act and the laws relating to the carrying of passes by Africans, in the course of which it advocated:

(a) the boycott of Bantu schools by the pupils thereof,
(b) that the inhabitants of the so-called Western Areas of Johannesburg should not voluntarily leave their homes,
(c) that African women should not voluntarily apply for reference books.

7. That the ANC, SAIC, SACOD, SACPO, SACTU and FSAW were strongly opposed to the apartheid policy and legislation of the government of the Union of South Africa and denounced the government in vigorous terms.

8. That the ANC, SAIC, SACOD, SACPO, SACTU and FSAW criticised the present constitution of the Union of South Africa.

9. That the ANC, SAIC, SACOD, SACPO, SACTU and FSAW demanded the substitution of a new and radically different government and in particular advocated:

(a) a system of government based on universal adult suffrage
(b) the abolition of all forms of racial discrimination.

10. That the ANC, SAIC, SACOD, SACPO, SACTU and FSAW accepted the view that extra-parliamentary activity

should be resorted to, and [they] advocated and carried on extra-parliamentary, activity.

11. That during the years 1954, 1955 and 1956, the ANC, SAIC, SACOD, and SACPO recruited or supported the recruitment of a body of persons known as the Freedom Volunteers.

12. That the ANC, SAIC, SACOD, and SACPO criticised the colonial system and sympathised with the efforts of colonial countries to obtain self-government.

13. That the expressions by the ANC, SAIC, SACOD, SACPO, SACTU and FSAW of their admitted policies were often vehement and repetitive.

14. (a) That all the above-named organisations co-operated with one another generally in the policies and activities above set forth, insofar as such activities took place during the period of existence of each organisation.
(b) That the ANCYL (African National Congress Youth League) and ANCWL (African National Congress Women's League) similarly co-operated with the ANC.
(c) That the TIC (Transvaal Indian Congress), and NIC (National Indian Congress) were constituent parts of the SAIC.
(d) That the TIYC (Transvaal Indian Youth Congress) and NIYC (Natal Indian Youth Congress) similarly co-operated with the TIC and NIC respectively.

Additional Admissions Made by the Defence

1. That the Defiance Campaign was directed against the following laws, namely
(a) pass laws
(b) stock limitation regulations
(c) the Group Areas Act
(d) the Separate Representation of Voters Act
(e) the Suppression of Communism Act
(f) the Bantu Authorities Act.

2. That the SAIC and ANC formed a National Volunteer Board as part of their activities in the Defiance Campaign.

3. That the Defiance Campaign was carried on in several parts of South Africa from 26 June, 1952 to December 1952.

4. That NACCOP (National Action Council of the Congress of People) established various provincial, regional and local action councils, consisting of representatives of the constituent organisations, namely the following:
(a) Natal Action Council
(b) Transvaal Action Council
(c) Johannesburg, Natal Midlands, Cape Eastern and Cape Western Regional Committees.

5. That the object of NACCOP was the co-ordination of the activities of the organisations in their sponsorship and organisation of the COP.

6. That the provincial, regional or local councils of NACCOP organised meetings at various places in South Africa in support of the COP.

7. That the COP campaign was conducted in many parts of South Africa.

8. That various joint consultative provincial and regional committees were established by the organisations.

9. That meetings of the National Consultative Committee or the provincial or regional committees were held to discuss:
(a) Publicising the Freedom Charter
(b) Passes.

10. That the campaign against the laws referred to (in paragraph 6 of the first set of admissions), constituted part of the policy of extra-parliamentary activity.

11. That the said campaigns were conducted in many parts of South Africa.

12. That these campaigns were regarded as part of the general activity of the organisations.

13. That the organisations advocated extra-parliamentary action as a means of achieving the change of government desired by them (as set out in paragraph 9 of the first set of admissions).

14. That Chief A J Luthuli, on behalf of the ANC, called for 50 000 Freedom Volunteers and that the other organisations supported his appeal.

15. That the TIYC and NIYC had all the policies and participated in all the activities which have been admitted with reference to the SAIC and that the TIYC and NIYC co-operated with the other organisations referred to in the admissions.

The Crown called some 150 witnesses, who testified to more than 4 000 documents. These consisted of constitutions and policy statements of the ANC, records of meetings held by the ANC; and notes made by certain of the police witnesses. Of these last, some were recorded or taken down in shorthand by those qualified to do so, but to a large extent purported to be records of what was stated at meetings taken down in longhand, in some cases by persons who were unable to understand English – and English was frequently spoken at these meetings.

Insofar as the crown case rested on the advocacy of violence as shown in documents or by speeches, it failed completely. I cannot do better than quote from the conclusion of the written 'Reasons for Judgment' given by Judge Kennedy. He confined himself to the question of whether, in the speeches made, there was evidence of a policy of violence on the part of the ANC. Both Judge Rumpff and Judge Bekker also dealt with this question and came to the same conclusion as Judge Kennedy, who said:

To sum up, then, on the speeches:

> 1. The evidence of the longhand writers fall to be rejected on the issue of violence.
>
> 2. The evidence as to the non-violent policy of the African National Congress far outweighed the isolated instances of speeches which indicated that certain members or branches of the African National Congress were prepared to adopt violent means, if necessary, to achieve their aims. In the face of this conglomeration of evidence, the court was not able to find that the African National Congress had changed its avowed policy for one of violence. For these reasons, therefore, I came to the conclusion that the case for the prosecution has failed in as much as it was based on the evidence of the speeches.

As is well known, the court found it unnecessary to hear the whole of the argument of the defence on the case and gave a short judgment acquitting the accused on 20 March 1961.

We had no quarrel with the findings of the court, with the exception of one finding (recorded in paragraph 1(f)). The judgment on 29 March 1961 stated that the formulation of the court's reasons would take a considerable time. In the result, three separate judgments were written. Dealing with the finding with which we did not agree, it is of interest to note that whilst both Judge Rumpff and Judge Kennedy, in their reasons, did not depart from their findings as set out in that paragraph, Judge Bekker did. He said:

> The evidence of Professor Murray makes it clear that no matter how many principles of Communist dogma, tactics or methods may have been followed or adopted, unless it is shown that the concept of a one party system – the dictatorship of the proletariat – had been advocated, it would be incorrect to find that Communism in the true sense of the word had been put forward. This evidence, in the circumstances, destroys the validity of the contention advanced by the prosecution and at the same time, apart from other considerations, shows why we were unable to find that it was proved that the African National Congress

had become a 'Communistic' organisation. In our earlier judgment we held, with reference to the Freedom Charter, that 'the type of state as seen by the Transvaal Executive Committee of the African National Congress is a dictatorship of the proletariat, and accordingly is a Communist state, known in Marxism-Leninism as a people's democracy.' We based our conclusion on the contents of a certain lecture which this committee made use of and which reads as follows:

'Before the Europeans came, the country was governed on the tribal system. The Chief was the head of the tribe. But when laws had to be made or decisions taken the chief called together the people in a pitso *or* lokgotla, *etc. That was "government by consent". The people agreed to the laws and obeyed them because they were consulted, and they helped to make the laws and run the government. Today, the power of government, of the state, which makes the laws, is not held by the people. Power is held by the ruling classes of white mineowners, living both in South Africa and in Britain and America; it is held by the wealthy owners of large-scale factories and financial concerns; it is held by the Afrikaner farmers. Those classes are represented by the National and United Parties. The power of state is not exercised for the benefit of the people. It is used to permanently subject the people. It is used against the people to ensure the profits of the few. Congress aims to replace this government of the few, with a government of people's democracy. In a people's democratic state, the power of state will be exercised by the people. That is, by the working people of all colours, together with all other democratic classes who will work for the changes set out in the Freedom Charter. This will be a government of the people as a whole; of the present oppressed and exploited classes used to achieve their maximum well-being, and to prevent the "few" exploiters from regaining state power.'*

I have since come to the conclusion that our earlier finding is erroneous, for reasons which follow immediately. The test to be applied in construing the document is in the light of Professor Murray's evidence a simple one, namely: does it advocate the concept of a one party system or not? He suggested 'people's democratic state' is defined as

> being one consisting of the oppressed and exploited classes and other democratic classes who will work for the changes set out in the Freedom Charter and in which the 'few exploiters' namely the 'white mine-owners', the 'wealthy owners of large-scale factories and financial concerns' and 'the Afrikaner farmers', who are represented by the National and United Parties, will be excluded from regaining state power. This definition does not in my opinion necessarily imply that a one-party system was being put forward since in the classes which remain after the exclusion of the 'few exploiters' as defined, there may very well be room, for instance, for a Communist party on the one hand and a socialist party on the other working for 'the changes set out in the Freedom Charter ... and to prevent the 'few exploiters' from regaining state power. The definition of the 'people's democratic state' as contained in this lecture does not in my opinion exclude such a result as a reasonable possibility and I am accordingly unable to agree that the one and only inference to be drawn from the document is that a dictatorship of the proletariat was being advocated.

In the second indictment, it was alleged[82] that the accused had organised and participated in various campaigns against the administration and enforcement of legislation relating to resettlement of Africans, 'Native' education and passes.[83]

The campaign against the Native Resettlement Act was directed in the first instance against the government's intention to remove Africans from the 'Western Areas' of Johannesburg to Meadowlands, a considerable distance away from the centre of Johannesburg. The Western Areas consisted of three townships, Sophiatown, Martindale and Newclare, and up to the time of the passing of the Act in 1954, Africans had been permitted to own land in freehold there; although comparatively few Africans could afford to own the houses they occupied. Nonetheless, their presence there showed that they were permanently resident in Johannesburg. These Africans, also, were mainly employed in Johannesburg.

It is quite true that many of the houses were really slums and that there were rapacious landlords, as there are today in Hillbrow where many Africans and Coloured people are now living. Nonetheless Africans living in these areas were free of many of the regulations typical of urban African locations.

Among those living in Sophiatown was Dr A B Xuma, a former President General of the ANC. According to him there were at that time 'in these areas registered schools and old-established missions, where our Churches stand, where we have cinemas and shops and the only swimming bath for African children in the whole of Johannesburg.'

I may add that Africans could not own land in Meadowlands but had to rent homes that were built there (which were undoubtedly of a better quality than the houses in which the majority of them lived in the 'Western Areas'). The real reason for removing the Africans from these areas was that the areas had become 'black spots': meaning African areas adjacent to or surrounded by the growing spread of White Johannesburg. Over and above that, of course, of particular importance to the National government was the importance of eliminating African rights to ownership of land.[84] After the Africans were removed from Sophiatown the whole of the Western Areas was rebuilt for occupation by Whites and renamed – in my opinion somewhat cynically – 'Triomf'.

On 22 November 1956, a private meeting of representatives of branches of the ANC on the Witwatersrand was called by the Transvaal Executive Committee. A number of speeches were made and part of the proceedings were recorded on a tape recorder that the police had installed without the knowledge of those present at the meeting. One of the speakers was the accused, Robert Resha, who was at the time a member of the National Executive Committee of the ANC and was the Volunteer-in-Chief of the Freedom Volunteers in the Transvaal. The recording took up the words of the chairman of the meeting, introducing Resha, and Resha's speech. In his judgment, portions of these proceedings were quoted by Judge Rumpff as follows:

> CHAIRMAN: So the one I am going to call upon to speak now is the Volunteer-in-Chief. You know that some time ago we said we want 50 000 volunteers. I think today we still want those volunteers, we want those volunteers to

be there. The one I am going to call upon to speak now is the Volunteer-in-Chief. He is just going to speak in his capacity as a Volunteer-in-Chief. I am very sorry because I've got no means – if I had the means I would be taking you and showing you what actually we mean when we say a man is a volunteer. When I was at PE I saw exactly what is meant by a volunteer, by saying so I wouldn't like to waste his time. So Mr Resha as the Chief Volunteer is going to address you, and he is the last speaker.

RESHA: Afrika!

AUDIENCE: *Mayibuye!*

RESHA: Afrika! (*Mayibuye!*) Afrika! (*Mayibuye!*) Afrika! Mr Chairman, sons and daughters of Africa, war has been declared, war has been declared, your leaders have spoken to you, but you must not be afraid. When war has been declared it is the duty of those to whom war has been declared against not to panic. War has been declared. The government has decided not only to oppress the African people but to exterminate them from the surface of this earth, their mother country. Your leaders have told you what the position is. Your leaders have told you that among other things the government of this country, the Strijdom, Swart and Verwoerd clique, want to arrest yet another 200. …

The time has come for congress to take the offensive. We are tired of the bluff of Strijdom and others, time has come now for congress to tell Strijdom and others what to do. Time has come for Chief Luthuli, for Moretsele and for Revd Gawe to say who must be arrested, who is this wanted. It must be congress which must give those wanted, not these fools to come and choose amongst us who is to be arrested. How can that be done? How can Chief Luthuli decide who must be arrested and when? Only when Chief Luthuli has … 50 000 volunteers, then 200 will be a simple matter, out of 50 000 volunteers he can give Swart 200 and that will cost Swart the whole of the Union of South Africa. Friends, my task this afternoon or this evening is not to speak to you about what is happening in this country, but my task is to give you duties. War has been declared and we must be ready. …

Volunteers are those people who do and die. Volunteers are those people who – who when they are given leaflets to do they go out and distribute those leaflets. Volunteers are those people who don't ask questions. A volunteer is a person who has pledged himself to carry out the work of the African National Congress whatever is involved without questioning. A volunteer is a person who has dedicated his entire life to the liberation of his African people during the whole time. A volunteer is a person who is disciplined. This is the key of the volunteer discipline. When you are disciplined and you are told by the organisation not to be violent, you must not be violent. If you are a true volunteer and you are called upon to be violent, you must be absolutely violent, you must murder! murder! That is all. …

Your leaders have told you that the government of this country, amongst other things, is planning to arrest 200 leaders and is attacking every day today leaders of the people. My direction to you is, if this government in its madness does one day arrest 200 leaders then 200 000 Congress members must emerge from those who are remaining in this country. You can only do that, my friends, if you are going to tell your brother. The first thing that you are called upon to do today is, that every Congress branch from tonight must form or revise its volunteer corps. The next thing you must do friends, it is the duty of every one of you who is a field worker, who is a volunteer – never to go to bed unless you have reported to your volunteer-in-chief in your area. When you go to your area in the evening, go to your volunteer-in-chief and say: 'I have come, is there any work to do?' It is the duty of you all who are here tonight to tell the people what you have been told. I want to say to you once more that the main thing in a volunteer – the thing in a volunteer is discipline. The second thing in a volunteer is to be vigilant. You must be sensitive towards anything that is happening to the African people. The third qualification

> of a volunteer is madness, and you can never be a volunteer unless you are mad. Because if you are a gentleman, or if you are a lady, you can never get into the train and speak about Congress, you can never get into the bus and speak about Congress, only mad people and only volunteers can do that because they are mad, and we need mad people to get our freedom in this country. …
>
> Well, friends, Mr Nkadimeng has said 'We are meeting here this evening at a most critical time in the history of South Africa,' and, in explaining that, Mr Duma Nokwe said: 'We are meeting at a time when it is in our hands to destroy or build our freedom.' Mr Masina showed us the way out when he said: 'Do unto your enemies as you would have them do unto you'. When you are a worker, the duty of an employer is to exploit you, and your duty to your enemy is to refuse the labour. If your leaders are going to be arrested it becomes the task of the volunteers, the task of those who are going to remain, what you are going to do with those who are remaining and those who have arrested our leaders. That becomes the task. …
>
> Friends, war has been declared, and I call upon you today to become volunteers, every one of you must go and sign in his branch, and I say to the leaders, that before you leave this meeting, please see the Provincial Secretary and tell him when you want me to get there. I will not be going there to discuss politics, I will be going there to find soldiers. I think we are called upon in this country to do directly the opposite of what is taking place in Egypt today. In Egypt it is the imperial forces that are moving into Egypt, but in South Africa we want the freedom forces to eradicate evil in this, our mother country South Africa.

A replay of the tape recording indicates that the injunction to 'volunteers' to murder if called upon to be violent was received with a roar of approval by those present. I have quoted this part of the judgment in full because so much attention was given to it by the prosecution. Resha himself was cross-examined on it, as indeed was Chief Luthuli. Resha gave evidence as follows:[85]

RESHA: The African National Congress has no policy in regard to violence. The policy is absolutely non-violent.

FISCHER: (*for the defence*) Has there ever been any question about that?

RESHA: There has never been a question about that policy at all.

FISCHER: And you accepted that policy?

RESHA: I have accepted and preached that policy.

FISCHER: Have you ever taken a hand in preventing violence?

RESHA: I have stopped and prevented violence.

FISCHER: Have you ever taken part in any violent action?

RESHA: I have never taken part in any violent action whatsoever.

FISCHER: Now I want to ask you whether you have ever departed from this policy in any of your speeches?

RESHA: I think I have.

FISCHER: Can you explain to the court why you have departed from it if you have?

RESHA: My Lords, when I think of the brutal methods used by the government in imposing its inhuman policy on my people, I sometimes have grave doubts about the policy of non-violence. Sometimes it seems to me that if the government is prepared to use this force and violence in stifling every endeavour by my people to improve their lot and to attain some political rights, then sometimes I feel we too have the right to use this violence at times.

FISCHER: You would like to use the violence at times? If you sit down and ponder about what the policy would be, what is your conclusion?

RESHA: When I sit down calmly, and consider the African National Congress policy, I realise that the only wise policy is the policy of non-violence.

FISCHER: But your other feeling, was that expressed in some speeches?

RESHA: I think it is expressed in some of my speeches, but not frequently. …

FISCHER: Now I want to turn to some of your speeches – you know by heart, probably, now, the end of the much-debated speech in which you suggested that if a volunteer were ordered to murder he should 'murder, murder'?

RESHA: I think I know that speech by now.

FISCHER: Can you reconcile that with African National Congress policy?

RESHA: The example I used in that speech cannot be reconciled with the policy of the African National Congress. …

FISCHER: Now I would like you to turn over the page, and have a look at a reference to madness at the foot of 8153, about two thirds of the way down the page. You say, 'The second thing in a volunteer is to be vigilant, he must be sensitive towards anything that is happening to the African people.' And then you say, 'The third qualification of a volunteer is madness. You can never be a volunteer unless you are mad.' What do you mean by that?

RESHA: I think I go further to show what I mean: 'because if you are a gentleman, or if you are a lady, you can never get into the train and speak about Congress, you can never get into the bus and speak about Congress, only mad people and only volunteers can do that, because they are mad.' What I was trying to put across was that Congress members must, wherever they are, preach the gospel of the African National Congress, even if people think they are mad, because when you stand in the morning on a street corner and speak about freedom, passersby think you are mad, there must be something wrong with you. If you get into a train and say to the people, the time has come for us to work for a defiance campaign, people think you are mad – and I was making that illustration here.

FISCHER: And you must do it even if people think you are mad?

RESHA: That was my point.

FISCHER: Now I want to ask you whether there were any consequences of your speaking in this fashion about 'murder, murder'. Did anyone approach you about this?

RESHA: I think a day after the meeting I was approached by Mr Sisulu, the then Secretary-General of the African National Congress.

FISCHER: Was he at that time Secretary-General?

RESHA: He was not, he was banned from participating in the affairs of the African National Congress, and he said to me that he had met Mr Nokwe who was rather unhappy about my speech where I spoke about murder, and he wanted to know from me what was this all about. I then explained – my explanation to Mr Sisulu was that it is likely that Mr Nokwe misunderstood me, I did speak about murder, but that was an example when I was dealing with the discipline of volunteers.

FISCHER: Was it ever raised anywhere else at an executive meeting or anything of that kind?

RESHA: It was never raised in any executive meeting, because there was no executive meeting between that day and the time of our arrest.

FISCHER: When were you arrested?

RESHA: About 14 days after that, on the 5th of December, 1956. …

Resha was thereafter cross-examined by the counsel for the crown:

TRENGOVE: At one stage you believed in violence as a means of achieving one's ends?

RESHA: I said in my evidence that it is the normal outlook of the youth at a given age to think that violence can solve their difficulties.

TRENGOVE: And I think you said – I am speaking subject to correction – I think you said that you shared that view at a certain stage?

RESHA: I did.

TRENGOVE: Did you ever change your mind?

RESHA: As I grew up I began to think much broader.

TRENGOVE: Did you ever at any stage decide for yourself that violence was a method that had to be discarded as a means of achieving your political ends?

RESHA: I have thought that way and I was convinced ...

TRENGOVE: Now when did you become convinced of that?

RESHA: I cannot put the date and time, but as I say, as I grew up and became experienced, took part in political activities, I was convinced that violence is not the method for one to achieve his political aspirations.

TRENGOVE: I just want to try and get a little closer to the date when you decided that or realised that. How long ago was that?

RESHA: Well, on a question like that, I would say since I joined the African National Congress.

TRENGOVE: As far back as 1944?

RESHA: That is right.

TRENGOVE: I am going to suggest that you never abandoned that idea and that you believe in violence as a means of achieving your political ends?

RESHA: My lord, that is not correct.

TRENGOVE: Dealing with the African National Congress Youth League, one of the aims of the ANCYL was to serve as a spearhead and shock brigade of the liberatory movement?

RESHA: The Youth League had no different aims from those of the African National Congress, its mother body. …

TRENGOVE: Now, how did you visualize the struggling masses of Africa were going to free themselves without the assistance of the white people?

RESHA: By struggling for their freedom.

TRENGOVE: Against whom would they struggle, against the white people?

RESHA: Against the government.

TRENGOVE: Against the white people?

RESHA: Against the government.

TRENGOVE: But now the white people constitute – ?

RESHA: Constitute the government of this country.

TRENGOVE: Oh, when you say the government you mean the white people?

RESHA: I do not mean the same.

TRENGOVE: Well, you are going to get your freedom, or you may get your freedom, you say here, without the assistance of the white people?

RESHA: With or without. ...

TRENGOVE: Now the only way to get [this] freedom would be to persuade the white electorate to bring pressure to bear on the government?

RESHA: The African people can themselves persuade the government to give in. The pressure does not only come through the electorate.

TRENGOVE: So that you distinguish here between the white people and the white government?

RESHA: That is so.

TRENGOVE: And how were you going to get the white government – which had behind it the support of the white people – how were you going to bring them to their knees?

RESHA: My Lords, in this country we have the government and its forces; we have thousands of Europeans who do not support the policy of the present government, but do nothing else – they say, 'Well, we don't accept that policy but that's about all we can say' – so that those people, quite apart from the fact that they say they do not support the policy, they do nothing. They render no assistance, to the African people to change this government.

TRENGOVE: Mr Resha, how many people does the government consist of?

RESHA: I don't understand that question.

TRENGOVE: You say you've got to bring the government to its knees; how many people would be standing alone against your liberatory movement in the end?

RESHA: I have not counted the number.

TRENGOVE: Surely, Mr Resha, you realise that on this passage as it is put here, that the government – at the time when you take power without the assistance of the white people – that the government would still have the support, the active support of a large number of the white population. That's what your message implies?

RESHA: What my message implies?

TRENGOVE: When you say 'The struggling masses will free themselves without the assistance of the white people'?

RESHA: Free themselves or take power, Mr Trengove?

TRENGOVE: Well, Mr Resha, I'll leave the choice to you?

RESHA: No, no – freeing is different from taking power.

TRENGOVE: All right, I'll accept that. When you free yourselves, you'll do it without the assistance of the white people?

RESHA: That is so.

TRENGOVE: At that stage you know that the government would still be able to call upon a large mass of white people to assist them in suppressing your struggle?

RESHA: In the same way we would be in a position, having attained freedom, to call upon a large number of Europeans to assist us in forming a government that will be for the people of South Africa. ... Anyone in this country, a multi-racial country, who opposes Congress – and that person being an African who opposes Congress in establishing a multi-racial society in this multi-racial country – is therefore a traitor in the cause for which we stand.

TRENGOVE: Such a person mustn't only be treated with contempt and suspicion but must be regarded as a traitor and an enemy of the people?

RESHA: In the sense that he supports the present government in its policy of preaching racial antagonism, in a multi-racial country. That person is not only a traitor, but an enemy of the people who seek freedom and harmony in this country.

TRENGOVE: And I take it that at an appropriate time the enemies, traitors, would have to be dealt with? By whom? By the people, when once they have achieved freedom?

RESHA: That I leave to the people.

TRENGOVE: You wouldn't have anything against it?

RESHA: Against? Against? Against what? A trial of traitors? The people are struggling for freedom, and once they have achieved freedom their work will be to reconstruct South Africa into a happy country for all who live in it.

TRENGOVE: And then those that were traitors and enemies of the people before freedom would have to be dealt with?

RESHA: That was your suggestion, Mr Trengove.

TRENGROVE: It wasn't an ANC suggestion?

RESHA: It never was. ...

TRENGOVE: Would the position then be, Mr Resha, that in the present type of state as we have it, where a minority group, the white people, have the government in their hands, that there is an inherent danger of that government being overthrown by the masses who do not enjoy those privileges?

RESHA: That is so.

TRENGOVE: And I take it that that danger is enhanced and increases as the masses are organised in a positive struggle for liberation?

RESHA: That is so.

TRENGOVE: So that whatever the inherent dangers were in the present situation, your activities had the effect of increasing the instability, the danger to the stability and safety and security, of the state?

RESHA: That is so.

TRENGOVE: And the more successful your struggle became, the greater that danger became?

RESHA: That is so.

TRENGOVE: Now, Mr Resha, in that sense the Defiance Campaign in itself in 1952, particularly if it had been developed to its final stage, would have been dangerous to the safety and security of the state?

RESHA: That is so.

TRENGOVE: And I take it, Mr Resha, that that factor, that ever-present factor of the inherent instability of the state was something which you sought to convey to the masses in raising the political consciousness of the people?

RESHA: That is so. ...

TRENGOVE: Now Mr Resha, when did the African National Congress realise for the first time that the government was determined to force through this [Western Areas] scheme at the cost, if need be, of violence and bloodshed, regardless of any consequences?

RESHA: My Lord, I am in difficulty in giving a date and time as to when Congress realised that, save to say that the possibility of the government using force and violence was always there; we have known this government through its years of rule [since 1948], and no less than 300 Africans have been killed by the police in that time, and whenever they decide to do anything, force and violence is one of their main features.

TRENGOVE: Would it be correct to say that as early as the middle of 1954 you already realised that the government was determined to force this scheme through regardless of the consequences, even if it required violence and bloodshed?

RESHA: I said it is correct to say by that time we did because that is about the period when the government decided to embark on a legalised robbery of the rights of the African people, in the Western Areas, by bringing into being the Native Resettlement Act. …

TRENGOVE: Did your organisation hold the view, as early as June, 1954, that the government was about to provoke a racial clash in the Western Areas?

RESHA: It has always been the main feature of this government to provoke racial clashes. It's one of its policies, main policies. …

TRENGOVE: Now, Mr Resha, this racial clash that the government was accused of wanting to provoke – that racial clash – would it be a violent clash?

RESHA: The government is always keen on a violent clash; as I have already mentioned no less than 300 of our people have been killed – and there is the situation of Sharpeville where innocent people were murdered cold-bloodedly by this government. …

TRENGOVE: Now, Mr Resha, did the fact that the government was prepared to resort to violence and bloodshed in forcing through this scheme – did that in any way deter the African National Congress and its allies from their objective, of making the Western Areas the Waterloo of apartheid?

RESHA: Not at all. But the congress and its allies did everything to avoid a bloodbath; and fortunately it succeeded.

TRENGOVE: Now, Mr Resha, I want to put it to you that notwithstanding your accusation that the government wanted to create a bloodbath and force through this scheme by violence against the wishes of the people in the Western Areas, that one of the objects of your campaign was to force the government to do just that; one of the objects was that you wanted to force the government to remove the people by intimidation and force?

RESHA: My Lords, that is absolutely incorrect and most unfounded.

TRENGOVE: You wanted to provoke the government into using as much force as possible and resorting to what you call intimidation of the people?

RESHA: We never wanted to provoke the government at all. What we did want was to get rid of the government, but insofar as the Western Areas was concerned our aim was to defeat the government from removing the people of the Western Areas. That was our express aim. …

TRENGOVE: I'm asking you a simple question, Mr Resha; did you want to compel the government to use intimidation against the people?

RESHA: I said yes long ago.

TRENGOVE: Now, Mr Resha, here you have a government that is only too willing to use force and intimidation you want them to use force and intimidation against the people in the Western Areas?

RESHA: What we want to do is to struggle for our rights, and no amount of force or intimidation on the part of the government is going to deter us from striving for our rights in the land of our birth.

TRENGOVE: I want to put it to you, Mr Resha, that you knew full well that the situation which you were creating in the Western Areas was such that it was the spark which started off the conflagration in this country?

RESHA: I knew full well what? That what the government did was intended to start a conflagration in the Western Areas – that was the intention of the government.

TRENGOVE: Now why would the government want to start a conflagration?

RESHA: Because it wanted to remove people by force, to rob them of their rights, and because it is natural that no person in this world wants to be robbed of his rights; as a result, no one takes it lightly. And the government says, 'If you don't do what we tell you we are going to use force.'

TRENGOVE: But the government were prepared to remove the people without bloodshed and violence?

RESHA: The government was never prepared to do that – sending 2 000 police, armed; do you call that a preparation to remove people without bloodshed?

TRENGOVE: But you regard that as a victory, that you compelled the government to do that?

RESHA: We regarded it as a victory, that they went away with their guns without shooting one person because of our perfect organisation on that day. That is what we call a victory, on our side. …

TRENGOVE: Mr Resha, you have as justification – for the steps that your Congress took in regard to the Western Areas campaign – you have from time to time referred to the alleged viciousness and brutality of the government; you went as far back as the strike in 1946. Is that correct?

RESHA: That is so.

TRENGOVE: Now, Mr Resha, I want to put it to you that you know that in all these campaigns that have been organised as far back as the 1946 mineworkers' strike, that if it had not been for the restraint and tact of the police you would have succeeded long ago in involving the whole country in bloodshed?

RESHA: My Lords. It has never been the policy of the African National Congress to involve this country in bloodshed. What the African National Congress has done, to the benefit of South Africa, and I think many right-thinking people owe that to Congress, is that we have avoided bloodshed right through all these instances you have quoted.

TRENGOVE: Mr Resha, do you know that in connection with the mineworkers' strike the then Minister of Justice in a statement reported in the paper praised the restraint and tact of the police in dealing with that situation [Minister Lawrence]. Do you know that?

RESHA: Do I know that he said so, after people were injured? That was the restraint used by the police that they injured innocent people. …

TRENGOVE: And I want to put it to you, Mr Resha, that what the Minister of Justice said about the attitude of the police and their actions in 1946, applied equally to the May Day strike of 1951, stay-at-home, the stay-at-home on 26 June, 1950, to the defiance campaign, and to the campaign in the Western Areas?

RESHA: You mean the same Minister made the same statement?

TRENGOVE: No; I said the actions of the police, the restraint with which they conducted themselves, and the actions they took to protect the public, that same type of statement would apply to every campaign up to the Western Areas campaign where you came in contact with the police?

RESHA: My lords, it would appear that the Crown and the Minister of Justice look at the brutal assaults of the people and the murdering of people as restraint, something to commend the police for. That is not how we look at it. If the Minister of Justice and the Crown are happy that the police baton-charge defenceless and harmless workers and that that is a very good thing, then that is their outlook. So far as we are concerned we condemn it. If the Minister of Justice and the Crown view the killing of 18 people on 1 May 1951, as a commendable thing, and that the police acted with restraint, then we differ. If the Minister of Justice says that in sending 2 000 police to the Western Areas, fully armed, to go and look for arms which were never seen by any policeman, to intimidate and frighten the people of the Western Areas – if that is acting with restraint, then, of course, we are at variance with the Minister of Justice and the Crown. We regard it as being a very vicious thing indeed to baton charge people because they want their conditions of work to be improved. We regard it as being very bad indeed to kill

18 innocent people without one policeman having been charged for the loss of life. But if the government thinks the police acted with restraint in killing 18 out of so many millions of Africans and that this was a good thing, then of course we differ, my lords.

TRENGOVE: Mr Resha, you and your organisation have over the years subjected the police – in having to carry out their very difficult task of maintaining law and order – you have subjected them to jibes and taunts and insults because you want these actions to take place?

RESHA: My lord, throughout the years that have been referred to, there is not a single case of violence where a Congress member has ever been charged. The difficulties that are placed before the police have been put there by the government, which is making the police to implement laws which the people of South Africa are opposed to. That is the difficulty which is facing the police, and the government, of course, can safely hide behind the machine guns of the police as if they are not responsible.

TRENGOVE: Mr Resha, your statement that not a single member of Congress has been charged is exactly the point that I want to make; because in the Western Areas you embarked on a vicious and ruthless campaign – in which you were using grievances of masses of people, and provoking action from both the government and those people – to suit your purposes?

RESHA: My lord, there is no evidence before this court, and anywhere else, to show that we have ever embarked upon such action. The evidence before this court is clear and simple. That our methods of struggle were clearly and completely non-violent, and we succeeded in demonstrating in a practical way what we mean by non-violence. That is why, my lords, the charges that are placed against me by the powers that be failed even before we could go before the magistrate. It is a clear demonstration. Insofar as the Western Areas is concerned, throughout that campaign, I make bold to say – and which I am very happy about – that not one Congressite was arrested for any action involving rioting, in spite of the fact that people were killed by the police during these raids – in spite of the fact that the police broke down doors and entered people's houses – all that is, of course, commended by the Minister and the Crown. …

TRENGOVE: Mr Resha, why did you give this example of discipline, that if people are told to be violent they must murder, murder?

RESHA: I gave this example, my lords, merely to illustrate the importance of discipline.

TRENGOVE: According to the tape recording which was played in court when you got to that point there was applause from your audience?

RESHA: According to the tape recording when I finished speaking there was applause. …

TRENGOVE: Yes, the sentence is, 'When you are disciplined and you are told by your organisation not to be violent you must not be violent; if you are a true volunteer and you are called upon to be violent, you must be absolutely violent, you must murder! murder! That is all' – and then the applause?

RESHA: That is so.

TRENGOVE: Now apparently the people at that Conference thought this was a very good example of discipline?

RESHA: I think so, insofar as it was an example of discipline.

TRENGOVE: And I put it to you, Mr Resha, that they applauded you because that is exactly the discipline that you want?

RESHA: That is completely unfounded and that is not the discipline which I want.

TRENGOVE: And that is why the people applauded?

RESHA: I do not know why the people applauded, but that was not the discipline I wanted; I was merely giving an example.

TRENGOVE: No non-violent organisation would applaud a statement like that?

RESHA: Congress happens to be known throughout the land *(sic)* and breadth of the world, to be a non-violent organisation; no one in this world has ever challenged that, and these people applauded.

TRENGOVE: And that was what Mr Nokwe was afraid about, if the true nature of Congress was brought to the surface people might change their views?

RESHA: If the true nature of Congress policy is likely to be misinterpreted by this example, Mr Nokwe was worried. ...

TRENGOVE: Mr Resha, I just want to put it to you that you were deliberately striving for a position where there would be a bloody conflict between the government, trying to maintain its position, and the masses, trying to get the demands of the Freedom Charter?

RESHA: Your wishes have nothing to do with the policy of the African National Congress; the policy of the African National Congress is clear in all the documents you have been going through; you haven't found one document to support your school of thought, however you might wish it. What we want to bring about in this country is happiness for everybody, and we have chosen methods of struggle which have indicated clearly what our aims were, and we have succeeded in those methods hitherto. That is why to-day you have political organisations in this country which did not exist before the defiance campaign, like the Congress of Democrats, like the South African Liberal Party, like the Progressive Party. Political organisations which believe that in order to make it possible for all to live happily in this country, the policy should be changed, and that we should all share. These political organisations consisting of politicians and thinking men – all of them, including the Nationalist government – have agreed that our policy is one of non-violence. We have never been accused in this country and I think the man has still to be born who wants bloodshed in this country.

TRENGOVE: Mr Resha, your statement that numerous white political groups have arisen as a result of your campaigns, I want to put it to you that the main reason for these white political groups to have arisen is because the

> Communist Party was banned in 1950 and its former members had to find a new political home, or homes?
>
> RESHA: My lords, I don't know if Mr Dadoo was a member of the Communist Party, I do not know if Mr Alan Paton was a member of the former Communist Party, and in fact it is incorrect to say that the Congress of Democrats is there because the Communist Party was banned. These statements are most unfounded. One wonders where you get them from.

In Chief Luthuli's evidence on Mr Resha's speech, he did not agree that the speech was subversive. Although he conceded that 'in parts' its was inconsistent with the ANC's policy of non-violence, he described it as 'a fighting speech', given at 'a time when the feelings of the people were high and therefore they could have been – applauding – actuated by the emotions of the times – not necessarily saying "We are foregoing Congress policy".' Resha's departure from ANC policy at that point in his speech did not in any way reflect a change in its policy, but a personal departure of one member at a given moment.

The judgment of Judge Bekker is of particular importance because of the historical review of the ANC as a political organisation, which he deals with in his judgment. He said:

> I commence accordingly with a brief historical survey of the organisation. The African National Congress came into being in 1912 shortly after the Act of Union. At the time it had as its objects the unification of the various Bantu tribes in South Africa, and the general advancement of the Africans in social, economic and political fields. To that end it sent two deputations overseas, the first in 1913 to lodge protest with the United Kingdom government against the 1913 Native Land Act and again in 1919, where, at the Peace Conference, it made representations to secure some measure of self determination for the people. In South Africa meetings were held from time to time; various topics, political and otherwise, were canvassed. In addition, protests and petitions were submitted to the government of the day in an effort to secure relief and greater political and

economic rights for the people. This state of affairs continued until 1943, when a committee of leading members of the organisation met at Bloemfontein under the Chairmanship of Professor Z K Matthews, where, after deliberations, the Committee formulated certain demands, which were later published in a pamphlet known as *Africans' Claims*. This document set out what the organisation termed its 'Bill of Rights' and 'The Atlantic Charter', from the standpoint of the Africans. The findings of the committee were unanimously adopted at the subsequent Annual Conference of the organisation at Bloemfontein in December 1946, and accordingly became the official policy of the congress. Amongst others, the demands included the extension of the vote to all adults, regardless of race, and the right to be elected to Parliament and to other legislative or representative institutions; the right to be appointed to judicial and to public service offices; the right to own, buy, live in, lease or occupy, in unrestricted fashion, all forms of immovable property; the right, with reference to land, to an equal share in all 'the material resources' of the country; the right of every child to enjoy free and compulsory education and of admission to technical schools, universities and other institutions of higher education. It condemned in no uncertain terms, all discriminatory legislation and demanded the repeal of all discriminatory laws, policies and practices. In the preface to *Africans' Claims*, Dr A B Xuma, the then President-General of the African National Congress wrote: *'In South Africa, Africans have no freedom of movement, no freedom of choice of employment, no right of choice of residence and no right of freedom to purchase land or fixed property from anyone or anywhere. Under the guise of segregation, they are subjected to serious educational, political and economic disabilities and discriminations, which are the chief causes for their apparent slow progress. ... We urge that if fascism and fascist tendencies are to be uprooted from the face of the earth, and to open the way for peace, prosperity and racial goodwill, the 'Atlantic Charter' must apply to the whole of the British Empire, the United States of America and to all nations of the world, and their subject peoples ... As African leaders, we are not so foolish as to believe that because we have made these declarations that our government will grant us our claims for the mere asking. We realise that for the African this is only the beginning of a long struggle entailing great sacrifices of time, means and even life itself. To the African people the declaration is a challenge to organise and unite themselves under the mass liberation movement, the African National Congress. The struggle is on right now and it must be persistent and insistent. In a mass liberation movement there is no room for divisions or personal ambitions. The goal is one, freedom for all …*

At the time there existed a statutory body, known as the Native Representative Council. It had been in existence since 1936. Amongst other duties this council was required to advise the government on proposed legislation affecting the rights of Africans. Although the African National Congress had initially been opposed to the legislative enactment which created this council, it subsequently decided to give the Council a trial, with the result that a number of leading African National Congress members, for example, Z K Matthews and A J Luthuli, served as members of the council from time to time. During the 1946 miners' strike on the Rand, a deadlock ensued between the council and the government of the day as a result of which Dr Xuma (President-General of the African National Congress) called an emergency conference of the organisation. This conference was held at Bloemfontein in 1946. The general consensus of opinion at the Conference was that the Native Representative Council could no longer be looked upon to satisfy the needs of the people and that the African National Congress should build itself up to emerge as a stronger political party to safeguard and further the rights of the people.

The learned Judge then quoted from a portion of the evidence of Professor Matthews and from the evidence of Chief Luthuli. (Here I may say that before Chief Luthuli became President of the ANC, he was recognised as chief in an area known as Groutville in Natal. He was told by the Secretary for Native Affairs that if he continued his membership of the ANC he would not be recognised as a chief.

He elected to retain his membership of the ANC, and as is well known was awarded the Nobel Peace Prize.)

It was accepted by the court that the ANC had no secret policy. On the policy of the ANC, Judge Rumpff said in his 'Reasons for Judgment':

> In its judgment of the 29th of March the court held that the prosecution had failed to prove that it was the policy of the African National Congress to overthrow the state by violence. This alleged policy of the African National Congress was the cornerstone of the case for the prosecution and failure to prove such a policy of violence on the part of that organisation inevitably meant a collapse of the whole case. The court arrived at its decision after the prosecution had addressed it on all the issues and after the defence had made general submissions on the policy of the African National Congress and on the issue of Communism. The court made no findings of fact on the policy of the organisations other than the African National Congress, or on the positions of the individual accused, and consequently those issues will not be considered in the reasons that follow. In view of the court's finding that the prosecution failed to prove a policy of violence, it was not necessary to decide whether the case of violence as argued by the prosecution was the case set out in the indictment. As indicated above, the prosecution approached the evidence on the basis that although the African National Congress purported to have a policy of non-violence this policy should be compared with what it published and taught and with the manner in which it conducted its campaigns. In dealing with the meaning of word 'policy' in this context the defence quoted the constitution of the African National Congress, which provided that the national conference should be the supreme body of Congress and should determine its general policy and programme; the defence contended that the court, in enquiring whether the allegation, that 'it was the policy of the African National Congress to overthrow the state by violence', had been proved, was confined to an enquiry whether the constitution had been

amended to that effect. In support of this contention, *dicta* in the cases of Wilkens *v* Brebner and others (1935 AD 175) and Kahn *v* Louw (NO 1951 S.A.(2) 194), were cited. In the former case, Chief Justice Wessels said (at p183): 'When we consider that we are dealing with the constitution of a political party it seems clear from the constitution that the individual member has abdicated to various committees and to Congress his individual right of determining what ought and what ought not to be done to further the political programme of the party. He has left it to the yearly Congress to say what the party thinks the political conditions of the country require the party to do'. The defence accordingly argued that when the prosecution bases its case on the policy of any organisation it is not enough to establish the policy of a number of individuals no matter how many there may be, or how influential they may be, in the councils, of the organisation. The policy of the African National Congress can only be proved, so it was argued, by showing the constitution and either a duly passed amendment of the Constitution or by the concurrence of all the members or a majority of members. As the members are bound only by the terms to which they have agreed the terms can only be varied by consent of all the parties to the agreement. Kahn's case, *supra*, and mere silence on the part of members, cannot amount to consent to an unconstitutional alteration. The prosecution submitted that where one is concerned with a political organisation which seeks to impose its demands by the use of illegal or unconstitutional methods, different considerations applied. In such a case the real policy of the organisation is best gleaned from utterances of its leaders, its publications and propaganda. It would be unrealistic to turn to its constitution in an endeavour to ascertain its true policy and, if it is a treasonable policy, to expect any mention thereof to be made in its constitution. I do not think that the meaning of the word policy raises any real difficulty. The policy of a political organisation or party is always a question of fact. One obviously looks to the constitution first, if there be one, with its amendments. One looks at resolutions taken at conferences, at declarations of responsible leaders and at any other relevant fact. If responsible leaders or publications issued by the party regularly, or over a lengthy period of time, proclaim or announce a certain policy, directly or indirectly, and the Annual Conference or General Meetings of the Party confirm such policy, either expressly or tacitly, the policy so proclaimed will be held to be the policy of the party. In order to draw a comparison between the professed policy of the African National Congress and its conduct, it is necessary to consider briefly what the organisation claimed its policy to be. In 1946 it formally decided that its objects would be the realisation of the demands contained in a document called *Africans' Claims*. In essence this document demands a general franchise and the removal of every form of discrimination based on race or colour. In 1949 a programme of action was adopted which, *inter alia,* described the methods or 'weapons' to be employed to achieve its objects as being 'immediate and active boycott, strike, civil disobedience, non-co-operation and such means as may bring about the accomplishment and realisation of our aspirations.' According to the defence evidence the African National Congress took up the attitude that it was compelled to use these methods because petitions and protests had proved ineffective. The evidence also disclosed that the African National Congress, in applying those methods, did not exclude the possibility of laws being breached and envisaged the possibility of the state using force to maintain law and order. Neither the constitution of the African National Congress (Exh MWS 34, rec p11426, Sched No), which contained in broad outlines the objects of the organisation set out above, nor *Africans' Claims* nor the 'Programme of Action' makes any reference to violent means or methods, and the evidence showed that on many occasions, at conferences and in declarations by leaders and at meetings it was stated that the African National Congress was a non-violent organisation.

Judge Rumpff pointed out that the contents of the documents put before the court could not be disputed, nor could the speeches recorded by competent shorthand writers or on a tape recorder be challenged. With regard to the speeches recorded by members of the police in ordinary handwriting, the learned judge disregarded them in no uncertain terms. He also made an important point: that although the court was referred to a considerable number of speeches made over the period of the indictment, the actual number was extremely small compared to the total number of speeches which, according to the evidence, must have been made over this period throughout the country. According to the evidence, about 15 000 meetings had been called by the various branches of the ANC over the period in question, and all the prosecution had done was to lead evidence of what was alleged to have been said by some speakers at about 225 meetings called under the auspices of the ANC. At 85 meetings, of a total of 149 meetings relied on by the prosecution, it was suggested that something had been said from which violence could be inferred. Judge Rumpff – in agreement with the conclusions arrived at by Judges Kennedy and Bekker – came to the conclusion that the proposition that the ANC had a policy to overthrow the state by violence, relying on the speeches alone, was without substance.

Nor did the Crown derive any assistance from the documentation that reflected the policy of the ANC nor its allegation that the ANC's policy was to overthrow the state by violence. It will be recalled that Pirow, in his opening address, had stated that the conspiracy upon which the Crown relied had had its origin in the so-called liberatory movement. This was alleged to be an international Communist inspired and supported movement, pledged to overthrow by violence all governments in non-Communist countries where sections of the population did not have equal political and economic rights. It was also alleged that in South Africa this liberatory movement sought to obtain its objects by stirring up trouble in disputes of national and local importance. This matter was dealt with by Judge Rumpff as follows:

> At the outset it must be stated that no direct evidence was led by the prosecution of the existence of an international liberatory movement. The evidence did disclose that the African National Congress considered itself part of the liberatory movement in South Africa, that it accepted that lib-

> eratory movements existed in other countries and that it had expressed solidarity with such movements. Professor Murray, who gave expert evidence on Communism for the prosecution, stated that he knew of no such 'international' movement. Whilst he agreed that such a movement might be regarded, according to the tenets of Communism, as an international phenomenon, the 'liberation' (and not 'liberatory') movements were separate and not part of any one movement. In the result, and apart from defence evidence to the contrary, there was no proof of the existence of such an 'international' movement in which it could be said the present conspiracy had its origin. Whilst therefore it was common cause that a liberatory movement existed in this country, as also in other countries, the prosecution failed to prove that it formed any part of an 'international' organisation, possessing the attributes contended for by the prosecution.

As the learned Judge correctly pointed out:

> The importance of this feature lay in the fact that the court would have to look elsewhere for the origin of the alleged conspiracy to overthrow the state by violence. If, notwithstanding the fact that its origin could not be said to be international, the prosecution had proved independently that there was a conspiracy to overthrow the state by violence, the shortcoming might have been of course, of no consequence.

The Crown thus failed entirely to prove 'a conspiracy to overthrow the state by violence.'

To revert for a moment to the question of speeches in which it was alleged that the audience was being incited to use violence against the state, Sydney Kentridge, in an argument referred to by Judge Bekker with approval, stated that 'insofar as political language is concerned – used either in public documents or from public platforms – courts have been slow to infer that catastrophic results would follow from strong political language.' Kentridge had argued 'that the courts have been careful in the past not to curtail the right to express unpopular political views even when expressed in strong language and furthermore that the courts have always made due allowance for emotional and metaphorical language.' The authorities cited by Kentridge fully supported his contention. They were Rex *v* Roux (1936 AD 270), Pienaar *v* Argus Printing and Publishing Company (1956 (4) SA 310), and Rex *v* Bunting (1916 TPD 578) – in which Judge Wessels said:[86]

> we must not judge of an article of this kind ('political') by its possible effect on a few super-sensitive individuals. We must ask ourselves what effect it is calculated to produce on the man with a normal mind and normal human experience.

It can be observed, from the judgment given on 29 March 1961 acquitting the accused, that there was a change in the attitude adopted by the prosecution – or rather, a change of approach by the prosecution. It became abundantly clear from the documentation and the oral evidence given – by persons such as, for instance, Chief Luthuli, Professor Matthews and Dr Conco – that there had been a total failure to prove that the ANC and/or its allies intended to overthrow the state by violence. As a result of questions put by the court after all the evidence had been heard, the prosecution stated that on the evidence its case was that the ANC intended to organise the masses against the state, and that it would make its demands through the process of campaigns, stay-at-homes and strikes; and if these demands were not acceded to, and if the circumstances were favourable (in the sense that the masses were sufficiently politically conscious), it would organise a nationwide strike that would be the final clash between the people and the state; that the African National Congress expected violence from the state to suppress the attack against it and that the African National Congress intended at that stage actively to retaliate.

Specifically with regard to the campaign against the removal from the Western Areas, the judgment reads:

> The prosecution also stated that in regard to the removal from the Western Areas its case was that the African National Congress was reckless in regard to whether vio-

> lence ensued or not and that as regards the freedom volunteers the case against them was not that they were expected to commit violence during the period of the indictment but in the ultimate and when the order would be given to be violent.

The defence submitted that the case presented by the prosecution, as set out in the paragraphs that I have quoted from the judgment, was not the case which the accused were called upon to meet. It was never part of the indictment nor in any of the particulars to the indictment or indeed in the so called 'Summary of Facts'. What in effect the Crown was doing was arguing the case which is rightly referred to in the judgment as 'contingent retaliation'. The failure of the Crown to prove the case set out in the indictment is stated by the court in strong words.[87] As to the case of 'contingent retaliation' as argued by the Crown, the court rejected this argument not merely on grounds that it was not the case set out in the indictment, but also – as I read the judgment – because there was insufficient evidence to find that the ANC had adopted a plan which revealed 'a general expectation of violence by the state and an intention to use the masses in retaliation'.[88]

It will be recalled that according to the second indictment in paragraph 4 (b) (iv), reference is made to the campaign against the Bantu Education Act. In their book, *From Protest to Challenge,* Karis and Carter state that the Bantu Education Act was a measure that potentially had a more profound and far-reaching impact than any other measure passed by the National government.[89] The then Minister of Native Affairs, Dr Verwoerd (often referred to as the arch apostle of apartheid), in moving that the Bantu Education Bill be read a second time, said: 'I want to add – and this is very important – that their [ie, Bantu] education should not clash with government policy',[90] and again on the same topic: 'it is therefore necessary for Native education to be controlled in such a way that it should be in accord with the policy of the state'.[91] He emphasised that:

> good racial relations could not exist when education was given under the control of people who created wrong expectations among the Bantu. ... Education must train

> and teach people in accordance with their opportunities in life. In terms of the government plan for South Africa there is no place for the Bantu in the European community above the level of certain forms of labour. Within their own areas, however, all doors are open. … I just want to remind honourable members that if the Native in South Africa today, in any kind of school in existence, is being taught to expect that he will live his adult life under a policy of equal rights, he is making a big mistake.

This speech of Dr Verwoerd is often referred to as one in which he condemned Africans, in areas outside their 'own areas', to being employed as 'hewers of wood and drawers of water'. In her study, Muriel Horrell quotes W A Maree, subsequently in charge of Bantu education, on the subject of Bantu Education as saying in 1959 that 'non-Whites must not gain a fallacious impression that academic training would remove discrimination in South Africa.[92] Ms Horrell, referring to certain aspects of the Bantu Education Act (No 47 of 1953, and amendments as passed in 1954, 1956, 1959 and 1961), observes that the Act and its amendments deal only with the government's decisions on the broad outlines of the new system of Bantu Education, it being left to the responsible minister to make regulations covering all other matters. The Acts provided for the transfer of the control of Bantu education, including teacher training, from the provincial administration to the central government. There were to be three types of schools: Bantu community schools, established or maintained by Bantu authorities or tribes or communities, which in approved cases might be subsidised by the state. Other state-aided schools (including mission schools) were provided for. It was illegal to conduct unregistered schools and registration was left to the discretion of the minister, who might impose conditions on individual schools. The minister could also cancel registration under certain circumstances. Teachers would fall under the control of the person or body vested with the control of the school. Generally, however, the minister was given extremely wide powers to make regulations covering control of the schools, conditions of service of teachers, syllabuses, media of instruction, school funds, and many other matters. With regard to mission schools, Dr Verwoerd said in the House of Assembly on 3

June 1964: 'If there is a church which is prepared to maintain schools entirely at its expense, then it is their affair. They have to be registered. For that purpose a church can train its own teachers but also entirely at its own expense. Or if it wants to use some of the teachers trained in our normal colleges it can do so. We, on the other hand, shall not necessarily employ persons who have been trained at such private schools'.[93]

The three Dutch Reformed Churches were in general agreement with the government's policy, but all the other major churches and missionary schools were opposed to the theory underlying the Bantu Education Act. Many of them decided – most reluctantly, however – that they had no option but to lease or sell their educational institutions to the government, since the result of their refusal would be to throw teachers out of employment and deprive large numbers of children of the opportunity of any kind of instruction. Some of these institutions with long and proud records were thus handed over, but were closed later by the Department because they were situated in areas declared 'white' under the Group Areas Act.

Adams College in Natal, which was run by the American Board Mission, was closed because the Department refused to register it. Insofar as the Anglican Church was concerned the dioceses were left free to decide for themselves; some of the controlling authorities decided to close the schools rather than hand them over. The nursery school teachers' training college in Sophiatown, run by the Anglican Church, had to close because registration was refused. No alternative training facilities for such teachers were provided until some 11 years later. The Roman Catholics, however, decided to maintain as many of their schools as possible as private institutions. During 1955 the sum of R1,5 m was raised and further donations were received later. In addition, African communities helped to pay the salaries of teachers. However, a number of those schools had to close because they were in 'white' areas or through lack of money, but, after long delays, the Department registered others on condition that no tuition fees were charged and the schools were subject to departmental inspection. The Department's curriculum had to be followed for all subjects except religious doctrine, and non-Roman Catholic pupils had to be taught according to the Department's syllabus for religious instruction.[94]

The results of these deplorable Bantu Education Acts were regrettably all too apparent. They resulted in thousands of African children being denied any proper education. The subsidies given for Bantu education were minimal. The facilities afforded by the government to these Bantu schools were virtually insignificant, certainly by comparison with the aid and facilities given to 'white' schools and to the pupils of those schools.

One of the obvious results of this miserable and disgraceful legislation has been to create a body of young African people who are not merely unemployed, but are unemployable by reason of the fact that they did not have a proper education. Instead of having an untrained force of workers we might have had a skilled force with benefits not only for themselves, but for the country as a whole.

In one of the documents handed in by the Crown there is an address given on 26 June 1954 by Professor Z K Matthews, President of the ANC in the Cape Province, which in my opinion is a fair statement of the situation of the African in South Africa at that time. In this document, Professor Matthews speaks of the African people like all other people claiming the right of self-determination.[95]

A portion of the evidence given by Professor Matthews when he was called as a witness for the defence is quoted in his judgment by Judge Bekker, in a passage referring to both Professor Matthews and Chief Luthuli. In having dealt with the policy of the ANC up to 1948 (prior to the change of government), Judge Bekker talks of the rights of the programme of action adopted by the ANC as a result of the change of government. The fact that this policy changed subsequent to the period of the treason trial is, in my opinion, explicable on the basis that – in the light of the judgment of the special court, and particularly having regard to evidence given by the defence witnesses, none of which was rejected by the court – one might have expected the government of the day to agree to attempt to reach some *modus vivendi* with the African people. Instead of this being the case all that happened was that there were further repressive measures against the Africans.

One often wonders what the economy of the country would have been like if it had not been for sanctions brought about because of the disapproval of the rest of the world (and I refer in particular to the western world) of the policy of apartheid, which was rightly regarded by the civilised world as being untenable and in its application inhumane and in many respects barbaric.

I have dealt with the campaign conducted by the ANC against the Native Resettlement Act (the Western Areas campaign), and with the Bantu Education Act. It remains for me to deal with the curiously named Native (Abolition of Passes and Co-ordination of Documents) Act (No 67 of 1952).

Anyone reading the name of that Act would think it concerned abolishing the necessity for Africans or Natives to carry passes. Actually all it did was to compel them to carry 'reference books' instead of 'passes'. But – what is more – whereas it had been held by the courts that the laws that compelled Natives to carry passes were designed to affect males only, this new piece of legislation compelled African women to carry these reference books. This legislation, compelling them to carry passes or reference books, was one of the most hateful and disgraceful pieces of legislation directed against the Blacks. The application of the so-called 'pass laws' are a constant example of man's inhumanity to man. The police, whose duty it was to enforce these laws and other inequitable legislation, came to be regarded as enemies of those whom they were supposed to protect and this perception, regrettably, prevails to this day. (It should be noted that the sadism and apparent enjoyment by many members of the police force which was displayed in enforcing those laws, was a sorry state of affairs.) The number of Africans jailed for failing to have a pass with them on their person entitling them to work in a particular area, is incalculable.

I have in an earlier chapter referred to the iniquitous farm labour system that had been introduced. In addition, it was quite common practice for the police to gain entry to a house legally occupied by a Black family in a township and – if the father of the family could not produce his pass or reference book – to arrest him in front of his children and march him off to a police station.

It is thus not difficult to understand why a campaign against this legislation was conducted – peacefully, not violently, as alleged by the prosecution. These were, by any standards, simply unjust laws. There was a famous march from Johannesburg to Pretoria of African women to hand in a protest at the Union Buildings, the seat of government, against the application of the pass laws to women, but like other protests, to no avail. A certificate had been issued by the African National Congress to women who burnt passes in demonstration against the pass laws. It read:

> Award of Merit. This award is conferred upon [*Name*] in the name of the oppressed people of South Africa for outstanding service given in a spirit of selflessness and courage in resisting oppression on the occasion of the Anti-Pass Campaign, 1958 pass burning. By this service the day of liberation from oppression has been brought closer. Signed A J Luthuli, President-General, D Nokwe, Secretary-General.

Trengove cross-examined Chief Luthuli at the treason trial on the question of the burning of passes.[96] Trengove put it to Chief Luthuli that incendiarism was regarded as a type of pressure one could bring to bear on the public or the government to change its policies. Luthuli responded that he came to a different proposition: that people ought to be free, and not have to carry a pass; and that, 'in order to demonstrate that, I must subject myself to whatever the law might do to me, and I just throw away my pass. That is all there is to it. In fact I am exerting pressure on no one, I am merely saying now as evidence of the fact that I hate a pass, I get rid of it.'

About the 'Award of Merit', Chief Luthuli commented that:

> at the time women throughout the country were agitating greatly and we supported them, as African National Congress, against passes. Now some of the women in that struggle voluntarily, without any instructions from us, burnt their passes, and I wouldn't take that really as an isolated instance – as an individual or a group burning a pass. Mind you, I think I must make it quite clear that insofar as the principle is concerned I am not against it. It was merely a question of saying well, if you do burn a pass, it must be furthering the struggle and I would interpret this as having been help in furthering the struggle, insofar as the pass is concerned.

Concerning the principal crown witness, Professor Murray, he gave evidence at some length and I cross-examined him for many days. In fact my cross-examination of him was the longest I have ever done in the whole of my career at the Bar.

His evidence as to principles of Communism, or perhaps one should use the term Marxism-Leninism, was not challenged by us. It was correct. What we did challenge, however, was his – at first – quite unequivocal statement that certain remarks made in speeches, or in documents found in the possession of the accused or their alleged co-conspirators, were 'in line with Communism': for example, a reference to the South African government as being a 'fascist' government was said to be 'in line with Communism'. Similarly, Murray had said that certain phrases popularly used, or tactics popularly adopted, by persons far removed from Communism were 'in line with Communism'. Indeed, some cases bordered on the ridiculous. The term 'united front' used by ANC speakers or found in some of the documents which had been in the possession of the ANC, the accused, or its co-conspirators, was regarded by Prof Murray as being 'in line with Communism'. He had some difficulty in maintaining that this was any evidence of the use of a Communist phrase when he was confronted with the fact the term 'united front' was used by Mr J G N Strauss, then leader of the United Party, in a speech made in Bloemfontein, and also in a speech made by the famous Group Captain Malan, (generally known as 'Sailor' Malan), who had stood as a United Party candidate in an election.

As a further example, Luthuli in one of his speeches had suggested that Congress should establish closer co-operation between itself and trade union leaders and organisations. This was said by Murray as being 'in line with Communism.' When it was pointed out to him that, through the activities of the late Dr Albert Hertzog, the National Party had by secret means obtained control of the white Mineworkers' Union, he answered that it was not a matter of the policy of the National Party. Being pressed on the point, by suggesting to him that the National Party had tried in this way to influence the membership of the Mineworkers' Union into its ranks, he finally admitted that possibly that was the purpose of the policy.

Another example was given in Murray's suggestion that a trade unionist addressing a meeting or starting a letter addressed to a fellow trade unionist using the word 'comrade' was 'in line with Communism'. We had to demonstrate to him that many of the things that he claimed were 'in line with Communism' were contained in his own writings – and he was certainly not a Communist.

A comment with regard to fascists and fascism. Originally the words derive of course from the movement started by Mussolini in Italy. However, by the time the treason trial took place, and for many years before that, the term fascist or fascism had become virtually a term of abuse. Murray was referred to examples of the word as used by people like Winston Churchill, President Roosevelt, eminent non-Communist academics, and innumerable non-Communist authors.

After many days of cross-examination, Murray made a final admission – really dragged out of him – that particular statements or phrases that he had found to be 'in line with Communism' could just as well have been non-Communist in origin.

During my cross-examination of Murray on a document in which Luthuli had expressed high regard for the late J H Hofmeyr, I asked him whether 'the ordinary person reading that document might believe that Mr Luthuli was expressing his high regard for the late Mr J H Hofmeyr?'

MURRAY: Yes.
MAISELS: Who was he?
MURRAY: Minister of Finance.
MAISELS: Former Vice Prime Minister?
MURRAY: Yes.
MAISELS: One of the leaders of the United Party?
MURRAY: Yes.
MAISELS: A great liberal?
MURRAY: Yes.
MAISELS: A Communist?
MURRAY: No.
MAISELS: Now wouldn't you regard it as significant that this man regrets the fact that white South Africans didn't honour a man like Mr Hofmeyr, and regrets the decline of liberalism? Do you regard that as some evidence of anti-Communism or non-Communism, to put it at its

lowest?

MURRAY: Not finally – necessarily. I would give it most value as being the honest expression of appreciation of liberalism, but I can see a Communist doing the same – a moderate Communist doing the same.'

At the end of the day Professor Murray's evidence turned out to be favourable to the accused. I refer particularly to the question of the 'Freedom Charter'. This was, in the early stage of the case, regarded by the prosecution as clear evidence of the intention of the ANC and its allies to form a Communist state. Murray admitted that this could not be said to be the case. As was said by Judge Rumpff in his judgment, dealing with the evidence of Professor Murray:

> I think that it is correct to state that on [Professor Murray's] evidence, Communism must be considered as part of a spectrum of belief. This spectrum extends from the most moderate forms of socialism, through extreme forms thereof, to Communism. Somewhere in this spectrum there is a dividing line between Communism and an extreme form of socialism but which falls short of Communism. The evidence of Professor Murray indicates that this line should be ascertained by a consideration of whether or not the idea of the dictatorship of the proletariat, the rejection of reformism and the inevitability of the violent revolution have been accepted.
>
> These must be considered as fundamental principles of Communism. If a party accepts these principles, then, on the spectrum, it has crossed the dividing line and is a Communist party. If it has not accepted these principles it may be an extreme left wing party ('left' in the sense of occupying a position on the spectrum of socialism), but not a Communist party.
>
> In view of the fact that Communism refers to itself as socialism the term 'bourgeois socialism' was at times used in this case to indicate a form of socialism which falls short of Communism. In the light of Professor Murray's evidence, and having regard to the nature of the charge on the issue of Communism, it was not sufficient for the prosecu-

> tion to prove that the African National Congress, or the Congress Alliance, had propagated ideas which corresponded with Communist ideas, or had applied an analysis to situations which was also a Communist analysis.

None of the judges made reference to words or phrases claimed by Professor Murray to be 'in line with Communism' – such as, for example, references to imperialism, fascism, and co-operation with trade unions. I think it is of some significance that none of the judges in his full 'Reasons for Judgment' made any reference to such words.

On 10 March 1960 the Crown closed its case and we opened our case a few days later. We called as our first witness, Dr W Conco, then Deputy President of the ANC.

Our next witness was Chief Luthuli, named as a co-conspirator and one of those arrested in 1956. He endured the whole of the preparatory examination, but although he was then President of the ANC, he was not indicted under the second indictment. Chief Luthuli's evidence was being led when 'Sharpeville' occurred.

The ANC had nothing to do with the events at the Sharpeville Police Station on 21 March 1960. In fact it had opposed the steps which the PAC, under the leadership of R M Sobukwe, had organised. The PAC had come into being in 1954 in opposition to the ANC's apparently increasingly closer ties with Indians and Whites. This opposition found expression in 1954 particularly among members of the ANC Youth League in Orlando, and it was from a circle of nationalist or 'Africanist' youth leaders under a schoolteacher named Leballo that the PAC was formed five years later. Robert Sobukwe – who had been a high school teacher at Standerton after he had graduated from Fort Hare in 1949 – became involved not long afterwards, when he took up a post as a language instructor at the University of the Witwatersrand.[97] (I never met or saw Mr Sobukwe, although I appeared on his behalf in the Appellate Division in the early 1970s).

Sharpeville occurred in the course of a campaign against the carrying of passes, intended by the PAC to be non-violent. The ANC (although opposed to the pass laws) did not wish to take part in this particular campaign because it felt that it had not been properly prepared and had no reasonable prospects of success.

Contrary to the expectations of PAC leaders, its call to hand in passes met with negligible support in Johannesburg, Alexandra and other parts of the country. Sobukwe, Leballo and other PAC leaders presented themselves for arrest at the Orlando Police Station. They were followed by some 150 volunteers. Nothing happened. In Durban, Port Elizabeth and East London, no demonstrations took place.

However, around Vereeniging, there had been a great deal of organisation by PAC militants. At Vanderbijl Park, several thousand protesters gathered at the police station and refused to disperse although the police threw teargas at them and aircraft dived at them. Some protesters threw stones, and police fired at them, killing two men. A police baton charge scattered the crowd. At Evaton, a short distance from Sharpeville, several hundred men presented themselves for arrest without passes, but police refused to imprison them – apparently on the basis that jail facilities were inadequate.

At Sharpeville, an industrial complex around Vereeniging, there was a large demonstration. Matters appeared to be getting out of control. There are, of course, conflicting accounts of what took place and of the numbers protesting against the carrying of passes. The size of the crowd was said to be between 3 000 and 10 000. (Police witnesses testified at a subsequent enquiry that the size of the crowd was about 20 000. The police maintained also that the crowd's mood was hostile and aggressive. Witnesses sympathetic towards the demonstrators stated that the crowd was amiable, well-mannered, and not at all aggressive.) The size of the crowd and the threats apparently shouted by individuals in the crowd, combined with the natural anxiety of the police – who were surrounded and outnumbered by people they regarded as enemies – brought police nerves, after several hours, to snapping point. Apparently no order was given to shoot nor were any warning shots fired, but in a moment of panic a line of policemen opened fire on the crowd and continued to fire for perhaps some 30 seconds.

In the event, 67 Africans were shot dead – a great majority of them hit in the back as they ran – and 186 others were wounded, including 40 women and 80 children. As Karis and Carter state,[98] if police had not shot into the crowd on that day, events might have marked just one more abortive campaign in the history of African protest.

Naturally the shooting at Sharpeville was widely publicised and the South African government was faced with a political crisis of unprecedented magnitude. Efforts by Dr Verwoerd, the Prime Minister, and other National Party leaders, to downplay the incident, proved futile. The United Nations Security Council passed a resolution banning the government for the shootings and called upon it 'to initiate measures aimed at bringing about racial harmony based on equality.' The United States voted for this resolution, which was carried 9-0, but with Britain and France abstaining. As I write this, over more than 30 years after Sharpeville, this day is still commemorated by the Africans.

The immediate result of Sharpeville was that a state of emergency was declared on 30 March 1960, and – with the exception of Wilton Mkwayi, who disappeared and was never seen again – all the accused in the treason trial then in progress were arrested: some in dawn raids, and most outside court. (Arrests were not confined by any means to those then being tried – hundreds of people in all parts of South Africa were arrested and detained without trial. Amongst others, members of the Liberal Party, and others in no way connected with the treason trial or with any alleged treasonable acts – or even breaches of the many laws then in operation – were detained without trial.)

The accused were held in jail for five months – throughout the emergency period – and numerous people were placed under restriction of movement. Professor Matthews was one of those in detention. Although he was not – at the time of the trial under the second indictment – one of the 30, he was liable to be tried later, as he had initially been committed for trial and indicted. Chief Luthuli, too, when called to give evidence, was confined by a restriction placed on him to an area in Natal, and special permission had to be obtained in order to enable him to give evidence.

A description of the conditions under which people were detained is to be found in Helen Joseph's *If This Be Treason*. It makes sorry reading.[99] In his *Guide to the Microfilm Record of the Treason Trial*, Dr Karis wrote of this period of imprisonment:

> Nokwe and others among the accused continued to exam-

> ine witnesses. The accused marked time by examining one White, one Indian, and one Coloured witness regarding conditions in South Africa and avoiding testimony on the ANC's policy. Many questions were asked by Mr Justice Rumpff, the presiding judge.[100]

We took the attitude that the government, by its statements in support of a state of emergency, had made a judgment on the case. We raised questions about the position of witnesses whose testimony might lead to judicial or administrative proceedings against them, and we queried the propriety of continuing with the trial.

Our application for a postponement of the trial was opposed by the prosecution, but the court decided to adjourn from the day we made the application on 31 March 1960 until 26 April. In so ruling, Judge Rumpff said:

> it is obvious to us that any witnesses called by the defence may reasonably apprehend that if he is called to give evidence, his evidence may result in certain provisions of the regulations being applied to him.

A number of official assurances were then given by cabinet ministers. We appeared on 26 April and stated that we were prepared to continue, but mentioned the difficulties of conducting our case during a state of emergency, not knowing where persons are: whether they have been detained, are out of the country or what has happened; and the virtual impossibility of consulting with our clients in the presence of members of the police 'special branch'. The court, however, decided that the trial should recommence, which it did, on 26 April 1960.

The accused, Nokwe being their spokesman, decided that our mandate to appear on their behalf was cancelled and that they would conduct their own defence – which they did until August. During the period when the accused conducted their own defence, Luthuli and other witnesses gave evidence. A large portion of Luthuli's evidence was given during the time when the accused were undefended. Luthuli was then a very sick man. He gave evidence for 16 days, but the court sat for only two hours on each day out of consideration for Luthuli's health.

After Luthuli had finished his evidence, Mrs Helen Joseph was called by Nokwe and she was examined-in-chief by other accused persons Adams, Kathrada, Leon Levy, Lollan, Mrs Lilian Ngoyi, Sibande, Tyiki and five others. She was then cross-examined by the prosecution for a number of days and questioned at length by Judge Rumpff.

After Mrs Joseph's evidence was finished, one Ismail Ahmed Cachalia, Secretary of the Transvaal Indian Congress before he was banned in 1954 (now special adviser to President Mandela), was called to give evidence. I happened to be in Pretoria that day on another matter and decided to have a look at what was happening in the synagogue where the trial was in progress. I sat in the gallery and was present when Cachalia was called. Kathrada told the court that it would be more comfortable if he gave his evidence in Gujerati. Judge Rumpff saw right through this ploy. Cachalia's English was as good as that of anybody in the court and he duly gave his evidence in English.

After Cachalia had been cross-examined, others of the accused gave evidence. Lollan's evidence concluded at the end of July. The accused then informed the court, through Nokwe, that they intended asking the counsel for the defence to return to the case, and – since counsel would not be available until 1 August – applied for an adjournment until that date. The court decided to adjourn until 18 July and eventually adjourned again from that day until 26 July, when certain members of the defence team returned. After it was announced at the end of July that the regulations imposing the state of emergency would be lifted on 31 August, all those forming the counsel for the defence returned to court and our clients through the month of August, depending on what other commitments we had previously undertaken.

I cannot speak at first hand on what occurred during the time when the accused were not defended by counsel. It would be wrong for me not to say that during the whole of the period and during all the proceedings at which I was present, the members of the court went out of their way to ensure that there was a fair and proper trial. All the members of the court displayed what I would venture, with respect, to call considerable patience and anxiety to ensure that as far as was in their power, the trial should be conducted in a manner which brought well deserved recognition of their impartiality and their desire to do justice.

However, while counsel were absent from the proceedings – essentially the period May-July – the conduct of the court, by the very fact that so many experienced lawyers were missing, took on a different tone. It was during this hiatus that events took place that, to my mind, provided a key turning point in the trial and possibly assisted the final 'not guilty' verdicts for all the accused.

Michael Parkington, with his extraordinary tactical skills, began to ring the changes so that, aside from the three key witnesses, Luthuli, Mandela and Professor Matthews, the accused would call the less informed members of their group to give evidence for the defence and many of them would then take turns in leading evidence from each of the accused. This was a huge waste of the court's time and led to great frustration on the part of the prosecution, as recorded by Professor Karis (*see* p202).

On our return to the defence case in August the accused complained to us that Mrs Joseph had been unfairly questioned by Judge Rumpff . During the course of Helen Joseph's testimony (she was called to the stand on 2 June 1960), Judge Rumpff took a rather inquisitorial view of the proceedings and began to adopt an active role in questioning her and others. Moreover, it appears that the prosecution moved to a new tack in the Crown's case (the 'contingent retaliation' mentioned earlier), and that, regrettably, the support for the prosecution's new position appeared to have been constructed through Rumpff's own questioning of the accused, something that is quite outside any judge's mandate.

Essentially, the prosecution began to suggest that there was a charge in the alternative, namely that the inevitable consequence of mass action and civil disobedience would be violence, arising from the government's intransigent attitude towards full rights of citizenship for South Africa's people of colour; and, further, it was understood by the leaders of the ANC and the leaders of the other extra-parliamentary groups, that violence could flow from confrontation between the police acting to curb and control such opposition and those involved in the protest.

On 19 August Bram Fischer interrupted his examination of Robert Resha to ask for a 'special entry' (a note in the court record drawing the attention of a higher court or review to an event or behaviour that one of the parties regards as abnormal), because, as he put it, 'the cumulative effect of the interventions by Judge Rumpff in the examination or cross-examination, particularly of Mrs Joseph, had created the impression in the minds of the accused that he had not approached their evidence with an open mind and consequently that they were not obtaining a fair trial.' The principles involved in our submission were:

> That the questioning of defence witnesses, including accused persons, ... constituted an irregularity in that (1) the frequency and extent of the interventions of the learned Judge hampered the defence in the presentation of its case; (2) the learned Judge's questioning appeared to constitute cross-examination of the witnesses by way of assistance to the prosecution; (3) the learned Judge appeared at times to be entering into a political debate with the witnesses; and (4) that certain of the learned Judge's questions gave the impression of constituting hostile comment on the evidence of the witnesses.

In all this, Bram specifically stated that the 'Judge's motive and object in questioning the witnesses are not raised in this application at all. The problem is whether the questions have created an impression that justice may not be done.' He quoted at length from the authorities and then gave this famous admonition to judges from Lord Denning quoting Lord Bacon:

> Lord Bacon spoke right when he said that patience and gravity of hearing is an essential part of justice, and an over-speaking Judge is no well-tuned symbol, it is no grace to a judge first to find that which he might have heard in due time from the Bar.

Bram then quoted at length from the court record, making specific reference to the interventions from the Bench in respect of the testimony of one witness, Albert Luthuli, and two of the accused, Dr Conco and Helen Joseph. He then introduced to the court a fifth reason for arguing that an irregularity had occurred:

> Your lordships will see that a considerable volume of pas-

> sages has been relied upon … these passages constituted an irregularity in that the cumulative effect of the said interventions by the learned Presiding Judge have created the impression that he has not approached the defence evidence with an open mind, and has given rise to a reasonable fear in the minds of the accused that they are not obtaining a fair trial.[101]

This fifth point complicated the argument because it moved from the more objective realm of the grounds for an irregularity as stated in points one to four to something that was more subjective ('given rise to a reasonable fear in the minds of the accused').

I won't hold up the narrative at this point to dwell on the legal argument that then engaged the Crown, the judges and the defence as to whether the various grounds cited by the defence for a special entry did, in fact constitute an irregularity demanding the attention of the court, or whether the objections of the defence should not have been preferably phrased as an application for the recusal of the presiding judge.

The consequence of the argument was that the application for a special entry was dropped and instead we applied for the recusal of the presiding judge. Judge Rumpff refused to recuse himself, saying that in his opinion the fear that the accused said they may have had – that they may not get a fair trial – was unreasonable and unfounded.

Ultimately the trial was turned in our favour by these events, which took place during our absence from the proceedings: first, Rumpff's refusal to accept a special entry or to recuse himself; and second, the possibility that a higher court, on appeal, would have paid special attention to the reasons giving rise to the defence objections and, particularly, to the part that Rumpff might have played in the construction of alternative charges through his interventions – charges not framed by the indictment. And, thirdly, this no doubt became still clearer to him once he had heard Crown argument and the commencement of our own defence argument.

After the failure to obtain a recusal, the case continued with the cross-examination of Resha and the further evidence given by other witnesses for the defence. There were frequent adjournments of this case, some largely due to the illness of Judge Kennedy.[102]

When, of course, the state of emergency ended at the end of August, further witnesses were called for the defence and cross-examined by the Crown, including important witnesses such as Mandela, Robert Resha and Professor Matthews.

I suppose it is fair to say that the three most important witnesses called for the defence were Chief Luthuli, Professor Matthews and Nelson Mandela. Luthuli, of course, was not an accused at the trial, he not having been indicted after the preparatory examination. Professor Matthews was also never tried, although indicted. Mandela, on the other hand, was in fact one of those who were tried and eventually acquitted. He was, at that time, President of the ANC in the Transvaal, and was the youngest of the three. Other important members of the ANC were on trial, and gave evidence, but though Mandela was one of the younger ones, he already stood out as a leader.

These three witnesses gave evidence on important aspects of ANC policy and in particular on the claim of the ANC that everybody should have the vote, subject to an age qualification, but irrespective of sex or of colour. There was no adverse finding by any of the judges in their reasoned judgment as to the credibility of these or indeed of any of the witnesses called by the defence.

In his evidence,[103] Luthuli confirmed the aim of the African National Congress: to secure a universal franchise, apart from a qualification as to age, so that every person would be entitled to participate in parliamentary elections. He confirmed that this was a claim on which the African National Congress was not prepared to compromise in any way. If there were negotiation with the South African government on this matter at any stage, this would be 'definitely a clear goal that we are striking for uncompromisingly'. But, explained Luthuli, should the government call negotiations and express an intention to improve wages and similar economic factors, but change nothing as far as the vote was concerned, this would not be acceptable. The ANC would not reject whatever might be done in the economic field, but the vote was a fundamental issue. Cross-examination continued:

> TRENGOVE: Mr Luthuli, negotiation was never contemplated, and you know that?

LUTHULI: It has been all along anticipated, my Lord – even at this moment, we would be very, very happy if the government would take up the attitude of saying, come let us discuss. We would be extremely happy, in fact even to discuss, even if at the end of the discussions we didn't agree.

TRENGOVE: Mr Luthuli, it is sheer hypocrisy to make a statement like that, and you know it. That was never your attitude?

LUTHULI: You may be allowed in court – I don't know what your rights are – but to call one a hypocrite, really it does hurt. And I will defend myself, my Lords, although if I recall – at the time when I was being led by counsel, reference was made to the fact that I wrote as President-General of the African National Congress a letter, in 1957 … to the Prime Minister, pleading exactly for what I am saying here now – and for me to be called a hypocrite, publicly be called a hypocrite, well counsel has the right to say so, but it does hurt one.

(I have little doubt that John Trengove, who is a friend of mine, would unhesitatingly apologise for having, in the heat of this long and wearisome trial, accused Luthuli of hypocrisy. He is a distinguished lawyer, and his distinguished son, Wim, was until recently Chairman of the General Council of the Bar of South Africa. It is interesting to note that John Trengove, since his retirement from the Court of Appeal, has given invaluable assistance to the important work of the Legal Resources Centre in Pretoria.)

Nelson Mandela, under cross-examination by Mr G G Hoexter of the prosecution,[104] confirmed that the state visualised by Congress could not be created by concessions increasing the proportions of representation of Africans, Coloured people and Asians in Parliament, instead of giving them the vote. That state could be created only if the vote were extended to all sections of the population.

In relation to the notion of a process of gradual reforms over a period of time – Mr Hoexter suggested ten or 20 years – Mandela responded that the Congress, to his knowledge, had never specifically discussed such a question. He thus stressed that the views that he gave were his own, not necessarily those of Congress.

His view was that – the demand being for universal adult franchise – Congress was prepared to exert economic pressure to attain this demand, using tactics such as defiance campaigns and stay-at-homes to compel the government to the point of negotiation. Should the government then be prepared to grant even a limited number of seats for a limited period, followed by a review of the situation, this, said Mandela, would in his view be a victory. It would be a significant step towards the attainment of universal adult suffrage for Africans. If such a process were initiated, and continued over successive periods, 'we would eventually be able to get everything that we want; we shall have our People's Democracy'. Civil disobedience could then be suspended in favour of educating Europeans to see that such changes were possible, and to bring about better racial understanding in the country. 'But, of course,' he added, 'I would not abandon the demands for the extension of the universal franchise to all Africans.' Congress expected, he said, that over a period it would realise its aspirations as a result of repeated economic pressures together with the pressure of world opinion – notwithstanding the government's attitude 'of ruling Africans with an iron hand'.

Mr Hoexter put it to Mr Mandela that the African National Congress held and propagated the view that the government *would* use violence and armed force against the Congress movement in resisting such economic pressures. When pressed to say whether the Congress alliance had discussed or considered whether white supremacy in South Africa would 'surrender that which if surrendered would mean its end', without a show of arms, Mandela replied that the Congress had considered the question from the point of view firstly of its experience – that Whites were eager to retain political power exclusively for themselves. It was also considered a realistic possibility that through exertion of economic pressure Whites would be forced – even against their will – by the numerical preponderance of non-Europeans to grant the demand for the vote. Mandela said:

> We worked on the basis that Europeans themselves – in spite of the wall of prejudice and hostility which we encountered – that they can never remain indifferent indef-

> initely to our demands, because we are hitting them in the stomach with our policy of economic pressure. It is a method which is well organised. The Europeans dare not look at it with indifference. They would have to respond to it and indeed, my Lord, they are responding to it.

Thus, Mandela's evidence shows that the ANC was prepared, at that time, to accept a gradual recognition of the rights of Africans to the franchise, and also significantly makes the point that economic pressures would compel the Whites to abandon the existing policy of white supremacy without franchise rights to people of colour.[105] I suggest it is not unfair to say that if there was any step calculated to create greater hostility among Africans against Whites, it was the deliberate exclusion of the Africans from the limited form of representation given to Coloured people and Indians through the attempts made, under the leadership of Mr P W Botha, to give certain franchise rights to Coloured people and Indians in the House of Representatives and House of Delegates (as those chambers were called), while at the same time retaining power in the hands of the Whites by the creation of the President's Council.

In his evidence,[106] Professor Z K Matthews said that the optimism of Congress that they would succeed in their goals was based upon the fact that other governments, equally relentless and determined to not to give in to popular demands, had subsequently done so. He cited India, and how, although Churchill had declared it impossible for the Indians to get their independence, they had done so within Churchill's lifetime. Under cross-examination by Sydney Kentridge (for the defence), he like Luthuli and Mandela expressed his confidence in the forms of action – economic pressures – that Congress had decided to adopt. He saw it as evidence that these methods had had some success, that there were White groups conscious of the existence of the problems, and who were 'working a change and changed outlook towards us'. Such groups included the Congress of Democrats, the Liberal Party, and the Progressive Party. Even in SABRA, a pro-apartheid organisation, there was a move indicating an awareness that things in South Africa were 'not as they ought to be' and that 'something ought to be done about it'.

When Judge Bekker asked Matthews if he thought that giving the franchise to everybody over 18 years would bring about the end of White supremacy in the country, he replied in the affirmative, saying:

> We think that even the White supremacy is not impervious to political pressure and economic pressure. The thing is that up to now it hasn't been used ... on a sufficiently wide scale, and sustained over a sufficiently long period. In other words, we feel that as the ANC, we are still a weak body, but if that we were stronger than we are now, even the White supremacists would talk. ... it is a matter of negotiation, of talking – I mean, the suggestion that you bring people to their knees is that we have the idea of wanting to dominate them and becoming the top dog. That is not the idea of the ANC.

Kentridge asked whether the leadership had not considered that it was advisable to restrain the expression of individual opinions:

MATTHEWS: No, we didn't think it was advisable to impose a kind of censorship, either of thought or of writing, on our members.

KENTRIDGE: Did you ever observe that sometimes in these journals the mode of expression was emotional?

MATTHEWS: Yes.

KENTRIDGE: Did you disapprove of that?

MATTHEWS: No, I didn't disapprove. I understood it. I can understand people writing under the conditions in which Africans do write, with feelings of resentment and a sense of humiliation, people writing from that point of view are sometimes apt to be emotional in writing, and one understands that.

KENTRIDGE: What about the young men in the Youth League, would that apply to them?

MATTHEWS: Yes. They would not be peculiar as far as youth are concerned. Youth in any group express themselves strongly and vigorously as compared with their fathers.

KENTRIDGE: When they use political expressions, let us say

in Youth League journals, do you think they were always carefully formulated?

MATTHEWS: No, I don't think so. That is now how political writers or political speakers work. They don't write as if they were writing academic theses. They let themselves go in their speeches. ... [A polemical political article or speech] is not a statute, you don't interpret a political speech the way you might interpret a statute, for example, looking at every word and trying to find out what the meaning is of that word. You get the general sense.

Matthews said, however, that it seemed to him that for the leadership to preach to the public a policy of non-violence, while it really wanted to pursue a policy of violence, would be futile; at some time the leadership would have to reveal this secret policy to their followers, with the result that they would regard the leadership as having deceived them all along, and consequently cease to support the leadership.

In the Crown's opening address, the statement was made that 'The Crown will ask the court to infer from certain evidence, for example happenings at a beerhall, Johannesburg, that the bulk of the country's non-European population is likely to respond more quickly, more irresponsibly and more violently to illegal agitation than would be the case with a group whose general standard of civilisation was higher.' In response to this, Matthews said:

> I'm a little sceptical about the use of this word civilisation being higher; I don't know in what sense the word 'higher' is used in connection with civilisation there, but my own impression would be that even the so-called more highly civilised groups, subject to the same conditions to which the Bantu are subject in this country, would I think react more violently than they do. I think the Bantu are a very patient people, a very law-abiding people. You will remember that General Smuts himself at one time referred to them as having the patience of an ass because of their very slow reaction to the conditions to which they are subjected.

Professor Matthews expressed the view that the agitation of the

African National Congress was 'not actually illegal'. If by 'illegal agitation' was meant agitation to break laws, he said, 'the Bantu would not readily do that sort of thing'. He felt that an audience might show approval of emotional speeches by giving applause, yet not react in a violent manner; and that this was, in fact, merely evidence of an emotional release of their frustrations on the part of the audience. He affirmed that Africans resented 'very much indeed' the conditions under which they lived in this country. When asked by Kentridge what form such resentment would take, if given expression, Matthews said:

> Well, there is a whole host of possible reactions to resentment, but the burden of our work in the African National Congress has been to canalise the possible reactions and to see that they are confined to what we consider to be non-violent methods.

He expressed the opinion that the African people were capable of understanding and responding to a call for non-violent methods. Yet, at the same time, the leadership of Congress had repeatedly stressed non-violence, 'because in the circumstances of this country, the temptation to do otherwise must be strong'.

In response to the Crown's allegation that 'the accused had deliberately created an explosive situation' by the time of the arrests in December 1956, Matthews said that the Constitution of the country was such that it contained within it the 'seed of dissension between the various sections of the population'. That, he said, was not a situation created by the African National Congress, but one that had existed since the state was created in 1910.

The special court, after this long trial, found that the ANC had no secret policy and that it was not a Communist body with the object of overthrowing the existing order by violence.

Subsequent to the treason trial Luthuli, as is well known, was awarded the Nobel Peace Prize in 1961. Professor Matthews became first Ambassador to the United Nations for the newly emergent state of Botswana. Chief Luthuli and Professor Matthews are no longer with us, but of course Mr Mandela was sentenced to life imprisonment in 1964 at the conclusion of the 'Rivonia trial'. As is well known, on his release from imprisonment in 1990 he became President of the now unbanned ANC, and, since April 1994, the first President of a democratic South Africa.

An analysis of the evidence, I suggest, reveals not merely the honesty of persons such as Professor Matthews, Luthuli and Mandela, but also their sagacity. One would have thought, after the acquittal of all the accused by the court, that a responsible government might really have considered it worthwhile to make an attempt to speak to and negotiate with the leadership of the ANC – having regard not merely to the outcome of the treason trial, but to the quality of the leadership of the ANC. The government of the day might have considered attempting to negotiate some suitable manner of overcoming the impasse in South Africa resulting from its policy of apartheid.

However, the government of the day did exactly the opposite. It embarked on a policy of endeavouring to maintain white supremacy in all spheres of life of the Blacks. The ANC was declared an unlawful organisation. There were restrictions on freedom, censorship, banning to remote areas, house arrests and, to crown it all, the notorious 90-Day Detention Without Trial Act, which enabled the government to detain persons without trial for this lengthy period, prohibiting access to them even by an attorney or members of their family. Detainees were kept completely *incommunicado*, states of emergency were declared from time to time, South Africa became an outcast among the nations of the world – and sanctions had such a disastrous effect on the economy of the country, that it is said that the country's economy was brought to its knees as a result of the relentless pursuit of the apartheid policy of the government, finally leading President De Klerk, in 1992, to abolish apartheid.

One must bear in mind that the failure of the government of the day – under leaders like Strijdom, Verwoerd, Vorster, P W Botha – to negotiate with Black leaders, led inevitably to 'the armed struggle' which Mandela himself and others like him were forced to undertake. The ANC formed a military wing, Umkhonto we Sizwe ('spear of the nation'), and sabotage became the order of the day. Today in this country we continue to pay the price of the oppressive policy of which I have written. This country is now almost in a state of anarchy, with murder – of Black-on-Black, Black-on-White, White-on-Black – a daily occurrence. One is entitled to wonder whether, without that succession of National Party leaders, the country would have been in its present state.

It was a week after Sharpeville that my client, David Pratt, attempted to assassinate Dr Verwoerd. He was found by the court – correctly so – to have been insane when he committed this act; but in his speech at the enquiry into his sanity, he predicted that the policy of Verwoerd would lead to disaster. Indeed, Mr Paul Sauer, then Minister of Lands and a senior member of Verwoerd's cabinet, delivered a speech shortly after Sharpeville in which he said that the 'old book' of South African history had closed at Sharpeville and that there was a need for the country 'in earnest and honestly' to reconsider its whole approach to race relations.[107] Paul Sauer's political life came to an end but we continued to have Verwoerd, Vorster and the likes of them in power.

After we had closed our case on 7 October, the Crown asked for one month's adjournment to enable it to prepare argument. This was granted and the Crown's argument began on 7 November, ending early in March 1961 – but, of course, between the commencement and end of the argument, the court's Christmas vacation took place.

As I was free to take on other work during that period, I was briefed to appear in a matter before the Water Court in Salisbury, Southern Rhodesia. During the course of that matter I saw, at his request, the Southern Rhodesian Minister of Justice. He offered me an appointment on the Southern Rhodesian Bench. I said I would have to think about it, but stated that in any event if I accepted the offer I would not be available until the treason trial had concluded. It was anticipated that our argument in the treason trial, which would commence in March, would last for some time. I remember telephoning my wife on the night the offer was made to me and she told me to accept the offer immediately. I did not then accept her advice and thought I should discuss the matter with people whose less emotional advice I would seek on the question as to whether I should accept the offer. When I came back to South Africa, among those whose advice I sought was Mr Justice Greenberg, undoubtedly one of the greatest judges before whom I had had the privilege of appearing (who had by that time retired from the Appellate Division of the Supreme Court). He thought that on the whole I should accept the appointment but said, with some prescience, that if I did not like being a judge in Rhodesia I could retire after two years. I did accept the appointment.

When the news that I had done so became public knowledge, I received a letter signed by all the accused, the contents of which, I must confess, moved me very much indeed. I had not, before I was briefed in the treason trial and learnt the true position of the non-Whites and particularly of the Blacks in this country, fully appreciated how unjust was the society in which I lived. Although it is a cardinal principle, and indeed necessary, for the advocate to maintain an entirely objective view of his client's case and not to make the client's case his own case, I must confess that I found it impossible to maintain this objective view because of the feeling that developed in me as the case went on, that this was an unjust trial and that the accused should really have filled the role of accusers. It is not necessary for me to say whom I think should have been the accused.

Chapter Thirteen

TWO CIVIL TRIALS WITH UNUSUAL FEATURES

During the period of the treason trial there were various adjournments. During one of them I was briefed to lead David Melamet, then a junior at the Pretoria Bar, in an unusual case which came before Mr Justice Williamson in the Transvaal Provincial Division.

Our clients were the executors testamentary in the estate of a person who had been a partner in a confectionery business, known as Geneva Confectionery, in Johannesburg. One of the executors was the widow of the deceased. The defendant, a Mr Boesch, had been in partnership with the deceased. Mr Boesch had wanted to extend the business but the deceased had been disinclined to embark upon this new venture. The partners thereupon agreed to dissolve their partnership upon certain terms and conditions – only one of which is relevant here. This term was that if the defendant, Boesch, should dispose of the business of the company, the shareholding of which was held equally by the deceased and the defendant, the sum of £2 500 would become payable by him to the deceased. There was, however, a proviso that if the company were to go into liquidation before 1 January 1957 on the ground that it was unable to pay its liabilities in full, and it paid creditors a dividend only in respect of their claims, the deceased's claim against Boesch would be waived *in toto*.

It had been settled at law in South Africa[108] that whoever deliberately and intentionally prevents the fulfilment of a condition upon which he would have become bound, is considered bound if it was an implied term of the contract that he should not frustrate the fulfilment of the condition.

Boesch placed the company in liquidation on the basis that it was unable to pay its debts and took up the attitude that he was no longer liable to pay the sum of £2 500. Hence our action. The case involved the reverse position of a resolutive condition being fulfilled under circumstances similar to those which would give rise to a suspensive condition being regarded as being fictionally fulfilled. We contended that the court should so find, and we were successful in our contention. There was no doubt, on the evidence, that Boesch had deliberately set about to cause the company to go into liquidation.

The headnote to the report of the case accurately reflects the finding of Judge Williamson. It reads as follows:

> If the court finds that, from the nature of a contract as a whole, a moral or legal duty has expressly or impliedly been placed on the debtor to act in a certain way, it would be *dolus* on his part deliberately to act in breach of that duty with the intention of gaining an advantage for himself: and *dolus* cannot enure for the benefit of the person guilty of it.[109]

The reason for my referring to this case is not because of the interesting legal question that was decided, but because of what occurred at the trial. It was a hot summer's afternoon, and the court in which I had to cross-examine Boesch did not have airconditioning. I had asked him only two or three questions when he fell flat on his face. I thought he had had a heart attack, and felt terrible that such a thing should have happened. However, he recovered – and went on to lose the case.

The matter was taken on appeal to the Appellate Division, but I was not available to take the appeal because of my commitments in the treason trial. My place was taken by Oscar Rathouse – a silk of undoubted standing at the Johannesburg Bar – and the appeal against the judgment of Judge Williamson was dismissed. I should add that the appeal court did not find it necessary to deal with the novel legal ground upon which we were successful before Judge Williamson, basing itself on the simple view that the condition had not been fulfilled and that the defendant had not shown that the company had been wound up because it was in reality unable to pay its debts.[110]

In another interesting case, Bill Trollip, QC, and George Colman were briefed with me on behalf of the plaintiffs. (Bill Trollip was appointed to the Transvaal Bench about the same time that I was appointed to the Southern Rhodesian Bench, and he went on to become a judge in the Appellate Division. If I may be permitted to say so, he made a valuable contribution to the law in this country. George Colman became a judge of the Transvaal Provincial Division. He, too, should have been appointed to the Appellate Division, but despite a most distinguished career on the Transvaal Bench, was never appointed to that court where, like Trollip, he would have been a tower of strength.) The defendant's counsel were Oscar Rathouse, QC, and Rex Welsh: formidable opponents indeed.

In this case, the action was brought by the plaintiffs against Daggafontein Mines Limited, a company mining for gold on the farm on which the plaintiffs had a trading site. The plaintiffs were 'concession storekeepers' – that is, they carried on a business as general dealers and eating house proprietors. Such general dealers were generally known as 'concessniks' because of the monopoly conferred upon them – by the provisions of the 'gold law' – to trade on mine property, which enabled them to overcharge the unfortunate black miners.

Under the gold law in force at the time of the action brought against Daggafontein Mines, a person carrying on mining was guilty of an offence if he was interested, either directly or indirectly, in a business whose premises were on the grounds where such mining was carried on and for which a general dealer's licence was required. The plaintiffs, who had obtained the right to trade under certain conditions stipulated by the government, complained that the defendant, the mining company, was in effect carrying on business in breach of the law and in this way causing damages to the plaintiffs in loss of custom. The defendant (like other mines) had established what were called 'clubs', not for any profit motive, but to enable the inmates of their compounds to purchase day-to-day requirements without having to leave the compound. Any profits made were to be used towards financing sporting and other entertainment activities for the inmates. The motive of the Chamber of Mines in establishing such 'clubs' was entirely laudable, namely to enable the black miners to buy goods at a reasonable price. The difficulty for the Chamber lay in the administrative problem created in the formation of 'clubs' and the explanation that this entailed to unsophisticated and illiterate people.

The law in the Transvaal, as laid down in earlier decisions of the court, was that a *bona fide* club on ground held under mining title, in disposing of articles to its members did not effect sales to such members. Such a club was, therefore, not carrying on trade or business within the meaning of the gold law Acts of 1908 and 1910. (This followed English decisions, which laid down as a general rule that in a club commodities – the stock of goods jointly owned by all the members of the club – were not 'sold' to club members, but 'distributed' to individual 'club members'.)

The importance of what is known as 'discovery' in civil trials was mentioned in the case of Central African Airways *v* Vickers Armstrong, where, it will be recalled, a document disclosed by Vickers Armstrong in accordance with the rules of court showed that a certain bolt used in the construction of the plane should have been cadmium plated. This constituted a discovery that assisted in a victory for the plaintiff.

In this case, Daggafontein Mines claimed that it had merely set up a club, and had documentation to show that employees of the mine living in the compound had actually signed applications for membership. These, of course, were disclosed in the defendant's discovery affidavit. The plaintiffs' attorney was Mr Charles Friedman of the firm Hayman Godfrey Inc of Johannesburg. Friedman thought it would be a good idea to inspect the membership forms alleged to have been signed by the 'members' of this club, and sent a professional assistant, Mr Basil Wunsh (now a judge in the Transvaal Provisional Division, and the first attorney to have been appointed to the Bench), and my son Keith, then an articled clerk in that firm, to inspect these membership forms. It seemed both to Basil and my son[111] that the thumbprints on certain of the forms were made by the same person, and they requested permission from the mine to take away a few of these forms for examination. (The reason, of course, why the forms had to be fingerprinted was that the Natives employed by the mine were wholly illiterate and were unable to sign their own names.) Their request was acceded to and a handwriting expert was called in. He found that there were different fingerprints on each one of these forms, but a further examination of a large number of other forms that we obtained from the defendant revealed the same fingerprint on them all. As is well known, no two persons have identical fingerprints. It thus formed part of our attack on the defence that no *bona fide* club had been established. In fact, in opening the case for the plaintiffs, I was able to point out that this was a unique case where, contrary to what had long been accepted, so many members of this club had identical thumbprints. When the defendant's witnesses were called it appeared that the compound manager, or his assistant, had thought that making a fingerprint on the application form was a mere formality, and that, rather than going to the trouble of getting each individual miner to make his own thumbprint on the form, it would be much easier for one of the compound manager's assistants to put his fingerprint on the form. There were some 15 000 membership 'application forms'.

EDITORS' NOTE: *Isie's son, Keith, who was present at the trial, writes: 'I shall never forget my father's cross-examination of the compound manager. The witness was tall, good-looking and (to begin with) confident. I subsequently felt a great deal of sympathy for him. After all, he had been instructed by head office to make the 15 000 black miners members of the 'club'. He had not fancied the idea of these persons parading through his office and, in order to avoid this inconvenience and to accelerate the process, he had instructed about ten* indunas *to put their fingerprints on hundreds and thousands of the application forms. He had himself thumbprinted a large number of forms. He was cross-examined for only 15 or 20 minutes, but left the witness box in a very different state to that in which he had been at the commencement of the cross-examination. He seemed physically to have shrunk about six inches. We later heard that he had that night telephoned the mine manager and asked the latter to take care of his wife and children as he intended to commit suicide. Fortunately, he was dissuaded from doing so.'*

Judge Marais held that the so-called club was not a *bona fide* club,[112] and the plaintiffs succeeded in their application for an interdict restraining the mine from continuing to operate the 'club' and also for damages which they had suffered. This case was a test case. The Chamber of Mines had apparently previously taken a decision to establish similar clubs at other mines – again with no intention to profit the mines, but only to benefit black miners. However, the clubs had the effect of causing damage to the 'concession store-keepers' and in addition, loss to the government of revenue to which it was entitled in terms of the 'concession' granted to such persons to trade on mining property.

I may mention that my friend, Oscar Rathouse, was under the impression that some employee of the mine had leaked to our side the irregular signing of the membership forms – it took a great deal of persuasion on my part to convince Oscar that our discovery of the irregularity was purely fortuitous.

EDITORS' NOTE: *This was one of many cases in which Isie appeared, in which he felt there was a great deal of justification for what 'the other side' had done. Another example occurred many years later when he was briefed to act for a mining house in the eviction of certain workers who were conducting an illegal strike. He personally did everything possible to persuade the attorneys and counsel representing the miners to use the correct channels for the purposes of voicing their dissatisfaction, and he felt sure that his clients would have accommodated them in every possible way. However, his pleas fell on deaf ears and the eviction proceeded.*

Chapter Fourteen

RHODESIA

At the time that a further offer of appointment to the Southern Rhodesian Bench was made to me, in December 1960, Southern Rhodesia was part of the Federation of the Rhodesias and Nyasaland, comprising Northern Rhodesia (now Zambia), Nyasaland (now Malawi) and Southern Rhodesia (now Zimbabwe). There were, at that time, great hopes that 'the Federation' would prove to be a success and that a society would be established where various races could live together in harmony.

By contrast the situation in South Africa was, in the opinion of Muriel and myself, worsening. B J Vorster was Minister of Justice, and it was a time when increasingly oppressive laws were being inflicted on the population. In South Africa during 1960 we experienced Sharpeville; the state of emergency from 30 March to 31 August; the detention during the state of emergency of nearly 2 000 political activists of all races; the banning of the ANC; the coming into effect of the Bantu Self Government Act (passed in 1959, but providing for the end from 1960 of the minimal African representation, by Whites, in Parliament). In addition, what I had learnt during the Treason Trial of the feelings of Black, Coloured and Indian citizens of the country who were disenfranchised, combined with all these factors, contributed to the very strong desire we felt to live in a different country.

The decision to leave the country of our birth, to leave our relatives and friends, and, for me, to give up my practice at the Bar, was not, of course, an easy one. We were obviously taking a gamble as to our future in Rhodesia. Yet I had been working very hard for some years, and the prospect of an easier life in a society such as was envisaged at that time had its attraction. The prospects of living in a country not governed by Verwoerd, Vorster and their ilk, was tempting and attractive both to my wife and me. Our two sons had already grown up and were no longer living with us, but neither of our two daughters seemed too pleased about the prospects of living in Rhodesia. Muriel and I were conscious of the fact that we would miss the company of our friends and, in my case particularly, of my colleagues at the Bar in Johannesburg. Before we left, our close friends, Willie and Gypsy Aronsohn (now both dead), gave us a farewell party at the Inanda Club, and my colleagues at the Bar gave us a lovely party at the old Carlton Hotel.

I was appointed to the Bench in Rhodesia to fill a vacancy caused by the retirement of Sir John Murray. He was one of South Africa's most distinguished judges, and had resigned from the Transvaal Bench in order to become Chief Justice of Southern Rhodesia. I need hardly add that he was knighted whilst in Rhodesia – such titles had been abolished in South Africa many years previously. I learned that I would be stationed in Salisbury (now Harare). Having from time to time, over the years, been briefed to appear there, I remembered it as a beautiful city with tree-lined suburbs where every possible beautiful shrub and flower grew in abundance.

The Rhodesian government had undertaken to provide us with accommodation, but it was very difficult to find suitable accommodation when we arrived. Sir John Clayden (as he then was) was at the time acting as Governor General of the Federation owing to the fact that he was Chief Justice and the Governor General was on leave. Luckily for us, Sir John and his wife Gwen, owing to their having to occupy the Governor General's residence whilst Sir John was acting as Governor General, very kindly let us have their house. It so happened that another one of the judges of the Court of Appeal, Mr Justice Forbes, and his wife, went on leave after this, and we occupied their house until such time as the government found us a suitable residence in Highlands, a beautiful suburb of Salisbury. Our next door neighbours there were the Howman family. Jack Howman was the attorney who had briefed me in the Central African Airways case and we were friendly with him and his family. He later became a member of the cabinet of Mr Winston Field.

Having appeared before the courts of Rhodesia, I knew all the members of the Bench. I had appeared before Sir Hugh Beadle, who was a tremendous worker and an extremely clever lawyer. Then there was my friend Anton Hathorn, who had accepted the appointment to the Bench after I had refused it when it was first offered to me. Other members were Hector Macdonald, who, although born in Rhodesia, had practised at the Johannesburg Bar; John Lewis, who had been one of the counsel on the opposite side in the Central African Airways *v* Vickers Armstrong case, and before whose father, as a judge of the Southern Rhodesian High Court, I had appeared; and Dendy Young, stationed in Bulawayo, whom I had both appeared against and had as my junior in cases in Southern Rhodesia. There was a High Court in Bulawayo and, from time to time, one or other of us stationed in Salisbury was seconded for duty in the Bulawayo High Court when Dendy was on leave. In addition, I had another well-known colleague in my friend Jack Clayden, who had resigned from the Transvaal Bench to accept an appointment to the Federal Court of Appeal, of which he subsequently became the Chief Justice. I think it is fair to say that all of us on the Bench got on well together and speaking personally, I enjoyed the advantage of being able to discuss any difficulty I had with my brethren.

It was the custom, on the appointment of a new judge, to hold a welcoming ceremony attended by the members of the Bar. On such occasions, a speech of congratulations would be made by the leader of the Bar, to which the newly appointed judge would reply. (The custom obtained for many years in Johannesburg; but – no doubt for good and sufficient reasons – this custom appears no longer to exist in Gauteng.) When we arrived in Rhodesia, having left Johannesburg on Ascension Day in May 1961, we attended such a welcoming ceremony in the High Court, when I was sworn in as a newly appointed judge. As was apparently customary in Salisbury, the dignitaries of the city were invited to be present on this occasion. The Chief Justice, Sir Hugh Beadle, made a welcoming speech, as also did Mr Peter Charles, QC, leader of the Bar in Rhodesia, and I duly replied, having been told by my friend Jack Clayden that I would have to do so.

After the ceremony there was a small sherry party, and in the afternoon I sat for the first time as a judge of that court. It was some criminal case the nature of which I have long forgotten. I discovered then that when the accused person was an African, he was tried by a judge and two assessors. Almost invariably these assessors were retired district commissioners who had a great knowledge of the customs and habits of the African people generally. Occasionally one of the assessors would be a member of the Bar and I was particularly keen on having members of the Bar to sit as assessors as often as possible. In the case of Whites and other non-Africans there was a trial by jury. There was also provision made for a special jury to be empanelled in cases which apparently were regarded as being out of the ordinary. It was, however, never clear to me what qualified persons to be members of a special jury.

There was a strong Bar in Salisbury at that time and, as in South Africa, there were advocates and attorneys. (This situation has now changed – in Zimbabwe today advocates and attorneys are known simply as legal practitioners, and can practise as advocates or attorneys or both.) Among the leaders of the Bar were Peter Charles – whose untimely death a year or two after I was appointed was a great loss to the profession; Michael May who eventually left the Bar to become a senior partner in the leading firm of attorneys, Scanlen & Holderness; Bennie Goldin; and Dick Christie, an extremely able advocate who decided later to become an academic. He became a Professor of Law at the University in Salisbury and has written a most valuable book on the law of contract. There was also a very able African advocate, Herbert Chitepo. Chitepo had built up a good practice at the Bar, but as far as I could see he did not get any briefs from the White attorneys. Overwhelmingly the attorneys in Rhodesia were White. Both Jack Clayden and I felt that it was a pity that Chitepo, whose ability was beyond question, never had a brief from a White firm of attorneys.

After I had been in Salisbury for about a year Chitepo came to see me in chambers and told me that he wished to apply for a position as Attorney General in the then newly independent State of Tanzania. He told me quite frankly that it was his hope that when the Blacks took power in Rhodesia, as he felt was bound to take place, he would like to be qualified, possibly to occupy the position of Attorney General. After I had returned to South Africa he apparently decided to join one of the Black Rhodesian parties and went into exile. He never realised his ambition of becoming a member of the Black Government of what eventually became Zimbabwe because he was murdered in Lusaka when a bomb was exploded in his car. (This occurrence, in March 1975, was obviously a political murder.[113] It so happened that I was in Salisbury at that time: the then prominent African Nationalist Party leader, the Reverend Ndabaningi Sithole, had been placed in detention by the Smith government, and I had been briefed to appear for him at an enquiry before Mr Justice Hector Macdonald on the question as to whether his detention should be continued or ended. The procedure at this enquiry was such that my client and I felt no purpose would be served by my appearing for him. The procedure adopted at the enquiry was such as amounted, in our opinion, to being a travesty of the elementary rules of justice. The government authorities were entitled to place information before the judge that neither the person detained nor his counsel were entitled to see; and this they did. The position thus was that the judge could determine the matter on information that might be completely false, and that the person whose conduct was being enquired into was not able to controvert. Consequently I was instructed to withdraw from the enquiry, and did so. When I went to see Revd Sithole at the jail where he was detained, he had just heard what had happened to Chitepo. He asked me to tell his immediate followers who were in contact with me to attend the memorial service to be held for Herbert Chitepo. Among the persons to whom I communicated this request was Mr Robert Mugabe, now Prime Minister of Zimbabwe, but then – as I understood the position – Revd Sithole's righthand man. I gathered from others that Mugabe did not go to the memorial service, for some reason best known to himself.)

Work on the Bench was interesting but not exciting. Generally speaking, the life of a judge is easier than that of a busy advocate. I rarely had occasion to work at night – which is not to say that in endeavouring to do justice in any particular case I did not, like other judges, have many anxious moments. This was especially the case when I had to decide on the guilt or innocence of a person accused of a crime, and frequently when I had to determine what was, in my opinion, a proper sentence. I am not certain that all members of the public appreciate that the question of an appropriate sentence is, in many cases, a matter of grave difficulty. As is well known the jury are the sole judges of the facts and the judge is the sole judge of the law applicable in any case. It is a judge's duty to explain the law and as far as possible to make a summing up to the jury without imposing his own feelings on issues of fact. Perverse verdicts by juries are not unknown and I suppose it may be said that perverse verdicts have been given by judges as well.

In this connection, I may be permitted to digress to recount some interesting instances. One concerns a case over which the late Mr Justice Krause presided. Judge Krause, before whom I had appeared in the Supreme Court in the first trial in which I was briefed, enjoyed a colourful career. During his practice at the Bar he had had by far the leading practice in criminal matters. It is said that he once directed the jury as follows: 'Gentlemen of the jury, you have heard the evidence of the witnesses for the Crown and that of the accused. If you believe the evidence of the Crown witnesses you will convict the accused. If you believe the accused you will believe anything.' The jury then acquitted the accused.

Another well-known story concerns someone tried on a charge of buying diamonds illicitly. The crown case was that at an isolated spot in the Northern Cape the accused had been 'trapped' into buying some diamonds. They were in a small drawstring bag that had contained pipe tobacco – for some unknown reason, such bags were apparently used by the police when setting a trap to apprehend someone buying diamonds illicitly. The crown case was that the transaction between the 'trap' and the accused had been witnessed by the police, in hiding some distance away. After money had been paid by the accused and the bag containing the diamonds handed over, the police rushed on to the scene, but could not find the diamonds on the accused. He was then asked to move his feet away and underneath where he had been standing the bag containing the diamonds was found. The crown witnesses duly gave evidence to that effect. An accused person is not obliged to give evidence and the Crown has to prove his guilt beyond reasonable doubt. The judge, in summing up to the jury, correctly pointed out to them that the Crown had to establish its case beyond reasonable doubt and, of course, that the accused was not obliged to give evidence. The judge told the jury that if the Crown evidence, which had not been contradicted (the accused having elected not to give evidence), was accepted as correct, the jury should 'find him guilty'. 'If, however,' said the judge, 'you think it reasonably possible that at the very time the accused was standing at this lonely spot in the veld, an aeroplane flew over and dropped the bag of diamonds at the very spot where this man had been standing, you will acquit him.' This the jury did. The next day the judge was walking up Adderley Street in Cape Town when he was approached by a man who asked permission to talk to him. He said that he had been the foreman of the jury in the diamond case in question and told the judge how grateful he and the other members of the jury had been to the judge for his suggestion that the diamonds might have been dropped from an aeroplane at the spot where the accused was standing. He added that if the judge had not suggested that, none of them would ever have thought of this possibility.

One criticism of the jury system is that they have to give no reasons for their verdict, whether 'guilty' or 'not guilty'. When, however, the accused person is tried by a judge, or by a judge sitting with assessors, reasons are given by the court for acquittal or conviction as the case may be. The benefit of this procedure is that the accused person, if the reasons for finding him guilty are found to be incorrect, may succeed in an appeal, and if the reasons given for his acquittal are bad in law, the State may appeal. Generally speaking, however, quite apart from these considerations, the language difficulty is a very serious one in South Africa. What I mean is that very often the evidence given by a witness or by the accused in an African language must be interpreted into English or Afrikaans. Interpretation at the best of times is a difficult task and very often mistakes occur: mistakes that may lead to the conviction or acquittal of an accused person. Even the most skilful interpreter may not be able, adequately, to convey a nuance in the words as interpreted. There are some who advocate 'people's courts' and the jury system, but in my opinion the language difficulty is an overwhelming argument against the reintroduction of the jury system in South Africa.

In the whole of my occupancy of the Bench in Rhodesia I had to direct a jury on three occasions. On one occasion the jury found the accused guilty and in the other two, for reasons which I shall never know, they acquitted the accused.

In one case in which a person was convicted by me in Rhodesia, the accused took the matter on appeal to the Federal Supreme Court and, with the leave of that court, to the Privy Council.

In Rhodesia, as in South Africa, judges went on circuit, accompanied by a 'judge's registrar'. The procedure in Rhodesia – which incidentally I think was an excellent one – was to give young men who had elected to join the civil service in the Department of Justice an opportunity of becoming a judge's registrar (or judge's clerk, as it is sometimes called). Three or so candidates would be sent to a judge, who would select one of them to be his registrar. One of the three young men sent to me for selection was an Indian. I selected him, as according to his *curriculum vitae* he was a barrister, having passed the English Bar examination. The first circuit that I went on was to the Midlands town then known as Gwelo. Shortly before the circuit court was due to sit in Gwelo, I had a telephone call from the magistrate there. He told me that he understood my registrar was an Indian, and said he thought there might be some difficulty, as the proprietor of the hotel at which we would stay, whilst he was agreeable to giving the registrar accommodation, stipulated that the registrar could not have his meals in the ordinary public dining room, but would have to have his meals in the private sitting room allocated to me, where I would ordinarily have meals. I told the magistrate that if that was so there would be no session of the circuit court in Gwelo. I discussed the matter, of course, with Sir Hugh and he agreed with the attitude which I had adopted. Needless to say the hotel proprietor changed his mind and my Indian registrar duly accompanied me and was treated as an ordinary guest in the hotel.

This, my first circuit, was an interesting and unusual one. When the circuit court sat in any town in Rhodesia in those days, the judge was met, before entering the town, by police outriders and was thus escorted to his hotel. I was told that at Gwelo I would have to inspect a Guard of Honour and would have to wear a full-bottomed wig and white gloves when doing so. I borrowed a wig from Jack Clayden and duly inspected the guard.

It was also the accepted custom for the local gentry to attend the opening session of the court and the procedure was that after certain formalities and pleas had been taken, the judge would express his appreciation at the attendance of the members of the public and their interest in the administration of justice and would then advise them that it would not be necessary for them to stay in court any longer, unless they wished to. The court would then adjourn for a short while before resuming the business of the court. On this occasion, after the resumption I noticed an elderly woman seated near the back of the court. She seemed, from time to time, to be eating sandwiches. As she was elderly I did not think it necessary to say anything about this somewhat unusual conduct. It turned out that she was the complainant, or the victim, of a robbery at the farm on which she resided. When her case was called she entered the witness box and, having regard to her age, I enquired whether she would not like to sit instead of standing whilst she gave her evidence. She indignantly turned down my suggestion, and proceeded to give evidence. She explained that the robbers had not been able to get away with the most valuable goods, for she had taken steps to ensure that the valuables could not be found by the robbers. I may mention that after the case was over I heard that she was rather an eccentric person. Her farm was very close to the base of an airforce squadron. She took strong exception to the planes – which had to fly fairly low over her property as it was so near to the landing ground – because they disturbed her cattle and the noise annoyed her so much so that she had from time to time taken a rifle and shot at these planes as they passed over her property.

I had one unpleasant experience on this circuit, when invited to dinner by a local attorney who was the Deputy Sheriff. Conversation at the dinner table demonstrated that my host was a strong rightwinger, and he endeavoured to draw me into discussions with him – which I, of course, refrained from doing. He must have known that it was highly improper to discuss political matters with a judge, and I left as soon as it was politely possible for me to do so. The attorney was Mr Clifford du Pont, subsequently President of Rhodesia.

My next circuit visit was at Fort Victoria, where the court was held in what one might call a tin shanty. The heat was unbearable and I arranged to sit from early in the morning and to adjourn at lunchtime. The last circuit town that I attended was Umtali, situated in the beautiful eastern highlands of the country. This was an uneventful circuit excepting for the fact that there was a trial by jury of a person charged with culpable homicide as a result of having killed someone in a motor accident. He was acquitted.

A great deal of my time was occupied in dealing with cases that came before me as a result of the 'automatic review' procedure then in force. The position was that if a magistrate sentenced an accused person to imprisonment of, I think, a month or more, and there was no appeal, the matter would be sent to a judge of the High Court for review. If the judge was satisfied that a substantial justice had been done, he would confirm the conviction or sentence. If he was not satisfied he would refer the matter to the Attorney General raising the difficulty which he had in confirming the magistrate's verdict. If the Attorney General had the same difficulty as the judge, the conviction or the sentence, or both, would be set aside. If the Attorney General did not agree with the judge's *prima facie* view, the matter would be set down for argument and decided by the High Court. This automatic review practice was, in my opinion, an important one in the administration of justice. It has to be borne in mind that many of the magistrates, especially those stationed in rural areas, had little or no access to authoritative text books or to law reports, and might easily fall into error. In addition, in many of these cases, the accused person was undefended or not properly defended and the review system was undoubtedly of great value and importance.

EDITORS' NOTE: *There was, at the time, a case which caused a considerable stir in the country, and particularly in a certain rural area. A farmer had inflicted a terrible beating, using a hosepipe, upon one of his labourers, who had nearly died. To the farmer's utter astonishment, he had been sentenced to two months' imprisonment by the local magistrate. He naturally appealed against the severity of the sentence and the appeal was heard by Isie. The prosecutor at this case later said that, as counsel for the appellant rose to his feet to commence addressing the court, Isie said to the prosecutor: 'I should like to hear from you after Mr X is finished, as to why the sentence in this matter should not be increased.' The appellant's counsel then attempted to withdraw the appeal, but it was too late. The sentence was increased from two months' to three years' imprisonment; but, according to the prosecutor, it put an end to that type of vicious assault, at least in that area, forever.*

When I went to Rhodesia in 1961, Sir Roy Welensky was the Prime Minister of the Federation.

He was a self-educated man who had considerable charm, was very popular and had what was known as 'the common touch'. Sir Edgar Whitehead, the Prime Minister of Southern Rhodesia, was a rather shy intellectual, and a bachelor – a brilliant speaker, and a leader of what one would call the liberal party then in power.

Not long after we came, there were signs that the Federation would break up. Dr H K Banda agitated for and brought about the secession of Nyasaland. There was also, of course, unrest in Northern Rhodesia which eventually resulted in Mr Kenneth Kaunda's becoming President of that country, now known as Zambia, and its seceding from the Federation. I was never certain why the Federation broke up. I was given to understand that it was because the people of Nyasaland and Northern Rhodesia – or their leaders – felt that they were being governed by the Whites in Salisbury, where the headquarters of the government were situated. Be that as it may, however, there was a general election about a year or so after we had arrived there. Whitehead's government was toppled and the Rhodesian Front party, with Mr Winston Field as its leader, came into power. This was what would be known as a rightwing party and it was the party of which Mr Ian Smith eventually became the leader.

It would be quite wrong of me not to mention the great hospitality and friendship which Muriel and I received from so many of the people we knew, or got to know, in Rhodesia. Our closest friends were the Goldins, Bennie and his wife Hansie. Bennie had been my junior in several cases in Rhodesia, and on my resignation from the Rhodesian Bench was appointed to succeed me. He eventually became a member of the Court of Appeal after the Federation broke up. It is not possible for me adequately to say how kind and helpful the Goldins were to us during the whole of our stay in Rhodesia. A few years after we left Hansie died, far too young. A kinder person it would be difficult to find.

Shortly after our arrival in Salisbury we were invited to dinner by Sir John Clayden and his wife, Gwen. This was a formal occasion: after guests had arrived, they waited for a short while in the lounge until Sir John and Lady Clayden came in. Then, as each guest was greeted, the women were required to curtsy to Sir

John Clayden. When Muriel did this I noticed that he winked at me.

In addition to there being a governor general, each one of the three states had its own governor. Sir Humphrey Gibbs was Governor of Southern Rhodesia, and he and his wife were most charming and hospitable to Muriel and myself. We were invited to dinner quite frequently and on occasions would meet some visitor of importance. There was, of course, a strict rule, namely that if one was invited to dinner at 7.30 pm that meant 7.30 pm and not 7.29 or 7.31 pm. The result was that one would arrive at Government House before 7.30 and wait in one's car until 7.30 pm. I should add that when UDI was decared, the treatment of Sir Humphrey and Lady Gibbs by Smith and his government was appalling.

As I have mentioned, the legal profession was then divided, as it is still in South Africa, into advocates and attorneys. As was to be expected, not all the advocates, or perhaps not all the arguments by all the advocates, were convincing or right. I have in mind a certain divorce case which was bitterly contested. The husband was an Irish Roman Catholic who was opposed to divorce as a matter of principle. His wife, who was a young widow, her first husband having died of cancer, was not a Catholic but had apparently promised to bring up any children in the Catholic faith. She was the plaintiff in the divorce proceedings claiming in effect that life was intolerable because of her husband's conduct towards her. Her husband was a poor witness and in his final argument his counsel addressed me more or less in the following manner. He said, 'Your Lordship may have found the defendant to be an unsatisfactory witness' (I did not feel called upon to comment on that). He continued, 'Your Lordship will bear in mind that he is Irish, I am English and your Lordship will doubtless bear in mind that Irish people do not deliberately tell untruths, they simply cannot help it.' Keeping as straight a face as I could, I said I did not think I could take judicial notice of that alleged fact. I gave judgment in favour of the wife and granted her custody of the child born of the marriage. The husband asked me to order her to bring up the child as a Catholic. This I refused to do saying it was the custodian parent's right to determine a matter of that nature.

One amusing case that came before me was that of a woman plaintiff who was seeking a divorce from her husband. The action was undefended. The usual question was put by counsel as to whether her married life was a happy one and the usual negative answer was given. Counsel then asked what was the cause of the trouble, to which the woman, without any expression in her voice said, 'Pigeons.' I was not sure whether I had heard correctly and she repeated this. Apparently her complaint was that her husband devoted himself to the pigeons instead of her. I found it impossible, when this evidence was given, to contain myself and rapidly adjourned court.

The Winston Field government passed increasingly harsh legislation, which I would have to enforce as a judge. One of the final pieces of legislation which led to my making up my mind to resign from the Bench was the amendment to the Act which, I think, was called the Law and Order Maintenance Act, in terms whereof if a person threw a petrol bomb into a hut or house (whether the hut or house was occupied or not) and was found guilty, there was a mandatory death penalty. Although the death penalty was enforceable in Rhodesia in cases, for example, where the accused person had been found guilty of murder, if extenuating circumstances were found the death sentence need not be imposed. The concept of a mandatory death penalty generally, and more particularly the fact that it had to be imposed even where no person could possibly have been hurt as a result of a petrol bomb having been thrown – for example, in an unoccupied house – was something I could not stomach. I felt that this piece of legislation was a forerunner of similar legislation.

I think I was at all times aware of the fact that the executive and the judiciary must be kept apart, but I felt so strongly about this matter that I took it upon myself to speak to my friend Jack Howman to explain to him how I felt on this latest piece of legislation. I ventured to suggest to him that the matter should be reconsidered; but anything I said fell on deaf ears. Although I wish to make it clear that I am by no means critical of the judges who took a different point of view to mine, or those who subsequently took appointments to the Bench of Southern Rhodesia, it seemed to me clear that the position had arisen, or was arising, where I would find it impossible to carry out my duties as a judge. I thereupon made up my mind that I would resign, and communicated my intention to the Chief Justice, Sir Hugh Beadle. He tried to dissuade me; but it seemed to me to be inevitable that Rhodesia was becoming a second South Africa and I could not, in all conscience, carry out my duties as a judge.

Muriel and I spent many hours discussing what we should do and we came to the conclusion that I should resign, which I did. One of the senior officials in the Department of Justice asked me to issue a statement that I was resigning for personal family reasons, being anxious, of course for me not to give the real reason for my not being prepared to remain on the Bench. I refused to accede to his request, but at the same time did not make known, publicly, the real reason for my leaving.

Chapter Fifteen

AFTER RHODESIA

Having made up our minds to leave Rhodesia, the question was what we would then do. In a lengthy discussion with my friend, Jack Clayden, as to whether I should go back to the Bar in Johannesburg, we agreed that it would be wrong for me to do so until some time had elapsed. There was a feeling that a person who had been a judge, or who had acted as a judge and returned to practise at the Bar, had an unfair advantage over his fellow members – certain attorneys might believe that because he had been a judge, he was better qualified than his competitors. The Bar, therefore, was out of the question for the time being.

I had met Dean Erwin Griswold, Dean of the Harvard Law School, when he came out to watch a portion of the treason trial, and after he learned of my resignation from the Bench, I received a letter from him offering me an appointment as a lecturer at the Harvard Law School. Apart from the fact that Muriel and I had both felt it would be difficult to establish ourselves in the United States, I felt that I would not be a very good lecturer, and would certainly not enjoy spending the rest of my life trying to teach law.

Before accepting the appointment in Rhodesia, I had been a non-executive director of the OK Bazaars, having followed in the footsteps of a dear friend of mine, B A (Sonny) Ettlinger, QC, who had died suddenly in London. I had at that time been offered an executive directorship of OK Bazaars, which I had refused. As things stood when we left Rhodesia, however, I could in all probability obtain an executive directorship at the OK Bazaars – which, in fact, is what I did.

However, Muriel and I decided first to take a trip overseas. I had been invited to a conference convened in Athens by an organisation called 'World Peace through Law', and we thought it would be a good idea to go to this conference and then to Israel, where we had not been for a few years.

The conference was attended by lawyers and judges from all over the western world, with a specially large contingent of American lawyers, and also one of African judges. The proceedings were opened by the King of Greece (this was, of course, before Greece became a Republic), and commenced with a Greek Orthodox religious service that consisted of a long and seemingly interminable Gregorian chant. We had to stand during this service, held in a large hall that was not airconditioned. Some of us were rather resentful of the length of the service. The Hilton Hotel in Athens, where the conference was held, has a magnificent lounge with marble floors and sunken pools, to which we adjourned after the prayers. There was a certain amount of naughty satisfaction amongst some of us when one of these magnificently attired priests took a step backwards and fell into one of the pools. On this occasion, Muriel was presented to the King and Queen of Greece and we still have a photograph showing her curtsying – which, of course, was the right thing to do.

There were some interesting sessions at the conference. The last event was a dinner held in a magnificent banqueting hall with a draped ceiling. As this was a 'peace through law' conference, the chairman who presided at the banquet thought it a good idea to let loose a number of doves. Some of them, however, settled in the drapes and constituted a hazard for the rest of the evening.

As is the habit in Greece, the dinner started rather late in the evening, by which time the person who was to preside at the dinner had already quenched his thirst. The first thing he had to do was to introduce the people sitting at the top table. Among them were the United States ambassador to Greece and a fair number of African judges. The chairman had difficulty, his speech being affected by the quantity of liquor he had consumed, in pronouncing the names of the African judges whom he was introducing. He finally ended up by saying 'this name I cannot pronounce'.

The last speech of the evening was made in French by a distinguished Greek lawyer. We were all provided with earphones with simultaneous translation. To crown the evening, when this speaker had finished his talk, the chairman thought it proper to thank him for his 'brilliant speech', adding, 'unfortunately I couldn't understand a word of it because my earphones were not working.'

I still remember this man (who, incidentally, was President Elect of the American Bar Association) at breakfast with his wife the next morning. He had rather a hangdog expression on his face and his wife looked grim. My friend, Sydney Kentridge, impishly went across to congratulate him on the manner in which he had conducted the banquet the night before.

From Athens we went, as arranged, to Israel. There I bumped into Edel Horwitz and Israel Dunsky, respectively President and Chairman of the South African Zionist Federation at that time. We had also met Mr Sharett, chairman of the Jewish Agency, who had been in Johannesburg shortly before our going to Israel. In addition, of course, we knew Louis Pincus, then treasurer of the agency, and who subsequently became chairman of the executive of that body. Edel and Israel asked me to come with the four of them to see Golda Meir, the Foreign Minister, to endeavour to persuade her not to stop El Al planes from flying to Johannesburg.

Mrs Meir was as strong an anti-apartheid person as I have ever met and whether it was because of that or for some other reason, she did not want El Al planes to fly any longer to South Africa. I was asked by Edel and Israel to present the case for the continuation of these flights to South Africa. This I did and apparently must have made some impression on Golda Meir, because on that same afternoon I had a phone call from the director general of the foreign office, Mr Gideon Rafael, asking to see me. When I called on him in his office in Jerusalem he told me that he had been instructed to offer me the Africa desk in the foreign office.

We were leaving for South Africa the next day and I told him that I would like to consider this offer, which had come as a complete surprise to me. I saw my friend Eli Kirschner, a former South African (and the son of Nicholai Kirschner, sometime chairman of the South African Zionist Federation), who was practising as an attorney in Tel Aviv. He warned me to take no notice of Rafael's offer until it was made in writing – and even then, he said, I should be careful. When I came back to South Africa I immediately wrote a letter to Mr Rafael making the usual enquiries as to where, if I accepted the offer made to me, we would be able to reside, where our children would be educated, what the emoluments attaching to the office were – in other words the normal questions that would be asked in these circumstances. I did not have this letter typed, but wrote it out, as I treated the matter as strictly confidential. Enquiries about me had apparently been made from the Israel ambassador in South Africa, because he knew of this offer. I never received a reply to my letter. When I was next in Jerusalem, I saw Louis Pincus (who knew about the offer) and he asked me what had happened. I then told him that I had never received a reply to my letter. Louis did not at first believe this, but I invited him then and there to telephone Rafael, which he did. Rafael confirmed that he had had a letter from me, but said that he could not read my writing. It is quite true that my handwriting is by no means of the best, but I have no doubt that this letter was perfectly legible. The reason, obvious to both Louis Pincus and myself, was that Gideon Rafael – who I believe, incidentally, was an extremely able and efficient director general of the foreign office – simply did not want me.

Incidentally I should add that El Al continued to fly to South Africa, and still does so.

I decided, therefore, to accept an executive directorship at the OK Bazaars. Shortly after this, I was invited by my friend, John Turnbull, then chairman of the South African board of the Norwich Union Insurance Company Limited, to join this board in a non-executive capacity, which I did. Soon afterwards, I was approached by Donald Gordon and asked to become a non-executive director of Liberty Life to which, of course, I agreed. I also became a founding non-executive director of Liberty Holdings Limited when that company was formed. I found these directorships extremely interesting. Donald Gordon was, in my opinion, a financial genius and both the companies to which I have referred proved to be outstandingly successful. The Liberty board meetings were interesting, the board papers were invariably well prepared, and altogether my experience on these boards was a very satisfying one.

Finally I was invited to join the board of Barclays Bank (now First National Bank) as a non-executive director. This was a rewarding experience in many ways. Among the board members were former general managers of the bank and it was interesting listening to their experiences – or rather, to the manner in which they applied their knowledge of clients of the bank when consideration had to be given to overdraft facilities. I need hardly add that the only overdraft facilities with which the board was concerned were always at least seven-digit amounts. In addition I learned something about banking.

The chairman of the board was Arthur Aiken, senior partner of Aiken & Carter, a dynamic personality who devoted his considerable ability to the interests of the bank. I had met him when I was elected to the council of the University of the Witwatersrand shortly after my return to Johannesburg. The manner in which he looked after the financial affairs of the university was a clear indication of devoted service to this great university. I should add, *en passant*, that later on the same day that I was offered a directorship at Barclays Bank, I was offered a directorship in another bank; which, of course, I was unable to accept.

While I was still in Rhodesia I was elected an honorary vice-president of the South African Zionist Federation. As all the directorships – with the exception of the one I held at the OK Bazaars – were non-executive, and as being an executive director of the OK Bazaars did not necessitate excessively long hours or hard work, I was able to spend considerable time on Zionist work, which I found most interesting and rewarding. (I deal with this subject more fully in the following chapter.)

I in fact left the OK Bazaars in the 1960s. I must confess that I did not find my work there interesting – nor do I think that I was able to make any real contribution towards what was then, by far, the biggest chain of retail stores in South Africa. After ceasing to be an executive director, I could have stayed on as a non-executive director, but this I was unwilling to do.

After I left the OK Bazaars, Donald Gordon was, I think, quite keen that I should become more closely associated with him at Liberty Life. Had I done so I might today have been a wealthy person, but I made up my mind that law was my real interest in life, and I decided to return to practise at the Bar in 1970. I should, however, mention that I was not entirely 'divorced' from the law from the time I left Rhodesia until the time I returned to the Bar. I sat as an arbitrator in various matters, two of the most important being arbitrations in which the City Council of Johannesburg was concerned. The first was the expropriation of what was then the City Deep Golf Course (the property of Rand Mines), by the City

Council for the purpose of erecting a market. The second was an expropriation, for other purposes, of property belonging to Sorec, a Schlesinger organisation in the southern parts of Johannesburg.

The City Deep arbitration, as I shall call it, was a most difficult and interesting one. It was held at a time when the National Party was trying to stem the flow of Africans to the cities by applying influx control laws. The City Deep site was undoubtedly an ideal site for industrial purposes, but the policy of the government was not to permit any further sites to be utilised in Johannesburg for industrial purposes. If permission were given to a would-be developer to establish a factory on a site, it would be done only if rights to another site, already invested with industrial rights, were abandoned. Counsel for Rand Mines submitted that the ground expropriated should be valued on the basis that it could be utilised for industrial purposes and would thus have a value considerably greater than if it were used for residential purposes. Counsel for the City of Johannesburg contended that the premises could not be utilised for industrial purposes, and could at best be utilised for residential, or busines purposes such as shopping centres. Towards the end of the evidence, Rand Mines' counsel called a property developer who said that, in his opinion, having regard to the proximity of the premises to the Kazerne railway station at City Deep, it would be possible to establish warehouses which would render the ground more valuable. I was impressed with this evidence and gave full weight to it in determining the amount of compensation which had to be paid by the City Council. Although not obliged to, I gave full reasons for the conclusion at which I had arrived.

The Sorec arbitration was less interesting. There was a mine dump on part of the property which was expropriated, and somebody came along with the idea that flats could be erected on top of the mine dump, and that these could easily be let, thus enhancing the value of the ground because of the use to which it could be put. I was not over-impressed with the evidence given on this aspect of the matter, and in due course made an award – without, I think, giving reasons for my decision.

There were a few other comparatively minor matters in addition to these two arbitrations. Sitting during these matters had the effect not merely of making me keep up with the law, but of convincing me that the best thing for me to do was to go back to the Bar. More importantly, early in 1967, Judge Edward Roper came to see me to ask whether I would accept appointments to the Courts of Appeal of Lesotho, Botswana and Swaziland. (Up to the grant of independence, all these states had had a common Court of Appeal.) Another member of these Courts of Appeal was Mr Justice Oliver Schreiner, then recently retired from the Court of Appeal of South Africa. Despite the fact that I was still at that time an executive director of the OK Bazaars, the chairman and managing directors had no objection to my proposed appointments. The sessions of each of these courts were not very long to begin with and having decided to go back to the Bar, this suited me admirably.

I was deeply honoured, and remain so to this day, by the fact that Judges Roper and Schreiner recommended me to appointment at these courts. His Majesty the King of Lesotho and the President of Botswana duly appointed me. Independence was granted to Swaziland a short while later, and I received a letter from the High Commissioner asking me whether I would be prepared to accept an appointment to the Swaziland Bench, which I was. This appointment was duly confirmed by His Majesty King Sobhuza. I had sat as a member of the courts of Appeal of Lesotho and Botswana and was officially to be appointed when the 'instruments of independence' were given to King Sobhuza.

My first visit to Swaziland was a memorable occasion. The ceremony at which the 'instruments of independence' were to be handed to King Sobhuza was held in a vast stadium, to which the King, the High Commissioner and the members of the Court of Appeal were driven in cavalcade. The British High Commissioner was dressed in his elaborate Colonial Office uniform, cocked hat and all. The judges were dressed in their red robes. Both Judge Roper and Judge Schreiner had been decorated for distinguished service in the First World War: Judge Roper wore the DSO and Croix De Guerre, and Judge Schreiner wore the Military Cross. I wore the medals awarded to me for my – largely unearned – services during the Second World War. King Sobhuza was attired in traditional dress, and on the upper part of his arm wore a bangle around a piece of cloth. The High Commissioner asked him: 'Your Majesty, what is the significance of the piece of cloth you have surrounded by the bangle?' The King looked him up and down and said, 'Oh, this is part of my ceremonial dress, much as you are wearing today.'

It so happened that, around that time, two gentlemen named Wolpe and Goldreich had been awaiting trial in what was to be known as 'the Rivonia trial'. They thought it would be a good idea to avoid the trial and managed, after certain arrangements had been made, to escape from custody. Disguised as Anglican priests, they fled to Swaziland in a red Ford car. A friend of mine, Leo Lovell, a former Member of Parliament in South Africa, had emigrated to Swaziland where in due course he became the Minister of Finance. An attorney by profession, he undertook to dispose of Wolpe and Goldreich's car when they had left Swaziland. It so happened that no purchaser could be found for the car; but Leo, having arranged a fair valuation, bought the car himself. This was the car which transported the three judges to the stadium.

The 'instruments of independence' were duly handed over to the King, who was accompanied by his numerous wives. A vast crowd of warriors in traditional dress encircled the whole stadium. When these warriors commenced to dance, the King walked down solemnly from the stand where the ceremony of handing over had taken place and walked in a most dignified manner to join his subjects, and slowly danced with them. This was, for Muriel and myself, an unforgettable episode.

A few years later I was introduced by Dean Griswold to the Chief Justice of the Supreme Court of the United States. Dean Griswold explained to the judge that I was a member of the Court of Appeal in Swaziland. The Chief Justice remarked: 'This must be a barbaric sort of a country.' I explained to him the ceremony which we had witnessed and added that there was no gun to be seen, nor a soldier dressed in uniform, and enquired of him: 'What is the position when the President of the United States is inaugurated?' We then had a friendly discussion for about half an hour.

We were soon joined in the Court of Appeal by Mr Justice Milne, retired Judge President of Natal, and later by Mr Justice Smit, former Judge President of the Orange Free State. (Judge Milne recently died in England, and tragically his son – then a comparatively young man who had not long before been elevated to the Court of Appeal – died a few days after him. The son had been an outstanding judge – both of first instance and of appeal.)

Among other activities that occupied me during this time was my membership of the Council of the University of the Witwatersrand. I served on that body for about ten years, but decided to retire when I found it increasingly difficult to attend meetings – which almost invariably commenced at 4.00 pm on Friday afternoons – a time when I might just have left court or been engaged in consultation. The idea of arriving late at any meeting, and more particularly at meetings of the council of the university, was unacceptable as far as I was concerned.

Politically I was a supporter of the United Party under Smuts, but when the Progressive Party was formed I decided to join it. As is well known, the sole member of Parliament of that party for many years was the courageous and redoubtable Helen Suzman, for whom I have always had the greatest admiration and respect. I had the privilege of being asked to preside at many meetings addressed by her, particularly at the Houghton School. The hall was always filled to overflowing whenever she spoke. I was also given the honour of being asked to speak at the last meeting she addressed to her constituents when she announced her decision to retire from Parliament. A portrait of her hangs in Parliament, and as far as I understand the position she is the only person who was not a cabinet minister to have her portrait hanging in Parliament. She was a champion *par excellence* of the underprivileged in this country, and one wonders whether those whom she sought to assist fully appreciate the magnificent work that she did on their behalf.

I may perhaps add that I spoke at meetings held by other candidates for the Progressive Party, the first of whom was Rene de Villiers, former editor of *The Star*. He beat his opponent Mr Emdin, who was a United Party candidate, and I had occasion to praise Mr Emdin's work, saying, however, that he was now in the wrong party. I had been on friendly terms with Mr Emdin, but after this meeting he cut me dead. I addressed a meeting on behalf of Colin Eglin one Saturday night in Sea Point, where he succeeded in defeating his opponent. I also chaired a meeting held by Mr Waddell. He was duly elected and served as a Member of Parliament for some time. He has since left the country and now resides in England.

Chapter Sixteen

RETURN TO THE BAR

When I returned to the Bar in February 1970 I was fortunate enough to be able to join the group I had left in 1961. I had apparently not been forgotten during the years I had been away from the Bar and firms of attorneys who had briefed me before I left the Bar gave me work to do on my return – for instance, Webber Wentzel, Werksmans, Moodie & Robertson, and Bell Dewar & Hall.

Among the first briefs that I had was one in which I was instructed by Bowens in arbitration proceedings that their clients intended to bring against the government. This claim was a very large one, and necessitated a trip to Paris, Stuttgart (I had never previously been in Germany) and England. Accompanied by my junior, John Coaker, and two partners in Bowens, Derrick Reid and Neville Matterson, we went first to Paris to receive instructions and certain information from our clients. We then went to Stuttgart to consult a German professor who was an expert in the particular field with which we were concerned. I may mention *en passant* that during the Second World War Neville Matterson had been a prisoner of war in a camp near Stuttgart. Armed with the information we received from the German professor we went to London to meet the consulting engineers who had advised our opponents. The evidence which we intended to place before the arbitrators doubtlessly induced the government and their advisers to arrive at a settlement completely satisfactory to our clients, and the envisaged arbitration proceedings did not take place.

Before this matter arose, indeed within a few days of my returning to practice at the Bar, I was briefed by a firm of attorneys in Cape Town to defend a person charged with murdering his wife. He was well spoken, had impeccable manners and had been married to an unusually beautiful young wife who bore him two children. His story, as told to me when I came to Cape Town to consult with him, was that an unknown intruder had entered his beautiful home and murdered his wife, who had been sitting with him in his study. He had previously given this account to the attorneys acting in the case and to Harry Snitcher, QC, who had been briefed before I was instructed to lead him, and M Odes. He persisted in this version of events when he gave evidence in court. I was briefed to attend the preparatory examination and after that I was asked by the accused's father, a prominent businessman, to explain to him what the case was against his son. He believed implicitly in his son's innocence, as did the murdered wife's parents, the latter even after he had been found guilty. The State's evidence proved beyond any reasonable doubt that the accused's account of the mysterious intruder was false. Indeed there was an overwhelming case against him, and he was duly found guilty by the Judge President of the Cape, Mr Justice Beyers, sitting with two assessors.

The trial was a long one, but the judgment was a particularly short one. It was given on a Friday morning. I asked the judge for an adjournment until the afternoon so that I might be able to lead evidence which would show that the death penalty should not be imposed. The judge said he would give me the whole weekend to think about the matter. I have spent many miserable weekends during the course of my career at the Bar, but this was undoubtedly one of the most miserable ones. Muriel offered to fly to Cape Town to keep me company, but I explained to her that both of us would be miserable and that no purpose would be served by her coming down.

Fortunately, long before his trial, the accused had been examined by a psychiatrist of considerable standing in Johannesburg and my attorney was able to get in touch with him and induce him to come to Cape Town. This psychiatrist, Dr Zalman Woolf, had given evidence in a case which I have mentioned earlier where the defence of temporary insanity was upheld by the jury. (The law as it then stood provided that a person charged with murder who could prove insanity had to be found 'guilty but insane'. The jury had wanted to return a verdict of not guilty and acquit him – which, of course, was not permissible in the law at that point, and so they had returned a verdict of guilty but insane. The law has since been changed in cases of this nature where, in a proper case, the verdict is 'not guilty by reason of insanity'. Of course in both such cases the accused would be detained at the president's pleasure.)

In this case there was no question of the accused being insane at the time the crime was committed by him. There was evidence to the effect that the accused's wife had spoken to his parents by telephone shortly before the murder must have been committed. It was a friendly chat with no indication whatsoever of anything wrong or any quarrel between the accused and his wife. She had returned from a short holiday with some friends. He had not accompanied her on this short break because he had a considerable amount of work to do. Rejecting the accused's version of the mysterious, or rather non-existent, intruder, the doctor gave evidence to the effect that the accused, who was ordinarily a well mannered and controlled person, had completely lost control of himself and committed this horrible crime. It seemed to be obvious that some words had passed between his wife and himself as a result of which the accused committed the crime. This theory was advanced by the psychiatrist and, I think, the judge had independently come to that conclusion. He thought that the explanation of the accused's conduct was in line with what the psychiatrist had stated. Notwithstanding an intensive search by the police, no motive for the murder was ever discovered.

The Attorney General of the Cape, Mr Lategan, now Mr Justice Lategan, who appeared as prosecuting counsel, cross-examined the doctor to no effect, and I think he missed the point. The question, in my opinion, was whether it was something said by the accused to his wife or something said by his wife to the accused that caused him to lose control of himself and bash in her brain.

This question was not raised by Lategan. He emphasised the use of the two ornaments with which the accused had bashed his wife's brain to show that the murder was a cruel one. He stressed that the murder was a cruel one, emphasising the fact that two objects, and not one, were used to cause the death of the accused's wife. There was no doubt that the murder was a cruel one, but to some extent it emphasised the fact that the accused had completely lost control of himself – probably because of what had passed verbally between his wife and himself. The only evidence that I was able to present to the court was that of the psychiatrist, Dr Woolf. The accused did not give any further evidence.

After the judge had sentenced the accused to twelve years' imprisonment, I went to pay my respects to the judge and to say goodbye to him. He told me that the accused was not likely, in his opinion, to commit any further crime and that he would be a useful member of society. The accused was released from prison after four years and shortly thereafter left for England, and he has indeed shown that he is a useful member of society. The explanation simply was that he temporarily lost complete control of himself and killed his wife.

Whilst I am on the subject of murder, I had two more murder cases after my return to the Bar. The first one was that of a sugar planter who, suspecting someone of having an affair with his wife, had shot him. Fortunately we were able to obtain the services of the same doctor who had given evidence in the Cape Town case and he was of the opinion that this was a case of temporary insanity. I may mention that this case was in Natal and I had a consultation with a local psychiatrist who had been a naval officer. He pooh-poohed the idea of temporary insanity, but when he listened to the psychiatrist who had come from Johannesburg to give evidence, he changed his mind and became an enthusiastic supporter of the theory of temporary insanity. The judge returned a verdict of guilty but insane.

It was interesting to note that counsel for the State procured the services of a psychiatrist who sat throughout the evidence given by the accused and Dr Zalman Woolf. This psychiatrist was apparently convinced by the evidence given by Dr Woolf and he left the court. He had sat next to the prosecuting counsel and after the psychiatric evidence called by me, he vacated his chair. My junior in this case, Mr R Cadman (who was interested in politics, became a member of Parliament and was subsequently appointed Administrator of Natal) made the point that there was an 'empty chair'; in other words the inference to be drawn was that the State psychiatrist had not been able to dispute the evidence we had led. The accused was committed to be detained at the president's pleasure. He wrote me a letter from the mental asylum thanking me for my services and deeply regretting what he had done.

The last murder case I had was of an almost unbelievable nature.

I was briefed in this matter by Mr B J H Irving, senior partner of the firm, Woodhead Bigby & Irving of Durban. A young man, the father of an illegitimate child who was living with her mother, asked permission to take the child out for a day. He took his child to the flat which he occupied. The child started crying and in a fit of irritation he strangled the child to death. Afterwards he went to the beach in Durban, spent a pleasant day there and late that afternoon casually mentioned to his mother, who had been divorced from her husband many years before, that he had killed his child. He gave himself up to the police and his defence was financed by his father (who had since remarried). There was a history of his behaviour as a child that led to the inescapable conclusion that he was in fact a psychopath. Judge President James commenced his judgment by mercifully saying, 'I do not intend passing the death sentence.' The man was, of course, found guilty and sentenced to a long term of imprisonment. This was the first case in South Africa that evidence of psychopathy was accepted as a mitigating factor.

Apart from these three murder cases I appeared in one criminal appeal to the Appellate Division, and my practice was otherwise confined to civil work – opinions, consultations, civil trials and arbitration.

In the latter part of 1971 I was briefed to appear with the late Ernie Wentzel for Mr Sobukwe and Another *v* The Minister of Justice in an appeal to the Appellate Division.[114] I did not appear in the court of first instance, which was an application brought in the Transvaal Provincial Division by both Sobukwe and Ms Naidoo, against the Minister of Justice.

Mr Sobukwe was the head of the Pan African Congress (PAC). After the events of Sharpeville he was found guilty of some offence and sentenced to three years' imprisonment. A special Act of Parliament was introduced whereby Sobukwe had to undergo imprisonment for a further term. Upon his release from prison he was prohibited in terms of the Suppression of Communism Act[115] from absenting himself from 'the area comprising the Kimberley municipality'. In the case of Ms Naidoo, she was prohibited from absenting herself from 'the magisterial district of Johannesburg.'

Sobukwe held several academic degrees and had been a lecturer at the University of the Witwatersrand. He wished to leave

South Africa permanently with his family to take up a teaching post that he had accepted at Yale University, which would also enable him to study further for a PhD. The American consulate-general was prepared to issue visas to Sobukwe and his family for permanent residence in the United States of America. Sobukwe applied to the Department of the Interior for permission pursuant to the 'Departure from the Union Regulation Act 34 of 1955, as amended' to leave the country permanently. The minister of the interior, although he knew that Sobukwe was restricted to Kimberley, gave him permission to leave the country permanently. Proceedings were instituted because this meant, in effect, leaving Kimberley to catch an aeroplane at the international airport in Johannesburg, whilst the minister of justice refused to give permission for Sobukwe to leave Kimberley. Ms Naidoo's case was similar.

An application was brought in the Transvaal Provincial Division for an order directing the Minister of Justice to permit Sobukwe and Naidoo to embark, pursuant to the departure permits granted in terms of the Departure from the Union Regulation Act (No 34 of 1955), as amended. When the matter was taken on appeal to the Appellate Division, the Chief Justice, Mr Justice Ogilvie Thompson, with whom four other judges concurred in his opinion, stated:

> At first sight it would certainly appear to be somewhat anomalous, that a permit to depart permanently from the Republic granted, with full knowledge of the circumstances, by one Minister of State functioning under one Act of Parliament should be wholly ineffective and nugatory because of the attitude adopted by another Minister of State functioning under another Act of Parliament.

The learned judge pointed out that a convicted person serving his sentence would not be entitled to leave the country whilst he was serving his sentence despite the permission similar to the one granted to Sobukwe and Naidoo. He discussed certain Roman-Dutch authorities such as Van Bynkershoek, Grotius, and Puffendorf, and pointed out that there was no absolute right for citizens to leave a country. I conceded that a person serving a sentence could not leave the country even if he was in possession of a permit to leave. It seemed to me to be unthinkable that a cabinet minister with full knowledge of the fact that a person was serving a term of imprisonment, would automatically grant this freedom. On the other hand, I argued unsuccessfully, there was a distinction between such a case and that of a case consequent upon the minister's action, pursuant to delegated statutory powers such as those enjoyed by the minister of justice. *Inter alia* I argued that the State is one entity, and it is merely for the convenience of the government that it is divided into ministries for the discharge of its functions.

Sobukwe was by no means a Communist in the strict sense of the term. He was undoubtedly what was called a 'statutory Communist'. The statute prohibited a person from advocating communism within South Africa, and if by any chance Sobukwe or the other appellant were to preach Communism, they would be preaching Communism extra-territorially. I argued that firstly no offence would be committed if Communism was preached by a person permanently outside the country, and secondly that the court would have no jurisdiction to try any person for an alleged crime committed extra-territorially.

It seemed to me, with respect, to be somewhat far-fetched to think that Sobukwe could commit acts in America that would render him liable to prosecution in the courts of South Africa. Apart from this, I would, with the greatest respect, suggest that an injustice was committed to Sobukwe and, of course, to Naidoo. The Minister of Justice, one Mr Pelser, had previously been a country attorney; but I have no doubt that the decision was that of the cabinet. Sobukwe died in Kimberley.

In a case in 1977 in the Appellate Division, in which I appeared with W E Cooper, SC, and W G Thring (who both became judges of the Cape Provincial Division), the opening words of the judgment delivered by Chief Justice Rumpff read:

> *Hierdie saak is gelukkig uniek in die geskiedenis van die Suid-Afrikaanse reg*. (This matter is fortunately unique in the history of South African law.)[116]

In the latter part of 1976 I was visited by John Kirkpatrick and

Colin du Preez, senior partners of the well-known firm of Lorentz & Bone of Windhoek. They were obviously in a distressed state and told me the following tale. Du Preez had instructed counsel Cooper and Thring to appear for certain members of the South West Africa Peoples Organisation (SWAPO), two being charged with murder and others with being accessories to the crime. The person murdered was a Kaptein Elifas. Two of the accused had been sentenced to death, others had been sentenced to terms of imprisonment. Yet others who had played minor roles were sentenced to pay fines. The trial was held before Judge Strydom in Swakopmund and Du Preez had a feeling that the State had acquired some knowledge, in fact almost perfect knowledge, of the defence that would be presented to the court. He had an uneasy feeling that there had been some leak of information from his own office in Windhoek to the police.

Upon his return to Windhoek, after the judge had passed sentences on the accused, he mentioned the matter of his unease to his senior partner, John Kirkpatrick. All the other partners and employees of the firm were called together and in the light of what Du Preez had suspected warned that there was to be no breach of confidence on matters in which the firm was consulted. The next morning a clerk in the employ of the firm informed Du Preez that his principal, a junior partner in the firm, was a police informer. This proved to be true and that junior partner was summarily dismissed from the firm. He had had nothing to do with this particular case. (I may mention that he was employed the next day by the registrar of deeds in Windhoek). Further investigation revealed that Du Preez's own secretary had been guilty of passing information to the police. In fact she had actually handed over copies of statements to the security police. It seemed to me obvious that the accused had not received a fair trial. I discussed this matter with my friend Sydney Kentridge and he suggested that an application be made for a special entry (which may be made by the court when there is an irregularity in the proceedings of such a nature that a failure of justice occurs). Judge Strydom (the trial Judge) happened to be on leave and the application for a special entry came before Acting Judge Hart. I was duly briefed. Du Preez's secretary, a 'Mrs E', was a receptionist, telephonist, clerk and telex operator. She was entrusted with the duty of opening the mail and was frequently in possession of the keys to the safe. Du Preez employed her to do confidential typing.

In the hearing before Acting Judge Hart, 'Mrs E' admitted, after a lengthy cross-examination, that she had given one Captain Nel, a member of the security police, copies of documents, statements made by the accused and other confidential information received by Du Preez, her employer. In certain instances she had handed over the original documents, which had been copied by the security police. Captain Nel admitted that he had passed on the information obtained from 'Mrs E' to a Lieutenant Dippenaar, who was in charge of the investigation in the case against the accused. In fact Dippenaar was to all intents and purposes the junior of Mr Jansen, the Prosecutor. There was no suggestion that Dippenaar or Nel had informed Jansen of the means whereby they had obtained the confidential information from 'Mrs E'. In the result Acting Judge Hart made the following special entry:

> Whether in connection with or during the proceedings there were irregular and/or illegal departures from and infringements of the formalities, rules and principles which the law requires to be observed for a fair trial, and which resulted in a failure of justice by reason of the fact that prior to and during the Proceedings: statements of accused and/or witnesses for the defence and certain other confidential and/or privileged documents relating to the defence of the accused, the identity of the said documents being to the accused unknown, were wrongfully and unlawfully extracted from the files of the attorneys for the defence by a member of the staff of such attorneys; that such documents were copied and such copies furnished to the Security Branch of the South African Police, the investigating officer in these proceedings being a member of the Security Branch.

The Chief Justice had no hesitation in finding that the privilege that had existed between the appellants and their attorney had been breached in a particular manner from the day upon which the instructions to defend had been received, to the end of the case. The security police, through Captain Nel (to whom the documents had been given by 'Mrs E') had completely penetrated the defence and the privilege had simply been eliminated. The Chief Justice said that the irregularity was an extremely gross one, which as far as it concerned privilege could scarcely have been surpassed. Granted the security police had to fulfil a task of ensuring that law and order was maintained with every lawful means at its disposal, the court held that public policy demanded, however, that an accused in a case ought not to be subjected to what had occurred in the present case.

My friend, Dean Erwin Griswold, had instructed Lorentz & Bone to undertake the defence of the accused and he, after the accused had been found guilty and the special entry was made, supplied me with a great deal of relevant American authority, which I used in argument in the case, but a Scottish case referred to in *Cross on Evidence* [117] weighed heavily with the judge, who said:[118]

> The law must strive to reconcile two highly important interests which are liable to come into conflict (a) the interest of the citizen to be protected from illegal or irregular invasions of his liberties by the authorities, and (b) the interest of the state to secure that evidence bearing upon the commission of a crime and necessary to enable justice to be done shall not be withheld from courts of law on any mere formal or technical ground. Neither of these objects can be insisted upon to the uttermost. The protection for the citizen is primarily protection for the innocent citizen against unwarranted, wrongful and perhaps high-handed interference, and the common sanction is an action for damages. The protection is not intended as a protection for the guilty citizen against the efforts of the public prosecutor to vindicate the law. On the other hand the interest of the state cannot be magnified to the point of causing all the safeguards for the protection of the citizen to vanish, and of offering a positive inducement to the authorities to proceed by irregular methods.

The Chief Justice said that in this case, considering the nature and extent of the breach of privilege of the appellants, that it had to be found that their protection by the privilege before and during the trial had disappeared totally through the action of the security police and that thereby the trial did not comply with what justice required in this respect; and that a failure of justice had thus occurred.

I may mention that Cooper argued on the facts but it was not necessary for the court to decide on the merits of the conviction because of the court's finding that the trial was not a fair one.

This case was, in those days, regarded as unique. One wonders whether some other convictions may have been obtained by similar dirty tricks played by the police, some of which were uncovered in recent commissions popularly known as judicial commissions.

Chapter Seventeen

ON THE BENCH IN NEIGHBOURING STATES

It will be remembered that early in 1967, Judge Edward Roper had asked me whether I would accept appointments to the Courts of Appeal of Lesotho, Botswana and Swaziland, all of these up to the grant of independence having had a common Court of Appeal. Botswana, Swaziland and Lesotho had been given their independence from Great Britain in the mid-1960s. There were identical constitutions in the three countries and provision was made for a parliament. There were monarchies in Swaziland and Lesotho, the first monarchs being respectively King Sobhuza and King Mosheshwe II, and in Botswana there was a president, the first of whom was Sir Seretse Khama. Of these countries only the last has adhered to its original constitution.

In Swaziland, as a result of a decision given by the Court of Appeal (of which I was not a member), declaring an Act of the local Parliament to be *ultra vires* the constitution, King Sobhuza simply overthrew the constitution, save in regard to the provisions for the judiciary. The attorney general, Mr David Cohen, SC, subsequently Judge Cohen, was instructed to read out a completely new constitution to an assembly of chiefs.

In Lesotho, Chief Leabua Jonathan was the first prime minister. When the time came for the first election to be held, he was defeated by a rival party. He did not accept this defeat and continued as prime minister. It was the custom of the Court of Appeal when the King was in residence to call on him and to pay its respects. At one stage we were forbidden to do so in the sense that the King was no longer entitled to receive visitors. Judge Roper, who observed every decent principle of etiquette, thought that although we were forbidden to visit the King we should sign a book which was kept outside the King's palace, but we were forbidden to do this as well.

Relations between the King and the government were so bad that the King left the country and went to Oxford. There was constant hostility between the various governments and King Moshweshwe II, who was eventually deposed and succeeded by his son. Generally speaking, affairs in Lesotho have been, for some years, completely unsettled, with various instances of military coups, and governments being deposed. On one occasion the Chief Justice, at that time a South African, closed the courts for a period and returned to South Africa. When things quietened down he resumed office.

When King Moshweshwe was the monarch, I was asked to swear in the first Lesotho-born African Judge, an extremely able man who unfortunately died shortly after his appointment. The ceremony took place at the royal palace, at that time the home of the former British High Commissioner (a new palace was later provided for the monarch). On this occasion the national anthem was to be played, and it was explained that as the army band was engaged in quelling an uprising in some part of the troubled territory, a gramophone record would be played instead.

My successor, as president of the court, was Judge Peter Schutz. In desperation with the inability to secure records of cases on appeal, he resigned from this post. He is now a judge of the Transvaal Provincial Division. At the time when Judge Schutz resigned, other members of the court also resigned, with the exception of Judge Ishmail Mahomed; he was then appointed President of the Court of Appeal.

I was extremely fortunate in having Judge Roper and Judge Schreiner as my initiators in those Courts of Appeal. I think it would be impossible to find better tutors, both from the point of view of their knowledge of the law and of the manner in which they applied themselves to the work of the courts. My friend Jack Clayden, of whom I have already made mention, once told me that when he was a member of the court of the Transvaal Provincial Division, of all the other judges whom he consulted from time to time on difficult points, Judge Roper, who was on the Transvaal Bench when he was a member of it, was the most helpful. Judge Schreiner's knowledge of the law was encyclopedic. My friend Peter Schutz once said that he 'regarded judges Roper and Schreiner with awe'.

Judge Roper was President of the three Courts of Appeal until he retired. He was succeeded in all three courts by Judge Schreiner. Upon the latter having retired from the Bench of all three courts, I was appointed President of the Courts of Appeal of Botswana and Lesotho. Although I was the judge next senior to Judge Schreiner, upon his retirement Judge Ogilvie Thompson, who had recently retired as Chief Justice of the Republic of South Africa, was appointed to succeed Judge Schreiner in Swaziland. Upon Judge Ogilvie Thompson's retirement, I succeeded him as President of the Court of Appeal in Swaziland as well and remained President in all three courts until my retirement. Incidentally I might add that Judge Ogilvie Thompson was a judge of appeal when I was President of the appeal courts of Lesotho and Botswana.

I would not say that my fellow judges were all and everyone of them regarded by me with respect and admiration. But I name with respect and admiration the following: Judge A Milne, former Judge President of Natal, generally known as 'Sandy' Milne; Judge A S Smit, former Judge President of the Free State Provincial Division; Judge Louis van Winsen; the inimitable Higgy Isaacs; the distinguished Rex Welsh who was in the Swaziland Court of Appeal; Sydney Kentridge, a member of the Botswana Court of Appeal; George Bizos; Austin Amissah, who succeeded me on my retirement from the judge Presidency of Botswana, had formerly been a judge of appeal in Ghana; Judge Agudah, former Chief Justice of Botswana, a distinguished Nigerian who had been a member of a Court of Appeal in Nigeria and was the author of a number of books; Dendy Young, formerly a member of the Southern Rhodesian High Court, who, being of the opinion that the appeal court in Rhodesia, as it was then constituted, had surrendered its powers to the Smith Government in certain respects, had resigned as a matter of principle when the Smith Government was in power. Upon his resignation he was appointed Chief Justice of Botswana and became a member of that court and subsequently was a member of the appeal courts of Botswana and Swaziland. In addition, in Botswana we had Judge Doyle who had previously been Chief Justice of Zambia and Leo Baron who had previously been a judge of appeal in Zimbabwe. I do not mention the names of other judges who from time to time acted as members of the Court of Appeal with the exception of Bennie Goldin who had been a member of the Court of Appeal in Zimbabwe, and last but not least, Peter Schutz who succeeded me as President of the Court of Appeal of Lesotho.

One of the first cases in which I sat, as the junior member of the court, with Judge President Mr Justice Roper and Mr Justice Schreiner, was a matter which ended up in the Privy Council. It was the case of Molefi *v* The Principal Legal Adviser, the Prime Minister of Lesotho and the Government of Lesotho.[119]

Molefi, the appellant, who had always lived in South Africa, was arrested in August 1961. He was charged before the Regional Court at Johannesburg with being a member of an unlawful organisation, the Pan Africanist Congress (PAC) and with furthering its aims.

The actual charge against him was that of a contravention of certain provisions of the Suppression of Communism Act.[120] The charges against him related to his alleged activities between April 1960 and July 1961. He was granted bail on 28 August 1961 by the Regional Court and was due to appear in that court on 26 October 1961. He left South Africa and went to reside in Maseru, a town in the territory then known as Basutoland, which subsequently became the independent sovereign Kingdom of Lesotho on 4 October 1966. In October 1968, by which time he had been in the country for seven years, he was informed that being an 'alien', as defined in the Aliens Control Act No 16 of 1966, he was required to leave the country. On being required to leave Lesotho, Molefi invoked the provisions of section 38, the relevant provisions of which are as follows:

> (1) If any international treaty or convention relating to refugees is or has been acceded to by or on behalf of the government of Lesotho, an alien who is a refugee within the meaning of such a treaty or convention shall not be refused entry into or sojourn in Lesotho, and shall not be expelled from Lesotho in pursuance of the provisions of this Act except with his consent or except to the extent that is permitted by that treaty or convention, subject to any reservation that may be in force at the material time.
>
> (2) If any question arises –

> (a) whether an alien is a refugee;
> (b) whether any provision of an international treaty or convention relating to refugees, applies to that alien; and
> (c) whether the expulsion of that alien from Lesotho is permitted by that treaty or convention,
>
> the High Court may on the application of that alien declare that he is a refugee, that that provision of the international treaty or convention applies to him, and may declare that his expulsion from Lesotho is, or is not, permitted by that treaty or convention, or may decline to make any such declaration.

He presented a petition to the High Court of Lesotho and was granted a rule *nisi* by the chief justice, calling upon the respondents to show cause why an order should not be granted interdicting them from expelling him. After hearing argument the chief justice discharged the rule. The consequence of that was that the interim interdict ceased to operate. Molefi then appealed to our court. Pending the determination of the appeal, the interim interdict was renewed. In May 1969 the appeal was dismissed and the court gave leave to appeal to the Judicial Committee of the Privy Council in October 1969. The interim interdict was renewed pending the determination of the appeal by the Privy Council.

The appellant claimed before the Privy Council and before our court that he was protected from expulsion from Lesotho on the grounds that though he was an 'alien', he was a 'refugee' within the meaning of an international treaty or convention relating to refugees – which had been acceded to by or on behalf of the government of Lesotho – and that accordingly he could rely on the provisions of section 38 of the Aliens Control Act. In Article 1 of this international convention is a definition of the term 'refugee'. So far as material for present purposes, the term applies to any person who:

> As a result of events occurring before 1 January 1951 and owing to well-founded fear of being persecuted for reasons of race, religion, nationality, membership of a particular social group or political opinion, is outside the country of

> his nationality and is unable or, owing to such fear, is unwilling to avail himself of the protection of that country; or who, not having a nationality and being outside the country of his former habitual residence as a result of such events, is unable or, owing to such fear, is unwilling to return to it;
> In the case of a person who has more than one nationality, the term 'the country of his nationality' shall mean each of the countries of which he is a national.

The Article also contains the following important provision:

> For the purposes of this Convention the words 'events occurring before 1 January 1951' in Article 1, Section A, shall be understood to mean either
> (a) 'events occurring in Europe before 1 January 1951'; or
> (b) 'events occurring in Europe or elsewhere before 1 January 1951'; and each Contracting State shall make a declaration at the time of signature, ratification or accession, specifying which of these meanings it applies for the purpose of its obligations under this Convention.

In signing the convention, the United Kingdom declared that for the purposes of its obligations the words 'events occurring before 1 January 1951' were to be understood as referring to events occurring in Europe or elsewhere before 1 January 1951.

The first question our court had to decide was that the convention relating to the status of refugees was one that 'is or has been acceded to by or on behalf of the government of Lesotho'. The second question is whether the appellant was an alien who is a refugee within the meaning of such a treaty. It was not strictly necessary for our court to decide whether the convention relating to the status of refugees was one that has been acceded to on behalf of the government of Lesotho. Judge President Roper and Judge of Appeal Schreiner, with whom I in the end respectfully concurred, decided that the appellant was not a refugee within the meaning of the words contained in article 1 of the convention. The reasons given by our court were quoted with approval by the Privy Council as follows:

> In considering the question whether the appellant is outside South Africa as a result of pre-1951 events, one or two facts additional to those already mentioned must be in mind. The charges preferred against the appellant in 1961 referred to the period between 8th April 1960 and July 1961. The charges included charges of performing acts calculated to further some of the objects of 'Communism' by participation in the affairs of an unlawful organisation, ie the Pan Africanist Congress. That body did not come into existence until 1959. On 8th April 1960 it was declared to be an unlawful organisation. Roper P. states in his judgment that by the Unlawful Organisation Act, No 34 of 1960, the Governor General was given power specifically to declare that body an unlawful organisation without notice so that 'it must have been fairly clear to its members, including the appellant, that an unfavourable climate lay ahead of them'. The view of the learned President was that properly regarded 'the pre-1951 South African legislation and the repressive government policy referred to by the appellant' were merely the background to later events. On the undisputed facts the appellant remained in South Africa for some 13 years after the 1948 Elections and for some 11 years after the passing of the Suppression of Communism Act in 1959. The charges which were formulated in the prosecution proceedings related to 1960 and 1961.

The Privy Council approved of the judgment of the Court of Appeal, dismissing the appeal for the simple reason that it had not been shown that the appellant was outside South Africa as a result of pre-1951 events. However, although it was not necessary for the purpose of the present case to consider the point whether the convention had been acceded to by the government of Lesotho, I thought it was desirable to express an opinion on this subject in the event of other cases being brought before the court. The appellant contended that there was an accession on 22 March 1967. If there was, then as from 1 March 1968 when the Aliens Control Act came into operation, an 'alien' in Lesotho who was a 'refugee' could claim statutory protection.

Lesotho has at all material times been a member of the United

Nations. On 22 March 1967 a letter was sent by the Prime Minister to the Secretary-General of the United Nations. The letter was in the following terms:

> Your Excellency,
> The Government of the Kingdom of Lesotho is mindful of the desirability of maintenance, to the fullest extent compatible with the emergence into full independence of the Kingdom of Lesotho, of legal continuity between Lesotho and the several States with which, through the action of the government of the United Kingdom the country formerly known as Basutoland enjoyed treaty relations. Accordingly, the Government of the Kingdom of Lesotho takes the present opportunity of making the following declarations.
>
> 2. As regards bilateral treaties validly concluded by the government of the United Kingdom on behalf of the country formerly known as Basutoland, or validly applied or extended by the said government to the country formerly known as Basutoland, the Government of the Kingdom of Lesotho is willing to continue to apply within its territory, on a basis of reciprocity, the terms of all such treaties for a period of twenty-four months from the date of independence [ie, until 4 October, 1968] unless abrogated or modified earlier by mutual consent. At the expiry of that period, the Government of the Kingdom of Lesotho will regard such of these treaties which could not by the application of the rules of customary international law be regarded as otherwise surviving, as having terminated.
>
> 3. It is the earnest hope of the Government of the Kingdom of Lesotho that during the aforementioned period of twenty-four months, the normal processes of diplomatic negotiations will enable it to reach satisfactory accord with the States concerned upon the possibility of the continuance or modification of such treaties.
>
> 4. The Government of the Kingdom of Lesotho is conscious that the above declaration applicable to bilateral

treaties cannot with equal facility be applied to multilateral treaties. As regards these, therefore, the Government of the Kingdom of Lesotho proposes to review each of them individually and to indicate to the depository in each case what steps it wishes to take in relation to each such instrument, whether by way of confirmation of termination, confirmation of succession or accession. During such interim period of review, any party to a multilateral treaty which has, prior to independence been applied or extended to the country formerly known as Basutoland, may, on a basis of reciprocity, relay as against Lesotho on the terms of such treaty.

5. It would be appreciated if Your Excellency would arrange for the text of this declaration to be circulated to Members of the United Nations.

Please accept, Sir, the assurance of my highest consideration.

(Sgd) Leabua Jonathan, Prime Minister.

On behalf of the respondents it was contended that the letter was not an executive act but was a mere statement of policy not having the effect of accession to, or confirmation of, treaties binding upon Basutoland. Attention was directed to the words 'on a basis of reciprocity'. It was contended that the language of paragraph 4 of that letter is very limited and that the effect of the paragraph was that an offer was being made voluntarily to accept reciprocal obligations contained in multilateral treaties which had affected Basutoland. So it was contended that the letter amounted to no more than an offer voluntarily and on a reciprocal basis to observe certain terms of some treaties or conventions.

I was of the opinion that, so far as it concerns multilateral treaties, the reasonable meaning of the letter is that they are to continue in existence and to be considered as binding in Lesotho until such time as decisions could be made in regard to which of them should be terminated and which should be continued. The Privy Council expressed agreement with my opinion.

The case was argued by the respondents in the appeal to the Privy Council founded upon the words 'on a basis of reciprocity'. In this case the Privy Council decided that the words were not to be read as meaning more than that: if there are any reciprocal obligations in a treaty or convention which Lesotho is, at least for the time being, acceding to; and if another state failed to adhere to one of those reciprocal obligations; then Lesotho was reserving the right not to adhere to that obligation. In the judgment that I gave I was of the opinion that a declaration pending individual examination (which would take time) of those multilateral treaties which had resulted in treaties between the country formerly known as Basutoland and other states, Lesotho would adhere to those treaties. The Privy Council expressed agreement with this view.

However, the Chief Justice of Lesotho had decided that the appellant was not a refugee as defined. Our court, as stated above, was of the same opinion and the Privy Council dismissed the appeal. Notwithstanding Molefi's failure to win his appeal, he was not deported from Lesotho. I recall seeing him on many occasions until I retired from the Lesotho Bench in 1984. He was then a correspondent for various South African newspapers.

The case of The State *v* Petrus and Another[121] in Botswana was a constitutional case of some interest. In 1982 the Parliament of Botswana, by Act No 20, amended certain sections of the penal code, including Section 305, to provide for penalties of imprisonment with corporal punishment. Another Act, No 21, amended the Criminal Procedure and Evidence Act by adding certain sub-sections that provided that a person sentenced to corporal punishment under certain sections of the penal code, including Section 305, should be given four strokes each quarter in the first and last years of his term of imprisonment, such strokes to be administered 'in traditional manner with traditional instruments'.

In terms of the constitutions of Botswana, Lesotho and Swaziland, Section 7 reads:

> (1) No person shall be subjected to torture or to inhuman or degrading punishment or other treatment;
> (2) Nothing contained in or done under the authority of

> any law shall be held to be inconsistent with or in contravention of this section to the extent that the law in question authorises the infliction of any description of punishment that was lawful to the former Protectorate of Bechuanaland immediately before the coming into operation of this Constitution.

The questions submitted to the Court of Appeal were twofold: first, whether this section of the penal code made it mandatory for the court to sentence an accused person to corporal punishment as prescribed by Section 301 (3) of the Criminal Procedure and Evidence Act; and secondly, whether in any event corporal punishment prescribed in Section 301(3) of the Criminal Procedure and Evidence Act is *ultra vires,* as being in conflict with Section 7 of the Constitution of Botswana. For certain offences the Parliament provided that there was to be imprisonment for several years with corporal punishment.

After hearing lengthy argument for the appellant and for the State, the court decided in cases where persons committed offences which were punishable by imprisonment and the imposition of strokes, that this was *intra vires,* but that the provision of Section 305 that the person convicted should be given four strokes in each quarter of the first and last year of his term of imprisonment in traditional manner was *ultra vires* to the Constitution and was to be treated as null and void.

After the judgment was given and on a subsequent visit, I enquired whether the general feeling was that members of Parliament resented the decision to declare portion of an Act *ultra vires,* and I was assured that the attitude of that Parliament was that if the appeal court decided that particular Act was *ultra vires* to the Constitution, this was perfectly acceptable.

A quorum for the courts of appeal of Botswana, Lesotho and Swaziland was three members, but constitutional matters had to be heard by five members of the Court of Appeal. The members of the Court of Appeal, apart from myself, who sat in the case of The State *v* Petrus and Another, were Judges Baron, Aguda, Kentridge and Amissah. Judges Aguda, a Nigerian, and Amissah, a Ghanaian, are mentioned above. Baron, born in England, practised as an attorney in Rhodesia and was detained for a number of years without trial by the Smith Government. After he was released from detention he was appointed a judge of appeal in Zambia and when the Smith Government fell he was appointed a judge of appeal in Zimbabwe. Kentridge, a silk at the Johannesburg Bar, subsequently became one of the leading silks, if not the leading silk, in Great Britain.

In Lesotho an attempt was made to declare the government of which Chief Jonathan was prime minister unlawful, he having been defeated in a parliamentary election. It was the custom in matters coming before the Court of Appeal, that heads of argument should be submitted by counsel for the appellant and the respondent. Appearing before us one afternoon, an attorney was asked why he had not submitted heads of argument. He answered: 'My Lords, I have one head.' He simply stated that the government was unlawful and that was his only argument. It was reported to us, after the appeal was heard, that he had boasted to the judges that he had only one head. I may mention that it appeared to be obvious to persons who were listening to the case that the attorney had had a liquid lunch and there was some mirth when he stated that he had only one head. Despite the fact that no argument was addressed to us, Judge of Appeal Sandy Milne wrote a lengthy judgment dismissing the appeal.

One of the counsel who appeared for the State in Botswana in the Petrus case and in many other cases was Mr Afful, a Ghanian who argued very forcefully. On one occasion he was unsuccessful when an appeal against a decision of the Chief Justice, convicting an appellant on a charge of murder and sentencing him to death, was overturned. The court was crowded and the decision was received with applause by the spectators. We learnt subsequently that the person whom it was alleged the appellant had killed was a police informer. The next day an ordinary appeal was argued and I commented on the fact that there must have been a lot of unemployment in Lobatse, where the court sat, if cases of no interest were attended by such a large audience. One of the judges of the High Court, Judge Hannah, explained that there was no real interest in the case, but whenever Mr Afful appeared he attracted large audiences by reason of his vigorous conduct of the cases and references to what are called 'blue lies' – whatever that may mean.

Before I leave the subject of these courts, I should mention that a Chief Justice was once sued for damages for defamation of character. We persuaded a former judge of appeal in South Africa to sit at the trial, but on technical grounds the action was dismissed. Our Court of Appeal set aside this judgment and the appeal was duly heard. We came to the conclusion that it had not been proved that the Chief Justice had in fact defamed the appellant and the appeal was dismissed.

Chapter Eighteen

RHODESIA REVISITED

It was a matter of public knowledge that the South African government, at no little expense to itself, propped up the Rhodesian Front government in Rhodesia under Ian Smith for a number of years. The Africans in Rhodesia vastly outnumbered the Whites, who were in power in the Rhodesian government. Smith had broken ties with Great Britain by a Unilateral Declaration of Independence (UDI) in 1965, and various attempts by the British government to bring about a more equitable division of power between the Africans and the Whites had met with failure.

Sanctions were imposed on Rhodesia, but South Africa took no part in that. On the contrary it attempted, at considerable cost to itself, to assist Rhodesia in every possible way. The civil war in Rhodesia, which intensified from 1972, involved offensives by Africans operating as guerrillas or freedom fighters and counter-offensives from the Rhodesian army, resulting in many casualties in all sectors of the population. It seemed clear that some attempt had to be made to bring about a peaceful solution in Rhodesia. Apart from the supply of equipment there was a loss of manpower from South Africa, and Mr Vorster, then Prime Minister, determined in the early 1970s to try to induce the Smith government to come to terms with the Africans through a process of negotiation between the Smith government and African leaders, and so to bring an end to what he rightly conceived to be a fruitless effort on the part of the Smith government to retain the *status quo*.

Pressure was thus put on the Smith government by South Africa to start negotiations with the African leaders and Mr Vorster conceived the idea of having talks in a train which spanned the Victoria Falls, the southern side being in Rhodesia and the northern side being part of Zambia.

I was briefed, with a London silk, to attempt to advise the Africans, should these talks take place. I flew up to Lusaka, and was met at the airport and taken to State House, the residence of Kenneth Kaunda, then president of Zambia. I was taken to a very large room where a number of Africans were seated around an oval table. As I walked into this room one of them rushed up to me and embraced me, asking me whether I remembered him. I had to demur that I was unable to do so. He persisted, asking, 'Don't you remember the last time you saw me?' But I simply could not remember him at all; whereupon he replied: 'The last time you saw me you gave me ten years!' He was a Mr Malindi, whom in my short spell of sitting on the High Court Bench in Rhodesia (1961-1963) I had sentenced to imprisonment for conspiring to commit arson and malicious injury to property. He had been headmaster of a school for Africans and had incited a number of his pupils to set farms alight and generally to damage property of White farmers. In fact he was sentenced to two terms of imprisonment, of ten years and five years, the sentences to run concurrently. He had appealed to the Federal Supreme Court and the majority, Chief Justice Clayden dissenting, had dismissed his Appeal. Clayden had been of the opinion that I was wrong in admitting certain evidence to be led against the accused and the Court of Appeal granted leave to appeal to the Privy Council. The Privy Council held that I had indeed erred in admitting certain evidence, but came to the conclusion that the evidence wrongly admitted had no real bearing on the guilt of the accused, and his appeal was dismissed.[122] Despite the fact that Malindi served his terms of imprisonment, he apparently felt no ill towards me and embraced me as a long-lost brother.

Although I was engaged by the Rhodesian African nationalists to act as their legal adviser in this matter, my fees were paid by the English company, Lonrho, which had, and still has, substantial investments in Zimbabwe. I was briefed by their attorneys, and not only did they pay my fees, but they also flew me in their private aircraft from Germiston airport to Lusaka.

My English colleague and I were flown from Lusaka to a hotel in Livingstone within walking distance of the Bridge. We were not present at the talks, but sat in a carriage next to the one in which the talks were to take place and a microphone relayed what was happening. Mr Smith was accompanied by a member of his Cabinet, Mr Van der Byl (pronounced 'bile') and the leaders of the Africans included Bishop Abel Muzorewa, Reverend Ndabaningi Sithole, and Mr Joshua Nkomo. I do not recall Mr Robert Mugabe, who eventually became Prime Minister and subsequently the President of Zimbabwe (the name having been changed from Rhodesia), having been present at these talks.

Mr Vorster made a few opening remarks and the question immediately arose as to where further talks were to take place. Mr Smith was adamant that the talks were to be held in Rhodesia and some of the African leaders were equally adamant that they should not be held in Rhodesia because of the fact that some of them had committed crimes which would have resulted in their being arrested when they set foot in Rhodesia. The only contribution that Mr Van der Byl made was to state, at some point or another, that the matter was 'irrevalent' meaning, I suppose, that he thought the matter was irrelevant.

After Mr Vorster had spoken and the question of the venue for future negotiations had not been resolved, the parties broke up, Mr Smith and Mr Van der Byl occupying one of the carriages and the Africans another, the dining car of the train being available to both parties. The dining car, coupled to the carriage in which the talks were to take place, was well stocked with liquor, wine and soft drinks. Both sides started to 'quench their thirst' early in the day, and indeed after lunch some of them were scarcely intelligible.

I was profoundly depressed by the outcome of the talks and the calibre of the negotiators, not merely on the Rhodesian Front side, but also on the side of my own clients. I found it incredible that the Rhodesian Front was not prepared to make even the slightest concession to the African nationalists. This was evidenced by what occurred in Lusaka and subsequently at the Victoria Falls. In the ranks of the African nationalists was a lawyer called Edson Sithole (who subsequently disappeared without trace during the war); he had drawn up a new constitution for the state to be called Zimbabwe, and he gave this to me for approval. I could only describe it as a work of astounding illiteracy and incompetence. Moreover, the contents – which provided for the immediate removal of every white man employed in the Southern Rhodesian civil service and his replacement by a black man – were 'pie in the sky'. I told Joshua Nkomo and the others that, although it was not my function to advise them with regard to political matters, I did not think that the constitution drafted by Edson Sithole had the slightest hope of consideration by the Rhodesian Front.

They told me that they were of the view that the Rhodesian Front would not accept any constitution which in any way derogated from the powers which it then enjoyed. I found this incredible. My clients then asked me to draft a constitution which I thought the Rhodesian Front would accept, and I and my English colleague drafted a constitution in the space of two days, which consisted of proposals at the very opposite end of the pole to those of Sithole. Indeed, had it been adopted, it would have resulted in the white minority government obtaining terms which were far more generous than those they were eventually compelled to accept at Lancaster House in 1978.

The African nationalists read this document and told me that it had no chance of acceptance by the Rhodesian Front. I could scarcely believe that this was the case and struck a bet with some of the leaders for a bottle of whisky that it would have to receive proper consideration because it gave the other side virtually everything. In the event, the African leaders were proved correct and I was proved wrong. The Rhodesian Front never considered the constitution I had drafted. Frankly, Ian Smith, had spoken to Joshua Nkomo as if he were a kitchen servant.

President Kaunda, accompanied by an adviser, took some part in these talks. At lunch time Mr Vorster invited the Africans only, and not Mr Smith and his companion, to join him at lunch at the hotel at which we were staying. On this occasion, the Africans argued among themselves, some of their arguments being directed by the exclusion from future talks – if these were held in Rhodesia – of some of the leaders, who might be arrested on entering the country. My colleague and I drew up a document in which we suggested that whilst the negotiations took place, any persons who might have been arrested for crimes committed in Rhodesia would not be arrested.

We sent a note to Mr Smith via President Kaunda's aide giving effect to this suggestion. Mr Smith was apparently playing bridge with some other persons who had accompanied him. He read the note and, so it was reported to us, he immediately turned down the suggestion. This was in contrast to Mr De Klerk's wisdom in initiating discussions at Groote Schuur with persons who *inter alios* were liable to be arrested the moment they set foot in South Africa. I sometimes think that Mr De Klerk profited by the lesson that he had learned from Mr Smith's unwise conduct.

When the negative answer was given that night it was received by the Africans with cries of 'We will show them, now this is war.' Needless to say, by the time this negative answer was given there was not a drop of soda water left in the dining car. To put it mildly there was an uproar, so much so that the next morning Bishop Muzorewa took it upon himself to make excuses to my colleague and myself for the bad behaviour of the Africans.

Eventually some sort of settlement on a temporary basis was arranged between the Smith government and Bishop Muzorewa, but the 'struggle' continued. My conviction that the war would intensify and that many lives would be lost subsequent to these events was proved correct. The threats made by the Africans after the abortive Victoria Falls Bridge meeting were indeed carried out and there was an ever-increasing loss of life. There were two so-called Zimbabwean liberation armies: that of the Zimbabwe African People's Union (ZAPU), under the leadership of Joshua Nkomo; and that of the Zimbabwe African National Union Patriotic Front (ZANU (PF)) under the leadership of Robert Mugabe (who had supplanted Reverend Ndabaningi Sithole). ZANU (PF), was considerably more active than ZAPU, and when, eventually, an agreement was reached at Lancaster House in London, an election was held which resulted in a victory for ZANU (PF) under the leadership of Robert Mugabe. The considerable loss of life in this useless struggle could have been avoided.

It is not irrelevant to mention, likewise, that if the South African government of the day had negotiated with the leaders of the ANC when the Treason Trial ended in 1963, the armed struggle by the ANC could have been avoided and the lives of many Whites and Africans could have been saved.

Following upon the abortive meeting on the Victoria Falls Bridge, attempts were made by the British government to achieve a settlement with the Rhodesian government. The Smith regime tried to launch a campaign to persuade the 5,5m Black majority to reconsider the Rhodesian government's rejection of the attempts made by Britain to achieve a settlement (based on grounds upon which it is not necessary to embark here).

To add to the Smith government's troubles, Mozambican Frelimo guerrillas attacked the Portuguese government in Mozambique through acts of terrorism and attacks on strategic installations. At this time, Peter Niesewand, a freelance news correspondent,[123] published a report in *The Guardian* which read:

> Frelimo guerrillas in ... Mozambique have launched a major new offensive on the railway line which runs from the port of Beira to Tete, site of the giant Cabora Bassa hydro-electric scheme.
>
> According to Rhodesian intelligence reports, Frelimo bands crossed the border from Malawi last Saturday (11 November) and laid landmines at about 20 points on the Tete line. The track had been cut in several places, the reports said.
>
> The guerrillas are operating from bases in Malawi, a few miles from the Tete line. All attacks had taken place along a 100-mile front where the track runs close to the border, Rhodesian sources said.
>
> The Rhodesians are watching the security situation in Mozambique with growing concern. For months now, the road from Rhodesia to Malawi which runs through Tete has been officially considered 'unsafe', even for vehicles travelling in Portuguese military convoys. These convoys proceed at walking pace, while troops test the road for mines. But even so, a number of vehicles in the convoys have been blown up.
>
> The guerrillas are staging hit-and-run raids on lines of communication in the area, and the Rhodesians fear that their vital supply routes to the ports of Beira and Lourenço Marques may soon be threatened.
>
> Military sources said the Rhodesians are already taking an unofficial part in the Mozambique guerrilla war, including supplying aircraft of the Rhodesian Air Force for specific tasks in the neighbouring territory, and sending patrols of soldiers across on request.
>
> In August, Rhodesia's Minister of Defence, Mr Jack

> Howman, said that if the Portuguese military authorities asked Rhodesia for help to fight terrorists in the Tete area, this would be granted.
>
> Mr Howman said: 'They have, of course, a serious, a difficult situation up there. I think if our Portuguese friends wanted assistance, we would help them. But so far, they have given no indication of this.'
>
> Military sources say that although the Rhodesian government is reluctant to officially admit its forces are already taking an active part in the Mozambique war, the true position is that security forces from this country have been involved for most of this year.

Despite the truthfulness of the report, Niesewand was detained in Gwelo in solitary confinement. There was a public outcry against Niesewand's detention without trial and eventually he was tried before a magistrate on a charge of contravening the Official Secrets Act, it being stipulated by Mr Lardner-Burke, the Minister of Justice, that the trial was to be held *in camera*.

The Rhodesian Secretary of Law and Order confirmed the truth of Niesewand's report. Niesewand's evidence was that the facts set out had been published in other newspapers and he consequently had no reason to believe that the authorities had regarded it as being 'Top Secret' information. He was tried by a Regional magistrate, Mr J E T Hamilton. According to the book subsequently written by Niesewand, entitled *In Camera: Secret Justice in Rhodesia*,[124] he stated that his experience of Mr Hamilton led him to believe that before five minutes were up he would be found guilty by Hamilton and the only question was the sentence which would be imposed on him. Hamilton duly convicted him and he was sentenced to undergo two years' imprisonment with hard labour, one year of the sentence to be suspended on the condition that Niesewand was not again convicted of any offence under the Official Secrets Act during that period. An international uproar followed announcment of the conviction and sentence. Britain's shadow Foreign Minister, Mr James Callaghan, said: 'This tainted conviction makes a mockery of any fresh efforts by Mr Smith to effect a settlement.' Sir Roy Welensky, former prime minister of the defunct Federation of the Rhodesias and Nyasaland, added his voice to the chorus of protest. 'This,' he said, 'is the darkest hour for Rhodesia since UDI.' Niesewand himself recorded that:

> The London *Sunday Times* called the sentence 'savage'. In an editorial, the paper added: 'That a man should be so sentenced in a so-called democracy which pretends to be the guardian of Western and European culture against the dark hordes of barbarism is perhaps the most graphic illustration yet of the real character of the Smith regime. It illustrates not simply its tyrannical nature, but also its blind stupidity ... Sir Alec Douglas-Home ought now to say, once and for all, that the government has ceased to have any wish to deal with a regime which to describe as medieval would be to insult the Middle Ages.' The Guild of British Newspaper Editors sent a cable to Mr Smith saying that the sentence was a 'negation of democracy and interference with the freedom of the Press'. Ken Morgan, General Secretary of the National Union of Journalism, thought it was 'bloody diabolical'.[125]

I was briefed to argue the appeal. I should mention that Michael May, then a partner in the firm of Scanlen & Holderness, and previously a distinguished silk at the Rhodesian Bar, appeared for Niesewand at the trial and, in my opinion, he destroyed the case of the prosecution.

Secret trials were apparently common in Smith's day, but the Rhodesian court had never before heard an appeal *in camera*. Chief Justice Sir Hugh Beadle, together with Judges Macdonald and Goldin, sat on this appeal. Despite the prosecutor asking the court to hold the trial *in camera*, the court was reluctant to do so. The court stated that it proposed hearing sections of the appeal in public, but the responsible Minister, Mr Lardner-Burke, had issued the necessary certificate under the amended section of the Criminal Procedure and Evidence Act, that the appeal was to be held *in camera*. When this certificate was handed in by counsel for the prosecution, Sir Hugh Beadle, after perusing the document said, 'Our hands are tied.' The court had been filled with journalists who had a special interest in the case, and members of the public, who, by order of the government, were prohibited from being present at the appeal: the court was cleared.

I do not think it necessary to set out the various grounds upon which it was contended that Niesewand was wrongly convicted. Apparently the judges who were to hear the appeal wrote to Hamilton asking him to submit reasons for points in his judgment raised by the defence and when he had done so they asked him to submit further reasons. According to what Niesewand wrote, Hamilton wrote to the judges describing them as *ex tempore* reasons whereas, in fact, he had considered the matter for 17 days and had read from a prepared speech.

The appeal started on a Friday, and as it was not concluded on that day the court adjourned until Monday. As far as I can recall the hearing on Monday was a very short one and upon the conclusion of the argument, the Chief Justice immediately gave the judgment of the court. The Chief Justice said, in giving the judgment of court, that the minister's order did not permit the court to make any references to the facts of this case:

> But I may say that, after anxious consideration of all the evidence led, and having heard the very full argument addressed to it, the court has come to the conclusion that the state has not overcome the first hurdle, of showing that the information which the appellant published falls within the meaning of Section 3(c)(ii) of the Act that is, information which is likely either directly or indirectly to be useful to an enemy. In the circumstances, the decision of the court on the main charge is that the Appeal against conviction is allowed, and the verdict on that charge is set aside.

The appeal court then examined the question of whether the evidence established Niesewand's guilt on the alternative charge, which was that he had contravened the Official Secrets Act by having in his possession information relating to military matters, and by having published such information for a purpose prejudicial to the safety or interests of Rhodesia. It was clear that the matter published related to a military matter and although the onus was on Niesewand to establish that the information was not prejudicial to the safety or interest of Rhodesia, the Chief Justice said:

> Whether or not the appellant succeeded in doing this is

> again a matter purely of evidence which cannot be divulged. However, the court is satisfied, on a careful examination of the evidence, that the appellant did succeed in showing on a balance of probability that the purpose for which he published the information was not a purpose prejudicial to the interests or safety of Rhodesia. The court is also satisfied that the information itself was not in fact prejudicial to the interests or safety of the country.

Naturally the BBC and many newspapers commented on the success of this appeal.

Yet, despite the fact that Niesewand was successful in his appeal, he was still kept in detention. Lardner-Burke undertook to re-examine the order for further detention. He stipulated that Niesewand would be free from further detention and could leave the country only if he agreed not to mention anything about the trial or Rhodesian military matters. Niesewand agreed to do that, and took a plane out of Rhodesia on the same day that he was released.

Chapter Nineteen

JEWISH AFFAIRS

I was brought up in an orthodox Jewish home. My maternal grandfather, Koppel Sieradzki, was one of the founders of the Jewish Old Aged Home in Johannesburg, now known as Sandringham Gardens. Until he suffered a disabling stroke, he was active in synagogue affairs, particularly those of the President Street synagogue. Dr J H Hertz, who subsequently became Chief Rabbi of the British Commonwealth, was rabbi at the President Street synagogue (now no longer in existence). I have a distinct recollection of being taken to that synagogue at an early age by my grandfather and hearing Dr Hertz preach. Rabbi Hertz was, of course, the author of the English translation of the Bible and the commentary therein contained which is in daily use in synagogues in English speaking countries.

My mother was a member of a committee – founded by Mrs Annie Landau, the wife of Chief Rabbi Landau – that saw to it that those Jewish patients in the Johannesburg Hospital who wanted kosher food got it. In fact it was on the occasion of a visit to the hospital in May 1939, in the course of her duties as a member of the committee, that she had a brain haemorrhage and died, comparatively young. She was also, of course, an active member of the Parktown branch of the Women's Zionist League in Johannesburg. The famous 'blue box' was always in our house.

My late father took no part in communal affairs generally, but was very interested in the synagogue. He was, I think, a member of three synagogues, one in Fox Street, one in Fordsburg and one at Park Station. None of these synagogues is now in existence. The Yeoville synagogue replaced the President Street synagogue and the Park Station synagogue was replaced by the Wolmarans Street synagogue. The seat that my father occupied in that synagogue was the same one that his father had occupied and that I now occupy.

When I myself was at university I naturally became a member of the Students' Jewish Association and was the first chairman of the Students' Zionist Association formed at the University of the Witwatersrand.

My wife, Muriel, was brought up in a strongly Zionist home. Her paternal grandfather was buried on the Mount of Olives and her father was a devoted Zionist worker all his life. He first visited Palestine, as it then was, in 1905, and he visited Israel for the last time, to my knowledge, in the 1980s, making a thorough tour of the country on that occasion. He had always been active, and continued with his Zionist work almost until the day of his death at the age of 92. The family lived in Bethal and Muriel, when still at school, would often accompany her father when he went visiting farmers to collect money. In those days monies collected were designated for the Keren Hayesod or for the Keren Kayemeth, funds created for the purpose of assisting immigration of Jews, first to Palestine and then, of course, to Israel, and for the reclamation of land and the settlement of Jews – particularly in what became known as kibbutzim. Since Muriel's father invariably led campaigns for Israel, any Zionist leader who happened to visit the small but vibrant Jewish community in Bethal was naturally in close contact with her father, and was always a guest at her parents' home.

As for Muriel, she was very active in Habonim, a Zionist youth movement, at the time when the family moved to Durban. When we were married and she came to live in Johannesburg, she immediately joined the same Zionist branch to which my late mother had belonged, and from that time has been actively engaged in Zionist work. She became the chairwoman of one of the branches of the Women's Zionist League, a member of the Women's Zionist Council, president of that Council and is today the honorary life president of the Women's Zionist Organisation of South Africa. She has been a recipient of the Rebecca Sieff Award from the Women's International Zionist Organisation (WIZO).

The late chief rabbi, Dr Landau, was a great Hebrew scholar, most learned and cultivated, and his wife was the founder of the Women's Zionist League in Johannesburg. Dr Landau wrote the first modern play in Hebrew. Unlike most orthodox rabbis of his time, he was a great lover of opera and music – a love inherited by his son Felix, who, as I think I have already mentioned, left the Johannesburg Bar after his mother's death to fulfil a lifelong ambition to live in Israel and to endeavour to play a part in the building of that state.

I may mention that Felix had an offer of a lucrative partnership in a foremost firm of attorneys, but made up his mind to serve the state. He took a comparatively minor post as a legal adviser in one or other ministry, but naturally worked his way up in the civil service until he reached the office of the attorney general. He was thereafter appointed a judge of the District Court of Jerusalem, of which he subsequently became president. A district court in Israel has virtually the same status as that of a provincial division in South Africa. On reaching the age limit, he retired from that position but remained actively engaged in work for the Hebrew University as a member of the board of governors of that body. He was also for many years on the governing body of the Israel Philharmonic Orchestra. He contributed regularly to the *Jerusalem Post* on interesting matters that have arisen in the courts of Israel and acted as an arbitrator from time to time in important civil disputes, often of an international nature. But quite apart from all his activities he was one of the most thoughtful, kindly and truest of friends that anyone could wish to have. We have always maintained a correspondence with each other and when Muriel and I were last in Israel we naturally spent time with him and his wife Laura. Laura, who of necessity had to augment the meagre salary which Felix earned when working in minor ministries, was a professional guide in Israel. Felix was the 'star' of a dinner party which he had organised for Muriel and myself, and to which were invited some of our friends in Jerusalem. Unfortunately Laura was unable to attend the dinner, and has recently passed away.

Shortly after we were married, I was asked by Dr Landau to offer myself for election to the committee of the Wolmarans Street synagogue which was part of the United Hebrew Congregation. I was duly elected to the committee, and eventually became chairman and then president of the United Hebrew Congregation. Muriel was later elected a member of the synagogue council, and took an active part in organising and assisting in the conduct of services held specially for the youth and younger children.

As successor to Dr Landau, we were very lucky to have the late Chief Rabbi Dr L I Rabinowitz. Early in 1939, Muriel and I were in London and went one sabbath evening to the Great Synagogue in the East End (destroyed by the Luftwaffe in the Second World War). We heard a youngish rabbi deliver a most powerful sermon. On my enquiring from the man sitting next to me who this rabbi was, I was told that he was Rabbi Rabinowitz, whom he followed around wherever he happened to be delivering a sermon. In the result, when towards the end of 1944 the question of the choice of a rabbi to succeed Dr Landau arose, I was able to give some information about Dr Rabinowitz to the meeting held for that purpose. Dr Rabinowitz had also been a chaplain to the forces in the Second World War and particularly in the war zone in North Africa. I have over the years heard many rabbis deliver sermons, but those of Dr Rabinowitz were quite remarkable. He was an orator *par excellence* and a man of great learning. He did not hesitate to express himself on ethical matters affecting the country and particularly those affecting the Jewish community. He left South Africa in about 1962 to live in Israel, where he became one of the deputy editors of that great work, the *Encyclopaedia Judaica*.

I last saw Rabbi Rabinowitz in Israel after he had been ill for some time and shortly before he died. Muriel and I spent a fascinating afternoon with him at the King David Hotel in Jerusalem. Although he was no longer his former self, the discussion with him was certainly, as far as we were concerned, a memorable one.

Fortunately for us, at the time that Dr Rabinowitz became our chief rabbi we had, in the Wolmarans Street synagogue, Chief Cantor Alter. He was a refugee from Hitler and after serving our congregation faithfully for many years, he left for America where he became an acknowledged authority and teacher of the cantorial art in the United States.

Both Rabbi Rabinowitz and Cantor Alter took an active part in creating and conducting the services for the youth and younger children, which were well attended. Our son, Jeffrey, used to act as the cantor at these services, particularly on the high festivals. It was due to the efforts of men like Rabbi Rabinowitz and Cantor Alter that many young people, Jeffrey being one of them, are able to conduct a service on any sabbath or festival. Jeffrey, who has an ear for music, has become somewhat of an expert in his incantation of the Haftorah,[126] and he has frequently been honoured by being asked to recite the Haftorah whenever he has visited us in Johannesburg; and in the United States, ever since he has been living there, regularly on the high festivals.

Jeffrey married his wife, Carol Elkin, in Johannesburg in 1961 but left the country in 1966 for the United States where he still resides. After qualifying in medicine at the University of the Witwatersrand, he spent his internship at Baragwanath Hospital. One of the students who qualified in the same year as Jeffrey was an African who also spent his internship at Baragwanath. The salary he received was half of Jeffrey's – which was in itself not great – but this discrimination was something which Jeffrey could not tolerate and he and Carol decided to emigrate. He was anxious to specialise in a particular field and he tried first of all to ascertain whether there was an opening for him in Israel. There was none (and it seems somewhat ironical that he has since been invited to deliver lectures in Israel in his field of neo-natology). Consequently they decided to emigrate to the United States, where he was able to obtain permanent residence. This was during the Vietnam war and Jeffrey, although not yet a citizen, was called up to serve in the United States Army, in which he eventually became a lieutenant colonel. Fortunately for him – no doubt because he was engaged in research work – he was not sent to Vietnam, but served at the famous Military Hospital in Washington, where General Eisenhower died. Jeffrey and Carol have four children, all of whom spent a year in Israel after leaving school and prior to their entering university. They, of course, have become entirely fluent in Hebrew. Their youngest child, took Hebrew as one of his undergraduate subjects at Brown University in Providence, Rhode Island. They have all retained their interest in Israel and take part in various activities in that connection in the United States. All Jeffrey and Carol's children have graduated at various universities. The eldest daughter graduated BA *Cum Laude* at the University of Pennsylvania in Philadelphia and is presently studying for a Masters Degree at Clark University in Worcester, a city near Boston. The second daughter, after a spell of work with the American Civil Liberty Organisation in New York, has graduated BA at Columbia University. The third daughter has a BA *Magna*

Cum Laude from Harvard, and to my joy applied successfully to enter Harvard Law School. Jeffrey's son, James, is a George Marshall scholar at Balliol College, Oxford.

I was elected to the executive of the South African Jewish Board of Deputies in the 1930s, and served on it until I joined the armed forces in 1940. The South African Jewish Board of Deputies is concerned with the protection of the interests of the Jewish community in South Africa. Its importance as a guardian of the rights of Jewish citizens in this country became more apparent and necessary during this period, with the rise of Hitler and the birth of Nazi-aligned groups in this country, particularly the body known as 'the Grey Shirts'. When the war was over I rejoined the executive of the board and was, after some time, elected chairman and then president. I ceased my active association with the board in the late 1950s, a few years before I went to Rhodesia.

One hears from time to time of people seeking political office talking of the 'Jewish vote'. In my opinion, save for one period to which I shall now refer, there never has been a Jewish vote in South Africa. The Jews have exercised their full rights as citizens to vote for whatever party they pleased. The exceptional case arose before the Second World War and for some time thereafter, when, in the Constitution of the National Party of the Transvaal (but not, curiously enough, in any other province) it was expressly provided that no Jew could become a member of the party. This was the first and only time, that I am aware of, that the Jewish Board of Deputies actively took steps to persuade Jews not to vote for the National Party; not that I think much persuasion was needed. I am not certain when this clause in the constitution was eventually scrapped.

When I was associated with the Jewish Board of Deputies it had the good fortune to have two of the most competent and able members of what I might call, for the sake of convenience, the 'Jewish civil service'. They were the late Gus Saron and the late Jack Rich. I should also make mention here Mr Lazer Druion, who rendered devoted service in the financial sphere of the work of the board.

Gus Saron matriculated in the same year as I did and we took a BA together at the University of the Witwatersrand. Gus then took a BA (Hons) and won a scholarship to Oxford. Professor Haarhoff,

Professor of Classics, once told me that Gus was the best student he had ever had. After taking a BA at Oxford he returned to South Africa to take an LLB, and joined the Bar. He stayed at the Bar until 1936. This was the year in which the Grey Shirt movement was at its peak. The Jewish Board of Deputies had already undergone a great change in its executive. The chairman, the late Cecil Lyons, who had come to Johannesburg from Durban, was a man of great ability and energy who really gave his life to the board. Acting on behalf of the board, he approached Gus Saron to become the secretary of the board. I remember Gus coming to discuss with me whether he should accept the appointment offered to him. I told him that I did not know how good it would be for him personally to give up the Bar and take up this new task, but that, in my opinion, it would certainly be a good thing for the Jewish community if he did. He accepted the appointment. His title was changed to that of general secretary in 1940 after the Jewish Board of Deputies, again through Cecil Lyons, was able to recruit Jack Rich as secretary.

In addition to his duties at the Jewish Board of Deputies, Gus Saron was a lecturer in the Department of Classics and the Department of Hebrew at the University of the Witwatersrand in the period 1929-1930. He used to write leading articles for the *Zionist Record* as well as for *Jewish Affairs*, of which, I think, he was one of the founders. He was joint editor with Louis Hotz of *The Jews of South Africa: A History*. He was also a regional editor for South Africa of the *Encyclopaedia Judaica*. Altogether, he was an intellectual giant. He was one of those who conceived the idea of the United Communal Fund, and upon his retirement from the board, he undertook to write a history of South African Jewry. He did a tremendous amount of work, but unfortunately died before the book was ready for publication.

Jack Rich, who had taken an MA and a law degree at Cambridge, and had been the editor of the *Jewish Chronicle*, was the perfect secretary. He was largely responsible for the administration of the board. He knew all sorts of things that other people did not. For example he was an expert on protocol. One does not always realise how touchy people are when they do not receive the right place at a table at an official function. Jack Rich could tell you without any difficulty what the order of precedence was and the proper thing to do. He was a tremendous reader and had a magnificent library. In addition, he was a lover of good music and had an enormous collection of gramophone records. He was also a most agreeable person, who got on well with everybody. He was, in short, a cultivated gentleman.

With regard to executive members of the board during this period, the two outstanding men were Cecil Lyons, and his successor as chairman, Gerald Lazarus. The latter was an attorney. He too devoted his life to the work of the board. His son, John Lazarus, like his father before him a man of character, became a brilliant advocate and was appointed to the Bench, but regrettably suffered an untimely death not long afterwards.

As far as the Zionist Federation was concerned, I was co-opted to the executive of that body in 1939. War broke out soon after I had been co-opted. After the war I discovered that the party system had been introduced into the election of members of the executive of the federation. I did not and have never believed in the value of Zionist parties outside of Israel. I did not stand for election nor was I asked to join a party in the various offices I subsequently enjoyed in the South African Zionist Federation. As I mentioned previously, during the time that we were in Rhodesia I was elected an honorary vice-president of the South African Zionist Federation. (I should also mention here that when we moved to Rhodesia, Muriel immediately became active in the women's Zionist work in that country.)

In 1939 Great Britain, the mandatory power over Palestine, issued the notorious White Paper designed to limit Jewish immigration to Palestine – despite the terms of the Balfour Declaration. It will, of course, be appreciated that when the Second World War ended, only a limited number of Jews were permitted by the British to seek entry and refuge in Palestine and this despite the fact that the thousands who had been released from the notorious concentration camps set up by the Germans were again temporarily housed in camps in Europe. Leon Uris's book *Exodus* is well worth reading on this subject, because it portrays not merely the hardships that these people had to endure after their release from the concentration camps, but also the steps taken by the British to prevent them from entering Israel.

There did, however, take place what was called illegal immigration in which the Haganah played a great part. They were rescuing Jews to enable them to settle in a land which it was hoped, at that time, would become their own; and of course it did become their own when the state of Israel was declared in May 1948. When that happened there was a flood of refugees from the camps into Israel. There was, of course, no suitable accommodation for the thousands who came, but the Jews already living in Israel welcomed them and did everything possible to help them in what was to be their new home. They had, of necessity, to be accommodated in camps. The burden of providing accommodation and supporting many of these new immigrants was, of course, too much for the Jews living in Israel and reliance had to be placed, to a considerable extent, on assistance from funds which could be collected from Jews in the United States of America, South Africa, England and other countries of the western world.

I have already referred to Verwoerd's embargo on the transfer of funds to Israel, but I may mention that in addition to his other qualities Verwoerd was an anti-semite. This had been demonstrated many years before when he was editor of *Die Transvaler*, having left his position as a professor at Stellenbosch University. In the very first leading article written by him, he proposed a *numerus clausus* for Jews who wished to enter universities. That he hated Africans, Asiatics and Coloured people was demonstrated by his Bantu Education policy, the Group Areas Act, and in many other ways. He has been called the arch apostle of apartheid and regrettably this policy was followed with enthusiasm by his henchmen, some of whom survive today, who were initiated into those policies which have caused inestimable damage to this country and its peoples.

Being embroiled in Zionist affairs, I had the good fortune to meet many distinguished Israelis. Accompanying Mr David Ben Gurion on his visit to South Africa was Chaim Herzog, who subsequently became president of Israel. I accompanied Chaim Herzog at meetings that he addressed in support of the campaign for the immigration and absorption of Jews in Israel, which was then in operation. He and his brother Yaacov were born in Ireland when his father was chief rabbi in that country. They had emigrated to Israel as boys when their father was appointed chief rabbi of what was then Palestine. He was educated at Cambridge and served in the British Army during the Second World War in north-west Europe, and was director of military intelligence in Israel for some years. He was, in addition, the first military governor of the West Bank of the Jordan in 1967, after the Six-Day War. His radio talks, broadcast all over the world during the Six-Day War, are indeed memorable. He has also written many books, and it is difficult to imagine a person more fitted to be president of Israel. In 1970 he was awarded an honorary knighthood. I had the pleasure of meeting him at the modest presidential home in Jerusalem. Interestingly, but not surprisingly, he has retained his Irish brogue.

We had the privilege of hosting his brother Yaacov on a similar campaign. He was accompanied by his charming wife, Pnina, to conduct a campaign for funds for the same cause. Yaacov Herzog had been personal adviser to Ben Gurion when the latter was prime minister. He was Israel's ambassador to Canada, minister plenipotentiary at the Israeli embassy in Washington, director general of the Prime Minister's Office and political adviser to the prime minister of Israel from 1965 until his untimely death in 1972. Muriel and I had the privilege of spending a good deal of time with Yaacov and Pnina when they were here, and were able to see Pnina on our last visit to Israel.

Before I met either Chaim or Yaacov Herzog, Muriel and I had the privilege of entertaining their father, then chief rabbi of Israel, and his wife, who was an extremely wise person as well. I happened to be ill in bed with a dose of flu and the chief rabbi came upstairs to visit me. Some years later I was introduced to the chief rabbi's wife and she immediately said that she had been to our home in Johannesburg. She must have met many hundreds of people since her visit to South Africa.

Pnina is presently deputy director-general of Israel's Ministry of Health. As a pharmacist, she worked in the ministry's pharmacy division from 1965 to 1985, and was re-appointed when Mr Yitzhak Rabin was re-elected as prime minister in 1993. Prior to a 30-year taboo against Israel's representatives being elected to senior positions in the United Nations, she had held positions in the World Health Organisation. The taboo was broken when she was unanimously named the representative of the European region in the World Health Organisation at an annual meeting held in Copenhagen in 1992.

Yaacov Herzog, when he was ambassador to Canada, had a famous public debate with Professor Arnold Toynbee at McGill University in 1961. This debate was subsequently published in a book containing some of his speeches and writings, entitled *A People That Dwells Alone*. In this book tribute is paid to him by Mr Zalmon Shazar, president of Israel from 1963 to 1973, and by the famous Sir Isaiah Berlin. I take the liberty of quoting one passage from Sir Isaiah's tribute. I do so because this is the impression which he left, I believe, on everyone who was fortunate enough to have met him. It reads:

> In appearance he was gentle and unassuming; but within that frail body there lived a firm and powerful spirit which, armed with a sharp, critical brain, fine perceptions, inexhaustible patience, a great and perpetually growing store of beautifully ordered, accurate knowledge, made him intellectually formidable. As a political analyst and observer he had few equals and, I should guess, no superior. But he was more than this. Because he understood and loved everything connected with the culture, the history and, above all, the religious experience of his own nation, he understood the quality of other nations and customs, and the inner life of individuals who belonged to other faiths. They, in their turn, felt this and responded to him as they did to few public servants or political officials of Israel.

Another distinguished prime minister of Israel to visit this country was Mr Yitzhak Rabin. As is well known he was chief of staff of the Israeli forces in the 1967 Six-Day War. After that war he was appointed ambassador for Israel to the United States. As soon as his period of office there ended he was persuaded to come to South Africa. This was in 1973. I was then the chairman of the South African Zionist Federation, and Muriel and I were lucky enough to be able to take him and his wife, Lea, to the Kruger National Park for a week. Rabin is not an orator, but he is a no-nonsense man and a thinker who can express himself clearly and succinctly – the latter quality not always observed by speakers from Israel, and elsewhere, to whom I have had to listen in the course of my communal life. He became prime minister of Israel shortly after he had visited South Africa, when Golda Meir had resigned as prime minister after the Yom Kippur War. Whilst Rabin was ambassador to the United States he naturally had a small bank account in Washington. When he came back to Israel the money in the American bank was left there. It was not a large sum at all and Mrs Rabin, on a visit to the United States, was seen to draw some of this money. In those days Israelis were not allowed to have foreign bank accounts without the necessary permission. Rabin had not obtained this permission. In fact he had probably forgotten all about the small amount in that account. When a journalist discovered that Mrs Rabin had drawn some money from this bank in Washington there was a tremendous outcry in the Israeli newspapers. Rabin consulted his minister of justice, a leading lawyer, Mr Zadok, and they came to the conclusion that the right and honourable thing for Rabin to do was to resign as prime minister, which he did. He thought it was wrong, albeit inadvertently, for a person occupying his office to have broken the law. I often wonder whether the same standard of morality is of general application to persons who hold high office in their respective countries.

As prime minister, Rabin used to have special meetings with the board of governors of the Jewish Agency when he briefed us on the state of affairs. The Jewish Agency was engaged in practical work for the citizens of Israel and in particular immigration and settling the immigrants. It was also engaged in other projects, and the importance of its work cannot be underestimated.

Shortly before one of these meetings the Syrians had entered and virtually occupied Lebanon. Rabin said that he had been urged by certain people to have Israel go into Lebanon. This he said he refused to do, his attitude being that his job was to defend the borders of Israel and not to get involved in Lebanon. It is a matter of lasting regret that the person who succeeded him as prime minister, Mr Menachem Begin, was advised (by a person who is undoubtedly a top-rate military man, Ariel Sharon) to send Israeli troops into Lebanon – an expedition which turned out to be harmful to Israel in the loss of lives and in many other ways. I have always had little doubt that Mr Begin's resignation as prime minister and his withdrawal entirely from public life, was largely, if not solely, due to the sorrow that he felt as a result of the ill-fated Lebanese invasion.

From the time of the establishment of the state of Israel until today, the country and its citizens have had to fight many wars. There was first of all the War of Independence when the United Nations had resolved to partition Israel, giving part of the country to be governed by the state of Israel and part by the Palestinians. This partition was accepted by Ben Gurion and the people of Israel, but not by the Palestinians, whose aim was to destroy the Jewish state; or rather, to prevent the creation of a Jewish state. Armed forces of Egypt, Syria, Iraq, Lebanon and Jordan set about trying to destroy the state at its inception. Even before that happened, during the time of the British mandate, the Arabs committed atrocities of an unspeakable kind against the Jewish population.

The general view held at the time was that it suited British interests to favour the Arabs. The notorious White Paper was evidence of this and indeed Mrs Margaret Thatcher makes reference to the attitude of the British Foreign Office, with which she did not agree, that Israel was the pariah of the Middle East. She refers, of course, to the time when the state had already been established. How misplaced was British policy, prior to the Second World War and when the Second World War broke out, was demonstrated by the fact that the Jews in Israel joined the Allies against the Germans, and fought in the British army and in the Jewish Brigade, whereas the Grand Mufti of Jerusalem was on the side of Hitler.

How the Israelis managed to defeat the united Arab forces in what was known as the War of Independence, remains a miracle. There were the constant incursions into Israel by terrorists who murdered civilians, women and children. There was the 'Suez Canal War' in which France and Britain joined with the Israelis, who reached the Suez Canal but were forced by the United States and Soviet Russia to withdraw. There was the Six-Day War in 1967. There was the Yom Kippur War of 1973 when Anwar El Sadat, then President of Egypt, chose the holiest day in the Jewish calendar to launch an attack against the Israeli forces who were then in occupation of the Negev as a result of the defeat of the Egyptians and their allies in the Six-Day War and which ended when the Israeli army crossed the Suez Canal and came within striking distance of Cairo. In this 'Yom Kippur War' the Egyptians had as their allies the Syrians. The Golan Heights, now occupied by Israel, which I visited a week after the Six-Day War had been concluded, was up to the time the Syrians were defeated in that war the place from which settlements in Israel were bombarded by the Syrians. The importance of the occupation of the Golan Heights by Israel is perhaps not as great nowadays as it was then. I say this because of the development of missiles which can be fired from great distances into Israel, as was demonstrated in the Iraq 'Desert War' in 1991, perhaps better known as the 'Gulf War'. These Scud missiles, which caused considerable damage in certain parts of Israel, particularly Tel Aviv, were fired from Iraq despite the fact that Israel took no part in that war.

The picture then is that the citizens of Palestine and then Israel have never been left in peace, either prior to the coming into existence of the state of Israel, or since it came into existence in 1948. Hamas terrorists, in particular, have been active and there is evidence that these terrorists, despite agreements concluded with them, are still active. They are opposed to the peace arrangement concluded by Yasser Arafat in which, for the first time, Palestinians acknowledged the state of Israel and its right to exist in peace. When Israel took steps to send 400 of them out of the country for a while, the wrath of the nations descended on Israel.

It is, I think, worthwhile going back to the events which preceded the Six-Day War. Egypt, under Gamal Nasser, had taken steps clearly indicative of an intention to start a war against Israel. The point I wish to make is that Israel had asked the United Nations Security Council to meet in order to deal with the situation that had arisen as a result of Nasser's action. The Russians opposed the security council meeting at that time. When, however, it became apparent that the Israelis were winning the war, Egypt and its allies having been completely defeated, Russia demanded immediate convening of the security council to get a resolution through calling upon the Israelis to stop the war. Russia, of course, had supplied Egypt and the other Arab states with arms, and has continued to do so. Russia broke off relations with Israel after the Six-Day War, and endeavoured to have the security council pass a resolution censuring Israel's conduct of the Six-Day War.

It is not difficult to see why Arafat was anxious to conclude some peace agreement with Israel, but I do not wish to go into that. I would rather revert to an article written by James Reston in the

New York Times commenting on the Russian 'motion of censure of Israel' after the Six-Day War. It reads:

> Mr Kosygin's request that the United Nations should pretend that two and a half million Israelis were a menace to eighty million Arabs and should be punished like a race of moral monsters, set the stage for the Israeli foreign minister, Abba Eban, who talked like a Cambridge Don and who came through like a tank commander. It is easy to understand after listening to this debate between Kosygin and Eban why the Russians are suspicious of free speech. Eban worked through Kosygin's arguments with all the gentility of General Dayan's tanks in the desert.[127]

I quote this especially because it is time that the world stopped talking about the 'poor' Palestinians or the 'poor' Arabs. The Arab refugees who are in Israel are there because the oil rich Arab nations who have plenty of money and space, won't have them in their own countries and the presence of these refugees, in camps in Israel, is something which is held against Israel. According to the terms of a recent peace agreement, Israel handed over control of the Gaza Strip to the Palestinians. After the Six-Day War Israel wanted to give the Gaza Strip back to the Egyptians, who up to then had been in control of it, but the Egyptians didn't want it. Incidentally I may mention that Israel had taken steps to improve the living conditions of the Palestinians in the Gaza Strip, but the Gaza Strip became a hotbed of the Hamas fundamentalists. The true miracle of the Middle East is that despite the hordes of Arabs hostile to it, despite the assistance which up until recently the Arabs received from the Russians, Israel exists and will continue to exist as a democratic state that has managed to overcome the acts of aggression against it over the years.

It is perhaps not inappropriate, having regard to such events, to refer to something Mr Eban said in June 1967, in the course of his address at the United Nations after the Six-Day War:

> The Arab states can no longer be permitted to recognise Israel's existence only for the purpose of plotting its elimi-

> nation. They have come face-to-face with us in conflict. Let them now come face-to-face with us in peace.

It took the Arabs 26 years, from the time that speech was made, to come face-to-face with Israel in what one hopes will result in peace.

From the time that I retired from the board of governors of the Jewish Agency in 1977, I did not take part in any aspect of Jewish communal life. I believed and still believe that older men must give way to younger men. Muriel, however, still continued her Zionist work. Our son, Jeffrey, who is in America, has worked for the United Jewish Appeal, our daughter Elizabeth who lives in England is active in the Women's International Zionist Organisation (WIZO), and our daughter, Helen, when she lived in New York, did work for Israel Bonds. Now that she is living in Johannesburg she has, of course, joined one of the branches of the Women's Zionist Organisation.

Occasionally one heard some strange remarks at Zionist meetings. There was an occasion when a member of the executive of the South African Zionist Federation, critical of the Jewish community, said the trouble was that they were 'chicken livered.' Another man, when enthusiasm for Israel seemed to weaken somewhat, said that 'they're jumping off the bandwagon'. Then there was a person who introduced the great Dr Chaim Weizmann as not only being a great scientist, but also as a 'performing Jew' and finally there was the chairman of a meeting who introduced a well-known kibbutznik by saying that the men in the kibbutzim were 'after all the scum of the earth.'

One of the privileges that I had as a result of my being engaged in Zionist work, and particularly as a member of the board of governors of the Jewish Agency, was in being able to meet every prime minister of Israel with the exception of Yitzhak Shamir. I have already mentioned Mrs Golda Meir and Mr Ben Gurion. Perhaps it is not out of place to say something about some of the others.

The first prime minister whom I met was Levi Eshkol. He was, in fact, prime minister at the outbreak of the Six-Day War in 1967. He was an amiable person with a wonderful sense of humour. I had the privilege of being one of a delegation of members of the board of governors of the Jewish Agency to have a meeting with him at which, I think, I have already stated there were other cabinet ministers present. Our discussions were on a most friendly scale, with humorous remarks every now and then by Mr Eshkol. He convened certain conferences of people from all over the western world. Sometimes at these conferences confidential matters were discussed – confidential in the sense that they were meant solely for the ears of those present. On one such occasion, a participant said that he wished to say something of importance but his problem was that it would probably be in the newspaper the next day, and this he found quite unacceptable. Eshkol quipped, 'Well, you can consider yourself lucky. In my case they report what I intend saying before I have even said it.'

I had met Mr Begin long before he became prime minister. In fact on one of his visits to this country he accepted an invitation to have dinner at our home. The local members of his party, then called Revisionists and now called Likkud, were so worried about his safety that they insisted that he have a guard with him at the dinner. Mr Begin was, of course, a fiery orator with an excellent knowledge of the English language, which, he said, he had acquired as a result of listening to broadcasts of the BBC when he was in the underground movement (the Irgun) fighting British control during the mandatory period.

I have also had the good fortune to meet prominent cabinet ministers like Shimon Peres, a former prime minister. He is an extremely able man and a clear thinker. As foreign minister, he negotiated a recent agreement with the Palestine Liberation Organisation (PLO). When he visited South Africa in the early 1990s he delivered a brilliant address in which he emphasised something that is not always appreciated: the necessity of solving the water problem in the Middle East.

Presidents of Israel with whom I have had discussions include Mr Yitzhak Navon, a cabinet minister in the government of Israel, a cultivated Sephardic Jew whose home I visited one Friday evening long before he became a member of the government and, of course, Mr Chaim Herzog, whose brilliant addresses during the Six-Day War will never be forgotten. President Ezer Weizman, a nephew of the first president of Israel, the great Chaim Weizmann, looks like his uncle – whom I met when he was in South Africa and whom Muriel got to know much better. Chaim Weizmann made the famous remark that the Kruger National Park as a home for animals was larger than Palestine, as it then was. Ezer Weizman was, of course, a pilot in the Royal Air Force during the Second World War and was head of the Israel airforce during the 1967 Six-Day War. He was then regarded as a 'hawk', but is now regarded as a 'dove'. He played an important role at Camp David when President Sadat and Mr Begin signed the peace treaty between Egypt and Israel, through the good offices of President Jimmy Carter of the United States. This 'fragile' treaty lasted for many years and Mr Sadat's successor President Hosni Mubarak seemed to have played a part in bringing about the peace agreement between Israel and the PLO of the early 1990s.

Apart from prime ministers, presidents and cabinet ministers whom I met over the years, there were a number of other Israelis whom I knew, or got to know. A lifelong friend of mine was Arthur Lourie. After obtaining a law degree at Cambridge, he came to the Johannesburg Bar, but decided to leave the Bar to become political secretary of the Zionist Organisation in London. The head, of course, of this office was Dr Chaim Weizmann. When Arthur later settled in Israel, the famous Abba Eban succeeded him as political secretary to the organisation. Arthur had a distinguished career in the diplomatic corps. He was ambassador to Canada, to the United Nations and to the Court of St James. I invariably visited him when he was in Jerusalem (where, incidentally, he had an apartment in the same building as Nahum Goldmann – to whom I shall make further reference later).

On one of my visits to him I met Professor Yigael Yadin, the world famous archaeologist. Before the War of Independence Yigael Yadin was the Haganah chief of operations. The mandatory authorities, that is the British, thought that he was merely an archaeological student who spent his time at the Rockefeller Museum. He also became chief of operations during the War of Independence. Ben Gurion was opposed to having any military men in his cabinet, but he made an exception by offering Yigael a position as a cabinet minister – which, however, Yigael declined. He had, when I met him at Arthur Lourie's apartment, become famous for his archaeological excavations at Masada. Any visitor to Israel who has not been to Masada should, in my opinion, remedy that error as soon as possible. A great deal has been written about that 'dig', including a book by Yigael Yadin himself. his name is also associated, of course, with the acquisition of the Dead Sea Scrolls, which form a permanent exhibition in Jerusalem. The content of the scrolls is still a matter of controversy amongst scholars and Yigael Yadin himself has written about them. In addition to the dig at Masada, he conducted other important digs such as the one at Hazor.

I made up my mind that I would try to get Yigael to come to South Africa to deliver some lectures here. With the assistance of Arthur, and after great difficulty, I was able to persuade him to do so. He made it a condition of his visit that he would give lectures only in venues which were open to all, in other words there was to be no apartheid. To this, naturally, I agreed and he came out to South Africa with his wife Carmella. Carmella, who was a person of strong character, and managed all Yigael's affairs, was a member of the Ruppin family. One of her brothers was the Israeli consul general in Tanzania when we lived in Salisbury, and he paid us a visit there one day. Her father, Arthur Ruppin, was a key figure in the development of what has been called 'the Jewish state in the making', from the time he opened an office for the Zionist Organisation in Palestine in 1908. He was a founder of the kibbutz and Moshav movements. He also became the first Professor of Sociology at the Hebrew University. An anthology of Arthur Ruppin's memoirs, diaries and letters, originally published in German, was translated into English through the initiative and generosity of an American Jew, Sam Rothburg.

To say that Yigael Yadin's lectures were a success in South Africa is an understatement. The first lecture (over which I had the honour of presiding) was held at the University of the Witwatersrand Great Hall. His lectures were accompanied by slides that showed various aspects of his work at Masada. The day before he was to give his lecture I had to take him to the university so that he could satisfy himself that the equipment available there was such as to enable his lecture to be heard and his slides to be seen. The Great Hall, of course, was packed. In fact queues of people waited from the early hours of the morning to get tickets to the two lectures which he was to deliver at the university. The principal of the university was then Professor I D MacCrone. I told him about Yadin's intended visit and also something about his work and fame. He asked me to show him some of the books that Yigael had written, which I, of course, did. There was then, and probably still is, a special committee at the university which decides on whom honorary degrees should be conferred. Professor MacCrone, who presided at the second lecture, at which I was a member of the audience, announced that the university had decided to confer an honorary degree on Professor Yadin, and in due course an honorary doctorate of science was conferred on him at a graduation ceremony. He also delivered lectures in the Cape.

Apart from his eminence as an archaeologist he was, if I may be permitted to say so, a fine human being. He made one error. He was persuaded, at one stage of the many political crises that occur in Israel, to start a new party. This party received quite substantial support, but he decided to form a coalition with another party and, generally speaking, his venture into politics was a failure. Both Yigael and Carmella had untimely deaths, but his work lives on. He was a scholar of the first rank.

Accompanying the Yadins to South Africa was Mrs Miriam Sacher, a member of the Marks family (of Marks & Spencer fame). Mrs Sacher's husband had been an attorney who practised in Palestine and her son, Michael, was a member of the board of governors of the Jewish Agency representing the English Zionist movement, at the same time that I was on the South African board of governors. On a trip to London, Yigael had visited Mrs Sacher, and she had enquired of him what he most wanted to do. He said he wanted to undertake a dig at Masada. Although Mrs Sacher offered to defray some of the expense entailed in this dig, he thought that it was unfair for her to undertake what may have been a great financial obligation. As it happened, in London he happened to meet a correspondent of the newspaper, *The Observer*, which was then controlled by the Astor family. In the 'silly seasons' in London there was constant reference to the legendary Loch Ness monster, which, although never discovered is popularly supposed to be in the Scottish Loch Ness. He mentioned to *The Observer* correspondent that he thought that instead of publicising the Loch Ness monster, it would be of great interest to *The Observer* to publicise the dig at Masada. He was invited to lunch by Lord Astor and was promised a large amount if he would render weekly reports to *The Observer* of the progress of the dig.

During his visit to South Africa, we took Yigael Yadin to the Kruger Park, where we spent a night at one of the camps. The next morning the chief warden, who had apparently learnt of the presence of 'General' Yadin, as he was also known, called to enquire whether we would like to be taken around the park by him. Naturally we jumped at this invitation. He took us to parts of the reserve off the beaten track and we saw every conceivable kind of animal. He also, of course, told us about the habits of certain animals. One of the things I remember was that he stressed the ability of elephants to hear from afar. One most remarkable sight we enjoyed was at sunset where, at a watering hole, there was virtually a Noah's ark collection of animals. Yigael was a keen photographer and he had with him top rate cameras. He must have taken at least 40 pictures of these animals at the watering hole, but to his disgust and horror he found out the next morning that he had forgotten to take the cap off the lens. After the warden had driven us around we had a drink together at the end of the day. He asked me whether he thought he could ask Yadin to do him a favour. I said I was sure that Yadin would have no objection. He then made a curious request. The visit of which I have been writing was shortly after the tremendous defeat of the Egyptian army during the Six-Day War in 1967. He asked Yadin whether he could possibly obtain for him a cap worn by the Egyptian soldiers. Yadin, of course, agreed to do so (and in due course the chief warden got his cap). I asked him why he wanted it. He then told me that he was collecting caps of various armies, having latched on to this hobby after he had got the idea from an American visitor whom he had taken around the park.

Another remarkable person whom I met in Israel, and whom I had met on two occasions in South Africa, was Nahum Goldmann, one of the cleverest men I have ever met. He was the person whose inspiration led to the publication of the *Encyclopaedia Judaica*, and the Museum of the Diaspora in Israel, known as the Beth Hatsefuthsot, has been rightly named after him. He was the founder and chairman of the World Jewish Congress. He was at one stage chairman of the World Zionist Organisation and of the Jewish Agency. His main achievements were his negotiations with Chancellor Adenauer to obtain reparations from Germany, for Jews who had left Germany because of Hitlerism, and for the state of Israel as well. He regards the obtaining of German reparations, in his own biography, as being one of his most important achievements. Firstly he established a principle with Chancellor Adenauer of compensating Jews who had lost their belongings as a result of the Hitler regime. It is by no means unusual for a state which has been defeated in war to make compensation to the victor, but Israel was not a state until 1948 and took no part in the war – save, of course, as I have mentioned, that many Israelis joined the Allies. The concept that a German state would pay compensation to a state that was not in existence at the time of the German defeat was new, and he managed to persuade Adenauer to pay reparations to Israel.

There was, of course, opposition, and as Nahum Goldmann says, understandably so, by many Jews to accepting any reparations from the Germans. In fact Begin's party led big demonstrations in Israel against accepting reparations from Germany. The figure already paid by Germany at the time Goldmann's biography was written in 1976 was DM 60bn, and Goldmann estimated that eventually this amount would come to DM 80bn. There is not the slightest doubt that these monies proved to be invaluable to the fledgling state.

To see Goldmann presiding at a conference was really quite an experience. He would sit on the platform and ostensibly read newspapers whilst conference delegates would speak on various topics and make their points. Anybody watching would think, as I had done, that Goldmann was ignoring what was being said. That was far from being the case. He was able, after the discussions had ended, to stand up and deal with every point made by every speaker. He himself had rather an informal manner of delivering an address, and I had the good fortune of listening to him on several occasions. It was as though he was speaking to an individual. He had the remarkable ability of saying, in the middle of a speech, 'By the way this reminds me of ...' – and he would go off at a tangent to deal with the matter of which he had been reminded, and then come back exactly to the point where the matter had first been raised by him. He was a wonderful raconteur. When I was in New York attending a meeting of what was called the 'Claims Conference', that is a committee set up to deal with reparations, we went after the conference to Goldmann's apartment. There he regaled us with anecdote after anecdote until the early hours of the morning. He had a marvellous sense of humour. One of the stories he told us was of when he had been a member of a delegation consisting of Ben Gurion, a certain Rabbi Maimon and himself. They went to see Ernest Bevin, then foreign secretary of the mandatory power, and generally regarded as an anti-Semite. Rabbi Maimon could not speak or understand English and he spoke in Hebrew. He was the first person to speak to Bevin and his complaints against the British and their administration of Palestine were of such a nature that even Ben Gurion was alarmed. The arrangement was that Rabbi Maimon's speech, after he had finished speaking, would be interpreted to Bevin. Rabbi Maimon's attack was a lengthy one, and included remarks such as that the British were worse, in his opinion, than the Roman Emperor Titus. When he had finished Goldmann interpreted his remarks as follows: 'The rabbi says that there are certain aspects of the British administration of Palestine of which he disapproves.' He said no more and the rabbi said, 'Have you already interpreted all that I have said?' – to which Goldmann replied: 'Yes, English is that kind of language.'

I may be forgiven if I do not mention all those with whom I had the privilege of working in the committees of the Jewish Board of Deputies, the Zionist Federation, and on the board of governors of the Jewish Agency. I have already mentioned the names of Cecil Lyons and Gerald Lazarus as being prominent in their work for the Jewish Board of Deputies. Although other persons too numerous to mention also contributed significantly to the work of the board, I should like to make special mention of B A Ettlinger, QC, Simie Kuper (who was appointed to the Bench and after serving for a few years was murdered by an unknown assassin), Namie Philips, QC, Arthur Suzman, QC, and Felix Landau, all of whom played prominent roles during my term of office.

I also mentioned, in the previous chapter, the names of Max Fisher and Louis Pincus in the positions that they held on the board of governors of the reconstituted Jewish Agency. I have since visited Max Fisher in his home in Detroit on visits to my son Jeffrey. He invariably invited me to be present at important discussions which he had with the then prime minister, Mr Rabin, and took me into his confidence along with a few leading

Americans in several matters of some importance.

I formed many friendships with American members of the board of governors of the Jewish Agency. In particular I mention Chuck Hoffberger, with whom I have corresponded regularly. He has been kind enough to visit me in Detroit from his home in Baltimore, and on one occasion when my son Jeffrey was in Hershey, Pennsylvania.

Morry Levinson, too, was a very active participant in discussions at the board. He and I were very close to one another and I am eternally grateful to him and his wife Barbara for the friendship and hospitality that they showed to my daughter Helen when she lived in New York. Whenever Muriel and I were in New York we visited them and were treated with great hospitality in their magnificent home on East 65th Street. Morry died on the eve of Yom Kippur in 1993 and many tributes to him were paid by persons such as Abba Eban, who was on terms of close friendship with him. Of the many occasions on which Muriel and I were entertained by Morry and Barbara there is one that I shall never forget. Both Morry and Barbara were benefactors of the Weizmann Institute and Morry was one of the governors and active workers for this cause. I mention that the Weizmann Institute is generally regarded as being on a par with Massachusetts Institute of Technology. Muriel and I were guests of the Levinsons at a dinner held in aid of the Weizmann Institute. Apart from the chairman, all the people sitting on the dais were recipients of the Nobel Prize in various fields. We were entertained by that great violinist Itzhak Perlman. He played classical music and, when the audience would not let him off the stage, he contributed to the occasion with numerous encores. I regard this as one of the most memorable evenings I have ever spent.

Another member of the board of governors of the Jewish Agency with whom I was friendly was Ray Epstein. He was one of the leading members of the board and I believe is now active in the work of the Joint Distribution Committee (JDC). Muriel and I stayed with him and his wife Betty in Chicago for a few days. They entertained us royally. I happened to be in Paris on one occasion when they were there. Ray is a *bon viveur* and he and Betty entertained me in the best restaurant in which I have ever been. Ray, who is now retired, was an engineer by profession. He was the head of a very large engineering organisation engaged in projects in both the United States and in many other parts of the world. Apart from that, Ray is a collector of first editions and a lover of classical music. He is altogether a cultivated man.

Among other Americans with whom I have had the privilege of working were Irving Bernstein and Phil Bernstein, both chief executive officers of giant American Jewish organisations such as the United Jewish Appeal and United Israel Appeal. On a visit to America I was invited to various cities to address meetings for the United Israel Appeal. Muriel and I flew from New York to San Diego. This was not, as far as I was concerned, a very successful meeting. It was, I think, equivalent to a meeting held in Boksburg, one of the smaller towns in the Transvaal. Next we flew to Oakland, a city near San Francisco, where there was a vibrant community and I duly made an appeal for funds which, I think, met with some success. From there we went to Philadelphia, where I had to address a very large gathering. The chairman was Mr Mann, after whom the Mann Auditorium in Tel Aviv is named. Muriel naturally accompanied me to this dinner, but it was for men only, whereupon Mrs Mann was hastily summoned to keep Muriel company. I spoke about our comparatively small South African Jewish community and emphasised what we had done by way of contributions to the Israel United Appeal. Apparently my speech was well received and the message that I got from the headquarters of the Israel Appeal in New York was an encouraging one.

Valuable contributions during my term of office on the board of governors of the Jewish Agency were made by Mrs Raya Jaglom, the president of the Women's International Zionist Organisation, Charlotte Jacobson, the acknowledged head of the Zionist movement in America and the late Mrs Fay Schenk.

I have already mentioned the names of Edel Horwitz and Israel Dunsky, respectively president and chairman of the South African Zionist Federation at one time, in connection with important work for the Zionist Federation. It would be wrong of me not to mention other names, in particular the doughty Harry Trope, Joe Daleski and Fritz Frank. Fritz, together with his brother-in-law Helmuth Hirsch, were chairmen and managing directors of the well-known firm of Frank & Hirsch.

If I must mention one person whose name was outstanding in raising funds for the World Zionist Organisation and the Jewish Agency it must be that of Fritz Frank. Whenever we had a biennial campaign he devoted himself, literally full time, night and day, to work for the cause. He had a computer printout of all contributors to the campaign and he alone raised the standard of contributions to the United Communal Fund. He was a remarkable man and he and his wife, Lisa, who is herself active in the Women's Zionist Organisation, kept open house for any Israeli who might visit this country – and, indeed, open house for almost everyone. I cannot speak too highly of the work that Fritz did for the Zionist cause. And in addition to this work, Fritz was a contributor to every fund or deserving cause that I can think of. I well remember his waiting late at night to welcome Edel Horwitz, Maurice Porter and myself after our meeting with Mr Vorster (*see* Chapter 15). The Rabbi Goldstein prize is awarded to a person outside America who has done exceptional work for the Zionist cause. If any person deserved this honour it was Fritz, and in a ceremony at the home of the president of Israel, this award was made to him. I had the honour, from South Africa, of making a speech on this occasion. (The prize is named for the head of the Keren Hayesod, the distinguished Rabbi Israel Goldstein, a charming and cultivated person, who left the United States to settle in Israel, and who was also one of the founders of the Brandeis University. He was rabbi to a conservative congregation, but despite this, when he was in South Africa, he attended services at the Wolmarans Street orthodox synagogue.)

Turning to the officials of the Zionist Federation, the first person I should mention is Mr Zvi Infeld, a cultivated person who emigrated to Israel. The second person with whom I worked closely was Sidney Berg. Sidney Berg had a BA LLB, but he decided that his work for Israel was more important. He was, to all intents and purposes, my mentor and adviser when I joined the executive and became chairman of the Zionist Federation and of the Israel United Appeal. He was efficient in all his work and above all brought his great talents to bear on the work that he did. He, too, fulfilled his life's ambition by emigrating to Israel accompanied by his wife, who unfortunately died fairly recently. They were as one person, devoted to each other. Sidney Berg was the equivalent of Gus

Saron and Jack Rich combined. He had the qualities of a thinker and doer.

Of chairmen of the Zionist Federation who have emigrated to Israel – that is, made *aliyah* – I mention Nicholai Kirshner, Israel Dunsky, Kalmanowitz, Liebgott and Solly Sacks. Apart from them, Jack Geri (known in South Africa as Jack Geering, who became a member of the first cabinet of Ben Gurion), Arthur Lourie and Michael Comay had distinguished careers in the diplomatic corps.

Chapter Twenty

RECOLLECTIONS

Isie Maisels's memoirs were left unfinished. He was to have written one further chapter on his profession in which, it seems, he would have related anecdotes and reminiscences of some of his peers and his many colleagues and friends. In a sense, Isie's failure to complete the manuscript as envisaged offered a certain consolation to his editors: an opportunity to speak on his behalf. To this final chapter, therefore, Isie's colleagues have offered their own recollections of the man; some reflecting his remarkable judgment and wisdom, others demonstrating his great wit and sense of irony. Isie's son, Keith, who is an attorney and instructed his father in certain matters, was able to provide a number of stories concerning Isie, some of which have already been incorporated into the body of the book in the process of editing it; others are recorded in these pages.

It was quite out of the question for him ever to indulge in any personal aggrandisement or self-flattery. He was a uniquely modest man when considering his own achievements. On the other hand, he often spoke with considerable admiration of, for example Oscar Rathouse, Sydney Kentridge, Harry Morris and, of course, Rex Welsh. Perhaps the very best example of his own humility lay in a story that only came about when Isie had finally been cajoled into writing his memoirs – and he most certainly had to be cajoled.

While Isie was in the process of collating his papers, his family found a book in his library, Helen Joseph's diary of the treason trial, *If This Be Treason*, kept throughout the time of her incarceration and trial. It recounts her unique recollection of the trial, which – as it was so momentous a legal event – has taken up by far the longest chapter in these memoirs. Towards the end of her diary she records how the trialists composed a letter to Isie, leader of the defence team, when they heard that he had been appointed a judge of the Rhodesian High Court. The letter (*see* exhibit) was passed to him in court, while he was listening to the Crown argument. In the letter, the trialists handsomely compliment Isie's 'unsurpassed contribution to our system of law' in the course of 'our struggle for justice in South Africa'. Helen Joseph recounts how the trialists watched Isie read the letter two or three times before he looked towards the trialists 'for a brief moment, deeply moved. He takes off his spectacles and puts his head in his hands, and thus he remains for a little while, before folding up his letter carefully and putting it away in his breast pocket.'

In all the years following that singular event, Isie Maisels never once referred to the letter. He did not tell his wife when he went home that night; he never said a word to any of his children. It was only in 1993 after his retirement from the Bar that this reference to it was found, and he acknowledged it. (Interestingly, the editors have never been able to establish who wrote the letter. All the trialists remember it but no one is quite sure who wrote it. Perhaps that is the way it should be – no particular author, just an acknowledgement from all the accused.)

Isie appeared in a number of civil and criminal cases in which he was consulted by attorneys acting for people whose situation appeared to be hopeless. But he had a marvellous ability to imbue such clients with optimism – obviously not false optimism – and also with courage to fight the good cause. One attorney who practised for many years on the East Rand said that one of the reasons why he always took his clients to see Isie was that they always came away from such consultations feeling 'considerably better than when they went in'. Although one cannot estimate how many of these cases finished favourably for his clients, the general feeling is that the balance fell heavily in that direction.

Julian Block (formerly a leading attorney in Johannesburg – has been practising in Australia for a number of years) once went to see Isie in a 'running down' case, his client having been run down while walking across Louis Botha Avenue. This was in the days before the Apportionment of Damages Act, when a party received 'all or nothing'. Isie, already a silk, took the case 'as if it were his first', displaying the same energy and enthusiasm for this case as for the hundreds of other cases in which he had been involved during his long career. It was, according to Julian, quite astonishing. After extraordinary application and preparation in the face of strong opposition from the third party insurer, the matter eventually went to court and was won by the plaintiff.

Although generally the soul of courtesy with clients, Isie could be very testy with crooks. In about 1985 Keith Maisels consulted him with certain C and D, directors of a company quoted on the stock exchange. On the strength of a prospectus containing a large number of misleading and fraudulent statements, 'C', a chartered accountant, and 'D' had collected R23 m from the public, of which some R7 m had already gone into their own pockets or to some of their cronies. C attempted, by convoluted explanations and concoctions, to explain that the misleading statements in the prospectus were in fact true, but to no avail. Increasingly irritated with these half truths and excuses, Isie eventually told the pair that he was satisfied that they were guilty of 'very serious crimes', and that their attempts to justify their actions made matters worse. They asked what he anticipated their sentence might be if they were convicted. He told them 10 to 15 years was about right, unless they thought that was too short. He did not think that he – nor anyone else for that matter – could do anything for them. A suggestion by C that Isie should be briefed to intercede with the Attorney General on their behalf was rejected, as Isie thought that this would result in immediate prosecution. He was aware, he said, that it sometimes took many years for the state to get around to prosecuting people who had committed crimes of this magnitude. An exchange then ensued between C and Isie, as follows:

> MAISELS: C, I understand you to say that you have an Irish passport as well as a South African one?
>
> C: Yes.
>
> MAISELS: Well, if and when you are prosecuted you may find it convenient not to be here. *(C then asked in a voice of whining desperation what further advice Isie could give him.)* Tell me, C, are you a churchgoer?
>
> C: I go occasionally
>
> MAISELS: Well, I think you should go more often.

Isie had many years before given the same advice to certain clients involved in criminal activities in the hide and skin business in Port Elizabeth. They were prosecuted by the authorities and were defended by Isie and Sydney Kentridge (a junior at the time). Whether they took his advice he never knew; they were given a heavy fine, but were not sent to prison, and he ascribed this to divine intervention.

In 1982 a larger-than-life Australian, Murray Quartermaine, consulted Keith Maisels with his attorney from Perth. Quartermaine and a number of doctors in Perth had given 'hot money' (as means of tax evasion) to one Christo Theo Moll for investment in Singapore and other places. Moll had then decamped with the money, but Quartermaine had by chance discovered that Moll was living in Pretoria. The attorneys issued summons against Moll for provisional sentence, based on two promissory notes amounting to about R500 000, and briefed Isie. So fantastic was the story of how Moll had cheated Quartermaine of his money that it sounded like a tale from the Arabian nights. Isie sounded a note of caution to Keith on the question of cover for his and other fees in the matter. He suggested Keith should have regard to the fantastic tale he had been told, and expressed his belief that 'most of these Australians are liars'. He proceeded to regale Keith with a number of stories about Australian conmen who had operated in this country between the wars.

Moll denied his signature to the promissory notes, so an expert witness had to be called for the purpose of proving his handwriting. This witness arrived in the shape of retired Chief Superintendent Leo Murphy of the West Australia Police, accompanied by his wife, Doris. After two or three days, Doris remarked to Keith's wife that she now realised 'that your darkies are in the majority here.'

Superintendent Murphy had served in the West Australian police force for some 30 years, and had been presented with the Queen's Police Medal for meritorious service on his retirement. He proved to be what Isie described as one of the best witnesses he had ever had the pleasure of meeting. His evidence in chief was lucid, authoritative, perfectly illustrated with photographic enlargements and diagrams, and supported by references to the leading authority on handwriting, one Harrison.

'The commencement of Murphy's cross-examination by counsel

for the defendant will always remain in my memory,' recalls Keith, 'as an example of how not to cross-examine a witness.' It has been emphasised by many learned authors on the subject that it is most inadvisable, indeed dangerous, to ask a witness a question if you are not certain, or almost certain, of what the answer is going to be. In this case the cross-examination started something like this.

DEFENCE: Now, you have told my learned friend that you served in the West Australian police for 30 years.
MURPHY: Yes Sir.
DEFENCE: I take it, however, that during that entire period of time you did not devote yourself to the study of handwriting for forensic purposes.
MURPHY: That is correct, Sir.
DEFENCE: For how many of those 30 years did you study handwriting, as such?
MURPHY: 28 years.
(Counsel then got himself into further difficulties.)
DEFENCE: Now, you have told the court that at the expiry of your service you were presented with the Queen's Police Medal.
MURPHY: Yes Sir.
DEFENCE: Am I not right in saying that virtually every police officer that retires after a certain period of service receives this medal?
MURPHY: No, Sir.
DEFENCE: How many of the many hundreds of police officers who retired during your period of service with the West Australia police force received such a medal on retirement?
MURPHY: Three, Sir.
(It appeared therefore, that the initial attack on the credentials of this witness had not succeeded. But when it came to the merits of the evidence on the handwriting, things got even worse for the defendant. Using the textbook, Harrison, counsel put a number of questions to the witness.)
DEFENCE: Do you agree that the loop at the top of the L is the second L of this photographic enlargement and appears to contain a dot?

MURPHY: Yes Sir.

DEFENCE: Now if you turn to this textbook that you have been so fond of quoting from, Harrison, at page 42, does he not say that this indicates … ?

MURPHY: Yes Sir.

DEFENCE: Well, doesn't this directly conflict with your evidence concerning … ?

MURPHY: No Sir.

DEFENCE: But the explanation given by Harrison conflicts directly with what you say.

MURPHY: No sir. If you will kindly turn to page 87 of the same work, you will see …

Murphy then quoted at length from that page – verbatim, and from memory. The passage quoted completely demolished the point that the defence had attempted to make against him.

Quartermaine gave evidence that the promissory notes had been signed in his presence at a hotel in Zurich in Switzerland and that one Robina Trowbridge, a former girlfriend of Moll, had also been present at the time. Miss Trowbridge, a very attractive and charming woman, gave evidence on this point and, although both she and Quartermaine were cross-examined by Moll's counsel, this was to no effect.

Moll then gave evidence in support of his case, and was cross-examined by Isie. His incredibly arrogant and offensive manner in answering the questions – quite apart from the evident falsity of his case – contributed considerably to his downfall. Isie had assiduously studied all the documents discovered by Moll, including credit card vouchers, one of which was for a flight from London to Zurich on the same date on which the promissory notes were signed.

Isie asked him first why Miss Trowbridge should have given evidence that he was at the hotel in Zurich on the day in question when he maintained that he was not there. He replied to the effect that, as it was well-known, 'hell hath no fury like a woman scorned'. This answer produced a deathly silence in the court and the judge, Mr Justice Van der Walt, looked at Moll incredulously. Isie, a master of these situations, allowed the silence to continue and then, in a voice that was almost inaudible, said: 'Is that your answer? Is that your disgraceful answer, that you impugn the integrity of a woman who has come from England to give this evidence? Do you suggest that she is deliberately lying?'

Moll did not answer. Isie then showed Moll the credit card voucher showing that he and one other person (Robina Trowbridge) had travelled to Zurich on the day in question. Isie asked him to comment on the contents of the credit card voucher. He pretended not to be able to read it, and when it was read out to him by Isie, he made the fatuous suggestion that the document was a forgery.

As the trial proceeded and it became clearer to Moll that his lies and stratagems would be of no avail, he suddenly produced a document purporting to be an acknowledgement of debt in his favour, signed in Switzerland by Quartermaine - in Moll's favour for 750 000 Swiss Francs. The document was given to the prosecution by Mr Moll's legal team, and they of course showed it to Quartermaine in the firm belief that his signature had been forged and that this was yet another of the fraudulent practices of Mr Moll. (Had the document been genuine, the prosecution's case would have been destroyed.) To their astonishment, however, Quartermaine freely conceded that the signature which appeared at the bottom of the document was indeed his. He explained that Moll had induced him on a number of occasions to give him pieces of paper signed in blank so that Moll could conduct negotiations with Singaporean and other authorities, and to escape the vigilance of the Australian tax authorities. This was such a document and Moll had used it to type the alleged acknowledgement of debt above Quartermaine's signature. The only difficulty that he had, however, was to fill the page and so the terms of the acknowledgement were extremely lengthy and prolix and contained a large amount of what can be called legal jargon and verbiage. Nevertheless, if he could establish that it was genuine, Quartermaine was in serious trouble. Isie studied this document very carefully overnight. Its opening words were:

'I, the undersigned, Murray Vernon Quartermaine, do hereby solemny (*sic*) and sincerely declare that I am indebted to Christo Theo Moll in the sum of Swiss Francs 750 000,00 …'

The following day, whilst he was cross-examining Mr Moll, Isie handed him the document and asked him to explain the circumstances under which it had been signed. Moll's explanation of how the indebtedness had arisen and how the document had been prepared, typed out and signed by Quartermaine in his presence was reasonable and plausible. Isie appeared to lose interest in this document and went on to question Mr Moll about other matters. Then, seemingly as an afterthought and without resort to dramatics of any kind, he picked up the document again, whereupon the cross-examination continued something like this:

MAISELS: Mr Moll, would you mind having another look at this acknowledgement of debt, exhibit B, which you have there, and will you please read out the first sentence of that document. *(Moll reads the sentence.)* Tell me Mr Moll, how would you spell the word solemnly?
MOLL: S-o-l-e-m-n-y
MAISELS: Are you quite sure about that?
MOLL: Yes, of course I am.
MAISELS: And you say that Quartermaine himself typed this document on a typewriter in your office?
MOLL: Oh yes, I could even produce the typewriter, if necessary.
MAISELS: Mr Moll, will you accept what I say when I tell you that the word 'solemnly' is spelled s-o-l-e-m-n-l-y.
MOLL: No, it is not.
MAISELS: I would like to put that question to you again – I cast no aspersion on the fact that your home language is not English.
MOLL: *(Getting angry)* My English is as good as yours.
MAISELS: That it may be, Mr Moll, but will you accept that neither of ours is as authoritative as the Shorter Oxford Dictionary? *(He produces it.)* The word solemnly is spelled *(emphasising each letter in a slightly louder voice)* s-o-l-e-m-n-l-y. *(No response from the witness.)*
MAISELS: *(softly)* Did you type this document yourself, Mr Moll? *(No answer.)* Are you going to answer the question?

There was again absolute silence in the court. The judge looked at the witness with what appeared to be not only full comprehension, but also dislike. The question was never answered and there was no need for cross-examination to continue.

At the end of the case the court gave judgement in favour of Quartermaine for the full amount of his claim plus costs. Moll immediately left the country via Cape Town (fearing arrest at Johannesburg airport) and was not seen for many years. His estate and a trust that he had established for his ex-wife (hoping thus to place this property out of the reach of his creditors), were sequestrated, and a house in Lynnwood, Pretoria, was sold. Although Moll would not face his creditor in this country, he expended large sums in opposing the original application for the attachment of the property and on an appeal to the Appellate Division, which upheld Quartermaine's contention that the house belonged to his trustee. The amount realised on its sale came nowhere near to compensating Quartermaine for what he had lost.

When Isie was already rather elderly, he appeared in a matter in Namibia in which he was instructed by a prominent attorney, Billy van der Merwe, formerly the senior partner of Hofmeyer Van der Merwe. The judge in the matter was a fine example of the kind of affirmative action appointment that the Nationalist government was wont to make to the Bench. Isie's etiquette was to pay a call on the judge, especially when a matter was to be heard in a court away from home. Isie was so frail by that stage that an aide to walk with him was certainly a great help. Accordingly, he visited the judge with his instructing attorney. The judge objected to the fact that Isie had brought his instructing attorney along with him and remarked, 'I do not see attorneys in my chambers.' Isie replied that, in that case, both he and the attorney would leave; but he could not resist a final riposte. In the anteroom to the judge's quarters, with a number of the judge's colleagues within earshot, he remarked loudly, 'I'm not surprised that chap does not have attorneys in his chambers. He certainly never had them there when he practised at the Pretoria Bar.'

Peter Reynolds, senior partner at Webber Wentzel Bowens, recalls that his firm briefed Isie many times over the years, and that, although they never lost a matter in which Isie was under instruction, he himself had nearly lost a secretary of 25 years' standing. He recounts that Isie had the habit of phoning up and shouting at his instructing attorney if preparation was not going ahead as he considered it should. If the attorney wasn't available the attorney's secretary was good enough. On one occasion the secretary was near to tears – 'Mr Maisels has just phoned up and he shouted at me, again.' Peter Reynolds responded, 'Don't worry, he is really like a kind uncle.' To which the secretary replied, 'He's more like Isie!' The next time she cried was when she heard of Isie's death. Peter Reynolds also recounts the two anecdotes following.

Many years ago Webber Wentzel Bowens was instructed to consider an attempted fraud on a bank by one of its senior and respected, but decidedly eccentric, employees. The employee said he had attempted the fraud to draw attention to certain unfair labour practices which he felt were being committed by the bank. Notwithstanding his protestations, the matter was reported to the police, who arrived at his home, searched it, seized documents, and – despite his protestations of innocence – frog-marched him to the police car in front of his wife and children.

Thereafter, the bank relented and sought to have the charges withdrawn. The prosecutor agreed and so did the magistrate, and the matter was about to be removed from the roll when the investigating officer objected. The matter was reinstated and eventually the employee was charged with the attempted fraud of a large sum of money. During a lengthy trial, the accused chattered to the police, tried to crack jokes with the magistrate and fell into the habit of passing 'ghost notes' (folded pieces of paper with nothing on them) to all and sundry. All this irritated the magistrate, who found him guilty and sentenced him to six years' imprisonment without the option of a fine. The accused, his wife and children were distraught. The defence lodged an appeal and briefed Isie. Isie read the record and summoned his junior, his attorneys and the accused (with his whole family) to his home one Friday evening, the appeal being due to be heard on the following Monday.

Isie told the assembled gathering that the case was hopeless and that the accused must prepare himself to go to jail when the matter was finalised. The accused, not to be deterred, said that he would get his 'prayer group together' and that they 'would work on it over the weekend'. Isie did not seem to think much of the accused's sense of humour, and showed it. On Monday the case was called and counsel, the accused and the family sat waiting in a state of tension. The presiding judge asked the state advocate if he had anything to say. 'Anything to say about what?' asked the state advocate. 'About the conviction and sentence being set aside,' said the judge. The state advocate clearly did not understand, and Isie, for once, was at a loss for words. The state advocate said that he had nothing to say and Isie half rose, mumbled something incoherent and sat down. The appeal was upheld (*'no mens rea'* – no criminal intention – said the court), and the accused's conviction and sentence were set aside. The judges filed out, the accused leapt to his feet and shouted 'Hallelujah!' and hugged his wife and anyone else who happened to be in the near vicinity. Peter Reynolds left by the side door with Isie, who had only this to say – 'Hallelujah? I don't know about hallelujah, but I'm going to give up law!' – and he stalked down the passage into the lift and back to his chambers – thankfully he did not carry out his threat.

Isie, as one might expect of an advocate of his calibre and standing, appeared many times in the Appeal Court in Bloemfontein. Peter Reynolds was instructing Isie in a large and important matter in such a case, and senior executives of the client had arrived to see justice done. Isie was leading. After Isie, for the appellant, had informed the appeal Bench that he had never 'in his entire life' come across such a scoundrel as the respondent (with which sentiment the entire bench appeared to agree), it was time for lunch. Peter Reynolds had already informed their clients that senior counsel would in all certainty select a smart restaurant and some fine wines for their anticipated victory. Imagine their surprise on finding themselves in the nearest corner café, regaled with a dry cheese-and-tomato sandwich and a milkshake, over which Isie told them that the case was a foregone conclusion and they had already won. Isie was right of course; and Peter Reynolds was forgiven for getting the lunch venue badly wrong.

Towards the end of his career, Isie's hearing started to fail. It was thought by some attorneys who instructed him, and some of his opponents as well, that his hearing was selective.

A young attorney, Derek Rabin, remembers an occasion when, at the insistence of his client, he had consulted Isie. The matter at issue was the purchase of a farm by his wealthy client – an industrialist, not a farmer. The seller of the farm had asked the client if he would permit him, for a short while, to keep a prize herd of cattle on the property. The buyer thought nothing of it and agreed quite willingly. Thereafter, the cattle contracted foot-and-mouth disease and the seller attempted to sue the buyer. Rabin had regarded the matter as clear-cut and told his client that the seller really did not have a leg to stand on. However, the client was not prepared to rely on Rabin's advice and insisted emphatically on going to counsel: only 'the great Maisels' would do.

At the consultation the client, despite his obvious success and eminence, was clearly in awe of Isie. Rabin introduced his client to Isie. He had a long Italianate name, something like Ravaselli (not his real name). 'Hello, Mr Ravioli,' said Isie. 'Ravaselli,' corrected Derek and his client in unison. Quite undaunted, Isie then listened again to the facts as set out by the attorney and frequently interjected with questions addressed to 'Mr Ravioli.' So frequent was his repetition of the name that, towards the end of the consultation, the attorney was hard put to keep a straight face and the client was desperate. Finally, it was time for the 'great man' to give his opinion. 'What has Derek advised you, Mr Ravioli?' asked Isie. The Italian, who, by this stage, had give up any hope of correcting Isie's mispronunciation, told him that he had been advised that he had no case to answer. Then Isie, said: 'Derek's quite right, Mr Ravioli. We shall write to him and tell him to f— off!'

Yet another story from Peter Reynolds concerns a matter in the Witwatersrand Local Division in which Isie was leading counsel for a bank that had paid out a large sum of money in error. One of his tasks was to discredit the defendant's main witness, a wily financial consultant whose name was, let us say, Blackley (not his real name). Isie got up to cross-examine and put his one foot up on the bench. Peter comments that Isie also took out his hearing aid and then started his cross-examination:

MAISELS: Mr Blackleg, I want to ask you a few questions about your evidence.
WITNESS: Blackley.
MAISELS: What's that, Mr Blackleg?
WITNESS: Blackley.
JUDGE: Blackley, Mr Maisels.
MAISELS: Black what?
JUDGE: Blackley.

MAISELS: My apologies Mr Blackleg.
JUDGE AND WITNESS: *(in unison)* Blackley.
MAISELS: All right then ... right, now I have these few simple questions. *(Having completely unnerved the witness, Isie started his cross-examination. The witness was recalcitrant.)* Mr Blackleg . . .
JUDGE AND WITNESS: *(in unison)* Blackley ...

And so it went on throughout the afternoon. The witness became so agitated about the incorrect pronunciation of his surname, that eventually he gave Isie all the 'right' answers. At the end, Isie said, with the ghost of a twinkle in his eye, 'Thank you – Mr Blackley.' All this may sound comic but it was a wonderful piece of advocacy, and contributed largely to the successful outcome of the case.

Advocate Anne-Marie Engelbrecht (whose name was not Labuschagne) tells the following story. She had been practising about four years when she was briefed in a trial with Isie. Beside herself with joy that she could work with the great Maisels, she phoned her father in Windhoek to tell him that she thought she might have 'arrived'. Isie and she worked together for ten days, from early morning till late at night, including a weekend. The matter was settled at the doors of court and, being there, Isie attended roll call. When he appeared and had to announce her, he looked at her for a long while and then told the court that he was appearing with 'Miss Labuschagne'. She was devastated! After ten days he didn't even know her name! Deeply disappointed, she told the story to Fanie Cilliers (one of Southern Africa's leading silks). Unknown to her, Fanie went to Isie and told him how devastated she was. Isie immediately came down to her floor and apologised profusely. For the next nine years he insisted on calling her 'Miss Labuschagne', with, she recalls, 'a lovely glint in his eye. The greatness of coming to know the man,' she said, 'later far outweighed the greatness of having been able to work with him.'

Attorney Cyril Michaelson recalls the following two matters with Isie.

A client of Michaelson's registered a company called Bow & Arrow (Pty) Ltd. He then went off to the Far East, purchased, at about R2.00 per shirt, a consignment of cheap plastic shirts from Hong Kong, and inserted labels displaying in very small letters the word 'Bow', and in huge letters 'Arrow', with the Arrow logo – obviously cribbing the 'Arrowshirt' logo. He flooded the market with them. He received a letter from Spoor & Fisher claiming that he had infringed the patent and copyright, and warning him please to stop, otherwise he would get an interdict. He went to Michaelson, very harassed, and asked, 'What must we do?' Michaelson said, 'We've got to pay.' He retorted: 'Let Isie Maisels tell me I've got to pay.' So the attorney duly sent a letter to Isie with a brief and raised a consultation. When Michaelson introduced his client to Isie, he opened his briefcase and showed Isie the offending shirt. Isie said, 'Don't do it. Goodbye.' He marked the brief at R2000, and said: 'Have a good day.'

Cyril Michaelson consulted with Isie when the latter was near retirement – that is, in his mid-eighties. Isie's chambers were at the farthest end of the corridor away from the reception desk at 836 Innes Chambers. When the consultation was over, Isie started walking to the door with Michaelson, who remonstrated with him that it was quite unnecessary for Isie to accompany him, to which he replied, putting his arm around the attorney: 'Thanks for your concern, my boy, but I want to make sure that none of my colleagues steals you away from me.'

A person present at the time, after the acquittal of Philip Manners (*see* Chapter 9), reported that Isie displayed some emotion in contrast with his previous phlegmatic attitude when Manners exclaimed, 'Maisels! I am really grateful, what can I do for you?' He replied: 'Keep some distance between us.'

A judge who was formerly Isie's junior on a number of occasions, relates the following two anecdotes. On being asked if a certain attorney was honest, Isie replied, 'Yes, but he is not a fanatic.'

While acting as a commissioner in a '417' enquiry, the following exchange occurred between Isie and a certain Mr Manfred Holtzman (a well known liquidator): 'Mr Holtzman, what is the time?' asked Isie. Holtzman glanced at his wrist watch: 'It is 12.30, Mr Commissioner.' Isie looked toward the clock on the wall: 'That,' he returned, 'is the first direct and honest answer I have had from you this whole morning.'

Theodore (Teddy) Sachs recalled a case in which he briefed Isie more than 60 years ago (*see* Chapter 15). His client, a jeweller carrying on business in a small way, was charged with illicit diamond buying – a crime much more prevalent in those times than it is nowadays. The accused was the victim of a trap set by plainclothes members of the police, in the persons of two white and two black detectives. The prospects of a successful defence were indeed bleak. The case was to be heard in the Supreme Court at Johannesburg before the late Mr Justice Saul Solomon. They found on arrival in court that they would have to wait for the end of another trial, then in progress; and learned, to their great surprise, that this prior trial was also concerned with a charge of illicit diamond buying in which the witnesses were the same police officers who were concerned in their case, and who had set a trap in the same way as in their case. In those days the jury system was in force. The accused in the prior case was found guilty after the jury had retired for a considerable length of time. After a short retirement, Judge Solomon pronounced his sentence: not only had the accused to serve a term of imprisonment, but in addition the infliction of lashes. The jury was visibly taken aback by the severity of this sentence, a fact which did not escape the eagle eye of Isie, who knew that the same jury would be hearing his case.

In his address to the jury, Isie went to great pains to impress upon them the seriousness of the case their client was facing. He impressed upon them that the degree of criminality involved varied from case to case and could be judged by the sentences that were passed. He stressed that the sentence for riding a bicycle without a rear light was minimal, while that for illicit diamond buying could be extremely severe, as they well knew. During the course of his address he made indirect reference to that sentence on more than one occasion. As a result their client, in the face of what appeared to be irrefutable evidence, was acquitted by the jury. Teddy Sachs and those accompanying him had no doubt that Isie's tactic in playing on the jury's reaction to the severity of the previous sentence had, at his urging, the desired effect.

A recently appointed judge, who knew Isie well, recalled another devastating opening from Isie in the case brought against Daggafontein Mines (*see* Chapter 13). When Isie opened the case, the court was packed mainly with people from the mining houses and the defendant mine. In his opening address, Isie said something to the effect that there would be evidence that the defendants' alleged club did not recognise something that is universally accepted, which was that no two people have the same fingerprints. He gave notice of his intention to lead evidence that large numbers of the application forms by which the so-called members of the so-called club had joined it, bore the thumbprints of a few individuals and were clearly forgeries. This had a dramatic impact on the unsuspecting mining house and mine officials.

The same judge also recalls that when he saw Isie in the month before his death, Isie related two stories to him about a Cape-based National Party appointment to the bench. Apropos of his intended chapter on his colleagues, it is probably rather to the good that Isie committed neither of these stories to print.

Isie, as all his peers agreed, was an absolute master of cross-examination. There can be no greater compliment that the one paid to him by Sydney Kentridge, now a leader of the English Bar, when he wrote to Schalk Burger, SC, chairman of the Johannesburg Bar Council, on the occasion of Isie's retirement. He said in that letter that 'Isie was undoubtedly the greatest advocate I have seen in action in court in any jurisdiction in which I have practised.'

B J H Irving, an attorney recalls being in Isie's chambers one evening during a murder trial (*see* p249–50), when Isie commented about cross-examination that 'There are many things that one can do with cross-examination, save that it is not possible to cross-examine book entries out of books, bullet holes out of bodies and seminal stains out of underpants.'

Around the same time as Isie commenced practising as an advocate, one of South Africa's leading commercial attorneys was, like Isie, starting off on what proved to be a long and eminent career, which lasted more or less the same length of time. He instructed Isie on many occasions, and he said of Isie that the most impressive features of working with him were that: he saw the point immediately; he was a quick thinker and worker; he concentrated only on the main issues and dealt with side issues only when and if it became necessary to do so; he was one of very few lawyers to show the great ability of being able immediately to find the relevant statement or decided case in a law book, and was able to go straight to a textbook or law report in order to do so; he never wasted time in consultation or preparation for a trial; and never went to court unprepared.

Another attorney, who briefed Isie only once when Isie was a junior, yet has vivid recollections of that case. It was a criminal matter where Isie undertook defence in the High Court of Swaziland of a client charged with fraud. It was alleged that the accused had altered the odometers of secondhand cars, to the prejudice of purchasers. The trial lasted some two weeks and Isie showed prodigious energy and application in the matter. They worked every night until midnight and over two weekends. Isie's cross-examination of the technical witnesses was masterly. He literally destroyed their evidence. As a point of criticism, however, the attorney comments that Isie would have been a superb judge in any difficult criminal or civil trial, but he would have been frustrated in dealing with matters such as a 'motion court roll' and with listening to inept arguments and reading badly drawn and/or incomplete documentation. It was this gentleman's opinion that 'there would have been many times when he would have nearly burst a blood vessel'.

Charles Friedman recalled that he was consulted once on behalf of a South African woman who wished to be rid of her English husband, 'a really bad egg', who subsequent to his prosecution in a fraud case (*see* Chapter 5) was to be deported to England. One child had issued from the marriage and the lady in question wanted to deprive the husband of his guardianship. There were serious problems in proving the necessary facts to obtain such an order, more particularly because guardianship at that time was determined under common law. Isie worked out the procedure by which such problems could be overcome and his handling of the matter and legal argument resulted in the necessary orders being granted. The ex-husband subsequently wrote to Charles Friedman while *en route* to Cape Town for deportation, telling him that if he should ever meet either of the two lawyers in England, he would have no hesitation in killing both of them. He asked Charles Friedman to pass this sentiment on to Isie.

Of course, Isie's reputation was not confined to lawyers and legal professionals. He had a reputation that stretched the breadth of the country and far beyond; even a man such as the former state President, F W de Klerk, acknowledged Isie's reputation in the letter he wrote for Isie on the occasion of his retirement saying:

> His name has become a household word, not only in legal

> circles, but throughout the country, because of the numerous notable trials in which he distinguished himself over five decades. He is a shining example of the country's proud traditions and legal eminence. I am sure the entire country joins me in wishing him health and happiness in his well-earned retirement.

A strange accolade indeed from those who had been his ardent opponents for so long!

Perhaps the most astonishing indication of the reach of Isie's reputation concerns an incident that took place only a few months before his retirement. His driver at that time was driving down Claim Street to fetch Isie from his chambers. It was 4.30 in the afternoon – effectively the rush hour. Extraordinarily, the driver was deliberately cut off by a car in front and three men got out of the car and pulled Isie's driver into the street. At first they took a few rands that the driver had, and then they told him that they were also taking the car. 'You cannot do that,' said the driver. 'This car belongs to Judge Maisels.' Thereupon one of the three hijackers said, 'Oh – I know Judge Maisels! That's all right then – you can go.'

At the occasion to celebrate Isie's long career and to wish him well on his retirement, Fanie Cilliers reminisced that the only man he had ever seen pull rank on Isie was Higgie Isaacs, a silk greatly Isie's senior in years. In 1986 Isie asked him whether he was going to get up early to see Hallé's Comet. Higgie replied, 'No, I saw it last time!' There is no better note on which to close this account of Isie's life, than with the compliment paid to Isie by Fanie Cilliers on this occasion marking his retirement:

> For those amongst us who were fortunate enough to have had our careers overlap with his, it will always be a matter of pride to say: 'I, too, appeared with Maisels QC.'

NOTES

1 H Morris, *The First Forty Years* (Cape Town, Juta, 1948), p23.
2 Editors' Note: The incident recalled in this paragraph is a reminiscence recounted in conversation with Isie's son, Keith Maisels.
3 She died in 1992 at the age of 95.
4 Editors' Note: This is not true. He graduated with distinction and won the major law prize of his graduating class. He also played cricket and soccer for the first XI and was in the first tennis team.
5 Editors' Note: The author's son remarks that he does not know about 'luck' but in 40 years of practice Isie Maisels was the hardest working advocate he had known. In many cases in which the son briefed his father with juniors half the author's age, Isie would work twice as hard as they did.
6 Benjamin Bennett, *Genius for the Defence* (Cape Town, Howard Timmins, 1959).
7 See *South African Law Journal*, vol 72 (1955), p4–5.
8 Morris, *The First Forty Years*, p257–95.
9 Editors' Note: It was wide of the mark.
10 Also referred to in Bennett, *Genius for the Defence*, p188–202.
11 Referred to in Bennett, ibid, p203–14.
12 Ibid, p210.
13 It has been wrongly reported as an appeal, whereas it was an application for leave to appeal. 1933 AD p165.
14 It is reported on p166 of the report cited above.
15 1934 AD p95. Editors' Note: At this stage Isie was 28 years old. It is indicative of his intellect and powers of advocacy that he succeeded in this matter – even though an authority as respected as Philip Millin, KC, had advised that the point had no merit; and this, furthermore, before a bench of the calibre mentioned above.
16 Cf Rex *v* Nafte 1929 AD p333.
17 Editors' Note: Isie's modesty and sense of propriety would of course, have prevented him from including the anecdotes recorded here in italics, but it was felt that – rather than bury them in the obscurity of the notes – they should be placed in the narrative at this point.
18 A full account of the circumstances which led up to Broughton's trial, and of the trial itself, is to be found in Bennett, *Genius for the Defence* (p229–49) and in Morris, *The First Forty Years* (p242–55).
19 Editors' Note: In putting down his memoirs, Isie's recollection was that he

and Kaplan had been regaled with whisky. However, he had often recounted the pre-dinner events of that evening to Keith, his son, who recalls Isie's oft recounted anecdote of the occasion as represented in the text.

20 EDITORS' NOTE: This paragraph was not originally inclued by Isie in his memoirs, but he typically mentioned this opinion when relating the anecdote to his family.

21 Morris, *The First Forty Years*; Bennett, *Genius for the Defence*, p229–59.

22 James Fox, *White Mischief* (London, Cape, 1982).

23 At p255.

24 EDITORS' NOTE: Before his children, Isie often referred with hilarity to this remark following the famous acquittal of Broughton. Isie did not originally include in his memoirs his personal misgivings, as reported to his family; but it is considered appropriate to insert them here. When asked about the case, he would say, affecting a Cockney accent, '*She* done it!'

25 EDITORS' NOTE: The habit of referring with amusement to the physical peculiarities of others was one of Isie's less fortunate but picturesque qualities. In his last or second last year of practice he told a story one evening that at lunch in the common room that day, he and some of the other 'chaps' had been discussing the question as to who were the three ugliest members of the Bar. The consensus of opinion obviously cannot be given here. An attorney who frequently briefed him used to keep a photograph of his son, a particularly ugly child, next to his bed. Isie would affect a look of mock terror and say, 'Can you imagine waking up and seeing that!' Isie's own father had some extremely picturesque expressions about some very short people which my father recounted, but most of which are not printable. One, which he applied to a very short-in-stature suitor of Isie's sister was that 'he could walk under a table with a tophat on'.

26 Ellison Kahn, *Law, Life and Laughter* (Cape Town, Juta, 1991), p254.

27 *South African Law Journal*, vol 88 (1971), p275–276.

28 Moshe Dayan, *The Story of My Life* (London, Da Capo, 1992), p50–51.

29 He was only 39 at the time.

30 EDITORS' NOTE:This reticence on the question of applying for silk is not, with notable exceptions, adhered to in modern times, with the result that a number of young and financially successful advocates are granted silk when they have neither experience, judgement or maturity necessary for the proper advice of their clients. It is sad to record that competent 'juniors' are choosing not to apply for silk on the grounds that the prestige of the honour has been debased.

31 Further reference is made to this matter in the last chapter.

32 1948 (4) *South African Law Reports*, 683.

33 Benjamin Bennett, *The Evil That Men Do* (Cape Town, Howard Timmins, 1950), p167-237; court proceedings reported on p213ff.

34 EDITORS' NOTE: This anecdote, not originally included in the memoirs, is vividly remembered by the author's family, and is included in the narrative at the discretion of the Editors.

35 The resolution is quoted in full in *Journal of the International Commission of Jurists*, vol 1, no 1 (1956), being the report of a speech made in London by an eminent English silk, Gerald Gardiner, who subsequently became Lord

Chancellor of England.

36 In his address at the time of a party given by the Bar on the Isie's retirement, George Bizos, SC, referred to this episode as one that he would never forget.

37 See *Consultus*, vol 5, no 1 (April 1992), p22ff.

38 1943 WLD, p215.

39 Reported in 1950 (1) *South African Law Reports* ,447.

40 EDITORS' NOTE: The episode recorded in these paragraphs was not originally included by the author in his memoirs, but has been included here as one of the marvellous anecdotes that Isie on occasion told against himself.

41 The attorney was the late Harry Goss and it should be mentioned that Harry's articled clerk, Gerald Horwitz, was 'winged' at the same time.

42 In my recollection of the events that occurred in the matter when it came before Judge Rumpff I have referred to reports in the *Rand Daily Mail*, *The Star* and *Die Transvaler*.

43 Cf Rex *v* Pratt 1960 (4) *South African Law Reports*, 743, 744.

44 A *curator ad litem* is the person, usually an advocate, appointed by the court to investigate the mental condition of someone whose mental capability is in question. A *curator bonis* is subsequently appointed to manage the affairs of such a person judged mentally incapable (or, as he is called in the Rules of the Supreme Court, 'lunatic'). I took no part in those proceedings. Lawrence appeared for Pratt together with George Colman, QC, and a junior. Mr W E McEwan was appointed *curator ad litem*. The question of a *curator bonis* was left over pending the outcome of the trial.

45 A nephew of Pratt's, who visited him several times while he was in prison, said that Pratt had been cruelly and regularly tortured by prison officers during his incarceration.

46 Cf H R Hahlo 'The great South West African diamond case: A discourse', *South African Law Journal*, vol 76 (1959), p151–186; and 1958 (1) *South African Law Reports* 572 at 594.

47 1958 (4) SA 572 (AD) p594–597.

48 Published in the official gazette of South West Africa on 2 January 1957.

49 1958 (4) SA 572 (AD).

50 At page 594.

51 Hahlo, 'The great South West African diamond case', p151.

52 Ibid, p161–162.

53 Ibid.

54 1958 (4) SA 572 (AD) p619–620.

55 At page 636.

56 At pages 609 ff.

57 A matter which is dealt with in Phipson on Evidence (S L Phipson, *Law of Evidence*, London, Sweet & Maxwell, 14th edn, 1990).

58 Cf p610.

59 At p636.

60 By Chief Justice Fagan, p597 BC.

61 At p593.

62 p598 F & G.

63 They appear at p579 BF.

64 At p598 in fine to 599 B.

65 Thomas Karis & Gwendolen M Carter (eds), *From Protest to Challenge* (Stanford, Hoover Inst Press, 5 vols, 1972-1997), vol 3, p273.

66 Gerald Gardiner, 'The South African treason trial', *Journal of the International Commission of Jurists*, vol 1, no1 (1957), p43–58.

67 Ibid, p48.

68 Frederick George Gardiner & C W H Lansdown, *South African Criminal Law and Procedure* (Cape Town, Juta, 6th edn, 2 vols, 1957), vol 2,p987.

69 Karis & Carter, *From Protest to Challenge,* p347.

70 Helen Joseph, *If This be Treason* (London, Deutsch, 1963).

71 Joel Mervis, *The Fourth Estate* (Johannesburg, Jonathan Ball, 1989), p333–335.

72 Such as F C Erasmus; and Jimmy-'It-leaves-me-cold' Kruger, who used this phrase when reporting on the death of Steve Biko to a congress of the Transvaal National Party. Biko's death at the hands of the police, and the inquest and trial that took place after his death, was probably one of the worst advertisements for this country internationally.

73 Counsel for the Crown: O Pirow, QC (with him J De Vos, QC, J C Van Niekerk, M O Barker, C N Van der Walt, J J Trengove, G G Hoexter, and J H Liebenberg). Counsel for the accused, 1-92 (save Nos 5, 6, 11, 16, 28, 29, 51, 55 and 65): myself as Senior (with me A Fischer, QC, H C Nicholas, R S Welsh, S Kentridge, A P O'Dowd, J F Coaker, V C Berrangé, C Plewman, and D J B Osborn); for accused No 5, H C Nicholas. For accused No 6, D J B Osborn. For accused No 11, A P O'Dowd. For accused No 16, J F Coaker. For accused No 28, C Plewman. For accused No 29, S Kentridge. For accused No 55, V C Berrangé. For accused No 65, A Fischer, QC (with him S Kentridge). Accused No 51 (Joe Slovo) , in person.

74 Fully reported in 1959 (1) SALR p646–678.

75 Curiously enough, a few years before the treason trial, I had been involved in a case in which our side had intended to call Professor Murray as a witness. I was briefed by the American magazine *Time* to appear in an action brought against it by Sam Kahn, then a Member of Parliament, before the South African Communist Party was banned. In one issue of the photographic magazine published by *Time*, called *Life*, there appeared one day a whole page of photographs of the alleged leaders of Communist parties in various parts of the world, Sam Kahn's photograph being one of them, with the claim (as far as I can remember) that these persons were determined to overthrow the existing order by violence, in accord with Communist doctrine. Somewhat unwisely Sam Kahn sued for damages for defamation of character. We called a witness from overseas to prove that what was said of these persons was true, as being in accord with Communist doctrine. The witness was cross-examined, and Professor Murray was to have been our next witness. However, before this happened, counsel for Kahn approached me and stated that Kahn wished to withdraw the action, but asked whether we would not pursue our claim for costs against Kahn. I reported this to *Time*'s American attorney, Mr Harold Medina. In the United States of America, as I understand the position, costs are awarded against an unsuccessful litigant only if the case brought could be shown to be frivolous – in

other words when attorney and client costs would be awarded in South Africa. That being so, Medina had no objection at all to foregoing *Time*'s claim for costs. As a result of this it became unnecessary to call Professor Murray.

76 Court record, p6821.

77 Rex *v* Heyne and Others, 1956 (3) SA 604 AD.

78 1959 (3) SALR p753.

79 As I write this account it is perhaps noteworthy how often the word 'democracy' is used or misused by the politicians engaged in negotiations or thwarting negotiations to bring about peace in this country.

80 Thomas Karis, *A Guide to the Microfilm Record of the Treason Trial* (Johannesburg, Contra, 1998), p55, 57, 64.

81 Abbreviations used in this section are as follows: ANC, African National Congress; SAIC, South African Indian Congress; SACOD, South African Congress of Democrats; SACPO, South African Coloured Peoples Organisation; COP, Congress of People; SACTU, South African Congress of Trade Unions; FSAW, Federation of South African Women; ANCYL, African National Congress Youth League; ANCWL, African National Congress Women's League; TIC, Transvaal Indian Congress; NACCOP, National Action Council of the Congress of People; NIC, National Indian Congress; TIYC, Transvaal Indian Youth Congress; NIYC, Natal Indian Youth Congress. All these bodies were concerned with the organisation of the Congress of People which took place in 1955 at which the Freedom Charter was adopted.

82 In paragraph 4 (b)(iv) of Part B of the indictment.

83 Respectively, the Native Resettlement Act (No 19 of 1954), the Bantu Education Act (No 47 of 1953), and the Native (Abolition of Passes and Co-ordination of Documents) Act (No 67 of 1952).

84 Karis & Carter, *From Protest to Challenge*, p24 ff.

85 A portion of the record is reprinted in Karis & Carter, *From Protest to Challenge*; Resha's evidence appears on p596–607.

86 At p586.

87 On p11 in paragraph 11.

88 Cf p12 paragraphs 13 (ii), 14 and 15.

89 Karis & Carter, *From Protest to Challenge*, p19.

90 Hansard, vol 10, col 3585, 17 September 1953.

91 Ibid, col 3576.

92 Muriel Horrell (comp), *Bantu Education to 1968* (Johannesburg, South African Institute of Race Relations, 1968).

93 Ibid, p10.

94 Ibid, p12–13.

95 It is interesting to note that these words, 'self-determination', are being increasingly used by opponents of the plan which seems to be afoot to have a democratic South Africa with rights for all. The essential difference between the Africans' claims, as propagated over the years by its leaders and by its policy statements, was that they visualised a government elected by all the citizens of the country irrespective of their colour. Nobody can accuse the AWB and its allies of similar ideas when they claim a right of self-determination.

96 This evidence appears in Karis & Carter, *From Protest to Challenge*, p584–586.

97 Ibid, p17–18.
98 Ibid, p332ff.
99 Helen Joseph, *If This be Treason*, p52–55.
100 Karis, *Guide to the Microfilm Record of the Treason Trial*, p16.
101 Ibid, p16510.
102 At one stage there was a fear that Judge Kennedy might die before the conclusion of the trial, and there might have to be a complete retrial of the whole proceedings. Fortunately this did not happen. Judge Kennedy survived the trial and retired from the Bench upon reaching the retiring age of 70. He then acted, for a short time, as Chief Justice of Swaziland.
103 Karis & Carter, *From Protest to Challenge*, p590–596.
104 Ibid, p592–596.
105 EDITORS' NOTE: It was Isie's realisation – that not even the then moderate and mild requirements of the ANC would meet with any acceptance by the Nationalists – that determined him to accept a position on the Rhodesian Bench almost immediately after the trial had ended.
106 Karis, *Guide to the Microfilm Record of the Treason Trial*, p618–623.
107 Karis & Carter, *From Protest to Challenge*, p343.
108 Cf Macduff and Co *v* Johannesburg Consolidated Investment Company, 1924 AD 573, and Gowan *v* Bowern, 1924 AD 550.
109 1959 (2) SAT 377.
110 1960 (1) SA 293 AD.
111 It was actually Basil Wunsh who first noticed the similarities.
112 1960 (2) SA 507 W.
113 EDITORS' NOTE: Isie had a strong suspicion as to who was responsible for this murder.
114 1972 (1) SA 693.
115 Suppression of Communism Act (No 44 of 1950), section 10 (1) (a).
116 The State *v* Mushimba and Others 1977 (2) SA 829, at 812.
117 D L Mathieson (ed), *Cross on Evidence* (Auckland, Butterworths, 4th edn, 1989), at p277.
118 p845 of the judgment.
119 The judgment of the Privy Council, delivered on 17 June 1970, is to be found in 1970 (3) AER p724.
120 Suppression of Communism Act.
121 1985, Law Reports of the Commonwealth (Constitutional and Administrative Reports) at p699ff.
122 The case is reported as Malindi *v* The Queen 1967 (1) AC 430.
123 Peter Niesewand was a freelance correspondent for the BBC, the London newspapers *The Guardian* and *The Daily Mail*, Agence France Press, United Press International, Reuters and various other media.
124 Peter Niesewand, *In Camera: Secret Justice in Rhodesia* (London, Weidenfeld & Nicholson, 1973).
125 Ibid, p194.
126 A passage from writings of the Prophets chanted on Sabbaths and Festivals in orthodox synagogues.
127 This appears in Mr Abba Eban's autobiography at p434.

INDEX

A V Roe factory 91
Act of Union 181
Adams (treason trialist) 203
Adams College 192
Adenauer, Konrad 300–1
Adler, Fritz 96
African Films 30
African Guarantee 85
African National Congress (ANC)
  129–216 *passim*
Africans' Claims 182, 186
Agudah, Judge 259, 267
Aiken, Arthur 241
Aiken & Carter 241
Aliens Control Act 260–7
American Board Mission 192
Amissah, Austin 259, 267
Anatomy of a Murder 98
ANC *see* African National Congress
Anglo American Corporation 108
Apportionment of Damages Act 308
Argus Printing & Publishing Co 189
Aronsohn, Gypsy 224
Aronsohn, Willie 224
Athineos *v* Lloyds 83
Atlantic Charter, The 182

Balfour Declaration 287
Banda, Hastings Kamuzu 233
Bantu Authorities Act 157
Bantu Education Act 156, 190–3, 194
Bantu Education Bill 190
Bantu Self-Government Act 223
Barclays Bank 240
Barker, M O 136
Baron, Leo 259, 267
Beadle, Hugh 225, 230, 235, 277–9
Begin, Menachem 291, 296, 301
Bekker, S 135, 146, 149, 159, 160, 181,
  187, 188, 193
Bell Dewar & Hall 211, 246
Ben Gurion, David 288, 292, 295, 297,
  302
Bennett, Benjamin 13, 64
Berg, Sidney 305–6
Berker, Hans 112, 115
Berlin, Isaiah 290
Bernstein, Irving 304
Bernstein, Phil 304
Berrangé, Vernon 129, 130, 131, 139,
  141, 154
Beyers, F W 28–9, 247
Beyers, General 71, 72
Bill of Rights 182
Bizos, George 69, 74, 139, 259
Blackwell, Judge 77–8, 101
Bliss, M 77
Bloch, H M 80, 89, 91
Block, Julian 308–9
Blumenfeld, Jesmond 57
Boberg, Ulf 64–6, 93
Boeing Aircraft Company 90
Botha, P W 210, 214
Bowens *see*
  Webber Wentzel Bowens
Brink, Jack 28
Britten, T F 17
Broughton, Delves 40–5
Broughton, Diana 40–5
Burger, Schalk 322

Cachalia, Ismail Ahmed 203
Cadman, R 249
Callaghan, James 276
Carberry, June (Juanita) 42
Carlson, Joe 69
Carter, Gwendolen M 190
Carter *see* Aiken & Carter
Central African Airways *v* Vickers Armstrong 86–91, 225
Chamber of Mines 219–22
Charles, Peter 225–6
Chaskalson, Arthur 139
Chitepo, Herbert 226–7
Christie, Dick 226
Cillie, P M 102
Cilliers, Fanie 319, 324
City Deep Golf Course 241–2
Claasen, P S 95
Clayden, Gwen 224, 233–4
Clayden, Jack 80, 225, 237, 258, 271
Clayden, John 224, 226, 230, 233–4
Coaker, John 130, 139, 141, 246
Cohen, David 257
Colman, George 63, 80, 125, 218–9
Comay, Michael 306
Companies Act 59
Conco, W 189, 199, 205
Congress Alliance 148, 199, 209
Congress of People 153, 155, 158
Consolidated Diamond Mines of South West Africa Ltd 108–24
Cooper, W E 252, 256
Courtauld, Simon 43
Cowen, Dennis 114
Cowle, Rhodes Cecil 13–16, 21–2
Cowle, William Alfred 13–22; *see also* De Melker, Daisy
Cranko, James 13
Criminal Procedure and Evidence Act 266–7
Curlewis, Judge 28–9
Currie, William 94, 95–6

Daggafontein Mines Ltd 219–22
Daleski, Joe 304
Daniel, Hector 41
Davis, Gordon 37, 38
Dayan, Moshe 52–3
De Klerk, F W 7, 214, 274, 323
De Melker, Daisy 13–22
De Melker, S C 14, 21
De Villiers, D P 118, 122
De Villiers, Etienne 28–9, 78
De Villiers, J A 27
De Villiers, Nick 139
De Villiers, Rene 245
De Vos, J 135, 143
De Waal, Judge 30
De Wet, N J 27, 29
Defiance Campaign (1952) 157, 158, 173
Departure from the Union Regulation Act 251
Deutsche Kolonial Gesellschaft 116
diamond buying, illicit 228, 320–1
Dison, Lewis 139
Dönges, Eben 124
Douglas, Rod 47
Dove-Wilson, John Carnegie 4
Doyle, Judge 259
Druion, Lazer 285
Dryden & Myburgh 102
Du Pont, Clifford 231
Du Preez, Colin 253
Dunsky, Israel 239, 304, 306

Eban, Abba 294–5, 297, 303
Edward Nathan & Friedland 31
Eglin, Colin 245
Elkin, Carol 284
Eloff, C F 69
Engelbrecht, Anne-Marie 319
Epstein, Betty 303–4
Epstein, Ray 303–4
Erleigh, Norbert 59
Eshkol, Levi 295–6
Ettlinger, B A 'Sonny' 237, 302
Evil That Men Do, The 64

Fagan, H A 110, 113–116, 120, 122
farm labour 69–72, 232
Festenstein, Melville 64
Field, Winston 224, 233, 235
First Forty Years, The 15, 18, 144

Fischer, A 'Bram' 80, 137–9, 167–9, 204–206
Fisher, Max 302
Fourth Estate, The 144
Fox, James 59
Frank, Fritz 304–5
Frank, Lisa 305
Frank & Hirsch 304
Franklin, Blen 112
Franks, Maurice 64
Fredricks, Joseph 116
Freed, Muriel 36
Freedom Charter (ANC) 158, 162, 180, 198
Freedom Volunteers 159, 163
Friedland, Philip 31
Friedman, Charles 57, 220, 323
From Protest to Challenge 190
Fulmer Research Institute 89

Galgut, Oscar 39, 41, 139
Gardiner, Gerald 131–2
Gardner, Charles 47
Geach, Carveth 112
Geering, Jack 306
Genius for the Defence 13, 15
Geri, Jack *see* Geering, Jack
German Diamond Company 116
German law 114
Gibbs, Humphrey 234
Gluckman, Emanuel 10, 30
Goldin, Bennie 63, 87, 226, 233, 259, 277
Goldin, Hansie 233
Goldmann, Nahum 297, 300–2
Goldsmid, Len 77
Goldstein, Israel 305
Gordon, Donald 240
Gordon, O 94
Gould, David 59
Greenberg, Leopold 9, 15, 17, 18, 27, 29, 33, 34, 127, 215
Grey Shirts Movement 285
Grindley Ferris, I 27, 29
Griswold, Erwin 237, 244, 255
Grosskopf, E A 119
Grotius 251
Group Areas Act 68–9, 156, 157

Haarhoff, Prof 8, 285–6
Hahlo, H R 111–113, 117
Hall, 'Foxy' 113, 121, 122, 123–4
Hamilton, J E T 276, 278
Harrigan, Walter 43
Hastings, Patrick 31
Hathorn, Anton 80, 225
Hayman, Ethel 18
Hayman Godfrey & Sanderson 57
Hayman Godfrey Inc 220
Heath, Neville 58, 323
Hellman, Ellen 130
Henochsberg, Edgar 49
Hertz, J H 280
Herzog, Albert 196
Herzog, Chaim 288, 289, 296
Herzog, J B M 5, 148
Herzog, Pnina 289
Herzog, Yaacov 288, 289–90
Hewitt Woollacott & Chown 89
Hirsch, Helmuth 304
Hoal, W G 28–9
Hoexter, Gus 137, 208–10
Hoffberger, Chuck 303
Hofmeyer Van der Merwe 315
Hofmeyr, J H 6, 197
Hofmeyr *see* Webber Wentzel Bowens
Holtzman, Manfred 320
Hope, Adrian 39
Horrell, Muriel 191
Horwitz, Edel 239, 304, 305
Hotz, Louis 286
Howman, Jack 224, 235, 275–6
Hughes, Howard 39
Hutchinson, Alfred 149

If This Be Treason 143, 201, 307–8
In Camera: Secret Justice in Rhodesia 276
Infeld, Zvi 305
Inns of Court, London 92
Insolvency Act 22
International Tobacco Company (ITC) *v* United Tobacco Company (UTC) 79–80
Introduction of Separate Represen-

tation of Voters Act 67–8, 157
Irving, B J H 250, 322
Isaacs, I 'Higgie' 259, 324
Israel, Louis 139

Jacobs & Co Ltd 62
Jacobson, Charlotte 304
Jaglom, Raya 304
Jarvis, Cyril 15
JDC *see* Joint Distribution Committee
Jewish Agency 239, 291, 295, 302, 304, 305
Johannesburg Bar 4, 28, 67–8, 72–4, 97, 136, 137, 141, 218, 224, 225, 268, 282, 322
Johannesburg City Council 241–2
Joint Distribution Committee 303
Jonathan, Leabua 257, 264–5
Joseph, Helen 139, 142, 201, 203, 204, 307
juries, the jury system 229–30

Kahanowitz, Reuben 26
Kahn, Ellison 48
Kahn *v* Louw 185
Kaplan, Lazaras 40, 41
Karis, Thomas 190, 201–2, 204
Kathrada, Ahmed 203
Kaunda, Kenneth 233, 271, 273
Kennedy, A A 143, 144, 159, 160, 187, 206
Kentridge, Sydney 138, 139–40, 188, 210–12, 239, 253, 259, 267, 307, 310, 322
Khama, Seretse 257
Kirkpatrick, John 252–3
Kirschner, Ellie 52, 239, 306
Kirschner, Nicholai 239
Kneen, Johnny 39
Krause, F E T 12, 13, 228
Kuper, Simie 302

Lancaster House agreement 273
Landau, Annie 282
Landau, Chief Rabbi 281
Landau, Felix 94, 282
Landau, Laura 282
Lardner-Burke, D 275–6, 277, 279
Lategan, Judge 248
Law and Order Maintenance Act (Rhodesia) 235
Law, Life and Laughter 48
Lawrence, Leslie 103
Lazar, L 101
Lazarus, Gerald 287, 302
Lazarus, John 287
Leibrandt, Robey 133
Levinson, Barbara 303
Levinson, Morry 303
Levy, Dennis 38
Levy, Henry 36–7
Levy, Leon 203
Lewis, John 91, 225
Lewis, V A 63
Liberty Holdings Ltd 240
Liddiard, E A G 89
Liebenberg, J H 136
Lindsay & Appleyard 8
Liquor Act 78
Livingstone, Albert 62, 146
Lloyds Underwiters 83–6
Lollan (treason trialist) 203
Long, Taffy 4, 20
Lonrho 271
Lorentz & Bone 253
Lourie, Arthur 297–8, 306
Louw, Eric 131–2
Lovell, Leo 244
Lowen, George 118, 119
Lucas, F A W 78
Lüderitz, F A E 116
Ludorf, J F 75, 102, 143, 146
Luthuli, Albert 130, 134, 159, 164, 166, 181, 183, 189, 193, 195, 196, 199, 201, 202–3, 204, 207–8, 210, 213, 214
Lyons, Cecil 286, 302

MacCrone, I D 298–9
Macdonald, Hector 225, 227, 277
MacRobert, Norman 51
Madden, Geoffrey 55
Mahomed, Ishmail 258
Maisels, Andzia 1, 37,280
Maisels, Elizabeth 57, 295

Maisels, Helen 57, 295, 303
Maisels, Henry 1, 4, 8, 280
Maisels, James 7, 285
Maisels, Jeffrey 37, 283–4, 295, 302
Maisels, Keith 36, 220, 307, 309
Maisels, Muriel 36, 57, 224, 236, 244, 247, 281, 282, 287, 289, 295, 303
Malan, A C 78, 113, 123
Malan, A G 'Sailor' 196
Manasewitz case 26–30
Mandela, Nelson 131, 204, 207, 208–10, 213–14
Manners, Philip 99–101, 320
Mansell, Victor 64
Marais, Judge 221
Margo, C S 64, 86, 87, 90
Marks, Fanny Beatrice 'Dolly' 5
Marks, Miriam *see* Sacher, Miriam
Matterson, Neville 246
Matthews, Z K 133, 182, 183, 189, 193, 201, 204, 207, 210–13, 214, 226, 277
May, Michael 91
McEwan, Bill 38
Measroch, Ovi 38
Meir, Golda 239, 291, 295
Melamet, David 217
Mental Disorders Act 102
Mervis, Joel 144
Metro Goldwyn Mayer 30
Michaelson, Cyril 319–20
Millin, Philip 27, 31, 61, 75, 81, 94, 95–6
Millin, Sarah Gertrude 9, 18, 96–7
Milne, A 'Sandy' 244, 268
Milne, Joseph 59, 259
Mkwayi, Wilton 201
Molefi, J S P 260, 266
Molefi *v* The Principal Legal Adviser, The Prime Minister of Lesotho and the Government of Lesotho 260–7
Moll, Christo Theo 310–15
Moodie & Robertson 246
Morgan, Ken 277
Morris, Harry 2, 13–25, 43–4, 307
Moshweshwe II 257–8
Mouton, C J 118
Mugabe, Robert 227, 274
Muller, G van R 118–9
Mulligan, George Angus 68, 96
Murphy, Doris 310
Murphy, Leo 310–12
Murray, Andrew 74, 135, 151, 160, 161, 188, 195–6, 197–9
Murray, Colin 8
Murray, John 81, 224
Muzorewa, Abel 271, 274

Nasionale Pers 119
Nathan, Chick 54
Nathan, Manfred 11
Native (Abolition of Passes and Co-ordination of Documents) Act 194
Native Land Act 181
Native Resettlement Act 156, 162, 174, 194
Navon, Yitzhak 296
Ngoyi, Lillian 203
Nicholas, H C 38, 139, 141, 142
Niesewand, Peter 275–9
Ninety-Day Detention Without Trial Act 214
Ninow, Frank 103
Nkomo, Joshua 272, 274
Nokwe, Duma 72–5, 133, 166, 169, 180, 195, 202
Norwich Union Insurance Company Limited 240

O'Dowd, A P 'Tony' 136,139,140,147
Odes, M 247
Official Secrets Act (Rhodesia) 276, 278
Ogilvie Thompson, N 251, 259
OK Bazaars 237, 240, 241
Oppenheimer, Ernest 108, 110–11
Osborn, David 139, 141

Parkington, Michael 141, 142, 146–7, 204
pass laws 69, 162, 194–5, 199
Paton, Alan 7, 181
Paul, Pieter 73
People That Dwells Alone, A 290

Peres, Shimon 296
Perlman, Itzchak 303
Philips, Namie 302
Pienaar *v* Argus Printing and Publishing Company 189
Pincus, Louis 239, 240, 302
Pirow, Oswald 37, 59, 77, 134, 151, 152, 187
Pitts & Weston 9
Plewman, Chris 139, 141, 142
Pollak, Walter 33, 130
Porter, Maurice 32, 36, 305
Pratt, David 102–7, 215
Pratt, Sarah Leonarda 103
Prussian Fiscus *v* The Town of Kolberg 114
Puffendorf 251

Quartermaine, Murray 310–15

Rabin, Derek 317–8
Rabin, Lea 290
Rabin, Yitzhak 289, 290–1, 302
Rabinowitz, L I 283
Rafael, Gideon 239–40
Ramsbottom, W H 8, 13, 31
Rand Mines 242
Raphaely, Siegfried 3, 9, 32
Raphaely & Gratus 9
Rathouse, Oscar 218, 219, 222, 307
Reichman, Dan 83, 86
Reid, Derrick 246
Rein, R W 103, 106
Resha, Robert 163–181, 206, 207
Reston, James 293–4
Rex *v* Bunting 189
Rex *v* Heyne and Others 151
Rex *v* Nafte 32
Rex *v* Roux 189
Reynolds, Peter 315–6, 317
Rich, Jack 285, 286, 306
Risean, James 88
Rivonia trial 213
Roman Law 113
Roman-Dutch law 114, 120
Roodepoort–Maraisburg Town Council *v* Eastern Properties 28
Roper, Edward 243, 257, 258–9, 260, 262
Rosenberg, N E 30, 31,40, 80
Rosenthal, Charlie 38, 100, 115
Rothburg, Sam 298
Royal Aeronautical College 89
Royal Aircraft Establishment 87, 88
Rubin, Leslie 145
Rudd, John 112
Rumpff, F 101–2, 104, 132, 135–6, 143, 144, 150, 159, 160, 184, 186, 198, 202, 203, 204, 206, 252
Ruppin, Arthur 298

Sacher, Michael 299
Sacher, Miriam 299
Sachs, Theodore 320–1
Sacks, Solly 306
Saron, Gus 285, 286, 306
Sauer, Paul 215
Scanlen & Holderness 226, 277
Schenk, Fay 304
Schlesinger, I W 30–32
Scholtens, J E 113
Schreiner, Oliver 8, 30, 113, 116, 122, 127, 151, 243, 258, 259, 260, 262
Schroeder, 'Bubbles' 64–66
Schutz, Peter 258, 260
Schwartz, Joe 57
Schwarz, Zvi 52
Seef & Co 62
Separate Representation of Voters Act 67–8, 157
Shamir, Yitzhak 295
Shapiro, Hillel 94, 99–100
Sharon, Ariel 291
Sharpeville (1960) 174, 199–201
Shaw, Frank 55
Shawcross, Hartley 88
Shazar, Zalmon 290
Sieradzki, Andzia 1
Sieradzki, Koppel 280
Simons, prosecutor 12, 125
Sisulu, Walter 169
Sithole, Edson 272–3
Sithole, Ndabaningi 227, 272
Six-Day War (1967) 289, 292, 294, 297

Slovo, Joe 133
Smit, A S 244, 259
Smith, Ian Douglas 233, 270, 273
Snitcher, Harry 247
Sobhuza II 243–4, 257
Sobukwe, Robert 199, 250–2
Sobukwe and Another *v* The Minister of Justice 250
Society of Advocates 73
Solomon, Saul 23, 32, 321
Sonin, Carl 30
Sorec 242
South African Jewish Board of Deputies 285–7, 302
South African Zionist Federation 241, 287, 290
South West Africa People's Organisation 253
Spoor & Fisher 320
Sproat, Robert 13–22
Sproat, William 19–22
Stallard, C F 4, 48–9
State *v* Petrus and Another 266
Steytler, Grimmer & Murray 8
Stratford, Judge 28–9
Strauss, J G N 11, 196
Strydom, Judge 253
Suidwes-Afrika Prospekteerders 109
Suppression of Communism Act 68, 146, 151, 250
Suzman, Arthur 302
Suzman, Helen 245
Swart, C R 126, 129, 143, 144

Tambo, Oliver 130,134
Taverner, Prof 89
Tennet, Benno 103–4
Theron, Charles 126, 127
Thring, W G 252
Tindall, Judge 27, 29
Titren, Harvey 76
Tobler, Eddie 39
Toynbee, Arnold 290
Treadwall, Geoff 38
treason trial 129–216
Trengove, John 137, 150, 169–81, 195, 207–8
Trengove, Wim 208
Trisk, Benjamin 57
Trollip, W G 'Bill' 80, 218–9
Trope, Harry 304
Trowbridge, Robina 312–3
Turnbull, John 108, 112, 114, 240; *see also* Webber Wentzel Bowens
Tyiki (treason trialist) 203

Umkhonto we Sizwe 214
United Tobacco Company 79–80
University of the Witwatersrand 6–8, 97, 241, 245, 298
Unterhalter, Jack 101
UTC *see* United Tobacco Company

Van Bynkershoek 251
Van den Heever, F P 63, 127
Van der Byl, P K 271
Van der Merwe, Billy 315
Van der Walt, C N 136, 312
Van Niekerk, J C 129, 136
Van Rhyn, G P 119, 123
Van Winsen, Louis 259
Vanderbijl Park Health Committee and Others *v* Wilson and Others 77
Verwoerd, H F 72–4, 75–6,102–7, 190–2, 201, 214, 215, 288
Vickers Armstrong Limited 86–91
Vorster, J B 73, 214, 223, 270, 273

Watt, Andrew 94
Watt, J M 17
Webber Wentzel Bowens 108, 246, 315, 316
Weber, F S 123
Weizmann, Ezer 296–297
Weizmann, Chaim 295–297
Welensky, Roy 233, 276–7
Welsh, Rex 139, 142, 219, 259, 307
Wentzel, Ernie 250
Werksmans 125, 246
Wessels, John 27, 28–9, 185, 189
Western Areas, Johannesburg 162–3, 174–8, 194
White Mischief 43
Whitehead, Edgar 233

Wilkens *v* Brebner and Others 185
Williamson, A Faure 86, 217, 218
Wise, Alec 14
Woodhead Bigby & Irving 250
Woolf, Zalman 247, 249
World Peace through Law, conference 237–9
Wright Rose-Innes & Wise 14
Wunsh, Basil 220

Xuma, A B 163, 182, 183

Yadin, Carmella 298
Yadin, Yigael 297–300
Yom Kippur War (1973) 291, 292
Young, Dendy 225, 259